From Italy to San Francisco

DINO CINEL

From Italy to San Francisco

THE IMMIGRANT EXPERIENCE

STANFORD UNIVERSITY PRESS 1982
STANFORD, CALIFORNIA

Stanford University Press
Stanford, California

Printed in the United States of America
ISBN 0-8047-1117-8
LC 80-53224

Published with the assistance of the Edgar M. Kahn Memorial Fund

Sources of illustrations:
1, by courtesy of the Byron Collection, Museum of the City of New York.
2, 4, 6, 11(bottom), by courtesy of Centro Studi Emigrazione, Rome.
3, 11(top), 16, by courtesy of Touring Club Italiano, Rome.
5, Oscar Handlin, *A Pictorial History of Immigration,*
by permission of Photoworld.
7–10, 12–14, 15 (Sbarboro, Fontana) by courtesy
of the Eureka Federal Savings North Beach Museum.
15 (Giannini) by courtesy of the Bank of America.
Endpapers, *Gli Emigranti*, by Angelo
Tommasi, by permission of the Galleria
Nazionale d'Arte Moderna, Rome.

TO THE MEMORY OF MY PARENTS

Acknowledgments

THIS BOOK was made possible by financial support from several institutions, the advice and criticism of American and Italian historians, and the cooperation of many Italians and Italo-Americans in both Italy and San Francisco. The History Department of Stanford University provided the technical training and stimulated the intellectual fervor that made the writing of this book an enjoyable happening.

An initial grant from the University Center for International Studies at the University of Pittsburgh allowed me to do some preliminary work in New York and San Francisco. Two generous grants from the Center for Research in International Studies of Stanford University made possible two extended visits to Italy to gather records and to do research. Stanford University was supportive beyond my expectations in providing unlimited funds for computer time and technical assistance when I went through the trials and tribulations of learning computer methods and analyzing my data. A Whiting Fellowship allowed me to enjoy a full year of reflective time to organize my ideas and write the first draft of this book. Tulane University too has been generous in providing financial assistance in the last stages of the preparation of the manuscript.

Among the historians who offered advice and criticism, David M. Kennedy was the most helpful. Because of his great interest in things Italian, and my curiosity for things American, he worked hard at introducing me to the intricacies of American historical scholarship. Then, as a good friend, he monitored the progress of this work through its various stages. Carl N. Degler provided intelligent and valuable criticism at a key stage in the preparation of the manuscript. On the other side of the Atlantic, Domenico De Marco, professor of history at the University of Naples, shared with me in several conversations his vast knowledge of the Italian south. Giuseppe Felloni, of the University of Genoa, introduced me to the study of the Italian northwest and to the archives of the city and province of Genoa. John S. MacDonald, of Chelsea College, University of London, read the manuscript and saved me from several errors. Finally, Gerald R. Lathrop, of the Stanford Center for Information Technology, provided much-needed advice on the analysis of my data; and Jeannie H. Siegman, of the same center, was generous in offering assistance in editing the manuscript through the computer.

Victor Filler, my editor at Stanford University Press, is responsible for greatly improving this book. His editorial skills polished my prose, and his probing precision saved me from many errors. I feel that this book is, at least in part, his too. J. G. Bell offered valuable assistance in the final draft of the last chapter. Of course, neither he nor any other person who provided advice and criticism is responsible for my errors. I will have to shoulder that responsibility on my own.

History books cannot be written without the advice and assistance of archivists. The staff at the Immigration and Naturalization Service in San Francisco was most helpful as I went through thousands of naturalization records. The archivists at the other California archives where I did research were most helpful too. In Italy my research was more laborious; but there too the archivists were a great help in locating important sources. With few exceptions, San Francisco Italians and Italo-Americans were willing to share their past with me in interviews. Through my research, I learned to be both critical and appreciative of Italian immigrants and of returnees to Italy. Yet I am left with the feeling that I still know so little about them, and that although I followed their journey from the Old World to the New, I only scratched the surface of their momentous passage from small traditional communities to cosmopolitan San Francisco.

D.C.

Contents

From Italy to San Francisco

CHAPTER 1

Emigrants, Immigrants, and Returnees

THIS STUDY in social history deals with change and continuity in the lives of Italians who immigrated to the United States, whether permanently or temporarily. Ordinarily, studies of immigrants in the United States focus mainly on events that occurred after the immigrants' arrival, and only tangentially on their societies of origin. This focus is often justifiable. Since most immigrants came to start a new life in the New World, historians have rightly concerned themselves with the processes of adaptation to the new society and interaction with it, and have studied the immigrants' background only to the extent that it helps understand their American experience.

If applied to Italians, however, this approach would ignore the impact American society had on more than half the migrants. In fact, about 60 percent of the Italians who arrived in the United States between 1908 and 1923 returned to Italy within a few years. In some years the returnees far outnumbered the immigrants. In 1908, for instance, returnees exceeded immigrants by 240,000 to 130,000; and again in 1911 many more returned than arrived.[1] As Robert Foerster, probably the most perceptive student of Italian emigration, remarked of the massive return migration from America: "No previous immigrants in this land of promise had done that."[2] How were the returnees changed by American society, and what effect did they have on their native land after returning? To answer these questions is to see the interaction between immigrants and American society from another perspective.

My interest in the returnees does not arise solely from the fact that return migration was common among Italians. Other evidence indicates that the desire to return home was shared by virtually every Italian immigrant, even those who never did go back to Italy. At least until the early twentieth century, and probably until the end of the First World War, most Italians considered their residence in the United States only temporary. As another American writer pointed out at the time: "It is doubtful if more than a few have given up the hope of returning at some period, after they have amassed abroad a sum sufficient to make the remainder of their lives easier."[3] Italian statistics corroborate this. For instance, of all who left Italy in 1909, only 20 percent declared that they intended to stay abroad indefinitely; all the others indicated that they would return inside of a year.[4] Moreover, about 80 percent of the Italians who arrived in the United States in 1907—a year chosen at random—were between the ages of 16 and 45, and almost all those who were married had left their families in Italy.[5]

We know that a large number of Italians eventually became permanent residents and citizens of the United States. Why and how did these Italians change their minds? We can speculate that returnees failed by and large to achieve their goal of a good life in Italy, and that this failure discouraged others from going back to Italy. Perhaps, too, life in the New World changed the immigrants' goals; despite nostalgia for the homeland, immigrants were realistic enough to compare the opportunities in the New World with the deprivations of the Old. In any event, a study of the Italians who remained in the United States must take into account the phenomena of return migration and reemigration—as well as immigration itself—and the general desire of virtually all Italians to go back to Italy.[6]

Following a practice common among immigration historians, I have examined the emigrants, immigrants, and returnees from selected areas only.[7] Originally, I intended to study Italians in San Francisco in order to see how regional differences survived and interacted in the New World. When the research revealed that almost half the Italian immigrants in San Francisco had come from the four provinces of Genoa, Lucca, Cosenza, and Palermo, I turned to the local socioeconomic conditions that had given rise to mass emigration in the late nineteenth and early twentieth centuries. In the process, I came to realize that return migration and subsequent reemigration deserved more attention. This study, as a result, is organized in two parts. In the first, I explore why emigration was common in some provinces but not in others; I deal with the numbers of emigrants and how the numbers varied over time; I follow the course of return migration; and finally, I assess the significance of the migrations in the light of the broad socioeconomic dynamics of Italian society. In the second part, I deal with the changes the Italians underwent in San Francisco, both in a quantitative analysis of certain aspects of their lives and in a more general study of community organization and development.

The History of a Family

The main sources for this study are the histories of almost 2,000 families over three generations, the second of which was the generation that moved from Italy to San Francisco. Of all these histories, I have selected one that illustrates both the nature of the sources and the themes of this study.

For our purposes, this family's history begins late in the nineteenth century with five people: Antonio and Margherita Torrano, both in their early forties, and their three sons, Carmelo, Pietro, and Franco. The family lived in Verbicaro, a commune [8] of about 5,000 people located in the mountains of the province of Cosenza, in the deep south of Italy. According to family records, Antonio owned two acres of land, hardly enough for a family of five.[9] Since 1888, four years after the couple was married and the year the second son, Pietro, was born, Antonio had balanced the family budget with money he made in Sicily. He would leave Verbicaro every spring, crossing the Strait of Messina to work until late October on an estate in the province of Palermo, while his wife worked the land at home.[10] Antonio Torrano was not the only seasonal migrant from Verbicaro; the prefetto of Cosenza (the prefetto was the representative of the central government in each province) reported in 1886 that for several years from 200 to 300 men had been leaving Verbicaro every spring to work either in Sicily or in other areas of the Italian south.[11] By the early 1890's, however, the migrations had begun to decline. "Few people can find work in Sicily now," the prefetto reported. "As I understand it, the once-flourishing agricultural economy of Sicily is going through a long depression. Those who still go to Sicily can hardly save half of what they used to save ten years ago."[12]

When internal migration of this sort failed to provide the additional income many families needed, the peasants of Verbicaro were forced to seek work across the Atlantic. Migration to America, rare in the 1870's, increased in the 1880's and reached mass proportions in the 1890's. The reports by the prefetto in the 1870's mentioned migration to America only in connection with the suppression of brigandage. In 1877, for instance, he stated that "those who leave for the distant Americas are either former brigands escaping prosecution or adventurers."[13] In the following decade, the prefetto noted that small landowners and day laborers were joining merchants and former brigands across the ocean. The mayor of Verbicaro, in one of his quarterly reports to the prefetto, wrote in 1887: "Emigration to the Americas was unheard of among us a few years ago. Now it has become almost a household word. Those who leave are still few, but they are increasing by the month."[14] By the 1890's the prefetto could report that "the movement to the Americas and back is massive. There is hardly a family in the province that does not have either the father or an adult member abroad."[15]

Both the mayor and the prefetto stressed that people left to escape poverty. The prefetto's report of 1887, for instance, noted: "It is only with money from America that some families can survive from month to month."[16] The following year the prefetto observed that "most families are in debt. It is unlikely that they will be able to pay their creditors, unless the local economy recovers from this long depression. But this seems unlikely. Only those families that have one or more members in America seem able to get out of debt."[17] Reports in the 1890's, exactly when the emigration rate soared, go beyond the theme of poverty. Emigration, these reports suggest, became a mass phenomenon when peasants realized that by working in America for three to five years they could save enough money to buy land in Italy. As the prefetto wrote in 1893: "The traditional migration to Sicily provided enough money to survive from year to year. The new migration to America brings bigger savings, which migrants invest in land."[18]

The determination to buy land in Verbicaro seems to have been at the root of Carmelo and Pietro Torrano's decision to go to San Francisco for a few years, as their uncle Nicola had already done. Antonio, their father, at first resisted the decision; he finally gave his consent when the children promised to be back in four years. In San Francisco, Carmelo and Pietro earned money shining shoes, like many other immigrants from Verbicaro.[19] Over the course of two years they sent their father 3,500 lire to buy land.* In 1909, three years after departing from Italy, Pietro returned home. Though the reason for the visit is not clear, subsequent events suggest an expla-

*Exchange rates remained fairly constant between 1880 and 1915, ranging from 4 to 5 lire per dollar. The First World War affected the rate of exchange between the lira and the dollar: 6.6 lire per dollar in December 1915, 8.4 lire per dollar in late 1917, 19 lire per dollar in December 1919. By January 1921 the dollar had reached 29.78. The rate stabilized in late 1927 at about 19 lire per dollar.

nation. Pietro may have wanted to convince his father that, since he and Carmelo were making good money, they should stay in America longer than the four years they had agreed on.

During Pietro's visit, Antonio complained that the two children did not write enough. Pietro answered that it was difficult to find a trustworthy person to write on their behalf; both Pietro and Carmelo were illiterate. Pietro suggested that Franco, the youngest brother, could go to school, and then come to San Francisco and write for the three. Antonio accepted the idea; Franco started school, and in 1911 he joined his brothers in California.[20]

Beginning in 1910 the goals of Carmelo and Pietro seem to have changed. They no longer sent all their savings to their father, but kept some; and in 1911 they rented a small shoe repair shop off Market Street. When Franco came to San Francisco, it occurred to the two older brothers that they could do more business if Franco knew English. Thus, a few weeks after arriving, Franco went back to school, this time to learn English. Their father, however, was not informed of the decision.

Two years later, a dispute between Antonio and his sons threatened to break up the family. Antonio insisted that it was time for them to return. The family now owned eight acres of land, and the aging father complained that to cultivate the land he had to hire labor, which was increasingly expensive owing to the high rate of emigration. Franco, writing on behalf of the brothers, repeatedly begged for time; but finally he disclosed that they had decided to stay in San Francisco, since their business was doing well. Only then did Franco reveal that he had learned English. Besides, Pietro had decided to get married—to an Italian woman who was not from Verbicaro. Franco concluded by suggesting that their father could rent the land in Verbicaro and join them in San Francisco.

For several months Antonio did not answer. When he did, he expressed resentment. He was upset that Pietro was going to marry without his consent and without returning to Verbicaro for the wedding. He could not understand how the children considered their business in San Francisco more important than the family land and how they could forget the promises they had made to return. He felt insulted by Franco's suggestion to rent the land and move to San Francisco. And most of all, Antonio stressed that he had sent Franco to school to have him act as correspondent for the brothers, in order to keep the family together. But educating Franco had backfired: it had helped him learn English and made him more comfortable in American society. Thus education had been for the brothers a major step away from Verbicaro into the larger world. Emigration had brought some material prosperity, as expected; but it had also brought changes that Antonio had not anticipated, and found hard to accept.

The refusal of the three brothers to return did not mean they intended to stay in San Francisco forever. They were simply making good money and wanted to take advantage of the opportunity. As a matter of fact, Franco said in 1975, it was only in the 1930's that he realized he would not return to Italy. But as he put it: "It was not because I wanted it that way. My children never liked the idea of returning." Carmelo did eventually return to Italy, and he raised his family there. It is interesting to compare what happened to the families of Pietro and Franco, who stayed in San Francisco, with what happened to Carmelo and his children in Italy.

Carmelo returned to Italy in 1914. It is likely that he considered the family's eight acres of land and his savings a solid financial base for himself and his future family. The following year, at age 29, he married; his marriage license listed him as *contadino* (peasant). He worked with, and for, his father until his father's death in 1928.[21] In the settlement of the family estate, Pietro and Franco traded their shares in the land for the shares Carmelo owned in the shoe business in San Francisco. Soon after returning to Italy, Carmelo built a house in the section of town that was popularly known as the American village because most returnees built there. Until 1968, the year he died, Carmelo made a living farming the land. But his two children, unable to make a living in Verbicaro, were forced to embrace the old solution of emigration. Antonio, the first child, migrated to France for the first time in 1937; and for nine years he returned every winter to Verbicaro, leaving again in early February. Then, in 1946, he moved his family to Grenoble, France, where he now lives. Nunzio, the second child, did not leave Verbicaro permanently. His family lives there, and Nunzio works as a seasonal laborer in Switzerland, leaving Verbicaro every March and returning in November.

For Carmelo and his family, temporary emigration to San Francisco failed to achieve what he had hoped for: a permanent, stable life on the land.[22] A British traveler who spent several months in a small northern Italian village wrote: "This money from America was by no means a solution to the economic problem. A man seldom remained long enough to save a sum sufficient for the next generation. He tried to make his savings last as long as he lived—but his son would have to go to America in his turn." [23]

Pietro and Franco eventually married in San Francisco, and both brothers became American citizens in 1936. For them, permanent emigration seems to have been a lasting solution. In 1913 Pietro married a woman from Palermo, Sicily. He was 25 and Assunta, his bride, was 21; [24] he had lived in San Francisco eight years, she only two. By 1936 Pietro had five living children, born between 1915 and 1929. The naturalization record shows that all five were born in San Francisco, an indication that the family had never left the city for long. The same record lists Pietro as a shoemaker; his address 1278 Amazon Avenue in the Outer Mission district. According to Franco's testimony, until 1929 Pietro had lived on Green Street, in the heart of Italian North Beach. In 1929, a few weeks after the birth of their fifth child, Pietro had bought a house.[25]

Before that date, Pietro had several times considered returning permanently to Italy. In 1927 he visited his aging father in Verbicaro and explored the possibility. He took along Assunta and the two older children, Sam, then twelve, and Angelo, ten. It was only then—fourteen years after Pietro's marriage—that Antonio accepted Assunta as part of the family. As a gesture of goodwill, Pietro left the two children in Verbicaro with their grandfather; they returned to San Francisco only after Antonio's death. It seems to have been during that visit that Pietro realized he and his family had a better future in San Francisco than in Verbicaro. Franco remembers that Pietro, after returning to San Francisco, seldom mentioned going back to Italy, and concentrated on the idea of buying a house. Until Pietro retired in 1963, his life was absorbed by hard work in the shop off Market Street; by the mortgage payments, which, his son Sam remembered, became a major concern during the depression; and finally, by the modest pleasure of going to North Beach on a Sunday afternoon for a bocce game with friends from Verbicaro or a bottle of wine at the Caffè Italia.[26]

The careers and marriages of Pietro's children can be described as a process of moving away. Eventually, almost all the children left the city, relocating either in the suburbs of the San Francisco Bay Area or elsewhere in the country. In choosing an occupation, none of them followed Pietro. Nor did they necessarily choose an Italian or Italian-American for a marriage partner.

Sam married at age 22 in 1937. According to the marriage license, he was then a clerk in a grocery store, and his bride, also 22, had been born in San Francisco of Italian parents.[27] For a few years, Sam and his family lived in San Francisco; then in 1946 they moved to South San Francisco where Sam opened a grocery store. In 1954 he had saved enough money to buy a small restaurant in nearby

Burlingame.[28] Another son, Angelo, married in 1938, when he was 21; his bride, a Jewish woman of 23, was a secretary in a law firm.[29] Pietro strongly opposed the marriage. But Angelo had always been the free spirit in his family; he married against his father's will in a civil ceremony. He left San Francisco on his wedding day to move to Burlingame, where he found work as a bartender.[30] When Angelo came back from the Second World War, he became a real estate agent, which proved financially rewarding for both him and his children. In 1942 Carmela, Pietro's third child, married a navy officer stationed in San Francisco. The marriage record indicates that Carmela had no occupation outside the house. Her husband Anthony, born Antonio Maffioletti, was an American of Italian parentage from Hoboken, New Jersey, where the couple moved at the end of the war.[31] In New Jersey, Anthony worked as a salesman for a small firm, then joined a larger firm that transferred him several times to different cities on the East Coast. Finally, he bought a hardware store in Tampa, Florida.[32] Pietro's fourth child, Anthony, died in the Philippines during the war. His fifth child, Santa, born in 1929, married an Italian-American in 1951. The marriage license lists her as a typist and her groom of 25 as a butcher. Of Pietro's four living children, Santa was the only one still living in San Francisco in 1975.[33]

The marriage of Franco, the other immigrant brother, was also opposed by his father, Antonio, because Franco married an Irish-American woman.[34] Franco had learned English quite young, and felt more comfortable than Pietro with non-Italians. In addition, Franco was more successful than his brother. The naturalization record lists him as the owner of a retail shoe store. In 1939 he left the city for San Mateo, in the suburbs, where he bought a larger store and built a house. David and Jonathan, Franco's two children, were as successful as their father in business. In 1938 David got married in San Francisco to a woman of Italian parents. He was then 22, and worked as a laborer for a moving company.[35] By 1975 he had become a partner in a large construction firm in the San Francisco Bay Area; he owned a house in San Mateo, and had three married children.[36] Jonathan, the other son, was married after the war in 1946, at age 26, to a woman of Russian parentage. At the time, he was a clerk in an insurance firm; [37] by 1975 he was a partner in the firm. He owned a house in suburban Marin County and had two college-educated children working in the electronics industry.[38]

Several themes that run through this study emerge from these stories. First, poverty in Verbicaro and economic opportunity in

America do not seem to have been the only reasons for the journey to America. The Torranos emigrated as a way to buy land in Italy. Second, Pietro and Carmelo did not intend to start a new life in San Francisco; they expected to stay only a few years. Third, though the savings from America enabled the family to buy land in Italy, the land failed to solve the problem of poverty. Carmelo, who clung to the original idea of temporary emigration, did not achieve security for his children. Fourth, life in San Francisco progressively changed the goals of Pietro and Franco, transforming their temporary stay into permanent residence and finally into American citizenship. But their decision to stay seems to have been more the product of circumstances than a clear choice. How their decision came about is among the most important questions to answer concerning their experience in San Francisco. Fifth, emigration forced Pietro, Carmelo, and Franco into new jobs. In Italy they had been peasants; in San Francisco they shined and repaired shoes. But their financial success was rather modest compared with what their children were able to achieve. Finally, emigration exposed Pietro, Franco, and their children to immigrants from other countries and other parts of Italy. Antonio, back in Italy, strongly resisted this process when Pietro and Franco chose their wives. His resistance found an ironic repetition one generation later when Pietro opposed his son Sam's marriage to a Jewish woman.

After three generations, the Torrano grandchildren living in the United States have in large measure achieved the financial security that Antonio hoped for when he allowed his three sons to go to San Francisco. But contrary to Antonio's expectations, the success was achieved by the sons who stayed and worked in the United States, and not by the son who returned. It was not only money, moreover, that Antonio, Pietro, Carmelo, Franco, and their children accumulated. They and their offspring changed in ways they had never foreseen.

The Torrano family is typical of the bulk of the families dealt with in this study. Although a very small number of Italians who settled in the United States made contributions to the arts or advanced the social thinking of their age, most were poor people whose main concern was to make a living.[39] Their energies were absorbed in coping with the daily problems of life: finding a job, raising a family, buying a house. Immigrants' children who went on to higher education often recalled how difficult the lives of their parents had been. Mario Puzo, in an essay on how he became a writer, described the limited horizons of the New York Italians living in Hell's

Kitchen, where he grew up. "Bent on survival," he wrote, "they narrowed their minds to the narrowest line of existence."[40]

Whoever deals with social history at this level is made painfully aware of how limited the available sources are. People who have to struggle to live do not have the leisure to leave records of their achievements, failures, or feelings. As in the Torrano family history, I have used three main types of sources: first, government records and statistics; second, written accounts, mostly reports by outsiders describing the experience of the migrants; and third, interviews with immigrants and their children. The most useful records were those of naturalization: not only did they offer detailed family profiles, but they pointed the way to birth, death, and marriage records for both the immigrants' parents in Italy and the immigrants' children in California.*

Historical Processes and Regionalism

Two broad historical questions underlie the themes of this study and the use of the sources. The first question concerns the nature of continuity and change in the immigrant experience; the second concerns the role of regional differences in the emigration of Italians and their acculturation to the New World.

The interplay between continuity and change, in a sense the very fabric of human history, has over the years been treated with various emphases by different historians. Among historians of American immigration, at least two important schools of thought have emerged. Historians of two decades ago clearly emphasized change rather than continuity. This interpretation was based on several broad assumptions: (1) that there was a vast difference between the traditional agrarian society the immigrants came from and the modern, urban, technological, industrial, and highly mobile American society; (2) that immigrants clearly broke with their past, driven by the simultaneous socioeconomic collapse in the sending society and the economic opportunity in the receiving society; (3) that in view of the great differences between the two societies and the distressing departure, the immigrants were by and large passive, unconscious victims of social and economic circumstances, both in the old country and the new; and (4) that immigration was a traumatic event that wiped out most of the immigrants' culture and forced upon them a

*How the records of the three generations were located, organized, and analyzed is explained in the first section of the Bibliographical Essay.

new identity by a painful process of assimilation in the New World. Oscar Handlin best expressed these points: "The history of immigration is a history of alienation and its consequences. I shall touch upon broken homes, interruption of family life, separation from known surroundings, the becoming a foreigner, and ceasing to belong."[41] Emigration was thus seen as basically a process of being uprooted from a personal identity shaped in a peasant society, and immigration became a long struggle to find new roots in the modern, dynamic American society. There was little or no continuity between the European experience and the American; emigration was an ordeal of painful change.

Recent historians, on the other hand, have stressed the continuity between the immigrants' past and their life in America. This interpretation too makes certain assumptions: (1) that the gap between premodern and modern societies was not as wide as once thought; and (2) that immigrants were not, on the whole, helpless victims of circumstances, but active and intelligent individuals controlling their own destiny. For instance, a study of Italians in Buffalo, New York, concludes that "the evidence we have seriously challenges the conventional model of change. The Italian families made a relatively smooth transition from the Old to the New."[42] A study of Italians in three other American cities argues that "the simplistic environmental explanation of success and failure is no longer tenable. The immigrants were not chameleons totally dependent on their surroundings for their character. They contributed to shaping their future rather than receiving their destinies wholly defined and packaged by others."[43] These and other recent works attempt to show "powerful continuities between Italian and American social life."[44]

The shift historians made from the model of change to that of continuity derived, to be sure, from scholarly considerations. John Briggs, for one, argued that an environmental explanation of immigration could not be accepted by the scholarly community of today, and those familiar with the current scholarship on human behavior and social change would probably agree.

But changing social attitudes also played a role in the shift. In the 1950's the common wisdom held that change was worthwhile, though sometimes painful, and that it was desirable to trade the characteristics of a premodern agrarian society for those of a modern industrial society. Of course immigration had been an ordeal, but a useful one. At the end of the rainbow stood the modern man, whose superiority to the old European peasant nobody ever questioned. Those were the years when American society looked with con-

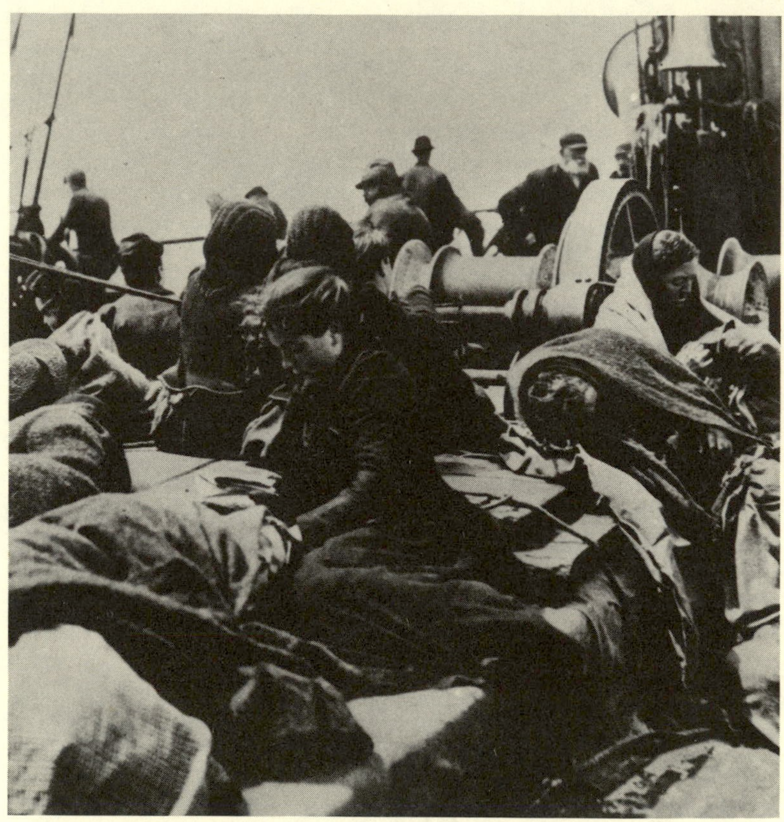

1. Italian emigrants aboard the U.S.-bound *Penneland*, 1893. Most of the photographic material we have seems to support the interpretation of the historians of change. Departing emigrants appear to be broken people, escaping an impossible situation, victims of circumstances beyond their control, with little or no knowledge of what awaits them in the New World.

fidence to the future the new technology promised. In the late 1960's and especially in the 1970's, Americans in general, as well as social scientists, lost this optimism and began to question the lasting value of a technological society and to doubt the future of America. In this new atmosphere it was only natural to look for continuities with the past, as a way to cope with the uncertainties of the present.

Both the model of change and that of continuity, though contributing to our understanding of the immigrant experience, are based on a process of reductionism that treats continuity and change as mutually exclusive categories. One cannot avoid the question of why much historical research seems to assume that there is only one, basic, logical explanation behind the complexity of human events. The historian's degree of intellectual sophistication seems to be measured by his ability to discover such an explanation and by his skill in refuting any other approach. Daily experience, however, teaches us that complexity, ambivalence, and even contradiction are a part of human life—should not history be concerned for these too? Possibly the zeal to discover a basic explanation for all human events represents an escape from reality in the name of logic. If we are uncomfortable with the ambiguities of the present, we create a refuge in our interpretations of the past.

Perhaps immigration historians have been wrong to pose a basic question of continuity versus change. The experience of Italian immigrants, as will be seen, included both major changes and powerful continuities. The first part of this study, centering on Italian society, asks whether emigration was at the same time a break from the past and an effort to preserve the traditions of Italian peasant society. Was emigration, in short, a conservative change? The second part of the study, centering on American society, explores how the Italians living in the United States and going through an accelerated process of change, used their native culture both to preserve their traditions and to cope with the challenges of the new environment. Traditions may even have been the strongest resources immigrants had for effecting change. Thus explaining the dialectical relationship between change and continuity may be more rewarding than studying either by itself.

The second major question I ask is that of regional differences. When mass emigration started in the 1880's, Italy had been a unified country for only about a decade, and regional differences were still profound. Metternich said that Italy was no more than a geographical expression; a later Italian observer said, "In no country of Europe are local differences so marked as in Italy."[45] Did these differences affect the processes of emigration and adaptation to American society? Is it possible to see the Italian emigrants as a homogeneous group, or did they react differently to the common experience of emigration? San Francisco was the ideal place to test this question. Of all cities in the United States, this was the only one in which both northern Italians and southerners were substantially represented. The question of regionalism is important in itself, and it also can shed light on the problem of continuity and change. If regional groups responded in different ways to the same American environment, it would point to considerable continuity between life in Italy and America. On the other hand, if regional differences disappeared, it would suggest that the impact of the environment made the previous experience of the immigrants irrelevant.

I have approached the questions of continuity and regionalism in three steps. The first treats Italian emigration as a development of Italian socioeconomic dynamics, in which most emigrants sought to go abroad temporarily in order to change their lives at home. I examine the success or failure of the returnees in achieving their goals, and I assess the impact of temporary emigration on the structure of Italian society in the early twentieth century, in order to see whether temporary emigration could indeed have been a realistic and lasting solution.

The second step is a microanalysis of certain patterns in the lives of 2,000 immigrant families in San Francisco. Only by dealing with the basic problems the immigrants had to face, such as finding a place to live, getting a job, and raising a family, can we have a realistic sense of how Italians coped with life in the New World. The focus of this section is the extent to which the changes the new environment forced upon immigrants were shaped by traditions the immigrants clung to. I compare Italians with immigrants of other nationalities who arrived in San Francisco around the same time, and I also compare immigrant groups from nine Italian towns located in the four provinces already noted.

Finally, the third step centers on a macroanalysis of the social and economic development of San Francisco Italians between 1848 and the Second World War. The purpose of this section is to outline the broad contours of San Francisco Italian life. The focus of the analysis is the extent to which every step in the direction of change was conditioned and shaped by the traditions the immigrants kept and cherished. I give particular attention to the gradual transition from *campanilismo* (the sense of loyalty to people from one's native town) to regionalism and nationalism, and finally to Americanization.

CHAPTER 2

The Old World and the New

IN A FREE society, wide social differences are likely to produce change that is both laborious and profound. Ordinarily, the encounter between immigrants and the host society changes both groups. But although immigrants have left their native country in search of change—in most cases better economic opportunity—they are likely to resist any change that threatens the social traditions they value. In order to understand what Italian immigrants were seeking in America and what changes they were likely to resist, we must first look at the differences between the California the Italian immigrants found and the world they left behind.

Both the Italian and the American literature that promoted migration to California commonly presented California as another Italy, minimizing any differences. In 1875, for instance, the California Immigration Union printed a booklet with the revealing title *California, the Ideal Italy of the World.*[1] Agents of Italian and foreign shipping companies in northern Italy depicted California as identical to Italy in climate, landscape, and working conditions.[2] In 1882 the prefetto of Genoa wrote: "Although geographically distant, San Francisco is the destination of many emigrants from this province. Emigration agents have been presenting San Francisco and the surrounding territory as a duplicate of our province, and returnees seem to agree."[3] But as immigrants found out, California and San Francisco were not another Italy. Indeed, the apparent similarities in climate and landscape masked profound social and economic differences.

The Economic and Demographic Growth of California

The economic differences were the most obvious. Diversification and rapid growth characterized the economy of California after 1848. Before then, the California economy prospered from stock raising on semifeudal ranchos, which, though self-sufficient, used primitive production techniques and lacked manpower and capital.[4] In 1848 the discovery of gold drew world attention to California. Gold mining became the state's major economic activity in the 1850's, creating new industries and stimulating old ones. Over 50 percent of the state's population, which grew from 15,000 in 1848 to 93,000 in 1850 and 375,000 in 1860, worked in mining in the early 1850's.[5] The 1860's saw a decline in gold mining as the more accessible surface deposits were exhausted. The discovery of silver in the Comstock Lode of Nevada, which lured miners away, and a series of floods and droughts between 1861 and 1864 contributed to a general slowdown of the economy. As mining declined, however, agriculture developed, particularly during the 1870's and 1880's. Industries such as metalwork, in turn, expanded to supply the machinery needed for agriculture, and a network of roads and railroads was built to link San Francisco to other parts of the state and the state to the markets of the East.[6]

A major change occurred in the early 1890's with a rapid increase in industrial activity. From that time until the 1950's, the economy of California developed in four cycles. The first, from the early 1890's until 1913, started with the discovery of oil in the San Joaquin Valley; oil, natural gas, and electricity became the sources of industrial power, and the construction industry expanded as a result of economic growth and the increase in population.[7] The second cycle lasted from 1920 until 1929. It saw the growth of the oil industry in the Los Angeles area, the further development of electric power, and an increase in agricultural output. The Japanese demand for petroleum products and the American demand for raw silk increased the volume of trade flowing through San Francisco. By the mid-1920's, however, San Francisco had lost its industrial hegemony in the state to Los Angeles.[8] The third cycle began in 1935, stimulated by the expansion of the aircraft industry, its auxiliary industries, and other manufacturing and services. The Second World War reinforced these developments because of government expenditure on military equipment.[9] The sharp decline of the California economy after the war, from 1945 to 1948, concluded the third cycle. The fourth cycle began with the outbreak of the Korean

War, which created a sudden demand for strategic goods and a wave of panic buying touched off by the fear of shortages comparable to those during the Second World War.[10]

Certainly until the earthquake of 1906, and probably for a few years afterward, San Francisco was the spearhead of the rapidly changing economy of California. The city's harbor made possible its near monopoly on the commerce stimulated initially by mining and later by manufacturing and agriculture. Moreover, San Francisco was the first city on the West Coast to be linked to the East by railroad, which opened the eastern markets to California products. By the end of the Civil War, San Francisco, with manufactures of $19 million a year, was already the ninth biggest industrial center in the nation, accounting for over 70 percent of the total California output.[11] Though manufacturing later declined in San Francisco, the city prospered as the center of a vast regional market.[12]

The development of the tobacco industry illustrates how rapidly San Francisco changed over several decades. Established in the early 1860's by German immigrants, the tobacco industry grew with the labor of Chinese, who made up about 90 percent of its workers in 1870. The industry expanded rapidly in the 1870's; by 1880 San Francisco counted 147 tobacco-processing businesses with over 3,500 laborers, almost exclusively males.[13] The output of the industry in 1880 was valued at four million dollars. By this time, Germans and Irish constituted the bulk of the labor force, now only 33 percent Chinese. Ethnic rivalries broke out during the 1880's; in 1885, in fact, the "White Labor League" demanded that the Chinese be fired and replaced with white cigar makers. Management complied, and white workers were imported from Europe and the East Coast. Few of these new workers remained in the industry, however, and by the end of the decade employers had hired the Chinese again. Labor disputes were not the only problems the industry had to face. Increasing competition from European cigarette manufacturers forced several businesses to close. By 1890 the yearly output had dropped to two million dollars, and the labor force was down to 2,500.[14] Five years later, there were only 750 employed in the tobacco industry. After the turn of the century, the industry expanded again: in 1905 it employed 1,250 workers and in 1910, 1,500. By 1910, however, the workers were almost exclusively women. Ten years later, the labor force had dropped to around 400, all women.[15]

Obviously, an expanding economy will attract new people. The growth of San Francisco's population in the late nineteenth century and the early twentieth was spectacular even in the United States, where rapid growth was the rule.[16] Although until 1910 California grew more slowly than the other western states, the rate for San Francisco was higher than that for any other western city, and one of the highest in the nation. The federal censuses showed the city with 57,000 people in 1860, 149,000 in 1870, and 234,000 in 1880. Ten years later the population had reached 300,000; it was 343,000 in 1900, and 417,000 in 1910. By the early 1920's the city had topped a half million.

This rapid growth resulted mainly from European and Oriental immigration. In 1870 American-born San Franciscans numbered 76,000 and foreign-born 74,000. From the mid-1880's until the 1940's, the total of foreign-born plus native-born-of-foreign-parents greatly outnumbered the native-born-of-native-parents. The census of 1890, for instance, showed 100,000 foreign-born, 110,000 native-born-of-foreign-parents, and only 62,000 American-born-of-American-parents. By 1940 the balance had shifted, with immigrants and their children outnumbered by native-born-of-native-parents, 320,000 to 310,000.

A cosmopolitan city since the days of the gold rush, San Francisco remained the meeting place of European and Asian immigrants for decades. Four groups comprised about two-thirds of all immigrants who settled in the city: Irish, Germans, Chinese, and Italians. The Irish were the first to arrive in large numbers; from the end of the Civil War to 1870, almost 20,000 of them settled in San Francisco. In the 1880's they were the largest foreign group in the city, totaling about 30,000. Later, from 1880 to 1900, about 25,000 Germans settled in San Francisco. According to the census of 1900, the Irish in San Francisco and their children totaled 70,000, the Germans and their children 60,000. The Chinese, like most other nationalities, had been in San Francisco since the gold rush. The major growth of the Chinese community, however, occurred between 1870 and 1880, when about 15,000 arrived in San Francisco. In 1890 the Chinese reached their largest number in the history of San Francisco, 26,000. A decade later, in part because of discrimination, only 15,000 remained.

Of the four major immigrant groups, the Italians were the last to arrive. In 1870 there were 1,600 Italians in San Francisco. The number grew to 2,500 in 1880, 5,200 in 1890, and 8,000 in 1900. Then, between 1900 and 1924, over 20,000 Italians came to the city. The census of 1910 showed 17,000 Italian-born and 12,000 Italo-

Americans; and in 1920 the figures were 24,000 Italian-born and 22,000 Italo-Americans. After the flow was stemmed by the Johnson Act of 1924, the census of 1930 showed 27,000 Italians and 30,000 Italo-Americans. The aging of the first generation was already noticeable in 1940, when there were 24,000 Italian-born and 32,000 Italo-Americans.

The growth of the Italian community fairly quickly altered the ethnic balance in the city. In 1900 the Germans made up over 30 percent of the foreign-born population, the Irish ranking second with 14 percent and the Chinese third with 9 percent. At that time, Italians were only 6 percent, a smaller community than the British. Ten years later, the Germans had dropped to 17 percent of the total foreign-born; the Irish were 16 percent; and the Italians ranked third with 12 percent. By 1920, however, Italians were the largest group among the foreign-born, 16 percent; Germans and Irish each made up about 12 percent. At that time, the Chinese were only 2 percent of the population. Clearly, the first two decades of the twentieth century saw the greatest expansion of the Italian community.[17]

When the era of free immigration came to an end in 1924, San Francisco had the sixth-largest Italian community in the United States, with 24,000 immigrants living there. According to the census of 1920, there were about 400,000 Italian-born in New York City, 60,000 each in Chicago and Philadelphia, 38,000 in Boston, and 27,000 in Newark, New Jersey. Detroit, Cleveland, Pittsburgh, Buffalo, Jersey City, and Rochester had Italian communities ranging from 10,000 to 20,000. But San Francisco was second only to New York in the proportion the Italians represented of the total foreign-born population of the city: 20 percent in New York and 16 percent in San Francisco. In Boston, for comparison, Italians made up 14 percent, and in Chicago less than 10 percent.[18]

The Regional Origin of the Italians

As early as 1867, the Italians in San Francisco were describing themselves as the "model colony of the United States." The San Francisco Italian newspaper *La Voce del Popolo* explained: "The Italians of San Francisco enjoy a better reputation among Americans than Italians in Chicago, New York, and New Orleans. Crime and corruption are unknown among them. Moreover, they are generally more successful than those of other cities."[19] After the early 1880's, however, the phrase was used invidiously in reference to the

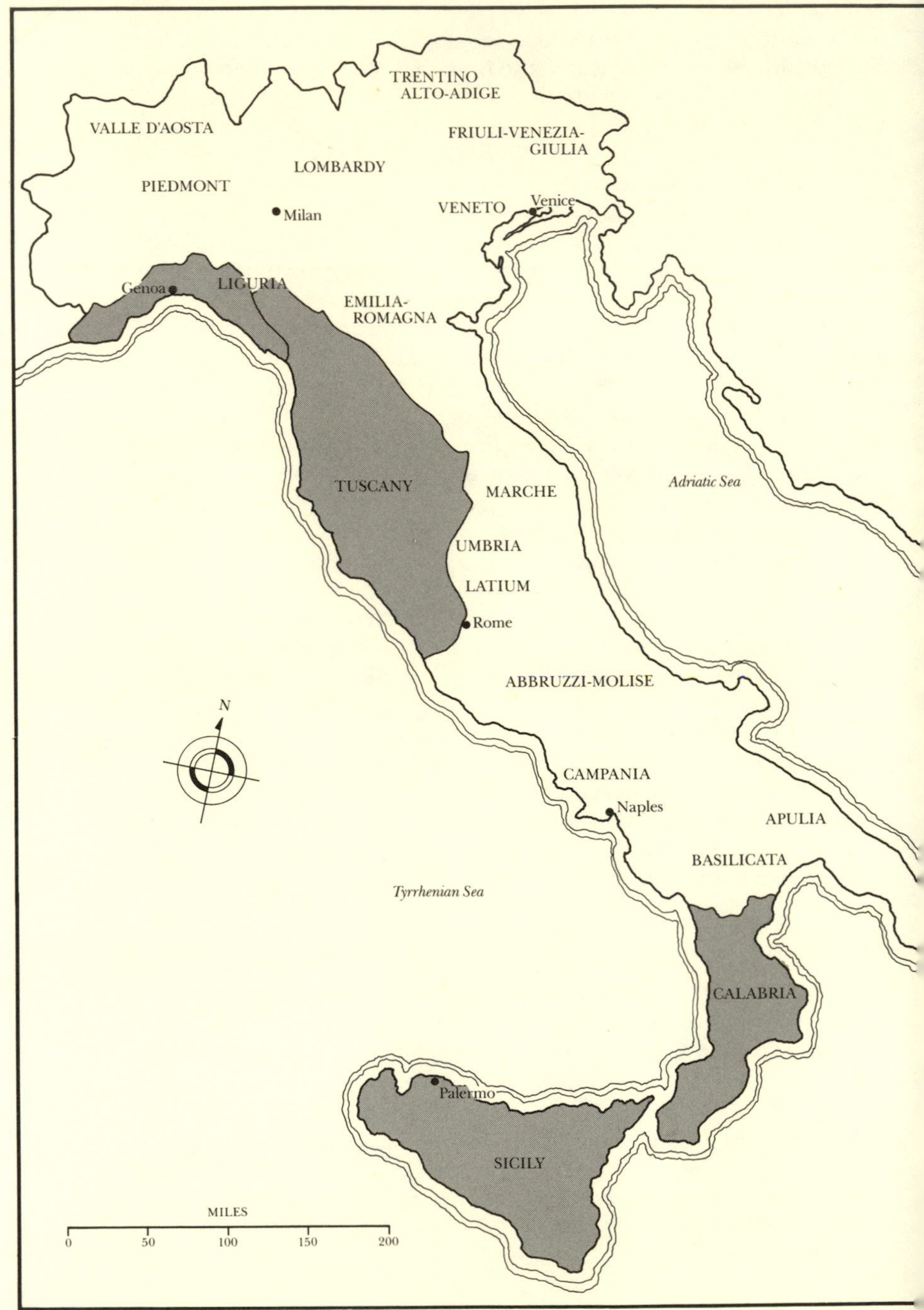

Map 1. Regions of Italy

regional origin of the immigrants. The San Francisco Italians felt they were a model colony because most of them came from the north of Italy; and the northerners intended to maintain their predominance.[20] Apparently they succeeded; at the end of the free immigration era, northerners still outnumbered southerners.

In this respect, San Francisco was unlike most American cities. Though northern Italians were the first settlers in most Italian communities in the United States, southerners formed the bulk of the subsequent immigrants. For instance, northerners, mostly from the province of Genoa and the Tuscany region, established the Italian community in Chicago and dominated it until the 1880's, when southerners took over.[21] The Italian consul in New York reported a similar regional shift in New York.[22] Even the Italian colony in New Orleans, which eventually became almost a Sicilian preserve, was originally settled by northern Italians.[23] By the end of the nineteenth century, almost all the Italian communities in the United States were predominantly southern.[24]

In the first two decades of the twentieth century, the balance in favor of southerners increased, with less than 20 percent of the Italian immigrants each year northerners. In 1902, for instance, 15 percent were northerners; in 1907, a peak year of Italian immigration, 17 percent; and in 1913, 16 percent.[25] It was only natural for Americans who wrote on immigration to associate Italian immigration with southern Italians.[26]

Clearly, California and San Francisco were exceptional. From 1899 to 1914, northern Italians made up about 70 percent of all Italians entering the state. When immigration resumed after the First World War, northerners still outnumbered southerners. Though we do not know precisely how much the figures for the state reflect the city of San Francisco, death and naturalization records suggest that northerners made up more than 60 percent of all Italians in San Francisco.[27] The consular reports of the 1860's and 1870's seldom mention the presence of southern Italians in San Francisco, and a report in 1869 noted that "the immigrants from Genoa and Lucca are definitely the majority in this city." [28] An extensive survey in 1887 by the Italian Geographic Society found northerners to be a clear majority in San Francisco.[29]

Four Provinces

The naturalization and death records indicate that about 45 percent of the Italian immigrants to San Francisco came from four provinces:* Genoa, Lucca, Cosenza, and Palermo. Together, the four provinces had about two million people, according to the census of 1881. Lucca was the smallest, with 284,000 inhabitants, 45,000 in the city of Lucca. Cosenza had a little over 450,000. Genoa had 760,000, one-third of them in the city of Genoa. Finally, Palermo had slightly over 700,000 people, over one-third in the city of Palermo.[30]

The four provinces were already parts of the Kingdom of Italy when mass emigration started in the early 1880's. But before 1870, the year Italy was politically unified with Rome as capital, they had been parts of independent states. The four provinces were very different when they joined, or were forced to join, the new nation. In 1870 only 2 to 3 percent of the inhabitants of the peninsula had Italian as their first language. To most Italians, the "national language" was unintelligible and the word Italy was unknown.[31] Politicians and social scientists pointed to deep, traditional regional differences as obstacles to the organizing of a national economy. Giustino Fortunato, a member of the Italian Chamber of Deputies from the Basilicata region of the south, told his northern colleagues in the 1890's that the south was so different from the north they could not even begin to understand its problems.[32] "In no country of Europe," wrote another Italian in 1902, "are local differences so marked as in Italy."[33] Fifteen years later Antonio Mangano, a naturalized American and head of the Italian Department at Colgate Theological Seminary, wrote after several visits to his native Italy: "The Italian provinces are unlike in everything, except the fact that they are different."[34] And a northerner who wrote extensively about the Calabria region of the south concluded: "Allegiance to the country is an unknown attitude among peasants."[35]

A brief description of the four provinces will illustrate their differences. First of all, they had different political and social histories. Genoa, located in the northwest between the Alps and the sea, had been an independent republic for centuries. In 1800, when Napoleon became emperor and king of Italy, the province became part of the French Empire. In 1814, after the defeat of Napoleon, Great Britain made it a province of the Kingdom of Sardinia, arguing that Genoa was the natural port of the Piedmont region. Genoa had three advantages over almost all the other Italian provinces: it was never under foreign domination, except for the few years under

*An Italian province was and is an administrative unit roughly similar to an American county, both in size and in function.

Napoleon; it was strongly influenced by the French revolution; and it had the most important commercial port in the nation.[36] But there were great differences within the province itself, as the prefetto pointed out in 1888: "The central government should be aware that Genoa and Chiavari [a large and relatively prosperous town along the coast] are not the whole province. In the hinterland communities poverty and ignorance are the inseparable companions of the peasantry."[37]

The city of Lucca, with the surrounding territory, was an independent duchy until 1847, when Duke Carlo Ludovico signed an agreement with Archduke Leopold II of Tuscany whereby Lucca and its territory became part of the Grandduchy of Tuscany. In 1860, by popular referendum, the region of Tuscany joined Italy. Lucca lacked the commercial resources of Genoa, and was also poorly connected to regional markets. The prefetto of Lucca described the province as "isolated from the surrounding regions"; its peasants, he said, were "reluctant to embrace any kind of change."[38]

The provinces of Cosenza and Palermo had a common political background: both had been provinces of the Kingdom of the Two Sicilies until 1860, when, following Garibaldi's campaign in Sicily and southern Italy, they joined the new nation. But Palermo and the cities along the coast of Sicily had a less conservative tradition than the cities in the deep south of the Italian peninsula, where the province of Cosenza is located.[39] The liberal ideas of the French Revolution had reached the educated elite of Sicilian cities like Palermo and Catania, but had barely touched the provinces of the deep south, including Cosenza.[40] A writer from the province of Cosenza lamented: "I would like to be able to say that I was born in a civilized province, or at least in a region aspiring to be modern. With bitterness, I have to admit that this province is still in the midst of barbarism."[41]

The rate of illiteracy is one measure of the differences between provinces. In 1882 almost 70 percent of all Italians making marriage contracts were illiterate; but there was a vast difference between northerners and southerners. The rate was 48 percent in the province of Genoa and 58 percent in Lucca, but 90 percent in Cosenza and 80 percent in Palermo.[42] Twenty years later, illiteracy among people making marriage contracts had dropped to 50 percent nationwide; but the regional differences were still pronounced. The rate was only 20 percent in Genoa and 39 percent in Lucca; but it was still 80 percent in Cosenza and 60 percent in Palermo.[43] By 1922 illiteracy had almost disappeared in the north; the rate seen in marriage contracts was down to 3 percent in Genoa and 5 percent in Lucca. The two southern provinces, however, showed a great variation within the south itself, as well as in contrast to the north: the rate had dropped to 17 percent in Palermo, but it was 40 percent in Cosenza.[44]

Economically, too, the four provinces were very different. In general, the provinces of the north were more industrialized than those of the south. In Genoa about 10 percent of the people worked in industry in 1890. About half of these were in mechanical and chemical industries and half in food processing, textiles, and smaller industries.[45] Twenty years later, the proportion of industrial workers in Genoa had doubled, to over 20 percent of the population.[46] In Lucca slightly over 5 percent worked in industry, almost half of them in textiles and food processing and the rest in mechanical and chemical industries.[47] By 1911 the proportion of industrial workers of Lucca had increased threefold, to 17 percent of the population of the province.[48]

In the south, by contrast, only 1 percent of the inhabitants of Cosenza worked in industry in 1898, mostly in food processing. A report on manufacturing in Cosenza concluded that there were very few encouraging signs of an industrial future for the province.[49] And in 1911, indeed, only 2 percent of the people of Cosenza were classified as industrial workers.[50] In Palermo only 3 percent of the people were industrial workers in 1891; most were in food processing, with small numbers in the chemical and textile industries.[51] By 1925 industrial workers in the province of Palermo made up about 4 percent of the total population. But at that time over 20 percent of the people of Genoa worked in industry.[52]

Though Italy had some industry, it was by and large an agrarian society, and one almost totally untouched by the modernization of agriculture that took place in Northern Europe and the United States in the second half of the nineteenth century. Many noted this difference between Italy and other European nations. In 1883 Senator Stefano Jacini presented to the Italian Senate the results of the most extensive survey of Italian agriculture ever made. Jacini concluded: "Italians are neither willing nor able to bring about the modernization of their agricultural economy so that it can compete with the more advanced European countries. The future is not bright."[53] Over the years, both the Italian government and the Italian people debated the issue of agrarian reform. Various measures were attempted, particularly in the south, but to little avail. The first land reform law, passed in 1861, was followed by others in

1884, 1893, 1902, and 1904. The purpose of the laws was to create small farms and small landowners. But breaking up the land into economically inefficient units to be worked by illiterate peasants did not lead to the needed modernization of agriculture.[54]

The last two decades of the nineteenth century saw the publication of many books and pamphlets by Italian economists and social scientists on the condition of the Italian agrarian economy and on ways to modernize it. Amid the great variety of subjects discussed and solutions suggested—none of which were carried out—one point was invariably made, that the greatest obstacle to the modernization of Italian agriculture was the mentality of the peasants themselves. Francesco Coletti, one of the most perceptive students of Italian peasants at the turn of the century, wrote extensively about what he called the "transcendental resistance to change of our peasants."[55]

Agricultural experts who toured the country on behalf of local agricultural committees to teach peasants new techniques met with suspicion and resistance, and finally gave up in frustration. One such expert wrote to the director of the agricultural committee in Lucca: "After trying to organize meetings in the evenings and visiting peasants in the fields during the day, I came to the conclusion that resistance to any kind of change is the very nature of these people."[56] Another expert, after visiting several towns in Palermo province, stated: "I believe the ancient Romans used more efficient farming techniques than the people of these provinces. There is no way to teach them to do things differently. Most of them do not even bother to answer a question. Those who do, argue that books and experts cannot be trusted, and that experience is the only valid guide. Of course, the only valid experience is their own."[57] The four social scientists who wrote the final reports for the Jacini survey on the provinces of Genoa, Lucca, Cosenza, and Palermo also concluded that the greatest resistance to change came from the peasants themselves.[58]

This picture of an Italian peasantry adamantly resisting any change can be misleading. Italian peasant society was indeed changing, and in ways that were important in the rise of emigration and return migration. A major force in Italian society was the peasants' desire to become small landowners. The Napoleonic reforms and the Risorgimento accelerated the decline of feudal entail. The process of forming free properties started as early as the third decade of the eighteenth century in the Italian south, where the land reform of the Bourbon dynasty added new land by means of draining swamps and terracing. Olive and vine planting also increased. The process continued, both in the north and in the south, but more vigorously in the north, from the Napoleonic era up to the unification of Italy. During the Risorgimento, Italian peasants showed a considerable revolutionary potential, both in 1848 and in 1860 when Garibaldi conquered the Kingdom of the Two Sicilies. Most peasants were more interested in acquiring land than in political independence; if they joined Garibaldi, it was very unlikely that they did so for the lofty ideals of national unity and independence. The seizure of land by peasants in sporadic rebellions took place before the unification of Italy and also after 1870. Subsequent land reform laws were mostly symbolic acts of governmental goodwill intended to placate rebels and prevent further outbreaks.[59]

In sum, Italy in the late nineteenth century was a complex society that can hardly be described by using the conventional categories of traditional and modern. On the one hand, the peasants showed an almost "transcendent resistance to change," on the other, a revolutionary potential that occasionally erupted in rebellion. The result was a kind of socioeconomic ferment not ordinarily associated with so-called traditional peasant societies. Finally, profound regional and social differences helped to create wide variations in culture and aspirations.

Nine Communities

From naturalization and death records it is possible to single out one or more communities in each province from which considerably more people came to San Francisco than from anywhere else in the province. I identified nine such communities: in the province of Genoa, the city of Genoa and the communes of Lorsica and Sestri Levante; in the province of Lucca, the city of Lucca and the commune of Porcari; in the province of Cosenza, the commune of Verbicaro; and in the province of Palermo, the city of Palermo and the communes of Trabia and Santa Flavia. The location of these communities is shown in Map 2.

The concentration of immigrants from the same town in an American city is hardly surprising. It was common for immigrants to send for relatives and friends to join them, thus starting a process of chain migration. In the 1880's the Italian consul in San Francisco pointed out that an increase in the number of immigrants had been made possible by tickets sent to Italy from San Francisco through the White Line Travel Agency. "Obviously," the consul noted, "tickets

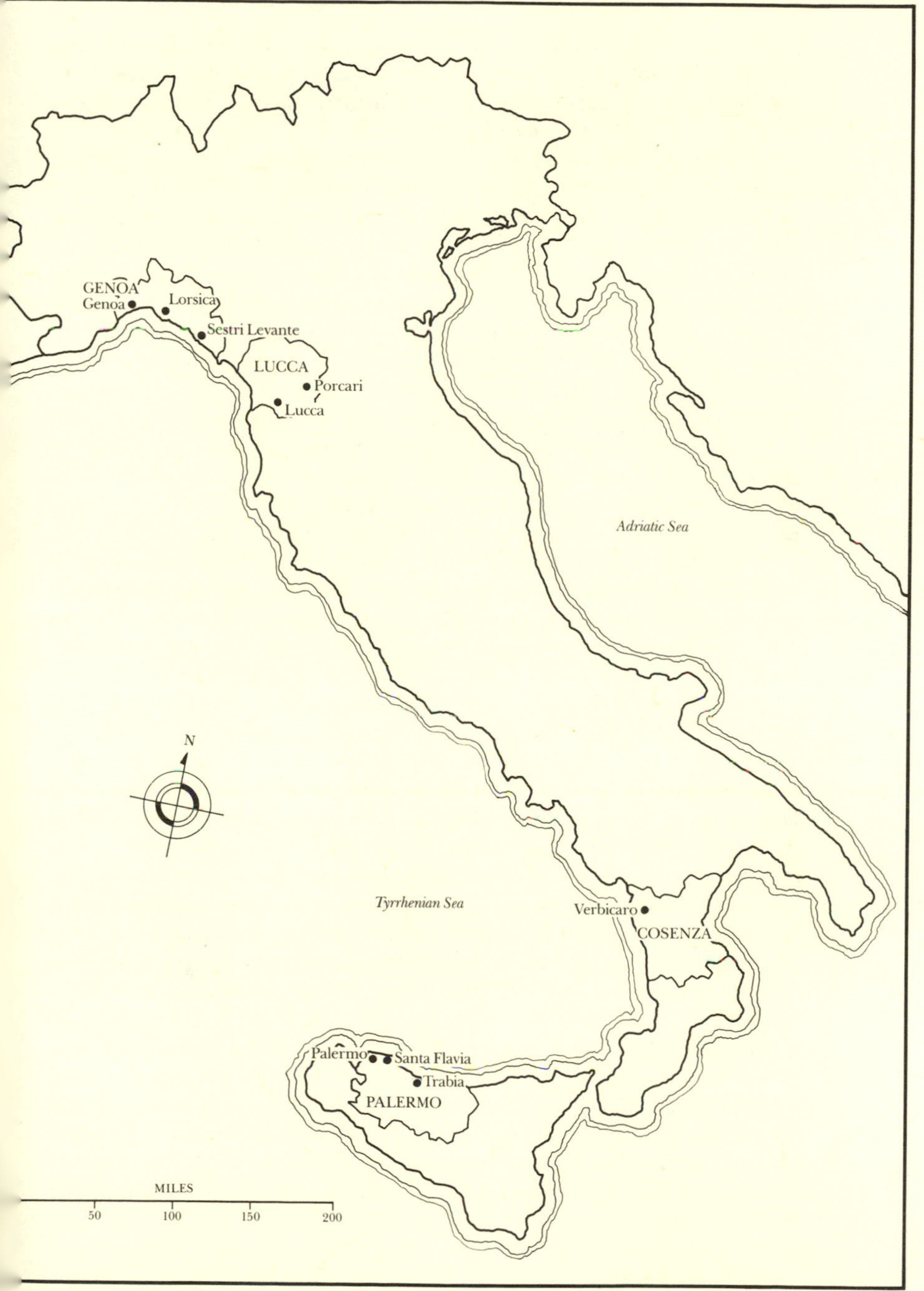

Map 2. Provinces and communes of Italy discussed in this book

are sent to relatives in the same town."[60] A few years later, the mayor of Lorsica wrote that "emigration to San Francisco has been on the increase recently. The major incentive to go is the tickets that relatives send from San Francisco."[61]

Chain migration was important in the movement of Italians to America. It affected the geographical distribution of Italians in American cities, their occupations, and their social organization. Chain migration can be defined as the movement of migrants who learn of opportunities abroad from previous migrants; perhaps the earlier migrants also pay the later ones' passage and provide initial accommodations and employment for them. Chain migration, based on primary social relationships, is therefore unlike organized migration, which is based on impersonal recruitment and assistance; an example of organized migration was the work of the International Refugee Organization after the Second World War. Impersonally organized migration brought many Italians to American cities, as will be seen in the next chapter, and perhaps an equal number came by chain migration.[62]

Immigrants from the same place often created distinct communities in American cities. As early as 1898 Jacob Riis found that immigrants from the Calabria region lived on Mulberry Street in New York, grouped according to their town of origin.[63] Immigrants from the Sicilian town of Sciacca concentrated in one part of the Italian section of Norristown, Pennsylvania.[64] In New Haven, immigrants from Amalfi and Scafati Atrani, two towns in the province of Salerno about fifty miles south of Naples, concentrated in one neighborhood.[65] A sizable part of the Middletown, Connecticut, Italian community had migrated from the Sicilian town of Melilli.[66] Sicilians from the large town of Termini Imerese in Palermo province gathered in Cleveland, Rochester, and Kansas City.[67]

In the many descriptions of the Italian community in San Francisco, the differences between northerners and southerners have often been discussed, but never those between immigrants from specific Italian towns. To form a profile of the immigrants from each of the nine Italian communes, I looked at naturalization records. The largest of my groups, with 250 people, was from Lucca, and the smallest was from Palermo, with 98 (see the Bibliographical Essay for a complete list). To obtain a clearer picture of the change over time in each of the groups, I used vital statistics on both the immigrants' parents who remained in Italy and their children, most of whom were born and eventually married in California. In this study, the immigrants' parents are designated the Italian generation and the immigrants' children the Italo-American generation.[68]

The nine communes were not only vastly different in population, but also in their growth between 1871 and 1921, the period of mass emigration.* As Table 1 shows, the city of Genoa grew the most; from 130,000 in 1871 to over 300,000 in 1921. Lorsica, on the other hand, declined; this small commune in the hinterland of Genoa had 1,907 people in 1871 and only 1,276 in 1921. Over the same period Sestri Levante, one of the largest communes in the province of Genoa, grew from 9,000 to over 14,000. Lucca more than doubled its population, from 36,000 to 78,000.†

Verbicaro was the only commune in the province of Cosenza from which a significant number of people left for San Francisco. Located at an altitude of 2,000 feet and almost totally isolated from the communes of the coast, Verbicaro was often described, at least in the late nineteenth century, as one of the most primitive communes in Italy.[69] By the end of the period of emigration, its population had declined from 5,200 to 4,500. Palermo was one of the largest cities in the nation, with over 200,000 people in 1871. Fifty years later, it had almost doubled in population. Trabia, a relatively small agricultural commune in Sicily, where 10,000 was the average size, grew slightly from 4,600 to 4,800. The fishing community of Santa Flavia, in contrast, had a major increase, from 3,400 to 5,200.

The Italian community of San Francisco was unique among the many that Italians established in the New World. Most Italians

*The following terminology is used in connection with the nine groups. The word commune refers to an incorporated territory enjoying administrative autonomy under a mayor and a council. Each commune was formed either by one town only, or by one town and a number of villages. The town was the major population center of the commune, and ordinarily also the seat of the commune's administration. A village, therefore, was a smaller community, separate from a town but forming with it and other villages an incorporated commune. A number of communes—from twenty to sixty—made up a *circondario*. Finally, several circondari typically formed a province; an exception was the province of Lucca, which had only one circondario.

†In presenting the nine communes, I stated that Lucca and Porcari were the two communes under study in the province of Lucca. Table 1 introduces another town, Capannori, and leaves out Porcari. The explanation is that Porcari was one of the 39 villages forming the commune of Capannori from 1871 until 1913, when Porcari became an independent commune. Accordingly, for the years before 1913, when data for the village of Porcari are not available, I will use data for the commune of Capannori. The table shows Capannori with fewer people in 1921 than in 1871; but the loss is misleading, since about 7,000 people broke off to form the new commune of Porcari.

TABLE 1

Population of the Nine Communes, 1871–1921

Commune	1871	1881	1901	1911	1921
Genoa	130,269	179,515	219,507	265,533	304,108
Lorsica	1,907	1,841	1,660	1,451	1,276
S. Levante	8,793	9,650	12,039	12,910	14,444
Capannori	43,313	43,673	48,217	47,650	41,828
Lucca	36,248	45,328	73,465	76,160	78,575
Verbicaro	5,199	5,108	4,624	4,517	4,507
Sta. Flavia	3,444	3,666	4,742	5,537	5,242
Trabia	4,618	5,176	5,601	5,108	4,765
Palermo	219,398	241,618	305,716	336,148	392,895

SOURCE: National censuses.

NOTE: In 1871 the city of Genoa was made up of the old *quartieri* (neighborhoods) of San Teodoro, Prà, Maddalena, Porto, Pretoria, Molo, and San Vincenzo. By 1881 the adjacent communities of Foce, Marassi, San Fruttuoso, San Martino d'Albaro, Staglieno, and Sezione Mare had been declared parts of Genoa. This explains some of the growth from 1871 to 1881.

who emigrated came from two specific parts of the nation, the northwest and the southwest. The northwesterners, from the Maritime Alps and the northern Apennines, typically went to South America, whereas the southwesterners, from the southern Apennines and the island of Sicily, typically went to the northeast and midwest of the United States. San Francisco was the only place in the New World where the two streams met and mingled. The city received few immigrants from the northern Alps of Piedmont and Lombardy, except from Valtellina and the province of Sondrio, two areas near the Swiss border. Nor did many come from the Veneto, the region in the northeast close to Austria and Yugoslavia. Alpine migrants tended to go to European countries and Australia. The peoples of the Po River Plains, especially those of Emilia-Romagna and the central hills of the Florentine and Umbrian regions, rarely left Italy.[70]

The backgrounds of the nine groups of San Francisco Italians differed in a number of ways. Three of the groups came from urban areas. Genoa and Palermo, in fact, were two of the largest cities in the country, and Lucca, although only a middle-sized city, was the capital of a province and the center of a regional agricultural market. Though immigrants from Lorsica, Porcari, Verbicaro, and Trabia all came from communes where agriculture was almost the sole economic activity, there were differences. Lorsica and Verbicaro were in the mountains, and thus did not produce two cash crops common in the lowlands, wine and wheat. In Porcari and

Trabia, on the other hand, wine and wheat were the basic cash crops. Finally, the communes of Sestri Levante and Santa Flavia had a mixed economy. About 80 percent of the workers of Santa Flavia were fishermen who, during the harvest season, left town to work on the large estates about ten miles inland. In Sestri Levante most of the inhabitants were commercial fishermen and also small landowners or renters who farmed their plots when they were not at sea.

Mass emigration seems to have had a greater effect on the communities in the mountains than on those in the lowlands and on the coast. Lorsica and Verbicaro, both mountain communities, had fewer people in 1921 than in 1871, with Lorsica showing a net decrease of about 33 percent and Verbicaro 13 percent. The other seven communes, notwithstanding the emigration, were all larger in 1921 than in 1871. The cities of Genoa and Lucca more than doubled; Palermo grew by 78 percent; and the smaller communities grew between 3 percent, for Trabia, and 64 percent, for Sestri Levante. Thus there was a substantial population decline in the mountain communities, particularly in the smaller places like Lorsica; a modest increase in the lowlands; and a great increase in the larger cities.[71] If the nine communes are representative of Italian emigration in general, the census figures reflect a population movement starting in the mountain communities and having its main impact there. The people of these areas first moved to the lowlands; some then settled in the large cities of the coast, and others crossed the Atlantic.

Timing and Previous Experience

There are two other important regional differences in Italy that can shed light on differences found in San Francisco. The first is that emigration to San Francisco did not begin in all four provinces at the same time. The second is that at the time the first emigrants left for San Francisco the people of each province had had different experience with both internal and international migration. These differences are important: earlier immigrants are likely to have an advantage over those who come later, and immigrants acquainted with the notion of geographical movement are likely to be more open to change than those never exposed to it.

The immigrants from Genoa, more than the others, enjoyed both advantages: they arrived first, and they had previous experience with internal and also international migration. A few Genoese came to San Francisco before the gold rush.[72] But most who left Genoa before 1848 went to South America, following the routes of Italian shipping companies. When rumors of gold reached Brazil and Argentina in 1848, some of the Genoese there left for San Francisco. These forty-eighters informed relatives and friends about California.[73] In 1871 the prefetto of Genoa reported: "Before 1850 people had hardly heard of California, and San Francisco was known only by the most adventurous merchants. California and San Francisco became household words when Genoese who had previously migrated to South America reached San Francisco and asked relatives to join them there."[74]

The first immigrants from Lucca arrived in San Francisco a few years after the Genoese. Luccans also had a long tradition of international migration, in both Europe and the Americas, as itinerant merchants of statuettes. The Italian consul in Antwerp, for instance, noted in 1866 that statuette merchants from Lucca had been passing through the city on their way to the large European capitals for over a century.[75] In the 1860's and 1870's statuettes of Garibaldi and Pope Pius IX apparently sold well among European liberals and Catholics, and Lincoln sold well in the United States.[76] When some merchants from Lucca decided to stay in San Francisco, instead of taking the usual route down the California coast to Mexico and South America, they formed the nucleus of what became the largest regional group in San Francisco.[77] By 1856 there were a number of Luccans in San Francisco, as an item in a Lucca newspaper indicates: "On July 5, 1880, A. F. Rocchicchioli died in San Francisco at the age of 52. He was born in this province, and had lived with other Lucchesi in San Francisco since 1856."[78] "Traditionally," a social scientist from Lucca reported in 1882, "our statuette merchants did not settle abroad. Now, even those who have never left the province want to join the merchants who have founded several communities of Lucchesi in Europe and the Americas."[79]

We know less about the first immigrants from the provinces of Cosenza and Palermo. Not until after 1885 do reports from the Italian consul in San Francisco and other documents mention immigrants from these provinces. In 1887, for instance, the consul wrote that "southern Italians, most from Sicily and the province of Cosenza, have been arriving in increasing numbers within the last few years. Before, they were only a few."[80] And in 1889 *La Voce del Popolo* reported "increasing arrivals of immigrants from other parts of Italy, especially Sicily and the deep south, so far almost unrepresented among us."[81]

It is likely that the first immigrants from Cosenza were former brigands. In the 1860's and 1870's brigandage was a vast and complex phenomenon in the deep south. Some brigands were the paramilitary retainers of nobles and bishops. After the annexation of the south to Italy following the Garibaldi campaign, some brigands fought for the Bourbon dynasty against the Piedmontese invaders. Others were peasants who became outlaws when the new Italian government did not carry out the social reforms that Garibaldi had promised them, especially in regard to land distribution.

Regardless of the origin of brigandage, all brigands shared a common handicap; they were wanted by the Italian government, which was determined to suppress political dissent. To avoid capture and execution, some brigands escaped, first to the mountains of the Sila and then out of the country. In 1879 the prefetto of Cosenza reported: "Conditions of internal security are much improved. I have been told that several notorious brigands who terrorized the region for years have left the region and, via Palermo, have reached New Orleans and the American west."[82] Three years later the prefetto wrote: "Some people are leaving for California now. Before, the few who left went to South America. A trusted source has told me that the tickets of the emigrants to California have been paid for by former outlaws who left this province years ago for Palermo and New Orleans."[83]

Unlike the provinces of Lucca and Genoa, Cosenza did not have a tradition of international migration. As the history of the Torrano family illustrates, temporary migration to Sicily and other regions of the south had been common since at least the 1850's. But when international migration started, the prefetto recognized it as a departure from tradition: "Some adventurers are leaving for the Americas now. There are only a few of them, and this phenomenon is totally new in the province."[84]

The people of Palermo themselves lacked any experience in either internal or international migration. The province had, however, traditionally been the destination of temporary migrants.[85] When Sicilians first began to emigrate overseas, they went to South America, but by the late 1870's some had reached the United States. As the prefetto reported in 1878: "Overseas migration was exclusively directed to South America until a few years ago. Now some emigrants leave for the United States, taking ships from Palermo to

New Orleans. I am told that most Sicilians stay in New Orleans. But a few go on to California by train."[86] Naturalization records show that some immigrants from Palermo who eventually settled in San Francisco had previously spent several years in New Orleans. Possibly Sicilians living in New Orleans heard of jobs in California from Italians who were on their way to California and decided to follow them, since most Italians reached California by train from New York via New Orleans.[87] In addition, many Sicilians had been brought to New Orleans as indentured servants to work on Louisiana plantations, where they were treated like slaves and in many instances actually took the place of the slaves. When federal authorities forced the release of these Sicilians, it is likely that many left Louisiana for California.

The Italians who came to San Francisco, more than simply the products of traditional peasant society, were a complex people. Italian society, to be sure, could not be equated with the more dynamic societies of northern Europe and the United States. But Italy was undergoing profound changes nevertheless, well before mass emigration started. The interaction between the Italian and American peoples, two groups changing in very different ways, is in large measure the story of the San Francisco Italians.

CHAPTER 3

American Money and Italian Land

EVEN WHEN undertaken under the most favorable of circumstances, emigration brings about major changes in the lives of individuals and groups. From the 1870's to the 1920's several million Italians opened themselves to such changes by leaving their villages for North or South America. Their decision to leave may be surprising if we recall that those emigrants were the same people Coletti described as imbued with a transcendent resistance to change. What forces, we may ask, broke that resistance and drove them to cross the Atlantic? Or perhaps another hypothesis comes nearer to the mark: that emigration was not so drastic a change as it seems, after all, but only the continuation of trends already present among the Italians of the late nineteenth century.

Most immigration historians of the last two decades would agree with John Briggs in discarding the notion that immigrants "were Old World minds and souls who either clung irrationally and at an unreasonable cost to an irrelevant past, or who submitted passively to the powerful forces shaping their future." On the contrary, most accept that "immigrants were rational, confident, capable, and talented individuals who contributed to shaping their future rather than receiving their destinies wholly defined and packaged by others."[1] Some historians have attempted to demonstrate the active role of the immigrants by pointing to patterns of continuity between the immigrants' lives in the Old World and the New. The emphasis, however, has been on the New World. Apart from the fact that the immigrants were poor, we learn little about how the social dynamics of the Old World shaped the immigrant experience.

To show continuity, moreover, it is not enough simply to document that certain Italian social institutions and patterns of living were similar in both Italy and America. This approach, in my opinion, uses marginal evidence to prove a central point. It seems obvious that any group of people forced to live in a strange land will seek security by trying to preserve some continuity with its past. But such efforts by immigrants to protect themselves were only palliatives masking the central fact that separation from the home country implied a basic break with it. To see a deeper continuity in the immigrants' lives we have to address this central question: was emigration only an apparent break with the past, despite the geographical distance between Italy and America? From this perspective, we will see that emigration was a strategy for achieving goals in Italy. It was an act in the larger drama of social change in late-nineteenth-century Italian society.

A Sudden Mass Phenomenon

Certain characteristics of Italian emigration suggest that environmental forces carried more weight in the departure of Italians than the personal choices of individuals. Emigration from Italy became a mass movement, almost a flood, within only a few years. The suddenness of the phenomenon suggests not a period of evolving social dynamics, but the unexpected breakdown of society. In the 1860's and early 1870's, overseas migration was still an uncommon event. Leone Carpi, one of the first to gather statistics on departing Italians, wrote that during those years most emigrants were either political refugees, merchants escaping the uncertain conditions after the liberal revolutions of 1830 and 1848, or people from the province of Genoa, which had a long history of overseas migration.[2] International migration gained momentum after 1875. From 1876 to 1880, about 100,000 Italians left the country every year. By 1887 the annual departures were over 200,000; in the 1890's they reached 300,000; and in 1900, 352,000. From 1901 to 1915, with the exception of 1904 and 1908, over half a million Italians left each year; and in 1905, 1906, 1907, and 1912, the departures exceeded 700,000. The exodus reached its peak in 1913, when almost one million Italians left the country: that was 2.85 percent of the total population.[3]

Until the 1880's most Italian emigrants set sail for South America, but during the 1880's an increasing number went to the United States. In 1879, for instance, 120,000 Italians left the country,

37,000 of them for overseas destinations. Of those departing for overseas, 13 percent went to the United States, 32 percent to Argentina, 16 percent to Brazil, and the rest to undetermined destinations. In 1890, by contrast, 215,000 Italians left the country, 113,000 for overseas. Of all those who went overseas, 44 percent went to the United States, 31 percent to Argentina, and 14 percent to Brazil. In 1906, 787,000 Italians left Italy, 512,000 for overseas countries. Of these, 67 percent went to the United States, 20 percent to Argentina, and 6 percent to Brazil. Only after the First World War did emigration to Argentina again greatly exceed that to the United States. In 1923, for instance, of the 184,000 emigrants, 57 percent went to Argentina and only 28 percent to the United States.[4]

Provincial prefetti, mayors, and other observers often pointed out this rapid increase in emigration.[5] The prefetto of Cosenza, for instance, wrote in 1894: "Going to America has become so popular recently that young men feel almost ashamed if they have not been overseas at least once. Ten years ago America evoked images of danger and distance. Now people feel more confident about going to New York than to Rome."[6] The prefetti of Lucca and Palermo sent similar reports to Rome.[7] The province of Genoa, though having a different past, was not an exception; as the prefetto reported in 1884: "Emigration to America has been a tradition for a long time in this province. Lately, however, the movement has assumed larger proportions."[8] A report of 1888 in Lucca gave this summary: "Emigration, not only from this province but from the country in general, has spread like a disease that nobody can control."[9]

One may rightly wonder whether the rise in emigration from Italy was indeed as sudden as the prefetti imply. Indeed, international emigration seems to have increased gradually over a period of 25 years: about 100,000 per year from 1875 to 1880, 200,000 per year during the 1880's, and 300,000 per year from 1890 to 1900. Internal migration, moreover, had been common in Italy. Emigration must be seen within the context of Italian society at the time. Today, modern organizational techniques make it possible to mobilize millions of people in a very short time. But in nineteenth-century Italy the departure within a year of 100,000 people out of a population of 25 million and the increase in emigration of another 100,000 within a few years were striking occurrences. Internal migration in Italy covered only a short distance, was seasonal, and did not involve many people. Going overseas, on the other hand, was perceived as a major departure from traditional migration.

The Escape from Poverty

Another characteristic of Italian emigration suggesting the power of environmental forces is that many emigrants had to leave Italy to avoid starvation. Many, in fact, were channeled to the United States by agents, who often did not even inform the emigrants of their destination. Students of immigration later documented the relationship between a push factor, poverty in Italy, and a pull factor, economic opportunity abroad. Harry Jerome, for instance, found a direct correlation between the rate of departures from Italian ports and the economic conditions in Italy and the United States: an increase in pig iron production in the United States or a poor harvest in Italy was usually followed by an increase in Italian emigration.[10] Others have pointed out that since poverty was less common in urban areas, emigration from cities or industrialized regions was nearly negligible, and most emigrants came from the poorest districts.[11]

All the literature on Italian peasants, including reports by prefetti and mayors, government and private surveys, and the accounts of immigrants themselves, testifies that extreme poverty was the main cause of emigration. In 1875 Pasquale Villari, one of the most perceptive students of Italian society in the second half of the nineteenth century, directed national attention to the peasants with a series of articles in the Milan newspaper *L'Opinione.* He wrote: "The social and economic conditions of millions of Italian peasants are incredibly poor and totally unknown to our government. It is unlikely that any change will occur as long as the peasants remain in Italy."[12] In another widely publicized essay at about the same time, Sidney Sonnino described conditions in northern Italy: "Our peasants live lives unfit for humans. Even in the more prosperous regions of the north, peasants work from sunrise to sunset, seven days a week. Regardless of how hard they try, they will never be able to improve their condition as long as they stay where they are. The odds against them are too great. A change in government or a social reform will not be able to humanize them."[13]

Turning to the south, Sonnino wrote: "Our peasants there are in worse conditions than the serfs of the Middle Ages." The landlords treated them like slaves. "Peasants live like beasts. Their sense of dignity seems to have died centuries ago. They have two equally hard choices before them—submission and work until an untimely death, or rebellion and a violent death—unless they are willing to escape to somewhere else."[14] At the turn of the century, Giustino

Fortunato, the representative of one of the poorest districts of the south in the Chamber of Deputies, described to his colleagues "the sadness of the physical and social landscape of the provinces of Calabria and Basilicata and the tragic reality of regions where peasants live months and years without ever seeing a happy face." And he concluded: "It is unlikely that these people will learn to smile as long as they stay in the deep south."[15]

Much was heard about the poverty of the peasants' housing and diet. In the province of Genoa: "Peasants who own larger farms live in better houses. But families with small holdings or no property at all live in houses not fit for humans."[16] Sonnino found as many as 30 families, including wives and children, living in a single large room. A survey of housing in the province of Cosenza in 1910 concluded: "Our people rot in these slums." Overcrowding was worse than what the official census of 1881 had indicated. Of the 1,400 dwellings described in the Cosenza survey, about 400 housed more than six people per room and another 400 from four to six people. Most houses had no windows; all of them lacked cooking facilities.[17] In the province of Palermo, the American consul wrote: "Peasants as well as mechanics live in one-room dwellings, ten or fifteen sharing the same room, and using the same bed, which is visible from the street day and night." And those who could afford such conditions were the more fortunate; many were homeless, "living in the streets for lack of shelter."[18] The 1881 census showed a ratio of one person per room in the more prosperous regions of the north. In the south the rate was three per room; and the one-room house was the rule in the poorest communities of the deep south, such as Verbicaro.[19]

As for the peasants' diet, a series of surveys taken between 1878 and 1917 revealed that the average family spent 75 to 85 percent of its income on food. The main foods were corn in the north of Italy and wheat in the south.[20] "We are all aware," said Jacini, "of the mental and physical diseases brought on by eating only corn. Yet even corn is becoming a luxury in some communities."[21] Villari wrote that laborers in the provinces of Cosenza and Palermo had to work from sunrise to sunset on a pound of bread a day. After following a group of them to the fields for several days, he remarked that he could not think of anything that could be added to the lives of those peasants to make them more miserable. In 1900 the life expectancy of a fieldworker in the province of Cosenza was 29 years.[22]

The prolonged agricultural depression from the mid-1880's through the 1890's hit the peasants hard. In the late 1880's the prefetto of Genoa reported: "The cost of oil and other items is so high that people are forced to leave for overseas to avoid starvation."[23] In the province of Cosenza the conditions were described as "extremely precarious," and those in Verbicaro as "alarming."[24] Crops failed in 1889, 1890, and 1893 in most communes of the province; during the winter of 1893–94 the people of several communities survived by eating roots.[25] In the spring of 1894 the prefetto wrote: "People are leaving in large numbers; they think they have no alternative, and they are unwilling to face another winter here. Poverty seems to have broken their will to fight. Their departure is like the flight of people who have nothing to lose by going."[26]

In Palermo at the end of 1888 the prefetto cabled Rome: "Conditions were bad last year. I have only to add that this year they are worse, and that starvation is forcing the peasants to go, although most of them are reluctant to make that decision."[27] The reports arriving in Rome from Palermo between 1888 and 1893 informed the government that wages were decreasing, foodstuffs were unavailable in a number of communes in the interior, and cholera epidemics were breaking out. The production of olive oil, a major commodity in the local economy, was falling off because of foreign competition and damage to the olive groves by an unknown disease.[28] Fishing too was hurt by the depression. In 1895 the mayor of Santa Flavia reported: "The fishermen of this town are forced to leave. The basic reason is that they cannot sell their catch. There is simply no cash in the region, and commerce has come to a standstill."[29]

The American Fever

Under these circumstances, it is no surprise that America became a household word. An American visitor to the south wrote: "There was constant talk of America on the trains, on the roads, and in towns. In a small southern town I saw a great throng of people. Upon inquiring, I was told that they had been to the station to say goodbye to 120 of their townsmen who had just left for America."[30] Even in the most isolated communities, emigration to America was the topic of lively discussion. There were people who could name the President of the United States but not the King of Italy.[31] In 1896 the prefetto of Palermo reported: "America seems to have an irresistible attraction for these people. Sicilians have traditionally been unwilling to leave the island, even to go to Italy. But America seems to be different. Or is it that they leave because they have no alternative, and anything is an improvement over their present condition in Sicily?"[32]

Adolfo Rossi, the commissioner of emigration, asked the president of an agricultural society in the province of Cosenza why America had become so popular in just a few years. The president answered: "Life was impossible here. When the first pioneers came back with money and told the peasants that it was possible to make a living across the ocean, desperation turned into hope. Why shouldn't they go? Or more to the point, do these people have other alternatives? America has become a disease, but out of necessity."[33] Letters from America and reports by returnees had a profound impact. The prefetto of Palermo, after visiting a ship about to leave for New Orleans, wrote: "There were over 300 people departing. As I talked to several of them, I realized that the most powerful arguments in favor of leaving had been the stories they heard from returnees and the fact that they had no alternatives left. It is either starvation or emigration."[34] A peasant was reported to have said: "If America did not exist, we would have to invent it for the sake of our survival."[35]

In addition to letters from America and stories told by returnees, the work of emigration agents was important in making emigration a mass movement even from remote villages. These agents, acting on behalf of Italian and foreign shipping companies and immigration agencies abroad, promoted the idea of emigration and also arranged for the departure of those who wanted to go. In the northern provinces emigration agents distributed pamphlets and made public appearances at local celebrations. In 1884 there were 34 agencies in the city of Genoa, employing several hundred agents throughout the province. The prefetto reported that promoters of emigration to California were active in Fontanabuona, Sestri Levante, and Lorsica.[36] Apparently, there were fewer emigration agents in the province of Lucca. The prefetto notified the Minister of the Interior that some were active in the southern communes of the province. But in the northern communes of Lucca the idea of emigration was mainly spread by word of mouth. The southern communes of Genoa province, such as Varese Ligure and Lignano, were only twenty miles north of the northernmost communes of Lucca, such as Giuncugnano, Sillano, and Minucciano.[37]

In the southern provinces, where literacy was rarer and outsiders not readily accepted, emigration was promoted by other means. Large posters were put up; agents were more often local people than in the north; and local leaders were paid by the agents to provide

2. Emigration agency, Udine, Italy, early 1900's. Emigration agencies supported by Italian and foreign shipping companies played an important role in the departure of large numbers of Italians. The agency pictured here, located in the Italian northeast, served emigrants leaving for North, Central, and South America. Its sign features two of Italy's largest shipping companies, Veloce and Navigazione Generale Italiana.

lists of families in great poverty.[38] The prefetto of Cosenza described how agents came to a celebration in Orsomarso, ten miles from Verbicaro: "Early in the morning, they erected a podium in the town square. From it, they addressed the people, offering explanations and especially dispelling doubts whenever peasants approached them and showed an interest in leaving."[39]

The rapid increase in emigration in the 1870's and 1880's, along with the widespread poverty of Italian peasants, suggests that departing Italians had little time to make plans, that they were forced to leave by events beyond their control. The vigorous activity of the emigration agents, who sent Italians overseas according to the demands of the American markets and the interests of the shipping companies, seems to support the idea that departing Italians were at the mercy of outside forces. On the surface, then, emigration seems a sudden, unplanned change, rather than a gradual and deliberate response to long-term social dynamics.

Regional Rates of Emigration

Yet despite the widespread poverty in Italy and the opportunity presented by the New World, there is reason to doubt any simple push-pull explanation for the massive emigration. Such an explanation is called into question by statistics that show virtually no emigration from some of the poorest parts of Italy.

Regional rates of emigration for the years 1902 to 1913, calculated from the number of passports issued for transatlantic travel and from shipping passenger lists, reveal some interesting contrasts. The rate of departures for those years was 39 per 1,000 for the Emilia-Romagna, Tuscany, and Umbria regions. Emilia-Romagna is located in the north-northeast of the Italian peninsula, and Tuscany and Umbria are in the center-east section. In the south the rate was much higher: 338 per 1,000 for Abbruzzi-Molise, 340 for Basilicata, and 368 for Calabria. All these are regions of the deep south. The south, however, was far from homogeneous. The rate for Apulia, a region in the southeast, was only 118 per 1,000. The two islands of Sicily and Sardinia had widely different rates: 263 per 1,000 for Sicily and 37 per 1,000 for Sardinia. These figures clearly show a marked difference between regions of the center-north and the deep south, and also differences within the south itself and between the two islands.

Further differences within the regions can be seen from Table 2, which shows the rate of departures from eight Italian provinces (the four that are the focus of this study and four others) in the randomly chosen years 1888, 1902, and 1919.[40] As the table shows, there was a great difference between Genoa, in the northwest, and Forlì, in the northeast, a difference that lessened only after the First World War. The gap between the provinces of Florence and Lucca was even wider. In 1888 about 25 per 1,000 left Lucca, whereas only 0.8 left Florence. The two provinces are located in the Tuscany region about 50 miles apart. Cosenza is in the southwest and Lecce in the southeast. The difference between them in emigration rate was

TABLE 2

Rate of Emigration from Eight Italian Provinces, 1888, 1902, 1919

Province	Rate per 1,000 inhabitants		
	1888	1902	1919
Genoa (North)	8.0	9.0	7.0
Forlì (North)	0.7	0.9	3.0
Lucca (Center)	25.0	19.0	14.0
Florence (Center)	0.8	0.4	8.0
Cosenza (South)	20.0	20.0	13.0
Lecce (South)	0.03	0.4	1.0
Palermo (Sicily)	4.8	15.0	10.0
Syracuse (Sicily)	0.09	5.0	8.0

SOURCE: *Statistica dell'Emigrazione Italiana all'Estero*, Italy [35], 1888, p. 28; 1902–3, pp. 65–66; 1918–20, p. 95.

great in all three years, and especially so before the First World War. Finally the Sicilian provinces of Palermo in the center-north and Syracuse in the southeast started out with markedly different rates and progressively grew close. These figures, although for three years only, show great differences that tend to level off after the First World War. The postwar emigration might well have been in part the outcome of social and economic dislocation caused by the war, which affected the whole nation. The prewar emigration was more likely to reflect long-standing provincial socioeconomic differences.

The intensity of emigration from the four provinces that are the focus of this study can also be seen from a comparison of the rates of emigration from these provinces with the rate from the country as a whole. In 1881, when the emigrants from the province of Genoa amounted to 2.2 percent of the total population of the province, the national rate was 0.6 percent.[41] In 1882 2 percent of the population of the province of Lucca emigrated, as against a national rate of 0.5 percent.[42] Ten years later, the rate from Lucca was 2.2 percent; the national rate was 0.7 percent. In 1906, the year 788,000 Italians left the country and 358,000 of them went to the United States, the emigrants from Lucca were 3.2 percent of the provincial population, and the national rate was 2.3 percent. In 1913, when almost 900,000 left the country, 376,000 for the United States, the rate was 3.1 for Lucca and 2.4 for the country.[43] From the province of Cosenza, from 1886 to 1890, the annual departure rate averaged about 2 percent, compared to a national rate of 0.7 percent. From 1901 to 1905 an average of 2.8 percent emigrated from Cosenza, as against 1.6 percent from all Italy.[44] In 1902 and 1903 the rate for the province of

Palermo was 2.2, that for the country as a whole 1.4.[45] Clearly, the rate of emigration from these four provinces, though it varied, was substantially higher than that from the entire country.

The rate of emigration varied throughout Italy, and not only in the eight provinces just discussed. It is possible, in a general way, to divide Italy into areas with low and high rates of emigration. The areas of low emigration were the Emilia-Romagna region, located south of the Po River and stretching from the Tyrrhenian Sea to the Adriatic, with the exception of the three provinces of Modena, Parma, and Piacenza; the central regions, like Tuscany, Marche, Umbria, and Lazio, with the exception of the province of Lucca; the Apulia region, located in the southeast; the Sicilian hinterland; and the island of Sardinia. The areas of high emigration were all the regions north of the Po; the three provinces of Modena, Parma, and Piacenza; the province of Lucca; except for Apulia, all the regions of the south, such as Abruzzi, Campania, Basilicata, and Calabria; and the coastal areas of Sicily. The four provinces of Genoa, Lucca, Cosenza, and Palermo all fall into this second category.

The evidence does not justify the conclusion that the regions of high emigration were poorer than those of low emigration. The survey conducted by Senator Jacini and the reports on industry in each province show that some regions of low emigration were among the poorest in the nation. For instance, Sonnino pointed out that the peasants of Emilia-Romagna—a province with a low rate of emigration—were among the poorest in the country.[46] Calabria, a region of high emigration, was not poorer than Emilia-Romagna.[47] Among the eight Tuscan provinces, Lucca, a major source of emigrants, was not poorer than Arezzo or Siena, from which few emigrated.[48] Sonnino did not find significant differences between peasants in the interior of Sicily and those along the coast, or between those of Syracuse and those of Palermo.[49] One Sicilian writer, in fact, found conditions in the province of Palermo, where emigration was high, to be better than those in the province of Syracuse, where it was low.[50] Other studies as well, by Coletti in 1911 and MacDonald in 1963, show that there was no direct correlation between poverty and the intensity of emigration from a province.[51]

The variation in the rate of emigration from different parts of Italy cannot be readily explained by other circumstances that prevented or facilitated emigration from specific provinces. From 1870 on, emigration was free from government restrictions in every region of Italy, and there is no evidence of government efforts to promote emigration in one region more than another.[52] Nor do faulty statistical methods explain the differences. Both Coletti and Foerster, who dealt with Italian emigration statistics more than any other scholars, considered the statistics fairly reliable, apart from occasional minor errors;[53] besides, statistics can be checked against other sources. A lack of information in parts of Italy about opportunities abroad does not provide an explanation either. By 1880 every Italian province had at least several hundred people overseas, many of whom reported on opportunities in America by letter or in person; and emigration agents seem to have missed no part of Italy.[54] Finally, the inability to pay for tickets does not seem to have prevented poorer people from departing. The money was often made available, usually as a loan from prospective employers or relatives and friends. It is estimated that over a fourth of all Italian emigrants had tickets prepaid by relatives and friends already overseas.[55]

The Returnees

If neither poverty nor the other factors mentioned can explain the differing rates of emigration from Italy, where does the answer lie? A clue may be found in the rate of return migration. After 1901 Italians applying for a passport had to declare whether they intended to stay abroad indefinitely or to return. The names of those leaving for good were canceled from the communal population registers, the names of the others retained. On the average, less than 25 percent of the emigrants declared that they intended to stay abroad. In 1909, for instance, 22 percent of all emigrants were canceled from the communal registers. The percentage was even lower in previous years,[56] and in both 1912 and 1913 only 19 percent of the emigrants were canceled.[57] Of course, a declaration of intent is not a guarantee of what will happen, but it is a strong indication.

Emigrants who had thus been canceled from the communal registers, if they returned to Italy, could apply for reregistration. The number of those reregistering was high, especially compared with the number canceled. In the two years 1908–9, for instance, when 243,000 Italians were canceled, a total of 155,000 asked to be reregistered; that is, 64 reregistered for every 100 canceled.[58] In 1912 there were 48 reregistrations per 100 cancellations. The following year the ratio was 39 per 100.[59] To summarize, over 75 percent of the Italians who left declared their intention of returning; and every year, for every two emigrants who declared their intention to stay abroad permanently, one emigrant who had made the same declaration before departing reestablished his domicile in Italy after a residence of one or more years abroad.

A breakdown of return migration by country of destination shows not only a fluctuating rate of return migration from the United States, but also similar rates of return from other countries of the Americas. In 1904, for every ten Italians who left for the United States, nine returned. In 1908 more returned from the United States than left for it. From 1912 to 1915 the number of returnees from the United States fluctuated between 110,000 and 150,000 each year; that was about 60 percent as high as the total number departing for the United States. The number of returnees declined sharply after the First World War: 36,000 returned in 1922, and this figure remained stable until 1929, when only 20,000 returned. After 1930 only a few thousand returned each year; in 1935, for instance, the total was 5,000.[60]

Return migration from Brazil and Argentina was just as frequent—about two returns for every three departures—and followed the same cycle. In 1902, for instance, the number of returnees from Brazil was about 75 percent as large as the total who left Italy for Brazil. In 1907 the departures and returns were equal; and in 1911 departures for Brazil were double the returns. Return migration from Brazil dropped after the First World War, and virtually ceased in the 1930's, when only a few hundred returned every year. As for Argentina, in 1902 about 40,000 Italians went there and half that number returned. In 1911 returnees greatly outnumbered emigrants, by 50,000 to 72,000. But that year was an exception. The number of returnees from Argentina dropped after the war to about 10,000 a year, and again in the 1930's to 2,000–3,000 a year.[61]

It is important to underline that the rate of return migration from the United States, Brazil, and Argentina was about the same. Had return migration of Italians been common only from the United States, it would suggest that the returnees had somehow been unable to adjust to the United States. A recent American historian concluded from the high frequency of returnees from the United States that immigrants returned because they were unsuccessful.[62] If this were true, it would give weight to the contention that Italian emigrants played only a limited role in the shaping of their future. It would suggest that their lives were determined by environmental forces not only in Italy, where poverty pushed them out, but also in the United States, where a strange environment pushed them back. This conclusion, however, hardly explains the many returnees from Brazil and Argentina.

To be sure, even in Brazil and Argentina Italians found problems of adjustment or had other reasons to return. Some, for instance, were trapped on Brazilian plantations as indentured laborers like their Sicilian counterparts in Louisiana.[63] In addition, a considerable number of Italians migrated to Argentina as seasonal laborers, working during the harvest season in South America and returning to Italy for the busy agricultural season there. More is needed, however, to explain the massive return of Italians from Latin America. In general, as social scientists have shown, the adjustment of Italians in Latin America was not as difficult as that in the United States, because of the similarity between the sending and receiving ends.[64] Thus, if return migration was a function of the failure to adjust, we might reasonably expect a lower rate of return migration from Latin America than from the United States.

Was it nostalgia for Italy that brought immigrants back in such large numbers? Foerster seems to support this idea. The Italian's affections, he wrote, "are warm and deep, attaching him to the family and the scenes of his childhood. When he breaks from these tugging intimacies, it is conditionally, not absolutely. He must live in them again, and he departs only that he may live in them more richly than before. Life abroad is strange and difficult for the unsheltered Italian, who tolerates it only for the promise of the return to Italy."[65]

In reality, Italian emigrants were not the nostalgic people Foerster made them out to be. In Calabria in the early 1900's a large number of returnees were polled, including many contemplating emigration for a second or third time. Nostalgia was seldom mentioned as a reason to come back to Italy. Most returnees said their decision to return to Italy had been based on economic plans made before they had departed for the first time. Emigration and return, then, were not decisions Italians took lightly. The returnees were for the most part neither rejected by American society nor spurred by nostalgia. Rather they were individuals actively pursuing goals they had set before departing.

Americans noticed the phenomenon of return migration, and they did not look upon it with favor. Italian migrants in the United States, and in Europe too, were called "birds of passage."[66] An American who studied several hundred Italian migrants wrote in 1913: "Many Italians come in the spring to work during the summer, when public works are undertaken, and return to Europe in the fall when the demand for labor diminishes. . . . In many cases immigrants have visited this country five, six, seven times, and cases of two, three, and four visits are common."[67] An Italian traveler reported on what he deemed the American impression of temporary migrants: "They come in the spring to escape poverty in Italy, they compete with our workers and accept minimal wages, and when winter comes they leave like birds of passage."[68]

The writer Giuseppe Giacosa, after crossing the Atlantic with a group of Italians en route to Texas, reported: "The children were in Italy with the grandparents because, it was understood, everybody intended to return. It was common everywhere in America."[69] Many of the Italians in Cleveland "dreamed of returning to Italy one day to establish themselves as independent farmers or small businessmen."[70] The Italian consuls in New York, Boston, and New Orleans all reported high return migration rates.[71] Foerster wrote: "After 1870, for the first time, it became evident that, following a somewhat indeterminate state, many Italians repacked their chattels and went home again. No previous immigrants in this land of promise had done that."[72] Immigrants of other nationalities did change their minds: for every 100 immigrants who entered the United States from 1908 to 1924, 38 were repatriated.[73] But of all the larger groups of immigrants, the Italians showed a much greater tendency to return home.[74]

Unfortunately, the Italian government—more concerned about how many Italians departed than how many arrived—did not count return migrants by province. The only detailed statistics on returnees we have, those collected by the Italians Alberto Beneduce and Luigi Rossi, cover the years 1905 and 1906.

Beneduce showed that returnees from the United States were in some ways unlike those from Latin America. About three-fourths of the returnees from the United States were single, whereas only one-fourth of those returning from Brazil were single. In addition, only one out of ten returnees from the United States was female in contrast to one out of two from Brazil. Beneduce's analysis by month showed that emigration to the United States reached its peak in March, April, and May; repatriation from the United States was most intense in October and November, a two-month span when about half the yearly total of returnees landed in Italy. Finally, Beneduce found that about 75 percent of the returnees were between the ages of 16 and 40, at a time when only 40 percent of the Italian population was in that age group.[75]

Elaborating on Beneduce's findings, Rossi remarked: "The study of the distribution of repatriates by age seems to show the periodic character of a large part of our emigration, which is becoming a back-and-forth flow of labor with the same people participating a number of times. As older people drop out of sight, younger ones join the emigration-return current; thus Italian communes are deprived of their best energies." Rossi's study made two other important points: first, that the average stay of Italians in the United States was about five years; and second, that the rate of return migration was higher in the south of Italy than in the north, the Calabria region of the south regaining as many as 80 percent of its emigrants.[76]

Most reports by prefetti and others on return migration stressed three points: first, that almost all emigrants, regardless of their destination, planned to return; second, that the goal of the emigrants was to save money abroad in order to solve problems at home; and third, that most returnees had improved their economic position while abroad. As early as 1878 the prefetto of Genoa reported: "Most emigrants go to South America, where living conditions are not very different from those of the province. Over half of those who leave return within a few years."[77] In 1881 it was reported that some emigrants sold everything they owned before departing but most did not, "since they plan to be back in a few years."[78] And in 1888 the American consul in Genoa wrote: "With few exceptions, peasants go overseas to make money, and once they have reached their goal, they go back to spend the balance of their lives in a quiet, frugal way."[79] In 1897 the prefetti still reported most emigrants from Genoa planning to return and eventually doing so.[80]

In the province of Lucca, too, only a minority of emigrants did not return. "Most go out with the intention of staying abroad about ten years," it was reported, "but some come back after five or six years."[81] As in Genoa, few sold their property before leaving, and from many families only the adult males departed.[82] An 1882 survey found that most emigrants from Lucca had returned; the same was true of the provinces of Cosenza and Palermo.[83]

In Cosenza, the prefetto wrote in 1881, most emigrants tried to find the money for their fare without selling their property; some who owned land mortgaged it. Even when entire families left, a relative or a friend was entrusted with the land until the family returned.[84] According to three northern Italians who took a survey of the province in the late 1900's, "the emigrants from Calabria are determined to return as soon as they have set aside the money they need to accomplish what they have decided they want to achieve. Unfortunately there are many circumstances that force emigrants to delay the date of their final return."[85]

An independent investigation of emigration and return rates,

3. Emigrants waiting to depart, port of Naples, ca. 1910. Reluctant as Italian peasants were to undertake a change that would separate them from their families, millions were forced to emigrate across the Atlantic when Italy and other southern European nations failed to provide an outlet for temporary migration. This scene was a common one from the 1880's to the 1920's at Genoa, Naples, and Palermo, the three major ports of departure.

which was compared with the national census findings, concluded that between 1875 and 1900 about 75 percent of the emigrants from Cosenza returned.[86] A survey of all the communes of the province in 1908 showed most emigrants staying abroad three to five years, and about 75 percent returning. In Roggiano Gravina, a town of 4,000 a few miles from Verbicaro, "almost invariably all emigrants return after two to four years. But most returnees emigrate again after a short time. There are people who have crossed the Atlantic four and five times." In Spezzano Albanese, another town in Cosenza, "emigrants return about three years after departure. It is not uncommon to see the same emigrants departing and returning within the same year. Returnees show a strong tendency to go back to America sooner or later. There are people who have been abroad five or six times."[87] The evidence on the province of Palermo largely agrees with that on Cosenza. The prefetto of Palermo, for example, reported in 1882 that family emigration was the exception. Emigrants did not sell the land or the house before leaving, since they were planning to return. If they needed money, they borrowed it.[88]

The Frequency of Return Migration

Since statistics on return migration by region or commune are not available, I have used two indirect approaches to gauge the return rate for seven of the nine communes that are the focus of this study.* The first approach, as seen in Table 3, is to examine the variation in birth and marriage rates from 1871 to 1920, on the assumption that a massive outflow of adult males is bound to affect those rates. The second, as seen in Table 4, is to compare data on departures by commune, gathered by the Italian Bureau of Statistics, with the actual numbers of people present in each commune at the time of the decennial census. This approach is based on the assumption that if large numbers of people leave permanently, this is going to show up at the time of the census.

Let us first look at the number of departures from some communes over the period of a decade. In 1901, for instance, the commune of Santa Flavia had 4,747 people, as Table 4 shows. According to the Bureau of Statistics, between 1901 and 1910 2,360 people left the commune; that is, 49 percent of the total population. In 1911 the national census counted 5,537 people in the same commune. The departures over the decade 1911–20 were 1,020, or 18 percent of the total. This was a massive outflow of population, and seemingly bound to change drastically the demographic profile of the small commune.

In the case of Trabia we do not know exactly how many people lived in the commune in 1891, since no census was taken in that year. But the population can be estimated at 5,500–6,000. The departures from Trabia between 1891 and 1900 were 2,370, about 40 percent of the total. The 1901 census reported 5,601 people living in Trabia; from 1901 to 1910, 3,810 people left, or 68 percent of the total population. Finally, in 1911 Trabia had 5,108 people; depar-

*The cities of Genoa and Palermo are not treated here because the emigration from them was very low in relation to total population; emigration and return migration would thus not have a clear impact on the demographic profile.

TABLE 3

Births, Deaths, Marriages, and Departures in Seven Communes, 1871–1920

(Yearly average for each decade and percentage of total commune population over decade)

Decade	Births No.	Births Pct.	Deaths No.	Deaths Pct.	Marriages No.	Marriages Pct.	Departures No.	Departures Pct.
Lorsica								
1871–80	54	2.8%	49	2.6%	10	0.5%	—	—
1881–90	54	2.9	37	2.1	15	0.8	18	1.0%
1891–1900	51	2.8	30	1.6	11	0.6	31	0.7
1901–10	45	2.6	33	1.9	10	0.6	42	2.5
1911–20	30	2.1	28	1.9	5	0.3	23	1.6
S. Levante								
1871–80	381	4.3	229	2.6	67	0.8	—	—
1881–90	392	4.1	259	2.7	75	0.8	124	1.3
1891–1900	437	4.5	243	2.5	70	0.7	70	0.7
1901–10	423	3.5	225	1.9	87	0.9	119	1.0
1911–20	357	2.8	212	1.6	67	0.5	97	0.8
Capannori								
1871–80	1,629	3.8	1,026	2.4	297	0.8	—	—
1881–90	1,596	3.7	1,068	2.5	348	0.8	2,392	5.4
1891–1900	1,558	3.6	975	2.2	354	0.8	1,881	4.3
1900–10	1,376	2.9	798	1.6	364	0.4	2,078	4.3
1911–20	945	2.0	655	1.4	229	0.5	1,148	2.4
Lucca								
1871–80	2,134	3.1	1,955	2.9	422	0.6	—	—
1881–90	2,110	3.1	1,785	2.6	494	0.7	1,605	2.3
1891–1900	2,153	3.0	1,684	2.5	524	0.7	1,664	2.4
1901–10	1,949	2.6	1,605	2.1	499	0.6	1,443	1.9
1911–20	1,613	2.1	1,684	2.2	400	0.5	1,148	1.5
Verbicaro								
1871–80	225	4.3	210	4.0	39	0.7	—	—
1881–90	191	3.7	169	3.3	45	0.9	73	1.4
1891–1900	210	4.1	142	2.8	50	0.9	94	1.8
1901–10	176	3.8	135	2.9	34	0.7	129	2.8
1911–20	130	2.8	127	2.8	25	0.5	122	2.7
Sta. Flavia								
1871–80	192	5.6	105	3.0	49	1.4	—	—
1881–90	209	5.7	94	2.6	37	1.0	9	0.2
1891–1900	216	5.6	96	2.6	37	1.0	11	0.3
1901–10	181	3.8	87	1.8	48	1.0	236	5.0
1911–20	147	2.7	79	1.4	36	0.6	102	1.8
Trabia								
1871–80	249	5.4	123	2.7	47	1.0	—	—
1881–90	264	5.1	147	2.8	51	1.0	56	1.0
1891–1900	244	4.7	132	2.6	51	1.0	237	5.0
1901–10	173	3.0	127	2.3	55	0.9	381	6.8
1911–20	128	2.5	125	2.2	36	0.6	174	3.1

SOURCE: Vital statistics from communal archives; departures from *Statistica dell'Emigrazione Italiana all'Estero*, Italy [35].

TABLE 4

Population Change and Emigration in Seven Communes, 1881–1921

Census year	Population in census year: Projected with natural increase[a]	Population in census year: Official count	Emigration in decade preceding census year: Expected[b]	Emigration in decade preceding census year: Official count
Lorsica				
1881	2,147	1,841	306	—
1891	2,011	—	—	180
1901	2,221	1,276	945	210
1911	1,780	1,451	329	420
1921	1,471	1,276	195	230
S. Levante				
1881	10,310	9,650	660	—
1891	10,988	—	—	1,240
1901	12,920	12,039	881	700
1911	14,019	12,912	1,107	1,190
1921	14,362	14,444	−82	970
Capannori				
1881	49,343	43,673	5,670	—
1891	48,953	—	—	20,392
1901	54,783	48,217	6,566	10,881
1911	54,087	47,650	6,437	20,780
1921	50,550	41,828	8,722	11,484
Lucca				
1881	69,994	68,063	1,931	—
1891	71,313	—	—	16,050
1901	75,003	74,971	32	16,440
1911	78,411	76,160	2,251	14,443
1921	76,089	78,575	−2,486	11,480
Verbicaro				
1881	5,349	5,108	241	—
1891	5,318	—	—	730
1901	5,998	4,624	1,374	940
1911	5,034	4,517	517	1,290
1921	4,547	4,507	40	1,222
Sta. Flavia				
1881	4,312	3,666	646	—
1891	4,816	—	—	90
1901	6,016	4,747	1,269	110
1911	5,682	5,537	145	2,360
1921	6,217	5,242	975	1,020
Trabia				
1881	5,878	5,176	702	—
1891	6,364	—	—	560
1901	7,466	5,601	1,865	2,370
1911	6,061	5,108	953	3,810
1921	5,138	4,765	373	1,740

SOURCE: Decennial censuses (there was none in 1891), vital statistics in communal archives, and *Statistica dell'Emigrazione Italiana all'Estero*, Italy [35].

[a] Census count ten years earlier, plus births over ensuing decade, minus deaths.

[b] Difference between columns 1 and 2.

tures from 1911 to 1920 were 1,740, or 34 percent of the total. By the end of this great exodus Trabia should have disappeared from the map of Sicily. Yet, in reality, as Table 1 shows, Trabia had more people in 1921 than in 1871: 4,765 in 1921 and 4,618 in 1871.

In Calabria, Verbicaro had 4,624 people in 1901. The departures between 1901 and 1910 were 1,290, or 28 percent of the population. In 1911 the same commune had 4,517 people; the departures for the decade 1911–20 were 1,222, or 27 percent of the population. The departure rates were not as high in the northern communes as in the south. For instance, Sestri Levante had 9,650 people in 1881; 1,240 departed from 1881 to 1890, only about 13 percent of the total population. In 1911 Sestri Levante had 12,912 people; the departures for the decade 1911–20 were 970, or 7.5 percent. Regardless of the differences between north and south, Table 4 seems to indicate, in both regions, an outflow of people so high that it could not occur without having a profound effect on the demographic profile of each commune.

Since most of the emigrants were young males, it seems logical to expect a substantial impact on the rate of births and marriages in each commune, except in the two large cities, where the emigration rate was lower. From 1900 to 1920, about 80 percent of the emigrants were male, and in the two previous decades it was 88 percent. Moreover, as many as 75 percent of these males were between the ages of 14 and 45.[89] A breakdown of these figures by province indicates that this pattern was universal. In 1886, for instance, of all the emigrants of 14 years or older leaving Genoa province, 21 percent were female and 79 percent male. In the province of Lucca, male emigrants outnumbered female emigrants 9 to 1. In the province of Cosenza, the ratio was 85 percent male to 15 percent female. Finally, from Palermo province the male emigrants outnumbered the female 72 to 28.[90] About two decades later the ratio had not changed significantly. In 1903, of the 5,000 people leaving Genoa, 80 percent were male; and of the 10,000 who left the province of Lucca, 75 percent were male. In the south, of the 8,000 leaving Cosenza, 80 percent were male; of the 16,000 emigrants from the province of Palermo, about 70 percent were male.[91]

Despite this outflow of young men, the marriage and birth rates in the nine communities were surprisingly stable, as Table 3 shows. The stability came to an end in the decade 1911–20 not because of emigration, but because of the dislocations of war. Marriage rates were particularly stable. In Santa Flavia, for example, from 1881 to 1910—the three decades of the most intense emigration—the rate was 1 percent in each decade. In Trabia too the rate was 1 percent from 1871 to 1901; the following decade it declined, but only to 0.9 percent. In general, the rate in the other communes was also stable. The reader will notice that the marriage rate was higher in the communes of the south than in those of the north: this difference will be discussed in Chapter 7, on the family.

Birthrates show less stability, especially after 1901. For instance, in Sestri Levante the rate dropped from 5.5 percent in the 1890's to 3.5 percent in the following decade; in Verbicaro from 4.1 to 3.8; and in Trabia from 4.7 to 3. The birthrate similarly dropped in all the other communes, with Santa Flavia the least stable and Lorsica the most. Emigration undoubtedly had an impact on the drop in birthrates. But two qualifications are in order: first, the decline was far from drastic; and, second, the birthrate was already declining in Italy before the onset of mass emigration. As some students of Italian demography have observed, the declining birthrate in the early 1900's must be explained as the continuation of a trend that started in the 1860's; emigration simply accelerated the trend, without, however, having a major impact on it.[92] The contrast between the relative stability of marriage and birth rates and the high rate of departures suggests that emigration occurred without substantially altering the cycle of life.

A second problem emerges from the comparison of the statistics on departures and the actual numbers of people present in each commune at the time of the national censuses, as seen in Table 4. For example, between 1901 and 1910 the number of departures from Trabia was 3,810, 68 percent of the population at the 1901 count. We expect this to show up in the census of 1911. In reality, however, the census indicates there were only 493 fewer people, a decline of only 9 percent.

Similarly, the departures from Santa Flavia between 1901 and 1910 were 2,360, 49 percent of the total population in 1901. Surprisingly, however, the 1911 census reveals that the commune had 1,210 *more* people in 1911 than in 1901, an increase of about 26 percent in ten years. Finally, between 1901 and 1920 2,512 people departed from Verbicaro, 54 percent of the total population in 1901. The 1921 census, however, shows only 117 fewer people in Verbicaro in 1921 than in 1901. Thus the large emigration did not result in the depopulation of these communes.

Why was the demographic impact of emigration so small? A possible explanation is that internal migrants replaced those who left for America. Santa Flavia and Trabia, for instance, might have been the focus of immigration as well as of emigration. There is no evidence, however, of significant internal immigration in the communes of Santa Flavia, Trabia, Verbicaro, Capannori, and Lorsica, though evidence suggests that Lucca, Genoa, and Palermo were indeed centers of immigration.[93] Sestri Levante also had a large immigration, at least in the late 1880's.[94]

Other possible explanations are that those who left came back before the end of the decade, and thus were counted in the national census, and that the same people applied more than once for a passport within the same decade or in successive decades. According to an Italian law of 1901, passports were valid for three years. If an immigrant returned and then reemigrated after the three years had expired, he applied for a new passport, and hence was counted as an emigrant as many times as a new passport was issued to him. From this, then, it seems likely that rate of departures was related to the high frequency of return migration and reemigration, which all agree was a common occurrence.

These statistics show two important aspects of emigration: the decades in which the rate of first-time departures reached its peak, and the different patterns of emigration and return migration in northern and southern Italy. Seemingly, Italian emigration reached its peak from 1901 to 1914, with an all-time record of 872,000 departures in 1913; immigration historians generally agree on this.[95] As Table 4 shows, however, although the highest numbers of departures were registered after 1900, most of the seven communes suffered the greatest population loss in the decade 1891–1900.

For instance, there were 2,512 departures from Verbicaro from 1901 to 1920, or 54 percent of the total population of the commune in 1901. But the actual loss of people was not of the same magnitude. For the year 1910, for instance, if we subtract the deaths and add the births that occurred between 1901 and 1910, we find out that the net decrease in population due to emigration was only 517. Similarly, if we perform the same computations for the decade 1911–20, we arrive at a real decrease of only 40. The picture for the decade 1891–1900 is rather different: the departures were only 940, but the net loss of people was 1,374.*

In the case of Santa Flavia, 3,380 departed from 1901 to 1920, 71 percent of the population in 1901. But the actual loss of people, after

*One may rightly wonder how the net losses could be larger than the actual departures—how could people be out of town if they never departed? The answer is that official emigration figures for most communes of the south are not very reliable for the years before 1901.

accounting for births and deaths, was 165 for the decade 1901–10, and 975 for the following decade. On the other hand, the commune suffered a net loss of population of 1,269 in the 1891–1900 decade, more than the combined losses for the two decades 1901–20. The departures from Trabia between 1901 and 1920 were 5,550, that is, almost 100 percent of the population of the commune in 1901. The net loss, however, was much lower: 953 in 1901–10, and 373 the following decade. On the other hand, the net loss for the decade 1891–1900 was 1,865. The commune seems to have lost more people in the decade of the 1890's than in the next two decades combined. But the rate of departures was higher after 1900, lower before 1900.

The figures for Capannori and Lucca need an explanation. Most emigrants from the two communes were seasonal migrants to France who returned to Italy every year; accordingly, they were counted as emigrants every time they applied for a passport. If the emigrants to France were subtracted, the figures for Lucca and Capannori would resemble more closely those for Lorsica and Sestri Levante than those for the communities of the south. In any event, the data show that all the communes, with the exception of Sestri Levante and Lucca, experienced their greatest loss of population in the 1890's, and that the high rates of departure for the decades 1901–20 were the result of counting in the same group both first-time migrants and returnees going back to America.

The data also reveal significant differences between north and south. The variance between the rate of departures and the net population loss was generally wider in the south than in the north. In Lorsica, for example, 420 departed between 1901 and 1910, and the net population loss revealed in 1901 was 329—a difference of 91. From 1911 to 1920, 230 departures were registered, and the net loss over the same decade was 195, a difference of 35. On the other hand, 3,810 departed from Trabia from 1901 to 1910 and the net loss was only 953 people, a difference of 2,857. The following decade the difference was 1,367. These figures seem to suggest that return migration and reemigration were quite common in Trabia, but less common in Lorsica: in Lorsica the net loss of people and the number of departures almost coincided, whereas in Trabia departures far exceeded population losses.

Reports from the mayor of Lorsica and the prefetti of Lucca and Genoa offer an explanation. In 1893 the mayor wrote: "A good number of migrants return after more than ten years. But most of them do not settle in their hometown. Rather they either buy or build a house in one of the coastal communes, where the climate is more pleasant and life less isolated in general."[96] And the prefetto of Lucca: "Emigrants return after a long residence abroad, ordinarily when they have enough money to spend the rest of their lives in relative comfort. It so happens they do not necessarily settle in their native town. Viareggio and other coastal communities are the places where returnees try to buy land or open a business. But very rarely do they settle in another region."[97]

To summarize, northerners usually returned only after a long absence and did not necessarily settle in their original communities; and reemigration seems to have been less frequent in the north than in the south.[98] In the south, emigration ordinarily lasted from three to five years; returnees settled in their original towns, and reemigration was common. The mayor of Santa Flavia wrote: "Emigrants usually return after three to four years. Those who cross the Atlantic every year are not exceptional. And most of those who come back cross the Atlantic again sooner or later."[99] As the prefetto of Cosenza put it: "There are a few who stay in America more than five years. But reemigration is the rule."[100]

Land Tenure, Emigration, and Militancy

Why did so many emigrate from the provinces of Lucca, Genoa, Cosenza, and Palermo, and so few from Forlì, Florence, Lecce, and Syracuse—at least until the First World War? And why did so many emigrants return and then reemigrate? The answers to these questions are suggested by several statements dealing with two regions in the south.

A social scientist from Cosenza wrote in 1883:

> One of the main characteristics of the economy of the south, and especially of this province, is the supply of land. When feudal land tenure came to an end with the ordinances of 1810 and 1811, the Kingdom of the Two Sicilies began dividing public land among the peasants. But the division did not go very far. It was only after 1860 that the division of public land was actively promoted. There is still a long way to go, and peasants are excited about the possibility of becoming landowners; but very few can afford to buy. Moreover, even those who have the money are often forced to resell because of a lack of funds for necessary improvements or for paying the mortgage.[101]

As Luigi Izzo noted, in a study of the Calabria region: "The supply of land exceeded the demand. Land was available for everyone, of course for a price."[102] Ettore Blandini, the director of the agency for setting up homesteads in Cosenza, supervised the sale of 500 acres of land in the province in 1900. Once placed on the market, the land was sold within a month. Blandini later wrote that "90 percent of the land was purchased with money coming from the United States." Most buyers, he added, were either farmers who had never owned land or small landowners whose purpose in going to America had been to enlarge holdings too small to support a family.[103] The sale of land, he concluded, came to an end in 1926 "as a result of the end of the free emigration to the United States and the consequent decline in savings arriving in the province from America."[104]

In the province of Palermo, in contrast, the mayor of Santa Cristina wrote: "Some people migrated to America from this commune. But when they came back and realized that they could not buy land because it was not for sale, they left forever. Few followed them, since there is no hope of buying land when they return. Those who come back and want to stay invest their savings in a house; but there are only a few such people."[105] The mayor of Piana dei Greci wrote: "Returnees are disappointed because they cannot convince landlords to sell them land. Unfortunately, there are no small properties in this town; this is a region of large estates. Frustrated in their hope of buying land, returnees leave forever. But since land is not for sale, only a few emigrate at all."[106] And the prefetto of Palermo wrote: "Not many peasants leave from the hinterland, which is the area of large estates. Emigration and return migration from the coastal communities are intense; this is an area of small properties, and returnees ordinarily invest in land."[107]

This seems to have been the general pattern in all Italy: emigration and return migration were much more frequent where land was for sale than where it was not. The land tenure system, then, is important to an understanding of emigration. In the late nineteenth century, two different systems of land tenure were present in Italy, with a virtually endless variety of regional adaptations. In one system, the large estate predominated and little buying and selling of land went on; in the other, small and medium-sized landholding predominated and there was an active market for land.[108] These two systems of land tenure derived from the ways that feudalism had come to an end in different regions, and the differences between the systems increased as a result of the sale of land promoted by the new government of the united Italy.[109]

The end of feudalism in Italy is a confused story because the laws abrogating feudalism in the various Italian states in the early nineteenth century were neither promulgated at the same time nor implemented in the same way. In general, the end of feudalism in Emilia-Romagna, Tuscany, Marche, Umbria, Lazio, Apulia, and the hinterland of Sicily and Sardinia did not bring about the subdivision of large holdings. Rather, it encouraged the transformation of the great landlords into owners and operators of estates. In those regions, as late as 1880, most land was worked by sharefarmers or gang laborers. Under the sharefarming system, every family received a relatively self-sufficient farm with a farmhouse. Small independent landholdings were rare in these regions and always threatened by large holdings. This system of land tenure, therefore, brought about a pyramidal social structure with a few large-scale entrepreneurs and a large class of sharefarmers and laborers.[110]

In other parts of Italy, though the end of feudalism did not bring the subdivision of all large estates, it did lead to the creation of a large number of small and medium-sized holdings. The result was a process of buying and selling land that became irreversible. This occurred mainly in the regions north of the Po River; the provinces of Lucca, Piacenza, Parma, and Modena; the regions of Campania, Abruzzi, Basilicata, and Calabria; and the coastal area of Sicily. In these areas the predominant unit was the small farm, which was cultivated by the owner and his nuclear family household, rather than the extended family household that ordinarily served as the labor force on large estates. The mixture of small, medium, and large holdings in these areas prevented the formation of a clear-cut pyramidal hierarchy, and a more differentiated society developed, based on the intense buying and selling of land and the consequent competition among peasants.[111] Contrary to common opinion, there were few large estates in regions of high emigration, such as Basilicata, Calabria, and Campania; this was pointed out as early as 1911 in the survey on conditions in the south, and later documented in studies of entrepreneurial activity in Italy.[112]

The breakup of church, state, and communal land increased the differences between the regions of large estates and those of small and medium holdings. Church land was confiscated by a series of laws passed from 1862 to 1873.[113] Land that had belonged to the former Italian states was put up for sale by the new national government, both to offset the national debt and to increase the number of small landholders.[114] Communal land—that owned by the communes—had been used in feudal times to support the poor.[115] Land from these three sources was divided into almost 300,000 parcels that were put up for sale between 1861 and 1899. Since there were fewer than half a million landowners in Italy in 1881,[116] the availability of 300,000 additional small farms had a national impact. The Società Anonima, the agency supervising land distribution on behalf of the government, divided the land into very small tracts of two to four acres each, as the 1867 law required, in order to offer as many peasants as possible the chance to become landowners.[117]

This goal of redistribution was not achieved everywhere. In the regions where small and medium properties were the rule, the sale of land increased the number of small holdings; but where large estates dominated, the sale increased the size of large estates. Although the letter and spirit of the law required that landholdings be sold to any propertyless peasant who could make a down payment, large landowners often bribed the officials supervising the sale or forced peasants who had bought land out of the market. Thus much of the newly distributed land was incorporated into large estates.[118]

The two different systems of land tenure arising out of the end of feudalism and the sale of public land had important political effects on the peasantry. In regions where small and medium holdings prevailed, and thus where the buying and selling of land was intense, peasants found themselves competing to purchase available land; their main concern was how to generate the necessary cash. In the regions of large estates, the polarization between the few landowners and the many sharefarmers and laborers led to peasant militancy, inspired largely by Marxist socialism, syndicalism, and anarchism.[119]

These differences help explain the phenomenon of emigration. In the regions of small properties, where there was land for sale and farmers were in competition, emigration became the way to generate cash to buy land. In the regions of large estates, with no land for sale, peasant militancy rather than emigration was seen as the solution. Militant farmers organized to obtain better contracts and working conditions, to prevent layoffs and lockouts, and most of all to increase their earnings. Only rarely did this militancy bring about land division, which was sometimes used by landowners or the government as a political strategy to defuse militancy.[120]

Although most observers saw Italian emigration as simply the flight from poverty, a few perceptive students did not fail to notice the relationship between land tenure, emigration, and militancy. As early as 1863 Giovanni Massari and Stefano Castagnola, in a study of banditry in the south, pointed out that "where holdings are large and controlled by a few people, land is simply not available, even for those who can afford it, and unrest is high." In the province of Foggia, in the Apulia region, where a handful of families virtually owned the entire territory, at least 8,000 bandits kept the province in a state of permanent unrest.[121] Twenty years later, analyzing the explosive situation in Sicily, the deputy Napoleone Colajanni observed: "I do not think that Sicily can be spared a rebellion by peasants. [A rebellion occurred only a few months later.] I am aware that in the hinterland of Sicily, where landholdings are large and most peasants are laborers, hatred has no limits and will lead to a revolution. A handful of landowners control the region, and small landholdings are not for sale."[122] In 1890 Massimo Pestalozza held that the creation of small properties was the best way to defuse peasant militancy, since competition among peasants would eliminate mass unrest.[123]

A survey by the Italian Association of Farmers in 1900 clearly showed a high incidence of unionism and strikes in Emilia-Romagna, Apulia, and the hinterland of Sicily, all areas of large estates and low emigration rates. At the same time, unionism and strikes were rare in Liguria, in the province of Lucca, in the Basilicata and Calabria regions, and along the coast of Sicily, all areas of small properties and high emigration rates; "in these areas," the study concluded, "emigration is a substitute for militancy."[124] Within regions, too, this pattern could be seen. Ernesto Marenghi, an astute observer of Italian society, wrote of Calabria: "Emigration started in towns marked by small properties in the early 1880's. Soon it became a mass phenomenon. But in the areas of large estates—like Crotone—emigration started only after the turn of the century and involved only a few people."[125] The province of Cosenza, for instance, had many small properties, and generally a high emigration rate; but from the few pockets of large estates in the province, the emigration rate was low.

Coletti, in a comprehensive study of Italian emigration, thus summarized the difference between a region of high emigration and the most militant region in Italy at the time: "In Calabria emigration occurs because land is available and the biggest problem is the lack of cash. In Emilia-Romagna the problem is sociopolitical; land is simply not available and peasants stay to bring about change."[126] After visiting Calabria in 1907, Leonello De Nobili noted: "Peasant organizations are weak in these provinces. As we well know, unionism is strong in Apulia, Emilia-Romagna, and the hinterland of Sicily. Where peasants are organized, they refuse to leave."[127] De Nobili was obviously sympathetic to the peasants who remained and fought; but he failed to take into account that they did not have the option of leaving and returning to purchase land in their own region. Their only solution was permanent emigration, and most peasants did not choose that course.

The four provinces of Genoa, Lucca, Cosenza, and, in part, Palermo, were all areas where there was land for sale, almost negligible peasant unionism, and a high rate of emigration; but they differed in the availability of land.* Much more land was available in the south than in the north, which helps to explain why return migration was greater in the south than in the north, and why northern returnees stayed abroad a longer time than southerners.

The province of Genoa illustrates these tendencies. As early as 1861 the Chamber of Commerce of Genoa described the local agricultural economy as one of small properties and intense buying and selling of land. By seasonal migration to the Po Plains, many Genoese earned enough to purchase or enlarge small landholdings.[128] The commerce in land continued throughout the 1870's and 1880's, but the demand for land far exceeded the supply. Returnees could buy land only from small landowners who for one reason or another wanted, or were forced, to sell their property. But these sellers were few: even those who left for the New World generally refused to sell. Meanwhile, there was little land for sale by the government after the 1860's.[129] Thus returnees to Genoa in the late nineteenth century had a hard time finding land to buy. This might explain why the Genoese emigrants stayed overseas longer than southerners: they were trying to save enough money so that they could either live on their savings or open a business in the rapidly growing Ligurian economy. For either of these purposes emigrants needed a larger sum of money than that needed to buy a few acres of land.[130]

In Lucca in the late 1870's there was land for sale, but few had the money for a down payment. Nor were banks willing to assist peasants who wanted to become landowners.[131] About a decade later, however, the prefetto of Lucca reported that the demand for small landholdings, stimulated by the arrival of American savings, far exceeded the supply. Many returnees, the report concluded, were

*The survey by the Association of Italian Farmers specifically mentions these four as provinces where unrest and unionism were almost totally unknown; see Società degli Agricoltori Italiani, *I Recenti Scioperi Agrari in Italia*, p. 27. The lack of unrest in the four provinces was further documented by the Italian Bureau of Statistics, which regularly published data on strikes in the provinces. See *Statistica degli Scioperi*, Italy [32], pp. 23, 81, 91; Italy [33], pp. 13–38; and Italy [34], pp. 17–25. Full authors' names, titles, and publication data for works cited in short form are given in the Bibliography, pp. 323–38. A list of abbreviations used in citations is found on p. 265.

leaving permanently because they were frustrated in their desire to buy land.[132]

There seems to have been more land available in the two southern provinces than in the north. From 1860 to 1880, 3,700 families purchased a total of over 10,000 acres of land in the Calabria region, mostly with American savings.[133] As we have seen, after 1860 the sale of public land was promoted in the south;[134] and in Cosenza land was generally available to those who could afford the price.[135] In Palermo the buying and selling of land along the coast was among the most intense in the nation,[136] despite a complaint by the prefetto in 1891 that a sound system of credit was lacking.[137]

Internal Migration as a Model

If Italians wanted land, one may ask, why did they not stay in America, where land was more plentiful and fertile than in Italy. Some did, of course, but to the great majority the idea had no appeal. According to Coletti, some emigration agents told peasants there was plenty of land across the ocean; but the negative reaction convinced the agents to drop the suggestion.[138] "When peasants cross the ocean," Coletti wrote, "they have only one goal: to come back and buy land in Italy. A piece of land somewhere else, no matter how fertile and large, does not interest them. When they return, they buy land regardless of the price. It is like a ritual the peasants think they have to perform; only in one's native village, where one's ancestors lived and died, does owning land have meaning."[139] A peasant in the province of Cosenza told an interviewer: "This is the only true land. We can live somewhere else for a while. But we can buy land only here."[140] Adolfo Rossi, the Italian commissioner of emigration, described a conversation he had with Rosa Granata, a peasant woman from Calabria. She explained how her marriage had ended when her husband Rosario, who had gone to South America, asked her to sell the two acres the family owned and join him across the ocean. She had refused to go, concluding: "Land in America is not good enough. This is the only land we can buy. I will never go."[141]

Coletti wrote at length about how the psychology of Italians made them reluctant to accept any change that would separate them from their communities. The peasants' world view was limited to the world they knew, around their villages. They would accept change only in order to cope with a temporary emergency such as a family problem. But any lasting solution had to be found at home.[142] In Italy this attitude was not unique to peasants; Italian society at large resisted for years the idea of permanent emigration. The Italian Bureau of Statistics had two categories of emigration: temporary and permanent. By temporary, the bureau meant emigration for less than a year; by permanent, it meant emigration of several years' duration. There was no word to indicate the definitive departure for another country—in Italy the concept did not exist.[143]

Another explanation for the peasants' reluctance to buy land abroad is that overseas emigration started when internal migration came to an end. Internal migration, common in some areas from the beginning of the nineteenth century, ended in the 1880's when Italian agriculture went into a long-lasting crisis as a result of American competition. In some regions of the south internal migration ended for another reason as well: the stabilization of the sedentary village population in the coastal flatlands. This occurred in those areas where railways and government roads were built, where sanitation was improved by the government, and in any case where the population exploded as great epidemics were eliminated. The surfeit of population made it impossible for seasonal migrants from the mountains to find work in the flatlands. At that juncture, peasants had nowhere else to go but overseas.[144]

The shift from internal to international migration, however, did not change the emigrants' basic goal. Emigration began as a temporary expedient designed to solve problems at home. It was only after several trips back and forth across the ocean that a large number of Italians began to entertain the idea of remaining in the United States.*

Emigration from Genoa to other regions of Italy had occurred from the time of the independent republic, before the Napoleonic occupation. Maria Marenco called this long tradition "one of the most active and persistent movements of population in the Italian peninsula since the seventeenth century."[145] Internal migration increased during the Napoleonic years, when the dislocation caused by the wars forced people to seek additional income as seasonal workers in Lombardy and Piedmont.[146] In 1819, for instance, the

*The reader should take note that some seasonal migrations never gave rise to international migration. For instance, the great seasonal migrations in the Po Plains and perhaps those from the Apulia region generated peasant militancy rather than emigration. The point here is not that internal migration always led to international migration, but only that international migration initially had the same goals as internal migration.

4. Crossing the Atlantic, 1898. Although the crossing of the Atlantic was an unprecedented ordeal, large numbers of emigrants to the Americas had already been temporary migrants, either to other regions of Italy or to Switzerland and France. For most Italians, crossing the Atlantic was certainly a more momentous decision than migrating temporarily to a nearby European country, but few of them doubted that the move was anything more than temporary.

mayor of Isola del Cantone reported that 300 people regularly left the commune every November to work in Lombardy and returned in the spring; another group went to the territories of Tortona, Novi, and Alessandria in the late summer. The mayor of Savignano remarked: "Without money from Lombardy, this commune could not survive."[147] When the opportunity for internal migration declined, there was no alternative but to go overseas. "International migration," the prefetto of Genoa pointed out, "is not a new phenomenon here; what is new is its intensity, owing to the failure of Lombardy, Veneto, and Switzerland to provide work for these seasonal migrants."[148]

From the province of Lucca, peasants and shepherds had a tradition of migrating to the islands of Sardinia and Corsica; some went as far as Marseilles and Algeria. A report of 1876 mentions shepherds leaving the mountain communities of Sillano and Minucciano to work in the flatlands of Lucca and Pisa.[149] Migration from the province of Lucca to Sardinia had a long history; as early as 1720 the complaint was heard that because of poverty the mountain population of Lucca could survive only by temporary emigration.[150] Later, the destination of emigrants from Lucca changed, as the prefetto explained: "Most emigrants still go to France and Sardinia; but these places do not attract as many as before. Yet these people need outside income to survive. Lately, emigration to South America has increased, and I believe it is a consequence of the declining opportunities in Europe."[151]

In Cosenza migration from the mountains to the flatlands of Calabria and Sicily or to Algeria and Tunisia was common in the 1860's and 1870's. The prefetto reported in 1874: "Migrants come back in the spring or the fall, according to when they emigrate, with savings of 200 to 300 lire. They pay their debts and eventually rent a tract of land that their families will work; the following year, they depart again."[152] Eventually, these opportunities came to an end and peasants looked elsewhere, as a member of the Cosenza Chamber of Commerce explained: "It is true that America fascinates the peasants. But some of them simply have to go, unless they choose to become outlaws. The peasants who relied on internal migration in the past are now forced to go abroad to make the extra money they need."[153]

Internal migration was less common in the province of Palermo. What there was of it occurred almost entirely within the island. During the harvest, agricultural laborers left the coastal zone to work on the large hinterland estates for two to three weeks. Only a small number of Sicilians left the island. In the mid-1860's some went to Barcelona, Madrid, Marseilles, and Cairo; some Sicilian fishermen, moreover, established temporary shelters along the coast of Tunisia and Algeria.[154]

To summarize, overseas migration from Italy often started as an alternative to the internal short-distance migration that many Italians had traditionally depended on. Such internal migration is a sign that the Italian society of the second half of the nineteenth century was more complex than the stereotype of traditional society, in which geographical mobility is virtually unknown. As Eugen Weber remarked: "The crux of traditional society is not immobility, but mobility of an impenetrable sort."[155] Perhaps it is impenetrable only because the modern mind has difficulty comprehending a basic concept of traditional societies, that every individual belongs in a geographical and psychological place to which he must always return. The modern idea of movement is linear: there is no way to return to the starting point. Though one may take a sentimental journey to one's native place, nobody really wants to go home; it is simply impossible. The traditional idea of movement was circular: every journey had to end where it had started. It is safe to say that psychologically our ancestors never left home. It seems to me that our modern fascination with the idea of alienation has a bearing here. Movement today is a one-way journey. We carry fond memories of our native places; but most of us live away from them.

In several ways internal migration was substantially different from the international migration that occurred later. First, internal migrants were ordinarily peasants going from one rural area to another; they underwent hardly any culture shock. Second, they nearly always migrated in gangs, which insulated them from the host society. Third, there is no evidence that sizable numbers of these seasonal migrants stayed in the areas where they worked regularly for several months every year. To us it might seem natural to relocate permanently where work is available, rather than travel there every year; but the seasonal migrants seem to have been completely unaffected by the environment in which they worked. They remained attached to their home society, with no thought of abandoning it.

The correlation that we have seen between the different systems of land tenure and either emigration or peasant militancy reveals the inadequacy of a deterministic push-pull explanation of emigration. Such an explanation fails to take into account social factors that influence how people respond to economic needs. There were three different responses to poverty in Italy in the late nineteenth century. One was to remain in Italy and attempt to change society by means of militant working-class organizations; another was to emigrate to the New World or elsewhere. The third alternative, to make no response and accept the status quo, has not been analyzed here; but it was generally adopted on the island of Sardinia, where neither migration nor militancy occurred.

The peasants' reluctance to buy land in America is another indication of the conditions in Italy that created both mass emigration and mass return. Emigrants might have escaped poverty more easily had they accepted permanent relocation overseas from the very beginning. That would have been a sensible decision from an economic standpoint. Their refusal to do so indicates that purely economic factors do not explain even those decisions that were basically economic.

No doubt the emigrants wanted change; but it had to be controllable, comprehensible, and clearly within the expectations of their peasant society. It took several decades and several trips across the Atlantic before Italians started to see emigration not as an extension of their lives in Italy, but as an end in itself.

CHAPTER 4

The Problems of Resettlement in Italy

RETURN migration from America, in the eyes of many Italians, was an unbounded success. "He who crosses the ocean can buy a house" was a popular refrain celebrating one goal of emigration.[1] Travelers reported hearing everywhere in Italy remarks such as: "The Americani have made a paradise of once-godforsaken regions."[2] As savings kept coming from America and emigrants kept returning, it looked as if the regions with high rates of emigration were securely on their way to an economic transformation. A government study of the peasants of the south concluded that return migration was bringing the only social renewal the country had seen in centuries. It concluded: "Mass emigration and return migration have become the most powerful force for social change in Italy."[3]

Does historical evidence bear out these optimistic views? In this chapter I will pursue two lines of investigation. The first concerns the returnees themselves—how were their lives affected by their stay in America? As we will see, their goals almost unnoticeably changed, and this introduced a totally new element into the equation of Italian overseas migration. The second line of investigation focuses on socioeconomic structures rather than individuals. In particular, it deals with the impact of return migration on the Italian economy. Returnees with their savings were bound to have an impact on communities, by stimulating the cash economy and the sale of land. Some historians have asked, however, whether these short-term economic benefits did not in fact retard more important social and economic changes, and thereby perpetuate the socioeconomic structures that gave rise to emigration in the first place.[4] According to this intriguing argument, return migration created a self-perpetuating cycle, forcing the reemigration of returnees and the departure of others who had never contemplated emigration.

The Conservative Expectations of the Liberals

Italian social scientists who studied return migration as it occurred were not unanimous in their assessment of its impact on Italian society. To most of them—Antonio Gramsci, Guido Dorso, Pasquale Villari, Sidney Sonnino, Leopoldo Franchetti, and Saverio Nitti were among the most prominent—emigration and return migration were destined to open up the backward Italian society to modernity, especially in the south, which many believed had not yet left the Middle Ages. The arguments these writers made in favor of emigration and return migration reveal that most of them—Gramsci and Dorso are the only notable exceptions—had a very poor and at times erroneous understanding of the socioeconomic transformation already under way in the industrial West, and of the conditions that were generating both emigration and return migration. They persisted in the belief that poverty could be eliminated by creating small farms and increasing the sense of individualism already pervasive in the areas of high emigration. As events were to show, these "liberal" ideas backfired; their proponents were not far ahead of the peasants in the ability to understand the social dynamics of Italy and of the countries to which Italians emigrated.

The analysis of Italian society by these writers began with a premise they all shared: that contrary to expectations the political unification of the country had not brought significant social change. As Villari, reflecting on the unification of the country, wrote in 1907: "Our Risorgimento has been almost exclusively a bourgeois achievement. The peasants had no part in it, just as they had no part in the previous history of Italy for centuries. They were always outsiders, and they still are."[5] When emigrants began to return, these writers thought it would touch off the social renewal that had been missing from the process of political unification. In a speech of 1911, for instance, Franchetti remarked: "While we were busy writing books and passing legislation to make Italy a modern state, the peasants who went to the United States to make money and returned became the real agents of change."[6]

These observers predicted that emigration and return would

bring about two changes. First, the accumulation of savings, given the peasants' determination to buy land, would expand regional cash economies and enlarge the class of small landholders. And second, the peasants' mentality would be transformed by the modern ideas and attitudes they had absorbed in more advanced societies abroad.[7]

The belief that creating small landholdings would solve Italy's economic problems sounds surprising today. By the second half of the nineteenth century, both Germany and England had reorganized or were reorganizing their agriculture by consolidating small landholdings into large estates in order to meet the demands of the new urban markets and to take advantage of new scientific farming methods.[8] Italian writers, nevertheless, persistently advocated the division of the large estates—the infamous *latifondi*—into small units. Coletti, in many respects a profound student of Italian peasant society, called on the Italian government to "assist the great effort of many returnees to buy land. Since the large estates have been the ruin of Italy, the future of the country lies with small property."[9] Villari said that it was not enough to create small holdings; they also had to be protected by the state against excessive fragmentation and against the power of the large estates.[10]

This insistence that Italian prosperity depended on having many small farms suggests a belief in a small-scale, agrarian, preindustrial capitalism. Most Italians apparently shared this belief. Large estates had a long history of bad, oppressive management by absentee landlords.[11] It made sense, seemingly, that if large estates had been the problem, small farms would be the solution. Italian economists did not realize, however, that the problem was more than size and ownership. It was also the inability to exploit the land with modern techniques and to use American savings to diversify the economy.

The transformation of peasant social attitudes was to be the second achievement. To those who kept repeating that the peasants' instinctive resistance to change would make any improvement impossible, Coletti answered that "returnees are going to be transformed, and they will be able to influence even those who will never emigrate."[12] Nitti envisioned a new social awareness: "By associating with the people of more modern cultures, emigrants will come in contact with labor unions, will witness the moral independence of more educated nations, and will live with the daily implications of popular democracy."[13] Nitti admitted that a few years in America, often in an Italian ghetto, was not likely to bring about a spectacular conversion to modernity. But he believed that even a small change could have great consequences. He noticed certain changes in regions of high return migration. Returnees refused to show the traditional deference to landowners and clergy; they were no longer totally ignorant of political matters, and some sought public office; they were no longer opposed to the education of their children, although still not encouraging it; and they joined voluntary organizations. "It is only because of the Americani," he wrote, "that our masses are making any progress."[14]

But the case for temporary emigration as a way to promote social renewal concealed a subtle contradiction. Many who celebrated the "new" Italian coming back from America also opposed any change that would upset the existing social order. Indeed, most who wrote on return migration regarded emigration as a way to prevent dangerous social change. Luigi Bodio, a government official, wrote: "We had to encourage them to leave. Security and tranquility at home could be maintained only by having large numbers of peasants emigrate."[15] Villari called emigration "a safety valve." It allowed peasants to make a living with money earned abroad; "thus it has spared the country from those savage peasant insurrections that terrorized Europe for centuries."[16] Another observer thought that emigration had to be viewed in reference to socialism. "Whatever we do to encourage emigration is a step in the direction of defusing social tensions and avoiding socialism. Emigration is the only way to keep change under control in Italy."[17] Apparently, these writers were unwilling to recognize that the very institutions that they did not want the returnees to disturb had created the backward conditions that brought about emigration.

Savings and Land

Money from America arrived in Italy before returnees did. The transformation of Verbicaro illustrates the effect the emigrants' savings had. In the 1870's Verbicaro was one of the poorest communes in the province of Cosenza; the prefetto reported on the squalor of the houses and the high rates of mortality and illiteracy.[18] By the early 1900's Verbicaro was changing rapidly. "There are more than 50 cottages already built and more in the process of being built; they are called the houses of the Americani," wrote the prefetto in 1905.[19] The older houses stood on the top of a hill, and the houses of the

Americani were built a third of a mile away on an open space.* Franco Ciccotti, an old resident of Verbicaro, recalled in 1975: "Most of the cash available in town was from America."[20]

Verbicaro was not exceptional in Italy. All communities with a substantial emigration received money from abroad—"more than this province has ever seen," the prefetto of Cosenza reported.[21] Reliable figures on remittances are not available, since most emigrants, especially early in their stay abroad, sent money to Italy only by means of friends.[22] But even the amount of money that arrived through banks was impressive. Leone Carpi, who based his estimate on the international bank notes issued by Italian consuls from 1869 to 1871, said that "the savings of the emigrants are the major source of income for many communities."[23] According to the Italian Bureau of Emigration, a total of 9 million lire (about 2.25 million dollars) arrived in Italy from abroad in 1902, over 7 million of them from the United States. The following year the remittances totaled 23 million lire (about 7.75 million dollars), 18 million from the United States. Except in 1906 and 1908 the remittances increased every year: 38 million lire in 1907, 25 million from the United States; 68 million in 1911, 48 million from the United States; and 84 million in 1914, 66 million from the United States. By 1916 remittances from overseas had passed 150 million lire, and in 1920 they reached the all-time high of one billion lire.[24]

The amount of money emigrants saved varied according to the time they had spent abroad. Luigi Rossi reported in 1910 that the average southern emigrant brought back "from 1,000 to 1,500 lire."[25] In 1912 an American wrote: "Returned migrants are in much improved economic circumstances, their average savings being from 250 to 1,000 dollars."[26] An Italian survey revealed that southern Italy received nearly two-thirds of the total savings entering the country.[27] The prefetti of Lucca, Genoa, Cosenza, and Palermo reported that savings arrived in different ways depending on what the purpose of the emigrants was. One Genoese reported that savings from America were the greatest source of income for the province.[28] According to the prefetto, however: "The savings are not as spectacular as it is often claimed. More emigrants leave every day for an indefinite period of time. These people do not ordinarily send their savings back to Italy if their families can manage to survive

*New houses are being built today; the only difference is that their construction depends not on American dollars, but on Swiss francs and German marks.

without them. Then there are emigrants who return after many years; most of them bring their savings back with them, either to open a small business or to retire. Only those who intend to buy land send their savings back, so that their families can buy land as soon as it becomes available."[29]

More savings probably came to the province of Lucca than to Genoa. As early as 1876 several communities in Lucca were said to be surviving on the savings of emigrants.[30] Over the years the remittances increased. In the early 1920's it was reported that "the savings entering the province have reached unexpected proportions. Migration is really the most important industry in this province. Some migrants come back with large fortunes; most come back with considerable sums, and this enables them to achieve their goals. In most cases it is a piece of land. But land is not available for all. Only a handful arrive without savings."[31]

Most emigrants from the province of Cosenza sent money to Italy as fast as they saved it and had it deposited in postal savings or cooperative banks.[32] In the early 1890's the prefetto observed: "If the local economy has not altogether collapsed, it is only because migrants keep sending money. Emigration seems to be almost the sole source of income in this province."[33] And the prefetto of Palermo wrote: "We can only be hopeful for the new generation, because never before has there been so much money here. I am confident that these savings will change the face of this province."[34]

An emigrant's first savings went to pay debts from before emigration and to help family members. Then the goal was to buy land. The pattern, already visible in the 1870's, was that wherever peasants had never had enough money to buy land, there the efforts by returnees to join the class of landowners were most determined.[35] Jacini told the Italian parliament that "the savings of the emigrants are used for two main purposes: first, to save small properties threatened by heavy taxation and to pay old debts; second, to create new small properties."[36] The purchase of land in this way first occurred in the north, and later, more intensely, in the south.[37] The desire to acquire property was so strong that some families bought land as soon as they had enough money for an acre or even less.[38] As the prefetto of Cosenza explained: "Most emigrants buy land while they still reside in America. What they can afford is ordinarily a very small piece of property; but to peasants who never owned anything, even one acre seems a fortune."[39]

Some noticed the strong tendency of returnees to buy the same tract of land they had previously worked as sharecroppers or laborers. Agostino Bertani said that returnees were so determined to achieve this goal that they bought the land regardless of the price.[40] In Cosenza some paid 200 percent more than the normal price in order to get a specific piece of land.[41] This was interpreted by some writers as an act of revenge against the old landowners.[42] An American told of a district in the south where the people of several towns had rented and farmed the land of a single landowner in the 1880's. After a series of crop failures, they migrated en masse to the United States. By 1905 many of them had come back and bought the same land they once worked.[43] As Agostino Caputo remarked: "Often the sense of revenge greatly overrides any economic consideration. I have seen people lose money to satisfy their pride."[44] Clearly, the goals of returnees were not strictly economic. Many returnees seem to have been eager to achieve immediate social status in the eyes of their former superiors, even when it conflicted with their best economic interests.

The increased supply of money naturally pushed up the price of land. Land speculation became a profitable business, as a government report pointed out in 1910: "When returnees began to arrive, speculators purchased large tracts of land at a low price; after dividing the land, they resold it at a much higher price."[45] An American wrote that some large proprietors in the south made "immense profits by dividing estates and selling plots to land-hungry peasants."[46] Friedrich Vöchting, a German student of land tenure in Italy, remarked: "Returnees were not well advised. Redevelopment areas were sold at a very high price, and real estate companies made fortunes. But returnees were determined to pursue their goals, regardless of how economically unsound they were."[47] Ironically, returnees were paying inflated prices for land at a time when the price of agricultural commodities was drastically declining in Italian markets.[48]

If returnees could not afford land because the price had increased during their absence, they often left a second time or even a third. Second-time emigration from Palermo and Cosenza was typically to save more money to buy land.[49] Second-time emigration from the north was ordinarily permanent. The prefetto of Lucca wrote: "Second-time migrations—rather common in the past decade—seldom occur. If a returnee leaves a second time, chances are that he will never come back again."[50] A member of the Chamber of Commerce of Genoa said: "Returnees either buy land, if available, or open a business. If they cross the ocean a second time, it is because something went wrong, and it is likely that they will never be back."[51]

5. Barber shop, Palermo, Sicily, early 1900's. Most of the emigrants who returned to Italy put their savings into land, but some used the money to open a small business, especially where there was little or no land for sale. From the name Coney Island, we can fairly assume that the man who set up this shop was a returnee and had made his money in the New York area.

Most historians agree that the savings of the returnees brought immediate benefits to the Italian economy, especially by providing peasants with much-needed currency; they disagree on the long-term effects. Concerning the immediate impact, Vöchting noted: "Until 1920 the demand for small holdings was almost completely dependent on the supply of American money, which was seldom used for anything else."[52] This is an overstatement; in both Genoa and Lucca returnees also used savings to start new businesses. But Vöchting was more concerned with the south, where return migration was more intense. A government commission supervising the sale of land in the south concluded that during the long depression of the 1880's and 1890's land transactions in the south were almost totally dependent on American money.[53] Another survey, on land transactions after the First World War, found that the number of transactions had increased in the early 1920's as a result of the favorable exchange rate, which jumped from 13 lire to the dollar in 1919 to 29 in 1920.[54] Land sales in the 1920's were stimulated by a postwar panic; when many middle-sized landholders decided to sell, American money promptly stepped in to buy.[55] The prefetto of Cosenza reported that families with money coming from America were able both to save their holdings and to acquire new ones.[56] And the prefetto of Palermo wrote: "In this province land transactions occur almost exclusively with American money."[57]

If Vöchting's observation is correct, the decennial national censuses should show increasing numbers of landowners in areas of high emigration and return migration. I examined the figures on land ownership for 1881, 1901, and 1921 in several *circondari.* (A circondario is an administrative subdivision of a province.) In the circondario of Genoa, 28 percent of the heads of households engaged in farming were landowners in 1881; in 1901 the figure was 41 percent, and in 1921, 48 percent. In the circondario of Chiavari, where Lorsica and Sestri Levante were located, 38 percent were owners in 1881, 54 percent in 1901, and 60 percent in 1921. In the circondario of Lucca, coextensive with the province of Lucca, the increase was from 27 percent in 1881 to 40 percent in 1921. The circondario of Paola, the area of Verbicaro, showed one of the highest increases, from 11 percent landowners in 1881 to 35 percent in 1921. In the circondario of Palermo the increase was from 25 percent in 1881 to 29 percent in 1901 and 40 percent in 1921. Finally, the circondario of Termini Imerese—the area of Trabia—had a small increase from 1881 to 1901, from 16 to 21 percent, and a major increase in the next two decades, from 21 to 40 percent.[58]

These data must be viewed in the light of the agricultural organization of the four provinces. In the previous chapter we saw the differences in land tenure in areas of high and low emigration. But there were also differences within the areas of high emigration. In the southwest, where the distribution of land was changing, a good deal of the land was owned by those who cultivated it, as in the Abbruzzi and Molise regions; in other areas, such as Calabria, little land was in the hands of cultivators. As a rule, middle-sized landowners did not cultivate the land themselves; this was done by workers under sharecropping contracts of a year's duration. These short-term contracts heightened competition and individualism among cultivators, and prevented them from banding together for collective bargaining. These farmers with short-term contracts had no consolidated farms; the plots they contracted for were fragmented and geographically dispersed. Generally, in the same year, a cultivator worked on several plots under a variety of contracts, both sharecropping and day laboring. The socioeconomic position of a cultivator in a community was determined by the contracts he was able to secure within a given year.[59]

The figures given above indicate that in 1881 the proportion of landowners was small in the three southern circondari under consideration, with Paola having the smallest. By 1921, however, the proportion had greatly increased, by 60 percent in Palermo and by over 200 percent in Paola. Two things made this change possible. One was the savings of emigrants, as already discussed. The other was that many middle-sized landowners were either willing or forced to sell. The wealthiest landlords of the south were generally absentees living in Naples, Palermo, or Madrid; they turned their land over to agents who entered into sharecropping or other contract agreements with cultivators. Middle-sized landowners, too, often despised active land management, preferring white-collar jobs in the cities. Surveys of the south in the late nineteenth century show the class of landowners producing an oversupply of lawyers, physicians, accountants, and scholars. These professional people had two characteristics: they were underemployed, and they had turned their back on farming. They were unprepared, by both temperament and training, to deal with the agricultural depression of the late nineteenth and early twentieth centuries. Some landowners were willing to sell to escape their problems; others were forced to sell to make ends meet and to maintain their status. Of course, selling was an attractive proposition, since returnees were willing to pay an inflated price for land.[60]

In the northwest the land distribution and agricultural organization were different, largely because land in that region had been subject to liberal laws and administrative policies since early in the nineteenth century. In 1881 there were many small family farms in the Maritime Alps and the northern Apennines. In this respect the provinces of Genoa and Lucca were akin to the southwest, although the farms were generally larger in the northwest than in the southwest. The large numbers of small holdings in Genoa and Lucca may have been a result of the pre-1880 seasonal mass migration to the Po Plains, to European countries, and to South America. As early as 1879 the prefetto of Genoa complained that much land had been subdivided into plots too small to be profitable. "I know of a case," he wrote, "where an acre of land is divided among nine owners."[61] Not only were there many individually owned and operated plots in the northwest, but there were also many cooperative credit funds, cooperative banks, and consumer cooperatives. The degree of economic integration made the small farmers of the northwest quite different from those of the southwest, where individualism prevailed. The combination of relatively high rates of individual ownership with cooperative farming practices explains why the increases in the rate of land ownership were not proportionately so great in the north as in the south: in the north, a good deal of land was already widely distributed and the small farmers were less in competition with each other than southerners were.[62]

Large estates did exist in the northwest, especially in and near the province of Lucca. But neither emigration nor return migration broke them up. In most cases these large estates were worked by *mezzadri*, that is sharefarmers, not to be confused with the very dissimilar sharecroppers of the south. The contract *a mezzadria*, which often lasted for decades or generations, gave each cultivator and his extended family household a relatively self-contained farm with a farmhouse. In most cases several of these farms were parts of one large estate called a *fattoria*. The owner or manager of the fattoria supervised the allocation of working capital and operated the estate's central flour mill, barn, wine and olive presses, and a variety of smaller services. The owners were seldom absentees: they took a direct interest in improving farming techniques, they created associations among themselves to foster common interests, and they organized agricultural discussion groups, magazines, and research institutes. Thus the large estate owners of the northwest, unlike those of the south, were able to confront the challenge of the agricultural depression of the late nineteenth century. Very few were forced to break up their estates, as returnees found out to their disappointment.[63] These two circumstances—the large number of individually owned and operated farms integrated into a system of numerous cooperatives, and the active interest of large-estate owners in their farms—help to explain why returnees to the north could not find land for sale as easily as returnees to the south, and why the increase in the rate of land ownership was proportionally lower in the northwest than in the southwest.

The figures on the increase of landowners between 1881 and 1921 show an interesting difference between north and south. The increase in land ownership was greater in the northwest than in the southwest from 1881 to 1901, and the opposite was true from 1901 to 1921. Several explanations can be offered for this difference. Emigration and return migration developed earlier in the northwest than in the southwest; northwesterners were accumulating the capital necessary to buy land as early as the 1880's. This showed up in the Italian census of 1901. By the end of the century land sales had slowed down in the northwest, either because temporary emigration was increasingly turning into permanent emigration, or because there was no more land for sale for the reasons already given. Probably it was a combination of both: with no land available in the northwest, emigrants thought more seriously about permanently relocating abroad.

In the southwest, it was only in the late 1890's that return migration and the arrival of American savings became mass phenomena. Their impact did not show up in the census of 1901, since that census gave cumulative data covering the years 1881–1900. (No national census was taken in 1891.) The intense buying and selling of land continued in the south in the first two decades of the twentieth century, both because the agricultural organization of the southwest made more land available than in the northwest, and because the many returnees and the great amount of American savings were matched by the willingness of middle-sized landowners to break up their estates and sell them in plots.

It is possible that the differences in timing explain why return migration declined earlier and more rapidly in the northwest than in the southwest. Since land was available in the southwest well into the twentieth century, migrants kept coming back without even questioning whether it was more advantageous to stay abroad permanently. As long as land was available, southerners neither questioned nor reassessed the final goal of emigration. On the other hand, emigrants from the northwest were forced to take a second look at their goal when land simply became unavailable.[64] Undoubtedly when the goal of buying land became impractical, Italians looked at emigration with different eyes and saw it as an end in itself. And there were other reasons, besides, for Italians to reassess the value of their real estate transactions, even before land became unavailable.

Disregarding for a moment the long-term consequences of these land transactions, the available evidence seems to show that many returnees, especially in the southwest, were able to achieve their goal. The increase in the number of small landowners represented a major change in Italian society, especially in the south. The change was so striking, and its promise so great, that hardly anybody questioned its lasting value. The prefetto of Palermo voiced the general optimism in 1912: "This province, notwithstanding pressing economic problems, will have a great future. The capital brought home by the returnees, the creation of small properties, and a general prosperity that this province has probably never known before are the best indication of the renewal that these people have been able to bring about on their own."[65]

The new clothes returnees sported were the most obvious sign of a newly acquired status. A British traveler thus described an Italian returning to a small community in the north: "When he came back from America, he arrived in a dark blue suit and the most wonderful yellow boots Campià had ever seen."[66] Italian writers of fiction joined in celebrating these transformations. Luigi Capuana, for instance, has one of the characters in a novel say to his grandfather: "Grandpa, do you know that Baldy has arrived from America? You could not recognize him: fine hat, new suit, shiny shoes; he looks like a gentleman. And he brought a lot of money. They say he has bought a piece of land at Faito from Garozzo."[67]

Problems

Despite the success stories, many Italian emigrants returned home in poverty.[68] The Italian government, it was reported, established three hospitals, in Palermo, Genoa, and Naples, to "take care of the invalids that the consuls send back each year because they are no longer of use to the country. The three hospitals take care of only a fraction of the returnees who need medical attention; most of the others are sent back to their own communities and become a danger to the people there."[69] The Comitato di Soccorso e Patronato, an Italian organization in San Francisco for helping immigrants to find work and assisting them in case of unemployment, sent 314 people back to Italy from San Francisco in 1906 with "charity tickets" because they were sick or destitute.[70] To be sure, 1906 was the year of the earthquake, but 314 people in a community of 15,000 Italians is a large number, especially since the Italians in San Francisco were considered better off than those in most other cities.[71]

Prefetti in Italy and consuls in the United States reported many cases of returnees in extreme poverty. In 1867, for instance, the consul in San Francisco asked the permission of the Minister of Foreign Affairs to repatriate five Italians who were unable to support themselves and wanted to return.[72] In 1879 the consul in Boston notified Rome that he needed additional funds to repatriate indigent immigrants.[73] In 1891 the prefetto of Cosenza wrote: "The poor and disillusioned returnees are more than a few. Their return is usually paid for by relatives in America, less often by relatives in Italy. The most desperate returnees are those who have nobody to go to."[74] And the prefetto of Palermo in 1896: "Public opinion tends to ignore those who have failed. And they usually have no desire to make

6. Involuntary returnees, Ellis Island, N.Y., ca. 1910's. Not all returnees went back to Italy with money and dreams for a better life. Some were not even allowed to enter the United States because of criminal records or physical disabilities. Others returned poor and sick, their return tickets paid for by relatives in Italy, mutual aid societies in the United States, or the Italian government. The group of Italians shown here had been denied admission to the United States and were awaiting repatriation.

themselves conspicuous. But some of them have joined socialist clubs and are sowing discontent."[75] Vöchting concluded: "The Americani who came back with savings and were able to settle permanently in Italy were only a handful."[76] And a study of return migration to Sicily found that even those who returned with money generally failed to maintain their status.[77]

It is worthwhile to expand on the reasons why returnees who bought land failed in the end to achieve a good life in their native communities. Small-scale agrarian capitalism seems not to have been a lasting solution. One reason was that returnees overestimated their financial assets and what they could do with them. After four or five years in America, they typically brought back from 1,000 to 3,000 lire (250 to 750 dollars), which seemed a large sum to people who, before migrating, had been paid from 50 Italian cents to one lira a day if men, and from 15 cents to 45 cents if women.[78] As Vöchting noted: "The success most emigrants achieved overseas was objectively very modest. But it was extraordinary for peasants who had never owned anything." For many returnees, moreover, the need to be recognized as successful led them to overestimate what they could do with their savings.[79]

Some returnees bought more land than they could afford. To avoid revealing that their success had been only modest, they borrowed money and soon found themselves in conditions similar to those they had originally left.[80] Some returnees spent all their money on buying land, without setting any aside for improvements.[81] Returnees who had not kept abreast of inflation in Italy while in America discovered with dismay that the purchasing power of their savings was considerably less than when they had made their plans before departing.[82] The prefetto of Cosenza reported: "Returnees show unrealistic expectations. Often they are frustrated because the price of land has increased during their absence. But they seldom accept the advice of others: they buy more land than they can afford."[83] The prefetto of Palermo was more caustic: "Because they wear new suits and have some money in their pockets, they think they have nothing to learn. Unfortunately, their arrogance is their worst enemy. Many are forced to resell because they cannot make a living on land they have purchased. Embarrassed, they leave on the pretext that they are unable to adjust to life in Italy."[84]

Some returnees seem to have behaved differently in the north. The prefetto of Genoa wrote: "Those who return are very careful in investing their money. If they cannot get land, they open a business. Those who buy land are careful to set aside some money for improvements."[85] But in general the evidence shows returnees unable to grasp the complexity of the economy, and therefore seeking short-term solutions.

Some returnees crossed the Atlantic a second or a third time because the money they had sent to Italy earlier had been spent by their wives or parents. One emigrant, for example, spent several years in California saving as much as he could. The first money he sent home was sufficient to pay off the family debts. "The money he sent home afterwards was to be put in a bank for him. He sent 3,000 lire in all, and when he came back he found hardly a penny left. His father had drawn it out and spent it." This was not the only such case in that small community of about 200 people.[86] Reports from prefetti tell similar stories. The prefetto of Palermo wrote about "endless family disputes and fights" when returnees came back and discovered that either their savings were not as much as they remembered or the land bought on their instructions was not what they wanted. "Some returnees left forever when they realized that their families had cheated them and taken advantage of them when they were in America."[87]

Besides the returnees' own misjudgments, Italian government policy contributed to the failure of many of them. Gramsci analyzed in some detail how the government offered returnees bonds in exchange for dollars. The dollars were then used not to modernize the agrarian economy of the south, but to expand the industrial sector of the north. Thus, Gramsci argued, "the silent socioeconomic revolution that the government promoted and seemingly protected by encouraging temporary emigration and return migration was killed at birth by the government itself."[88] Vöchting showed that when the Italian Savings Association failed, following some risky investments in northern industries, most of its 400,000 creditors were returnees.[89] Gramsci sadly concluded: "Every attempt by the returnees to create a bit of capital in their regions failed, because the Italian government, which preached the necessity of temporary emigration in order to increase local capital, never allowed those regions to achieve that goal."[90]

New Men

Liberal writers hailed the returnees from America as "new men," and indeed they were noticeably different from the peasants who had never been abroad. In this section I look at three areas in which returnees had an impact on Italian society. First, returnees questioned the deference to the local elite that they had been raised to give, and asserted the freedom to choose one's place of residence; second, they promoted literacy, education, and political participation; and third, they strengthened mutual aid societies and made them more effective politically.

The returnees' questioning of social deference greatly expanded the limited freedom Italian peasants and small farmers had had before mass emigration began. The first emigrants faced the moral condemnation of a society that did not recognize the right of peasants to move about. In Genoa in the late 1870's, for instance, a writer lamented the "spreading evil of emigration and the dangerous idea that people are free to move; these new ideas will undermine the stability of our society."[91] A writer in Tuscany attacked "the immorality of the younger generation in this region," which claimed the "right to abandon the noble commitment to the land and to move to the city or to go overseas."[92] Priests condemned those who, "attracted by a handful of gold, dare to forget the sacred commitment to their families and to the land."[93] A series of articles in *La Civiltà Cattolica*, the leading Catholic journal, attacked the principle that one had the right to choose to leave one's country.[94] The peasants themselves were generally apologetic about leaving. Members of a group leaving Genoa for America declared that they would be back as soon as they had saved enough to pay their debts. After all, one of them added, emigration was morally justifiable only under extreme circumstances and for a limited period of time.[95]

The attitude returnees brought back with them was different. They openly claimed the right to choose whether they would live in Italy or abroad. As a peasant from the south put it: "When we left for the first time, we were made to feel guilty. Landowners and priests told us that it was wrong to abandon the land they owned. But now we know better; nobody can tell us to stay somewhere if we do not want to."[96] It was reported that returnees were brave enough not to take off their hats in front of the local gentry,[97] and that they showed less willingness to defer to priests and to join in the religious ceremonies of those who had never migrated. In a little southern town a city clerk complained that the returnees "come into my office and look at me as no better than themselves. They do not take their hats off. In America they lost all respect."[98] Emigration had become a way to express social protest, to find a new sense of freedom, to express personal independence. It became a sign of a new manhood. As a Calabrian observed: "In this region the man who has not been brave enough to cross the ocean at least once is not considered a free man. As a matter of fact, those who have never migrated have a hard time finding a wife."[99]

It was also reported that returnees showed a greater interest in education than those who had never migrated. It was during the decades of mass emigration, from 1871 to 1921, that the Italian government established a public school system, and in that period illiteracy in the country dropped from 70 percent to 33 percent. Yet profound differences between the north and the south remained.[100] In the provinces of Genoa and Lucca, people responded eagerly to educational opportunities, and illiteracy declined rapidly even in small and isolated communities.[101] In Lorsica, for example, only 14 percent of the men and 22 percent of the women who signed marriage contracts in 1911 were illiterate.[102] In the south, however, the response was different. One mayor wrote: "We fear a popular rebellion if we dare to open a school." And in Verbicaro: "We closed our school because the owner needed the building for his cows."[103] In the south illiteracy declined less rapidly than in the north. In 1911, for instance, 72 percent of the men and 85 percent of the women signing marriage contracts in Verbicaro were illiterate; and in Trabia the rate at that time was 51 percent for men and 63 percent for women.[104]

The returnees' new attitude toward education was seen everywhere. Asked whether returnees showed a greater interest in education than those who had never migrated, 125 southern mayors, out of 147 interviewed, reported that returnees did.[105] In 1910 a government official remarked that returnees were willing to send their children to school because they had suffered discrimination abroad on account of their own illiteracy.[106] The secretary of one of the mutual aid societies in Cosenza reported: "Returnees have, besides money, a new sense of personal dignity that stimulates an increased interest in education even among those who have never migrated."[107] In the province of Cosenza, a survey found that returnees, although not totally converted to the idea of education, had relaxed their opposition to mandatory education for their children.[108]

This increased interest in education was reflected in the rate of school attendance. During the school year 1871–72, only 37 percent of the children of school age attended school in the province of Cosenza, and only 32 percent in Palermo. In 1901–2 the rate had risen to 63 percent in Cosenza and 64 percent in Palermo. And in the two northern provinces, though the rate had been higher than in the south since the 1870's, by 1901–2 100 percent of the school-age children attended school.[109] The returnees from the United States perhaps had a specific reason to favor education. They were aware that groups of Americans opposed to free immigration had proposed literacy tests; this proposal had the strong support of the Dillingham Commission in 1911.[110] In 1909 the prefetto of Palermo commented: "There is a great interest in schools among returnees. I suspect, however, that fear is what stimulates this interest. Returnees want their children to learn to read and write so that the children can take their parents along when they grow up if the United States adopts a literacy test."[111]

Returnees themselves often expressed their new interest in education. A 45-year-old Calabrian peasant, who had worked in the mines of West Virginia for several years, told an interviewer: "Those who have been abroad understand better than others the need for an education, and some go back to school. I am illiterate, but I certainly will see to it that my children, if they have to go out into the world, do not suffer what I did, just because they are illiterate."[112] An American traveler reported that returnees were probably the most fervent advocates of education in Italy.[113] As Ernesto Marenghi wrote: "Until a few years ago the peasants of the south were in no way different from the serfs of the Middle Ages. Returnees have taught even those who have never migrated to lift their heads and become socially and politically independent by making good use of the schools."[114]

Finally, returnees joined fraternal organizations more readily than those who had not migrated. The impact of emigration and return migration on fraternal organizations deserves special attention because it sheds light on the socioeconomic structures in the regions of high and low emigration. In the late nineteenth century many Italian fraternal organizations were mutual aid societies, whose purpose was to give their members financial and medical assistance in case of sickness and to assure them a decent burial in case of accidental death. First established in the 1850's among urban industrial workers in the north, the mutual aid societies spread slowly among peasants. In 1860 there were only 181 societies in Italy.[115] The reason for the peasants' reluctance to join mutual aid societies was that there was no tradition of voluntary association in Italy. In fact, during the restoration period following the Congress of Vienna in 1815, the right of free association, which the French Revolution had affirmed, was either abolished or severely restricted in all the Italian states. Giuseppe Mazzini, the liberal thinker, met with strong resistance, especially from the peasants, when he preached the importance of voluntary association.[116] The only model the new associations could rely on was that of the guilds of the Italian Renaissance; the new societies began exactly where the guilds left off.[117]

The number of Italian mutual aid societies increased rapidly after 1860. In 1878 there were 2,091, with about 350,000 members. By 1885 the number of societies had more than doubled, to 4,896.[118] In Calabria, a region where there had been no societies before 1860, ten were created between 1861 and 1865. At one of the first Italian conventions of voluntary associations, in Rome in 1871, the existing societies drafted a declaration of principles and created a national organization to promote the establishment of new societies.[119] In the city of Rome alone, 43 were established between 1871 and 1873.[120]

Initially, political goals were expressly excluded from the mutual aid societies. The bylaws of the society of Porcari, for instance, stated: "Our society forbids its members to get involved in politics, or even to discuss politics, at the meetings of the association. Our sole purpose is mutual assistance."[121] The absence of political concerns should not come as a surprise; as late as 1880, only 2 percent of Italian males had the right to vote.[122] Politics was the province of the educated. The Calabrian Agostino Caputo wrote in 1910: "Even the more aware among our peasants—that is, those who belong to societies—do not know what politics is all about. The organization of a modern state and participatory democracy are beyond the realm of their interests."[123]

The great increase in the number of societies and their shift from fraternal to political goals occurred during the period of mass emigration, and earliest in the provinces where there was little emigration. Some figures will illustrate the difference between the areas of high and low emigration. In 1885 the province of Lucca had 35 societies with about 1,500 members; Ferrara, a northeastern province similar in size to Lucca but with low emigration, had twice as many societies and members. The province of Cosenza had 39 societies with only 500 members; Bari, a southeastern province slightly larger than Cosenza but with low emigration, had four times as many societies and sixteen times as many members. Of course, the provinces of Genoa and Palermo both had many societies—223 in Genoa and 148 in Palermo—but most were societies of artisans.[124] Peasant societies were rare in the two provinces.[125] Clearly, there were more associations, with larger memberships, in the areas of low emigration than in those of high.

As for the goals of the societies, the Italian Association of Farmers pointed out in 1900 that by 1880 the peasant associations where emigration was low had already become militant political organizations. In the areas of high emigration this transformation of goals occurred mostly in the late 1890's, principally as a result of return migration.[126]

An explanation for this difference can be found by comparing the two most markedly contrasting regions with respect to emigration and return migration: the southwest and the northeast. In the southwest, where emigration was high, the individualism and competitiveness stimulated by the active land market created a familistic society and economy, in which people withdrew from extrafamilial relations. The only strong extrafamilial tie was the patron-client relationship, which had large landowners and local gentry on one side and laborers, sharecroppers, and small landowners on the other. The patron presumably took care of his clients' needs directly; it was on this ground that patrons in the southwest resisted the establishment of fraternal organizations. The only other hierarchical structuring of this society came from outside the community, as a direct extension of the central government or the church.

In this context, without organized social classes, a militant labor movement could hardly arise. Yet at the same time the lack of an organizational infrastructure or social classes made economic development difficult. In an individualistic and familistic society of this sort, individuals are dispensable. Since there is no strong social solidarity, the likely result of economic pressure is that individuals will leave the community. Leonard Moss put it this way: "The traditional peasant society of southern Italy does not work well at any level."[127] It is safe to say that strong associations did not develop in the southwest because there was no sense of a society as we understand the term today.

The northeast was the classic area of large estates, sharefarming, and low emigration rates. Peasant militancy was common in this part of the country, with the Emilia-Romagna region the reddest area of the northeast. Two distinct and sharply conflicting classes arose. One was that of the owner-managers, who banded together to direct the economy. This class used the services of managers and technicians trained in schools of agriculture, and often organized agricultural forums; it held political power in Rome through elected deputies and senators. The other class was that of the sharefarmers, who had much to gain by uniting to curtail the power of the landowners. The relatively high literacy rate of the northeast helped sharefarmers to organize. At the same time, the extended family household prevalent in the northeast ruled out the narrow familism characteristic of the southwest. These two discrete and organized classes provided the basis for social conflict. In such a society, individuals were not dispensable. Since there was a strong sense of group solidarity, economic pressure was likely to result, not in the pursuit of individual economic gain, but in increased organization and militancy.[128]

In the areas of high return migration, and more specifically in the four provinces under study, returnees showed that their stay in America had changed them. They manifested a vigorous interest in organizing societies where there were none, and in making people who had never migrated aware of what organization could achieve. In Cosenza, Caputo reported: "Returnees greatly influence the growth and political organization of our societies. Where societies exist, the returnees make them stronger and politically more aware. Where they do not exist, they create them. It is because of the returnees that we now have societies in all the communities of the province."[129] Large landowners of the south complained that returnees had introduced the idea of cooperation among small farmers, which threatened the patron-client relationship.[130] The prefetto of Lucca reported that returnees had established mutual aid societies even in the mountain towns.[131] "Returnees are aware," he wrote, "that associations are important for their economic interests."[132]

In respect to personal independence, education, and voluntary associations, then, returnees had shed their resistance to change. They had outgrown the traditional peasant-client relationship, and now had some interest in political participation. Much of the individualism that had marked the areas of high emigration and return was gone. And not only did returnees themselves change, they brought change to their communes.

We should not, it must be added, attribute to the returnees all the social change that occurred in Italy around the turn of the century. The rise of individual freedom and the decline of the traditional deferential society, the increased interest in schooling and education, and the growth and politicization of the mutual aid societies were also the result of complex social dynamics within Italian society itself. As Moss noted, the Italian peasant society, especially in the south, had at least since the mid-nineteenth century been a surprising mixture of revolutionary movements and ultraconservatism. This aspect of the Italian society must be borne in mind if one is to assess realistically the impact of return migration.[133]

The Limitations of Change

If returnees were indeed motivated to seek social change, the question arises why they generally failed to accomplish the change they wanted most, to establish themselves permanently and successfully in their native communities. The evidence suggests that the social change that returnees effected, although real, was not profound enough to allow a lasting resettlement in Italy, just as their

American savings did not provide a lasting solution to their financial problems.

Events proved very quickly that the optimism of the liberals was ill founded. It was useless to expect major social change to spring from people who had been overseas only a few years and had had only marginal contact with American society.[134] Moreover, it became increasingly evident that the individualistic solutions that emigrants and returnees were pursuing could not work in the end. These problems were noticed as soon as large-scale return migration became evident. In Cosenza Caputo reported: "Returnees established associations; but there is little evidence that the social awareness of returnees has been deeply affected by their residence overseas."[135] One returnee was described thus: "Bortolo had been in California four years, but he showed no trace of Americanism. Had he not told me, I would not have guessed it. The returned emigrants of other nationalities I have seen have always something American about them. Not so with Bortolo. He went and returned the same old Bortolo."[136]

There were three main reasons that return migration did not bring significant social change to Italy, and especially to the south. First, there is no evidence that the patron-client relationship was replaced by other lasting social arrangements, particularly with regard to economic cooperation among farmers. Second, emigration did not sufficiently break down the extreme individualism characteristic of the areas of high emigration and return. The returnees' interest in mutual aid societies, for instance, was superficial, and aimed more at uniting the Americani as a distinct social class than at harnessing their new social awareness for the betterment of the community. Third, and probably most important, returnees were perplexed people. They were caught between the nostalgic desire to live in Italy in the old way, with the added prestige and money from having been abroad, and the inability to adjust to the old way of life. And yet they could not make the decision to stay in America.[137]

The ambivalent attitude of the returnees kept them from making a definite commitment to either Italy or America. As Foerster put it: "Life abroad was strange and difficult, and tolerated only for the promise of return. Once back, the returnees found their towns less beautiful than they had expected and the memories of America more seductive than they had ever anticipated."[138] A returnee told the prefetto of Palermo: "I was so disappointed when I came back to Italy that even New York became beautiful to me. Yet, when I was in America I wanted to return."[139] As one historian concluded: "At home their dream was of America; in America their dream was of home."[140]

Carlo Toti said he had returned to Calabria because he could not live anywhere else but in Italy. Once back, he was haunted by memories of America: "In America I was happy. Yet I wanted to return. And what did I find here? Disappointment."[141] The prefetto of Palermo wrote: "Returnees strongly identify with things American. Theodore Roosevelt is more popular among them than our King. But regardless of all their admiration for America, they feel they have to come back and establish themselves in Italy."[142] An American visitor to a small village in the Italian south told of seeing two women comparing shoes; one of them proudly displayed a pair of shoes from Michigan "for a dollar ninety-eight guaranteed."[143] The identification with America was strong, though not enough to cause a final break with Italy. The commitment to Italy, on the other hand, was not deep enough to keep Italians away from America. The tension between these two impulses persisted many years, and is one of the keys to understanding both return migration and the socioeconomic organization of the early Italian settlements in the New World.

The restlessness of the returnees was not purely sentimental, for they realized that they had a higher standard of living in America than in Italy. It became almost a litany, especially in the south, that one could make more money in one day in the United States than in a week in Italy.[144] As a returnee to Palermo said, in 1908: "In America I made from 11 to 15 lire a day as a mason and about 7.50 as a gardner. In twenty months I saved almost 3,000 lire. Like everybody else, I came back to buy land. But the land I bought is not enough to make a living on, and I have to hire myself out as in the old days. I make only 1.50 lire a day as a laborer. How can I stay here?"[145] And another returnee: "I came back because my family and my aging parents are here. But it was a mistake. Here I can hardly live off the land, and in America I made 8 to 10 lire a day. No, it does not pay to come back. Yet I could not stay there without my family." Asked whether he was contemplating leaving with his family, he answered: "I do not know."[146]

In interviews I had with returnees who had remained in Italy permanently and with others who had later gone back to the United States, many elaborated on how difficult it had been to decide whether to settle in America permanently. Of 25 Italians in San Francisco asked about the first time they had emigrated, thirteen said they had stayed two or three years more than they had originally planned because of the money they were making. Of those thirteen, nine said they had later returned to San Francisco, after going back to Italy for a while, for the same reason.[147] Observing the mixed feelings of the migrants, Foerster concluded: "There is a strife between the desire to continue to earn and that to return to Italy; so there arises a contest between the old and the new: the old calling, the new seducing."[148] It was virtually impossible for returnees to have both land in Italy and a job overseas. And their inability to make up their minds generally kept them from achieving either goal fully.

Many returnees, although willing to join mutual aid societies, were unwilling to associate with people who had never migrated. Often returnees were highly critical of their communes, and their attitude was cordially reciprocated by those who had never left. But the returnees seemed unwilling to work in order to bring about those changes they so vigorously demanded. Resentful that newly acquired social and economic status gained no recognition from the local landlords, returnees joined to form exclusive clubs that had no meaningful social goals. The prefetto of Palermo wrote: "Returnees seem to believe that everything is wrong with our society, and that they have all the solutions for our social problems."[149] Another observer from the south wrote that "the pride of the Americani is unbearable: they have become so annoying that those who have never migrated do not want to deal with them."[150] Returnees particularly resented being reminded of their origins. They liked to display their success in the way they dressed and the cigars they smoked.[151] But as Foerster observed, the local gentlemen would publicly ask: "Who were they before they went away?"[152]

Returnees, Gilkey notes, were often criticized as "lazy, wasteful, uncooperative individuals who did nothing to improve their land or promote agricultural progress, people who regarded the homeland as a place of vacation, and their return a sentimental journey."[153] It is difficult to assess how common these attitudes were and to what extent the criticism expressed envy by those less fortunate. Serious scholars like Foerster and Giuseppe Scalise, however, voiced the same criticism.

The children of returnees also sometimes made resettlement more difficult. At least until the turn of the century, emigrants who took their families along were a minority. Those who did, and then brought their children back from America, apparently expected the children to adjust to life in Italy with no problems.[154] But the children had no sympathy for the old country. To an American visitor's question, "How do you like it here?" a 15-year-old boy who had been brought back to Calabria from New York answered: "I do not like it at all. My father brought me back to help him in the barbershop and to live here. But this will not happen. In a year or two I will be back in New York by myself." And the visitor concluded: "Children of returnees, one and all, are not interested in the towns of their fathers. They want to return to the United States where they feel they belong."[155] De Nobili considered the children of returnees the most restless group of people in the region, and totally indifferent to local affairs.[156] As Foerster put it: "When children have been abroad they become the most powerful of all forces to sever the ties with Italy."[157]

In sum, returnees had varying reactions to emigration and return. With time, they felt the conflict between their different goals. On the one hand, in their determination to find a solution at home, they had committed themselves to purchasing land in Italy; on the other hand, they realized more and more that working a small plot of land in Italy was financially less rewarding than having a job in the United States. The old goal of land ownership was not as appealing after seeing New York as when they had first left Italy. Emigrants probably did not foresee that America would change them; emigration was to have been a parenthesis, a means to achieving an end in Italy. But returnees could not be the same after being in America; their perceptions of both Italy and America changed. Their commitment to both countries seems to have been strong, and this made the choice of where to live difficult. Returnees, then, were pursuing goals that proved increasingly unsatisfying the more they came within reach.

The Crisis of the Old Order

Return migrants, whatever their attitude, probably had little chance of making a living by purchasing and farming small plots. In the late nineteenth century the agriculture of the Western world was undergoing a transformation that made such small farming in Italy almost certain to fail. The main impact of this transformation on Italian agriculture was the invasion of Italian markets by American and European agricultural commodities, which successfully competed with local production. The American advantage resulted from three factors: the increased use of machinery, which enabled American farmers to cultivate more land and raise larger crops; improved methods of food processing and the use of refrigeration, which allowed shipment over longer distances; and a drastic drop in transatlantic freight rates.[158] To illustrate this last point, in 1860 it cost 37 cents to ship a bushel of wheat from Chicago to Genoa; 20 years later it cost only 10 cents. Freight rates did not decline proportionately in Italy: in the early 1880's it cost less to ship a ton of wheat from Chicago to Genoa than from Turin to Venice, about 300 miles. The wheat-growing regions of Italy like the Po valley and the old Neapolitan provinces were unable to stand the competition.[159]

The drop in the price of wheat, olive oil, and wine, the three main cash commodities of Italian agriculture, is a good indication of the changes that occurred. A quintal of wheat sold for 38 lire in 1873, and three decades later for 19 lire, the main drop occurring in the mid-1880's. As a consequence, Italian wheat production declined, the exporting of wheat ended, and imports, mostly from the United States, soared from 147,000 tons in 1881 to over one million in 1887.[160] The competition in olive oil and wine came from Spain and France. Olive oil sold in Italy for 159 lire per hectoliter in 1873 and 108 in 1894.[161] Wine fell from 85 lire to 34 lire per hectoliter in the same period.[162]

Prices did not fall simultaneously in all Italian markets; they fell first, for example, in Genoa, later in Florence, and still later in Palermo.[163] This time differential reflects the regional fragmentation of the Italian economy at the time. It parallels, moreover, the rise of emigration, which also started first in the north and progressively moved south; this adds weight to the findings of Harry Jerome, that Italian emigration to the United States fluctuated partly in response to the Italian and American economies.[164]

The price of other commodities in Italy also fell. Indian competition depressed the price of silk. In 1870 a kilo of cocoons sold for 10 lire; the price was 5 lire in 1887 and 2 lire in 1894. The total Italian silk production declined an average of 100 million lire per year from 1884 to 1894. The price of hemp dropped from 110 lire per quintal in 1876 to 65 in 1883. Iron production decreased too, at a time when the industry was expanding in Great Britain, France, the United States, and Germany.[165]

The impact of these changes must be assessed in the light of the Italian small-farm economy. A collection of budgets of about 300 Italian families, published in 1880, is revealing.[166] Most of these families owned or rented a piece of land producing either wheat, wine, or olive oil. These commodities served as cash crops; as the itemized budgets indicate, few families made extensive use themselves of wine, olive oil—ordinarily replaced by lard—or even the better quality wheat. Generally, northern families used the profits from cash crops to buy the wheat they lived on, and saved the extra cash for other family expenses. The southern staple was wheat of inferior quality. Incidentally, several budgets of families owning very small properties show the main source of income to be a family member who had temporarily emigrated.[167]

About half of the 300 families broke even at the end of the year or had a surplus of a few lire; this was more common in the north. The other half were in debt. An economist who collected family budgets in several northern provinces observed that "regardless of how hard they try, even though both women and children work, few families reach the end of the year in the black if they rely exclusively on the land. Most families are heavily in debt either to the local grocery store or to moneylenders. Tenants are often unable to pay the rent, and landowners have to provide them with food to prevent starvation. It is difficult to say whether there are domestic solutions to these problems."[168] In Genoa the Chamber of Commerce reported that "most families would be in debt if a member of the family did not emigrate for a season every year."[169] Similar accounts came from other provinces, north and south.[170] This economy was described as precarious as early as the 1870's, when Italy was relatively prosperous because of increased exports stimulated by the Franco-Prussian War.[171]

The fall in prices disrupted this already precarious economy.[172] Cash crops no longer generated the income to meet family expenses. And because of declining prices, the wages of laborers also dropped. Some absentee middle-sized landowners from the southwest, unable to maintain their status on their income from the land, sold their estates in small parcels. Owners and managers of large estates in the northwest tried to cope with the depression by increasing the financial burden on the sharefarmers. The reports arriving in Rome from the provinces are an endless tale of struggling families unable to overcome their poverty. According to these reports, many farmers thought that by increasing the size of their holdings or by buying new ones they could increase production and also profits.[173] As land became available, therefore, overseas migration was increasingly seen as the way to buy land in order to cope with falling prices.

The way out of the depression for Italy was to modernize its agriculture as other European nations had done or were doing. But such an expectation was unrealistic. The Italian people lacked both the capital and the technological know-how to do so. The only ingredient Italy had in abundance was labor. It was within this context that would-be emigrants, deeply committed to small-scale agrarian capitalism, made their plans to purchase small farms.

Regardless of how much money the returnees could bring back, however, Italy could not avoid the impact of the modernizing economies of the United States and the northern European nations. And the more that competition forced the modernization of the Italian economy and Italian agriculture, the less realistic were the plans of the returnees, who sought a traditional solution for problems that were largely the outcome of modernization and industrialization in other nations. As Robert Michels pointed out, Italian emigration and return migration, if judged in terms of their lasting social and economic impact, were artificial, premodern, and ephemeral phenomena.[174] The main problem of Italian agriculture was not poverty and overpopulation, but the inability to exploit modern techniques.[175] The returnees, with their idealization of small property, simply helped prolong that problem.

But temporary emigration was not an unmitigated disaster. It did teach Italians a lesson, that temporary emigration could not cure the long-term social problems in Italy. When Italians realized that emigration had to be an end in itself, and not simply a way to preserve their traditional way of life on the land, at that moment emigration ceased to be a function of Italian social change and instead became permanent.

Italian returnees were not the only group that was caught between traditional goals and the new social dynamics of modernization. Broadly speaking, modernization in North America and Europe brought about the slow and irreversible absorption of regional cultures and economies into the national culture and economy. As the historian Eugen Weber wrote in regard to France, "The unassimilated rural masses had to be integrated into the dominant culture."[176] But the French peasants, as Weber showed, had ambivalent feelings about the transition: the better life that modernization brought was desirable; but the demands of change were not equally welcome. Return migration by Italians can be seen as an unsuccessful attempt to resist the disintegration of Italian regional cultures and ways of life. The failure of the returnees could not be blamed entirely on the impact of modernization. It was also the result of the returnees' own ambivalence about whether their regional culture was worth saving, in view of the promise of modernization.

Though unique in its large numbers, Italian return migration was not the only such migration that failed to fulfill the hopes of its advocates. No return migration in Europe in the nineteenth and twentieth centuries seems to have brought about a social transformation such as that expected to come out of return migration in Italy. Since the Second World War, for example, major change has been expected from the mass movement in Western Europe between the industrialized countries of the north and the less developed countries of the southern and eastern fringes. "First, the migrants' remittances have been thought to provide critically needed foreign exchange; second, the migrants themselves are supposed to develop industrial skills that they then return to apply, overcoming in this way barriers to development generated by the shortage of skilled manpower." But "the returnees' contributions have proved in actuality to be rather elusive."[177] Other studies have reached similar conclusions.[178] On the whole, return migration seems to arouse unrealistic expectations in the countries of emigration and among the emigrants themselves.

CHAPTER 5

Italian Settlements in San Francisco

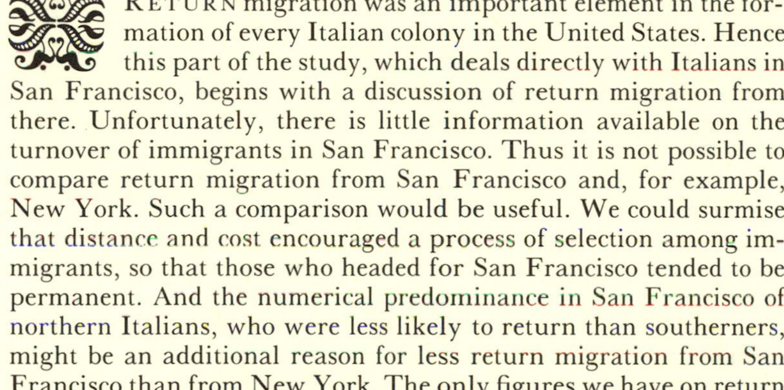

RETURN migration was an important element in the formation of every Italian colony in the United States. Hence this part of the study, which deals directly with Italians in San Francisco, begins with a discussion of return migration from there. Unfortunately, there is little information available on the turnover of immigrants in San Francisco. Thus it is not possible to compare return migration from San Francisco and, for example, New York. Such a comparison would be useful. We could surmise that distance and cost encouraged a process of selection among immigrants, so that those who headed for San Francisco tended to be permanent. And the numerical predominance in San Francisco of northern Italians, who were less likely to return than southerners, might be an additional reason for less return migration from San Francisco than from New York. The only figures we have on return migration from California before the end of the nineteenth century are lumped with data for Oregon and Washington. They show that between 1882 and 1891 about 22,000 Italians entered the three states, and that about 11,000 departed for Italy.[1]

Return Migration from San Francisco

Whatever the differences between California and eastern states, most San Francisco Italians intended to return to Italy, and many did. When plans were made in 1866 for an Italian hospital in San Francisco, the main objection was that it was an unwise investment since most immigrants intended to return.[2] In 1868 the consul reported: "Only a few have renounced their Italian citizenship and become Americans, since the common sentiment is in favor of returning, and most immigrants, sooner or later, do return."[3] An extensive survey in 1887 by the Italian Geographic Society found this still to be true. Twenty leading Italians answered a long questionnaire. One wrote: "There are those who keep delaying the day of their return, and since they are the most successful, it is likely that they will remain here indefinitely. But they are a small group. Most Italians want to, and in fact do, return."[4] In the 1890's return migration increased. Indeed, Carlo Dondero complained that the turnover of Italian immigrants had been increasing since the 1880's and was causing social problems the colony had never experienced before.[5] In 1903 the mayor of Capannori wrote that in the past returnees from San Francisco had been few, but that the number had increased since the turn of the century.[6] In 1908 the mayor of Verbicaro wrote that about one-half of the immigrants who had gone to California had returned, and that the movement back and forth showed no sign of abating.[7]

Reports on return migration made two other observations: the number of returnees who went to San Francisco again was growing; and the longer an immigrant stayed in San Francisco the more difficult it became to return to Italy. As the consul wrote in 1911: "Italians arriving here are not all first-time immigrants. There are those who come for the second or third time. Some of them come with their families; most likely they will never return to Italy. The general sentiment is still in favor of returning, but how much this will happen is questionable."[8] Two years later the prefetto of Palermo wrote: "San Francisco has been the destination of many emigrants from this province for over twenty years now. Many have returned. But among those who left last year were some who had been in San Francisco before. I have been told that these former returnees, unsatisfied with what they were able to accomplish here, migrated permanently."[9] When 25 San Francisco Italians were asked in 1976 whether they intended to return to Italy when they first migrated to San Francisco, nine said that they had at some point returned to Italy with the aim of remaining there, but had later changed their minds; eleven said they had gone back once to Italy to explore whether they could resettle there, but then had decided to return to America; and only five said they had never contemplated going back to Italy.[10]

From these accounts, we can identify four categories of Italians who came to San Francisco. The first consists of the permanent immigrants, people who moved to San Francisco with no intention of returning to Italy; this was probably the smallest group. The second consists of the permanent returnees, those who returned permanently to Italy after one or more stays in San Francisco; this group was probably larger than the first. The third consists of the returnees who later decided to go back to San Francisco. Finally, the largest group consists of those who intended to return to Italy—some even returned to explore the feasibility of moving back—but finally remained in San Francisco. Thus, among all Italians who came to San Francisco, those who settled there with no intention of returning to Italy were a small minority.

From this point on, our study concerns itself only with those Italians who made their final home in San Francisco, and with their children. The combined total of Italians and their children never surpasses 60,000. In 1930 there were 27,000 Italians and 30,000 Italo-Americans in San Francisco. Ten years later the Italo-Americans outnumbered Italians 32,000 to 24,000. All of them lived within the city of San Francisco; thus they shared the same social and economic advantages the city offered. The focus of the following pages is the changes that the San Francisco Italians and their children underwent, willingly or unwillingly, and the ways in which these changes were stimulated or obstructed by the immigrants' efforts to maintain some sort of continuity with the Italian past.

The Historiographical Question

A distinguishable and separate Italian settlement in San Francisco took form with the arrival of the first immigrants in the early 1850's. A handful of Italians who had been working for some time in the gold mines of California were forced out by Americans, and sought refuge in San Francisco. Together with Frenchmen, Basques, Mexicans, and Spaniards, they settled in the area later called the Latin Quarter, not far from Telegraph Hill, attracted by cheap rents and the freedom to live relatively undisturbed. Within a few years Romance languages dominated the district, where the Latin culture clearly set off the area from the rest of the city.[11] Although all Latins, these people were not terribly congenial, and interethnic fighting was part of everyday life. The struggle for survival, however, and a shared bitterness over the recent defeat of their attempt to control the mines, softened differences and cemented loyalties.[12] Frank Norris described this "aggregate Latin community" as reluctant to mix with other groups, quarrelsome, and addicted to heavy drinking. His description of the Latin quarter suggests a southern European village: men talking on the sidewalk, women standing by the doorsteps and chatting while watching their children at play.[13]

Italians soon carved out a little settlement of their own within the Latin Quarter; as other Latins spread to the south, Italians moved north. The first Italians had settled south of Broadway, between Pacific and Clay streets. The new immigrants who arrived in the mid-1850's moved across Broadway, around Du Pont Street (now Grant Avenue). By the late 1850's the community of Du Pont Street was known as Little Italy. In the following decade the Italian district expanded farther north toward Telegraph Hill and North Beach.[14] But the Du Pont area remained the historical center of the community, which already numbered 400 people by 1860.[15]

The establishment of separate neighborhoods by immigrants speaking the same language and sharing common traditions is hardly surprising; this pattern was typical of all immigrant groups that settled in urban areas.[16] Italians, however, showed a more pronounced tendency to create enduring separate settlements. Four-fifths of the Italians in the United States lived in cities in 1910, when only two-fifths of all Americans lived in cities.[17] In some sections of Chicago the Italians made up 50 percent or more of the total population.[18] In New York there were two distinct Italian settlements by the 1880's. The first was New Italy, the old Irish section of New York between Pearl and Houston streets east of Broadway; and the second was in a slum fringe of East Harlem between 109th and 111th streets.[19] Italians in Buffalo, Rochester, Utica, Kansas City, and Cleveland also concentrated in certain areas.[20] The censuses of 1910, 1920, and 1930, according to one analysis, show Italians in the major American cities to have higher indices of segregation than any other immigrant group; in seven of the nine cities analyzed, the Italians were more segregated than the blacks.[21] A recent study of ethnic neighborhoods in Omaha similarly found Italians to be more segregated than any other group.[22]

It was once common to call these urban enclaves ghettos: homogeneous, distinct, and separate areas where immigrants recreated their Old World way of life as a defense against the new society. Oscar Handlin called his chapter on residential patterns "The Ghettos."[23] More recent historians have questioned that interpretation, however, arguing that most immigrants never lived in ghettos, and that such ghettos as existed were far from being uniform environments sealed off from the influence of American society. Even in the most concentrated pockets, Italians shared their streets with people of other nationalities.[24] Unlike the "airtight cages" of the ghetto hypothesis, these settlements were seen as rather heterogeneous environments, where the traditions of the Old World were gradually reshaped under the influence of American society.[25]

The analysis of the formation and transformation of these settlements has undergone a similar process of revision. Early researchers saw "a regular sequence of settlements in successive areas of increasing stability and status."[26] The first-settlement area was a low-rent industrial district near the center of the city, where immigrants lived in compact and stable colonies, and in almost total isolation from Americans. If many immigrants settled in one city, several first-settlement areas were created in various industrial sections. In later phases, immigrants started to move out of these areas into second-settlement areas, which were desirable residential districts, with less physical concentration and less cultural solidarity, and with living patterns more like those prevailing in America.

Recent historians have challenged this model on several counts. The first-settlement areas, they maintain, had high rates of internal movement and a significant outflow and inflow of people from the very beginning.[27] In Buffalo, for instance, new Italian immigrants were constantly arriving, and others were leaving for other parts of town or other American cities.[28] In general, unskilled immigrants were geographically more mobile than more prosperous Americans. As Thernstrom has shown, immigrants formed a "flowing proletariat" that roamed American cities in search of jobs.[29] In addition, even in first-settlement areas immigrants lived intermingled with immigrants of other nationalities and with Americans. And when immigrants left the first-settlement areas, they did not necessarily move into more desirable residential districts, nor were these districts located at a considerable distance from the low-rent industrial areas. Finally, the second-settlement areas were not inhabited only by immigrants who had spent a few years in first-settlement areas and by well-established Americans. On the contrary, many first-settlement areas were not in or near industrial sections of town. And many second-settlement areas attracted not only better-established immigrants, but also recent immigrants "who brought their own outlook and made their demands in a first-settlement way."[30]

To historians who reject the ghetto hypothesis, therefore, the urban life of the immigrants was not a process of assimilation in which the ghetto was the last desperate effort to hold onto an outdated rural culture. On the contrary, they argue, it was a process of give and take in which the old rural culture was transformed but not wiped out. And that process in turn transformed American society. As more evidence becomes available, through detailed studies of immigrants in American cities, we are increasingly made aware of the variety of ways in which the immigrants responded to the American environment.

Settlements, Not Ghettos

Italians in San Francisco established two major settlements and one minor. The first and by far the largest was in the North Beach–Telegraph Hill area. In the 1850's the hill was first an Irish settlement and later predominantly German. When the Germans and Irish moved out to Bernal Heights and the Mission district, Italians took over. Photographs of Telegraph Hill from the 1860's and 1870's show dense settlements on the western and southern slopes.[31] Italians eventually spread to the adjacent North Beach area, between the hill and the bay. By the mid-1880's the blocks north of Broadway and east of Montgomery Street housed large numbers of Italians.[32]

The other main Italian settlement was in the Mission district. The first pioneers were farmers who had originally settled in the area where City Hall now stands in the early 1850's. As the city expanded and the value of real estate rose, they moved south, most of them to the Mission, and the rest to Noe Valley, the Outer Mission, and Visitacion Valley.[33] The third and smallest settlement was started in the 1870's when some Italians moved to the Old Potrero district. From there, the settlement expanded to Portola and Bayview. The Portola district was predominantly Irish in the 1850's and German in the following decade. When these two groups began to move out, Italians moved in and found housing similar to that of Telegraph Hill.[34] With the mass immigration between the 1890's and 1924, the concentration of Italians in these areas became greater; but no new settlements were created.

Data derived from the federal censuses allow us to assess the geographical distribution of Italians in the city. In 1900 about 13,000 people lived in assembly district 45, bounded by Montgomery and Kearny streets and the bay: half were American-born and half foreign-born. There were fewer than 2,500 Italians in that district, or about 40 percent of the foreign-born in the district and 20 percent of the total Italian population living in San Francisco.[35] Ten years later the same assembly district had 22,000 people, an increase of about 75 percent since 1900. Of that total, 18 percent were native-

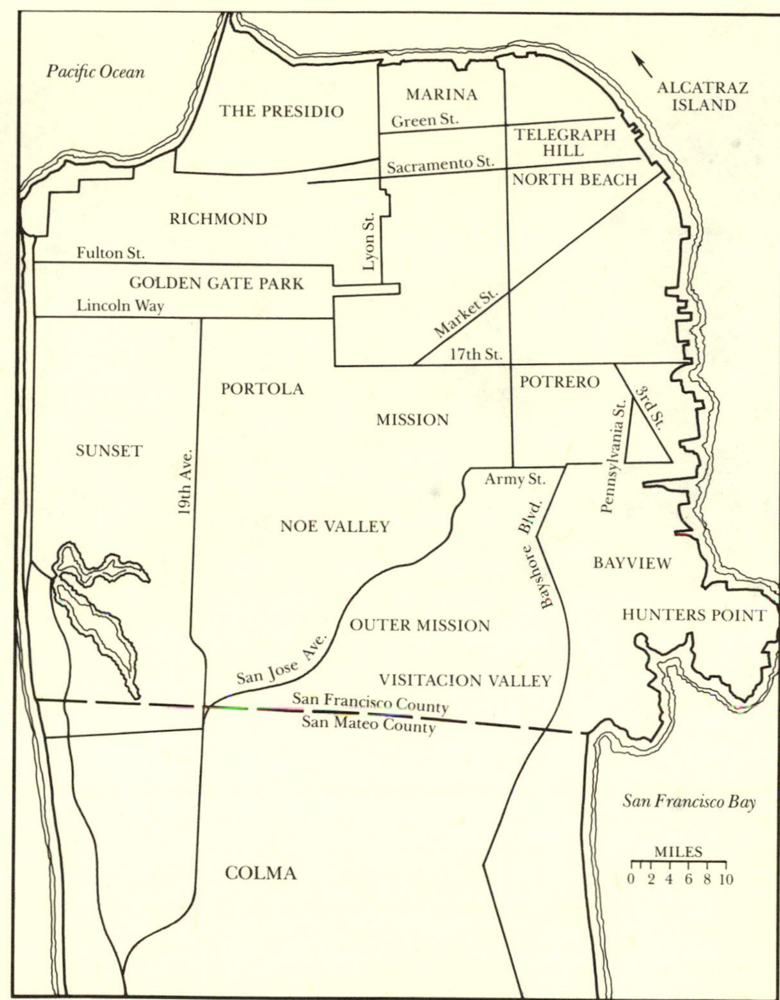

Map 3. Districts of Italian settlement in San Francisco

born-of-native-parents, 32 percent were native-born-of-foreign-parents, and nearly 50 percent were foreign-born. The 6,700 Italians were by far the largest foreign group in the district, making up about 30 percent of the total population and almost 60 percent of the immigrants. There were also 550 French, 450 Germans, almost 400

7. Telegraph Hill (view from Vallejo Street looking west), 1868. The Hill was the first area of Italian settlement. Originally an Irish and German neighborhood, it became increasingly Italian in the 1860's and 1870's. From here the Italians spread to North Beach, between the Hill and the Bay, and to the Mission and Potrero districts.

Irish, smaller groups of Austrians, English, and Norwegians, and 1,300 immigrants of other nationalities. In assembly districts 31, 32, and 33, the Mission district, Italians made up 5 percent of the total population and 15 percent of the total foreign-born. There were about 15,000 foreign-born in assembly district 33: about 20 percent Irish, 25 percent Germans, 18 percent Italians, and the rest from various other national groups.[36]

In 1920, 10,000 Italians lived in assembly district 33, roughly the former 45th district; this was about 40 percent of all Italians in San Francisco. The district also had over 1,000 French, 1,500 Spanish, about 1,200 Mexicans, 900 Germans, and representatives of thirteen other nationalities. Some 25,000 native-born whites—that is, a larger group than the Italians and the other immigrants combined—lived in the same district, and also 7,000 Chinese. In assembly districts 21, 22, and 23—formerly 31, 32, and 33—the Italians made up only 20 percent of the foreign-born population, Irish and Germans being the two largest groups.[37] As these figures indicate, from 1900 to 1920, in all districts where Italians lived, there were also sizable numbers of Americans and immigrants of other nationalities.

Naturalization records of the 1930's, moreover, indicate that, with the exception of the western section of the city, Italians lived in all districts in some measure.* About 10 percent of the city's Italians lived in a rather small settlement in the Richmond district. Another 9 percent formed a little enclave in a few blocks of the Mission district, close to the Italian Church of the Immaculate Conception. About 15 percent lived in the southwestern section of the Outer Mission; and about 9 percent in the southeastern section of the Bayview district. Another 15 percent lived in a rather compact settlement in the Old Potrero district, north of Army Street and west of Pennsylvania Avenue.

The remaining 40 percent lived in North Beach, three-fourths of them in five tracts later classified by the Census Bureau as tracts A1, A3, A4, A5, and A6 (see Map 4). A4 was the core of North Beach, bounded by Columbus, Chestnut, Montgomery, Greenwich, Sansome, Vallejo, Kearny, and Filbert streets. In it lived as many as 10 percent of the total number of Italians in the city, or about 2,700 people living in 32 blocks. Unfortunately, it was impossible to determine how many people, immigrants or American-born, lived in each tract. A3 consisted of 26 blocks bounded by Columbus, Leavenworth, Mason, and Green streets; 7 percent of the Italians, or about 2,000 people, lived there. In A5, 24 blocks lying to the south of A4 up to Columbus and Pacific streets, lived another 5 percent, or 1,600 Italians. A1 stretched from Leavenworth to Pacific along the bay; 4 percent of the city's Italians, or about 1,200, lived there. Another 1,200 lived in A6, a triangle bounded by Columbus, Pacific, and Mason. Together the five tracts made up of about 170 blocks contained slightly over 9,000 Italians, more than one-third of all the city's Italians. And a few hundred more Italians lived along the fringes of these tracts, most of them concentrated in tracts B4, B5, and A8, west of Leavenworth, south of Bay, north of Vallejo, and east of Steiner streets.[38]

Many contemporaries noted the unusual dispersion of the Italians in San Francisco. In 1913 an Italian from San Francisco commented that "unlike most other Italian colonies in the United States,

*The federal census began to use census tracts only in 1940. I have taken the census tracts adopted in 1940 and supplemented them with the data provided by the naturalization records of the 1930's.

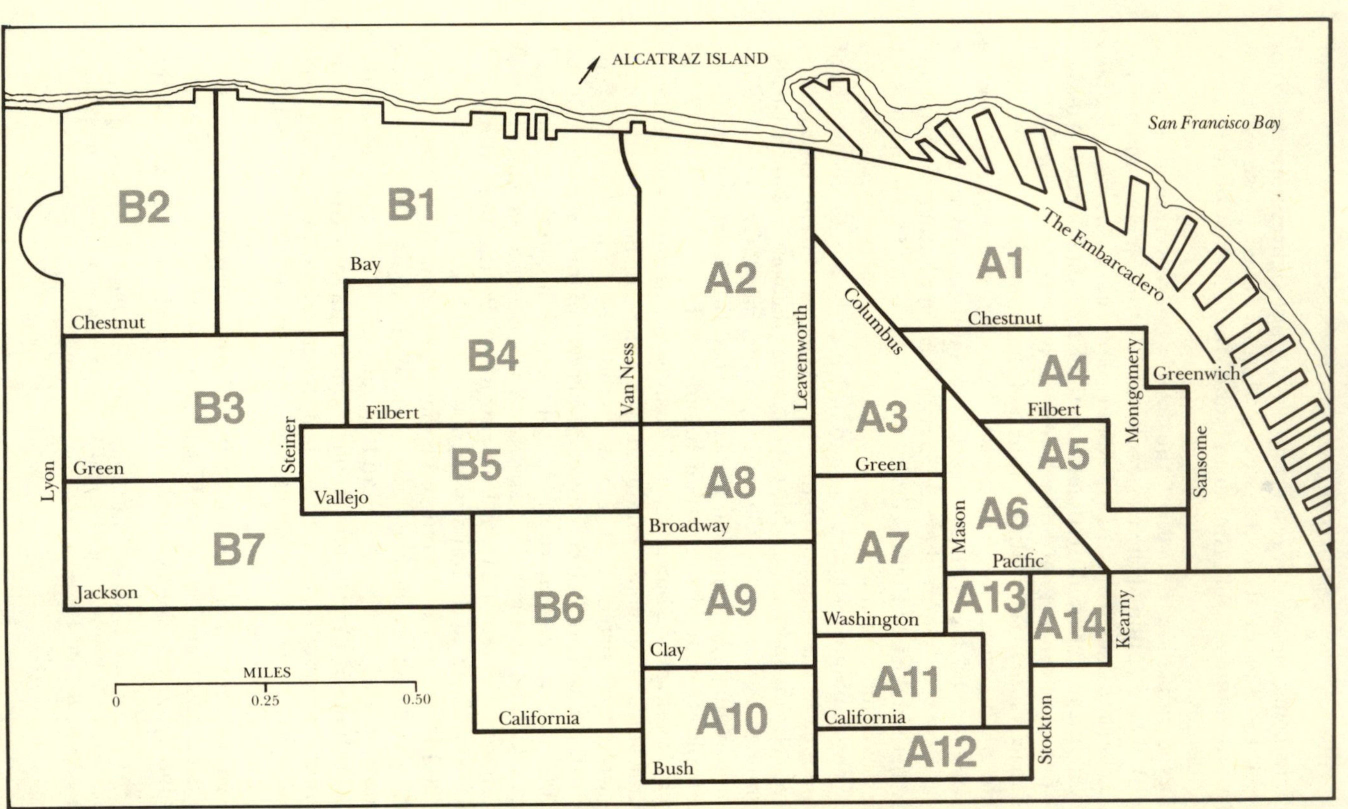

Census tracts of San Francisco discussed in this book

that of San Francisco does not show a high concentration in one area. Even North Beach, which is popularly known as the Latin Quarter, is hardly an Italian enclave."[39] The same year, Consul Daneo reported that the Italians in San Francisco had not created the exclusively Italian settlements found in New York and Chicago.[40] Simon Lubin, the president of the California Commission on Immigration and Housing, told Governor Hiram Johnson that this was a fortunate condition and should be maintained, since more Italians were expected with the opening of the Panama Canal.[41]

The residential pattern of the Italians three to four decades after immigration may usefully be compared with the pattern of other immigrants, especially the Germans and Irish, who in numbers most closely resembled the Italians. The comparison is rather difficult to make; the United States census published residential statistics by ward and nationality only in 1910 and 1920, when many Germans and Irish had already been in San Francisco twenty to forty years. Most Italians were just arriving in those years, and thus were likely to be at the same stage as the Germans and Irish in the 1880's and 1890's. This time lag may be partially corrected by comparing the 1910 and 1920 data for Germans and Irish with the 1950 data for Italians.

In 1910 there were 24,000 Germans and 23,000 Irish in San Francisco. But in no single assembly district was there more than 15 percent of the total Irish population of the city or more than 10 percent of the Germans. We should keep in mind that at the time about 40 percent of all Italians lived in assembly district 35. Compared to the Italians, the Irish and Germans were more evenly distributed throughout the city's districts. Six districts each contained from 8 to 10 percent of the Germans, and four others from 3 to 8 percent, with smaller groups elsewhere. As for the Irish, three districts each contained about 13 percent of the total Irish population, and six other districts from 5 to 7 percent each.[42] The Russians, English, French, and other groups were as spread out as the Germans and Irish. A decade later, in no single assembly district was there more than 10 percent of the total Irish or German population of the city. At that time, 45 percent of the San Francisco Italians lived in district 33. Among San Francisco immigrant groups, only Mexicans and Greeks were as highly concentrated as the Italians.[43]

By 1950 most Italians had been in San Francisco as long as the Germans and Irish had been in 1920. Of the 20,000 Italians living in San Francisco in 1950, almost 5,000, or 25 percent, lived in census tracts A1 to A10 of North Beach, an area considerably smaller than an assembly district of 1920. Another 3,000, 15 percent, lived in the southern section of the Old Potrero district. And finally, about 2,700, over 13 percent, lived in the Mission.[44]

These population distribution data show that in San Francisco, Italians lived in only a few districts, and that this pattern continued over the years. Immigrants of most other nationalities, especially Irish and Germans, were more evenly distributed in almost all of the city's districts. Moreover, to judge from what studies have shown about Italians in New York, Buffalo, Kansas City, Utica, and Omaha, the San Francisco Italians appear to have lived more intermingled with immigrants of other nationalities and with Americans than Italians in other cities.

Several factors explain the difference between Italians and other immigrants in San Francisco. Italians seem to have settled in some areas rather than others because of the availability and cost of housing. Virtually no Italian arrived in San Francisco able to make the down payment on a house. Italian sources, mostly the reports of mayors and prefetti, agree that most emigrants left with only what they needed for the trip, and no cash.[45] As already noted, this was not only because they were poor, but also because they refused to sell their land and house before departing, even if they were owners. Newcomers to San Francisco, after spending the first few weeks with relatives or friends, rented a house or an apartment. But rent was high in San Francisco compared with Italy. The Italian Geographic Society reported in 1887 that it was 400 percent higher, and at the turn of the century it was reported to be 300 percent higher.[46] In 1921 the Italian Welfare Agency noted that newcomers were appalled at the high rents and that their main concern was to find the least expensive apartment.[47] Since most immigrants intended to save money and return to Italy as soon as possible, their goal was naturally to spend as little as possible for rent.

North Beach, the section with the lowest rents in town from the 1860's, was where most Italians headed.[48] Carmelo Santoro, for instance, who arrived in 1912, spent a few weeks with relatives on Green Street and then rented a one-room apartment on the same street. As he put it: "I could save more by renting in North Beach than by renting in the Mission or Potrero districts."[49] As late as 1940 the census found that rents in the North Beach tracts where many Italians lived were among the lowest in town. For instance, the average rent in tract A4 was $31 a month, as against $56 in A11 and $52 in A12, two tracts only a few blocks south of A4.[50]

Rents were low in North Beach because the housing itself was poor. The Telegraph Hill–North Beach area had been developed haphazardly since the 1850's. After the earthquake of 1906 many San Franciscans hoped that the temporary quarters erected after the earthquake would be demolished and new houses built. One wrote: "We will build a new Greece under the skies of California."[51] But new structures were instead built alongside the old. In 1911 Alice Griffith, the secretary of the San Francisco Housing Association, complained that the North Beach housing was so poor as to compare unfavorably with the worst areas of New York and Chicago.[52] There was little new construction in North Beach after 1915; in 1950, of the almost 2,000 dwellings in tract A4, almost 1,600 had been built before 1915.[53] As new immigrants arrived and settled in North Beach, the concentration of Italians there increased.[54] A similar concentration, although on a smaller scale, occurred in the Outer Mission, where housing was poor and rents were traditionally low.

Apparently, almost the only buildings erected in North Beach after 1915 were speculative ventures promoted by Italian developers, most of whom were directors of the newly created Italian-American Bank. Since the demand for apartments was high and space was limited, developers came up with the idea of the Romeo Flats. These were miniature apartments, usually nine per structure, crammed into small lots where city ordinances allowed only two to four apartments. The San Francisco Housing Association denounced what it saw as the exploitation of newly arrived Italians by other Italians. Nothing, however, indicates that the denunciation stopped the developers. When Alice Griffith approached a number of Italians to have them testify in court against developers, she found no support. Most Italians were in San Francisco to save money, and as long as rent was lower in North Beach than elsewhere, immigrants were willing to put up with almost anything.[55] After all, as an old Italian remarked in 1976, "What I got in North Beach was much better than what I had in Italy."[56]

Italian immigrants did not go to North Beach or the Mission solely because of cheap housing. One reason they did not settle in other low-rent districts is suggested by the process of chain migration that brought many Italians to San Francisco. This process sharply limited the number of settlements Italians created in the city. The difference between Italians and other immigrants in the way they reached the city is striking. About 90 percent of the Italians came directly to San Francisco from the same city or village where they were born. This was true of only 30 percent of the

Germans, 20 percent of the Russians, and 40 percent of the Irish. Moreover, 95 percent of the San Francisco Italians came there directly from Italy, and only 5 percent had lived somewhere else in the United States before settling in San Francisco. In contrast, 38 percent of the British, 20 percent of the Irish, 27 percent of the Russians, and 41 percent of the Scandinavians reached San Francisco after living in other parts of the United States or in other countries.[57]

Non-Italians, then, were far more likely than Italians to have migrated, before reaching the United States, either within their own country or in other countries, and to have moved within the United States before reaching San Francisco. Italians, coming directly from their native place to San Francisco, were perhaps more likely than other immigrants to be following relatives or friends, and not arriving on their own. Non-Italians, because of migration prior to coming to San Francisco, may have had less need of the protection of compatriots in America.

That Italians went directly from their birthplace to San Francisco, in a process of chain migration, is an enduring theme in contemporary accounts. In 1868 Consul Cerruti noted that "almost all newcomers have someone who has sent for them and often advanced the money for the ticket." The point was repeated in 1887 in the survey of the Italian Geographic Society.[58] And in 1903 *L'Italia* explained a sudden increase in immigration (which will be discussed later) by many letters that were sent from San Francisco to Italy, "not infrequently with money."[59] When immigrants reached San Francisco they lived with relatives for a time; it was only natural that they settled in the same neighborhood when they took a place of their own.

Part of the explanation why Italians did not disperse throughout the city as quickly as other immigrants is found in the way they came to San Francisco, as well as in their goals in coming. Because Italian immigrants did not intend, at least at first, to stay in America, most of them secured only temporary employment, usually seasonal, through well-established compatriots who mediated between the new arrivals and American society. Under these circumstances, Italians were under no compulsion to move out of their settlements. On the contrary, as an 1887 consular report noted: "Most newcomers settle in North Beach, where some blocks are inhabited almost entirely by Italians. Since most immigrants intend to return, North Beach provides a home-away-from-home during the exigencies of temporary emigration."[60]

Discrimination against Italians undoubtedly had an impact on the creation of segregated neighborhoods.[61] A 1920 University of California master's thesis gives a hint of popular attitudes: "The idea that Italian immigrants came from an inferior race is not merely a matter of popular opinion; but one which has received substantial corroboration from careful investigation."[62] Discrimination against Italian laborers reached its peak between 1900 and 1915. By 1900 the city's unions claimed 40,000 members, an impressive organization, the sympathy of city authorities, and a good press. The unions felt threatened, however, by the arrival of thousands of Italians, whom the Employers' Association could and did use to break strikes and keep down wages. The Italians were denied admission to the unions, and were the victims of a discrimination that some likened to the persecution of the Chinese by the Workingmen's Party in the 1870's.[63] It is likely that by the time most Italians experienced any discrimination in America they had already made their choice of where to live. Thus discrimination probably played a larger role in the evolution of the Italian settlements than in their original formation. That is, immigrants who became aware of discrimination were less likely to move out of the settlement.[64]

Finally, there are some indications that the way Italians regarded American society became a conservative impulse that held the settlements together. Many Italians disparaged the quality of life in American society and urged resistance to assimilation. In 1902, for instance, the issue of Americanization was debated among San Francisco Italians for several months. Surrounding this debate was the larger concern of whether emigration to San Francisco should be discouraged or not. One local newspaper, *L'Italia*, argued against Americanization, the other, *La Voce del Popolo*, argued in favor.[65] *L'Italia* maintained that American values were not suited to the Italian temperament, and that Italians therefore had to preserve their traditions by living with other Italians.[66] Of course, the refusal to mix with American society might have been an expression of resentment owing to a failure to achieve material success. But regardless of origin, such perceptions of America might have played an important role.

In the old country, life had been patterned by tradition and by the belief that the cycle of nature was sacred and untouchable. Change, on the other hand, seemed to be almost sacred in the New World. It was the key to personal advancement. Many immigrants, caught between the old and the new, perhaps sensed in the challenge of the new a kind of immoral seduction, and felt a moral obligation to preserve the old way of life. The close Italian settlements made this task easier. As Consul Francesco Lambertenghi reported: "Only in North Beach do Italians feel completely at home. On Sunday afternoons the Italians who live in other areas of town get together there: it is a way of recreating the security of the Italian village they have left behind."[67]

The best explanation of why the Italian settlement in San Francisco was less concentrated than in other cities lies in the geographical location of the city. San Francisco, surrounded by water on three sides, simply had insufficient space for new immigrant groups. The proximity of different nationalities in San Francisco forced them to compromise with one another more readily than the groups in other cities, who interacted less. Moreover, the predominance of northern Italians that distinguished San Francisco from other cities probably made a difference. Americans loved to point out that northerners were especially adaptable to American society.[68] As Edna Dessery put it: "Northerners are capable of great progress in the social organization of a modern society."[69] Notwithstanding the discredited racial assumptions of her study, northerners were indeed likely to have had more exposure than southerners to the urban industrial world; this would have happened either in the province of Genoa or along the coast between Livorno and Pisa. Finally, internal migration was more common in the north of Italy than in the south, which might in part explain why northerners were more adventurous in moving out of their ethnic enclaves.

The process by which Italians reached San Francisco, the relatively high concentration of Italians in some areas of the city, and the stability of their settlements over a long period of time resulted in a preservation of Old-World customs and a resistance to dispersion that were clearly stronger among Italians than among other immigrants.[70] At the same time, San Francisco Italians were more exposed to the pressures of the host society, and thus subject to a faster pace of change, than Italians of other cities. A San Francisco Italian wrote in 1913: "The dispersion of the Italians throughout the city is the major reason why this is a better colony than any other Italian colony in the United States. Dispersion brought about assimilation, modernization of the less desirable traits Italians brought from the Old World, and a healthy competition between immigrants of different nationalities."[71]

Mini-Settlements Within the Italian Settlement

Thus far we have compared Italian immigrants with other immigrant groups in San Francisco and with other Italians elsewhere.

Certain differences can also be found within the large Italian settlements. One short study on the San Francisco Italians concluded, though with little evidence, that immigrants from the same province or village settled together in certain blocks and districts.[72] Others have shown, more convincingly, that Italian immigrants from the same region clustered together in American cities. A study of Italians in Cleveland, for instance, concluded that "village groups characteristically dispersed among settlements deriving from their districts and regions," and that the only important distinctions among Italian settlements were regional; thus the Sicilians and Abbruzzesi, two regional groups, created two distinct settlements in Cleveland.[73]

My concern here is not whether or not immigrants from different communes intermixed in a common regional settlement, but whether immigrants from communes with different residential patterns recreated in some measure those patterns in San Francisco. This analysis is possible only for the 1930's, 1940's, and 1950's, for which we have naturalization and marriage records for the immigrants and their children. I am concerned with the same nine communes as before, moving from north to south, and with two characteristics: the number of mini-settlements created by each group, and the percentage of the group in each settlement.

Immigrants from the commune of Lorsica established two main settlements: one in the Richmond district, where about 30 percent lived in a few blocks north of Geary, and the other in the two tracts A3 and A4, where another 37 percent lived in the Columbus Avenue area along Greenwich and Filbert streets. Other Lorsicans lived in the Mission district (10 percent), Portola (9 percent), and Potrero (6 percent). This distribution in San Francisco can be explained by the geographical distribution of the population in their native commune of Lorsica. This commune consisted of the town of Lorsica and seven villages. The largest of the eight was Lorsica, and the second largest Verzi. Most immigrants from the commune of Lorsica in tracts A3 and A4—69 percent of them—were from the town of Lorsica. Those in Richmond were mostly from Verzi: 73 percent. The Lorsican immigrants in other districts, like Mission, Portola, and Potrero, were from four of the other six villages. Almost no one migrated to San Francisco from the villages of Costafinale and Barbagelata; most from there went to South America.[74] The conclusions that follow from this are that the immigrants from Lorsica settled in San Francisco according to their village in mini-settlements; but that all people of the same commune did not necessarily migrate to the same destination, as Barbagelata and Costafinale demonstrate.

The immigrants from the commune of Sestri Levante settled in a similar pattern, in two main areas: 38 percent in tract A1 and A3 between Bay Street and the next street south, Francisco, and 40 percent in A5, on the south side of North Beach around Sansome Street between Vallejo and Pacific. In this case too the distribution can be explained by the immigrants' Italian background. Most of those who settled in A1 and A3 were fishermen from Riva Trigoso, a village of Sestri; those in A5 were from the main town, called Sestri Levante.[75]

By contrast, the immigrants from Porcari and Lucca lived in almost every section where Italians settled. Moreover, in no district of San Francisco was there a significantly larger settlement of immigrants from the two towns than in any other district. The immigrants from Porcari and Lucca were generally dispersed among other Italians and people of other nationalities. Of those from Porcari, about 5 percent lived in Richmond, 8 percent in Mission, 10 percent in Bayview, 9 percent in Potrero, 12 percent in the two tracts B4 and B5, located south of the Marina, 9 percent in A4, 6 percent in A5, and smaller percentages in other parts of town. Of the immigrants from Lucca, 7 percent lived in the Richmond district, 10 percent in Mission, 11 percent in Portola, 13 percent in Bayview, 10 percent in Potrero, 11 percent in B4 and B5, where immigrants from Porcari also settled, 10 percent in A4, 7 percent in A5, and the rest in other parts of town.

The immigrants from the three southern communes created settlements that had two main characteristics. First, each group, with the exception of that from Santa Flavia, created one main settlement where over 60 percent of the immigrants lived; second, the immigrants lived close to each other in those settlements in an area of a few blocks. About 60 percent of the immigrants from Verbicaro, for example, lived in the three converging edges of tracts A7, A8, and A9, the area around Leavenworth south of Green and north of Washington. Together, the three tracts encompassed about 60 blocks, but the immigrants from Verbicaro lived mostly in 10 blocks between Vallejo and Jackson east of Leavenworth Street. There were also smaller groups from Verbicaro in the Mission district (6 percent), Richmond (6 percent), Portola (5 percent), Potrero (3 percent), and other areas. Finally, 74 percent of the immigrants from Trabia lived in one settlement between Army and Pennsylvania streets. Few from Trabia settled in North Beach, less than 7 percent; 8 percent lived in Mission, and about 10 percent in Richmond.

Immigrants from Genoa and Palermo tended to gather in more than one large settlement. About 45 percent of those from Palermo settled in the southwestern section of the Potrero district and another 35 percent in North Beach, mostly in tracts A5 and A3; the remaining 20 percent were divided between the Mission and Richmond districts. About 35 percent of the immigrants from Genoa settled in one area in the southwestern section of Potrero, 20 percent in Richmond intermixed with immigrants from Lorsica, 15 percent in Mission, and the other 30 percent in North Beach.*

Thus we find three distinct types of Italian settlement in San Francisco: the multiple-nucleated type (Sestri Levante, Lorsica, and Santa Flavia), consisting of more than one main mini-settlement of high concentration; the dispersed type (Lucca and Porcari); and the single-nucleated type (Verbicaro and Trabia), with one main mini-settlement of high concentration. The differences between these types reflected differences between the Italian communes from which immigrants came.

In Italy the multiple communes of Sestri Levante, Lorsica, and Santa Flavia had two common characteristics. First, they were composite; that is, made up of several villages, some of which were considerably larger than the others. Second, they were nucleated; that is, the people of each village lived within a limited area, with families constantly interacting. For instance, Lorsica, a commune of about 2,000 people, consisted of eight villages in 1871. Three were about equal in size, with 450 people each, and the other five had from 50 to 200. In each village the population inhabited a limited area. Thus in the village of Figarolo there were 427 people in 1871, 403 living in a nucleated settlement and the other 24 dispersed about a fourth of a mile from the village. Monteghirfo, another village, had 129 people in 1871, 122 in a nucleated settlement, the rest dispersed. The 1871 national census showed 96 percent of the population of Lorsica in nucleated settlements. This pattern did not change over the years; in 1921, 91 percent of the population of Lorsica still lived in nucleated settlements.

Santa Flavia closely resembled Lorsica, though this made Santa Flavia an exception in the south. Santa Flavia was made up of four villages: Santa Flavia, Sant'Elia, Porticello, and Solanto. They were about half a mile apart, and about 97 percent of their inhabitants lived in the four nucleated settlements. In San Francisco, immi-

*It is impossible here to pursue the comparison between settlement patterns in Genoa and Palermo and the patterns in San Francisco, since the records do not show where the immigrants came from within the territory of these large cities.

grants from these communes reproduced the two main characteristics of their native communes, establishing more than one closely concentrated settlement.[76]

Most families in Lucca and Porcari lived in houses built in the middle of the property they farmed; thus their houses were ordinarily removed from other houses. The major centers of population in these areas were formed by a comparatively small number of families. Capannori, for instance, was in 1871 an incorporated commune of about 43,000 people living in 39 villages, of which Porcari was one. But only 2,500 of those 43,000 people—under 6 percent—lived in nucleated settlements, the rest on separate farms. Over the years the pattern changed little; by 1921 those in Capannori living in nucleated settlements were still only 7 percent of the total population. Though Lucca, as the capital of the province, naturally had a large part of the commune's people living in the old medieval walled city, about 50 percent of the commune's population lived in 79 small dispersed villages. In San Francisco the immigrants from Capannori and Lucca did not form one or more distinct mini-settlements as the other Italian immigrants did, and even in the districts where these two groups settled they showed a strong tendency to be dispersed.[77]

Finally, Verbicaro and Trabia had the typical settlement pattern of the south. They had only one highly concentrated settlement, and families dispersed in the countryside were an exception. In 1871 the commune of Verbicaro had about 5,000 people, 99 percent of them living in a small and dense settlement on top of a 2,000-foot mountain. Only nineteen families lived in the countryside. This concentration apparently increased over the years. The 1921 census reported that 100 percent of the population of Verbicaro lived in the central district, the few rural families having disappeared. Trabia was almost the same as Verbicaro: 99 percent of the people lived in a densely settled central district. The percentage did not change over the five decades 1871–1921.[78] In San Francisco the immigrants from these areas were similarly concentrated in one main mini-settlement, and only a few lived apart from it.

Thus in San Francisco the larger subgroups of immigrants created their own settlements within the general Italian settlement. Though I have not tried to document how each mini-settlement came about, the evidence on chain immigration suggests a plausible pattern. When immigrants from a certain commune settled in San Francisco, they sent for relatives and friends, and these were likely to settle close to those who had sent for them. The immigrants from the same commune, then, were likely to form settlements in San Francisco that reflected what they had known in Italy.

Elements of Change

Though the Italian settlements and mini-settlements in San Francisco were on the whole stable, the lives of individuals living in them were considerably less so. Almost all immigrants, for instance, at some time had to move from one dwelling to another. For them this was a new element in their lives.

The movement of the immigrants within San Francisco can be gathered from immigration and naturalization records and the files of the Italian Welfare Agency, as well as from the recollections of older Italians. A comparison between the records of petitions for naturalization and the actual records of naturalization reveals that 40 percent of the Italians lived at a different address at the time of naturalization than at the time of petition; this time span varied from one to nine years. In most cases they moved within the same settlement. There were group differences, however. Some 55 percent of the immigrants from Verbicaro and Trabia changed address between the two dates, only 25 percent of those from Lucca and Porcari, and 35 percent of those from Sestri Levante, Lorsica, and Trabia. Seemingly, geographical dispersion such as we have seen decreased individual movement, and geographical closeness increased it. The files of the Italian Welfare Agency help us follow the movement of several hundred families over two or three decades, since every year the agency updated the addresses of the families it assisted. Of about 300 files consulted, only 29, about 10 percent, reveal a family that never moved. The average family, in this sample, moved once every three years; and some families moved every year.[79]

The reasons for moving were usually economic, and only rarely social. Most families moved either because they were unable to pay the rent and had to look for a less expensive apartment, or because as new children were born they needed more space. Arturo Camilli, for instance, was paying $27 a month in 1931 for a two-bedroom apartment in North Beach. When his wages were cut from $2.50 to $2.20 a day in 1932, he could no longer afford that apartment, and asked a social worker from the agency to help him find a new apartment for himself, his wife, and their five children.[80]

Sometimes, although rarely, social problems forced people to move. The files of the Welfare Agency provide a few examples.

After Carmelo Sanfilippo's oldest boy was arrested on Market Street while stealing mail from a mailbox, the Federal Bureau of Investigation began looking into the family, since the boy had been arrested once before. The family was abused and snubbed by neighbors, and children wrote offensive words on the door of the Sanfilippo apartment. A social worker then stepped in and persuaded Carmelo to move the family to the Potrero district to avoid further trouble.[81] Friction between northern and southern families occasionally forced families to move from one neighborhood to another. When Rosario Cugnidoro, from Cinisi, province of Palermo, moved in 1927 from North Beach to the 2900 block of Green Street, where many Genoese had settled, he felt so unwelcome that at the end of 1929 a social worker advised him to move back to Potrero, where there were many Sicilians.[82] Franco Miraglia, an immigrant from Palermo, complained of discrimination when he moved to 1200 Bay Street, a block, he told the social worker, that was "as Genoese as Genoa itself."[83]

Italians moved for other reasons as well. Families sometimes moved to a less expensive place in order to save money to make a down payment on a house. People ordinarily moved from North Beach to the Mission district when they bought a house. When I asked 25 people about their experience with moving, three answered that they had moved to a less expensive place once, two to set aside money to buy a house and one to pay for the medical expenses of his aging father in Italy. Ten said they had moved to a better place or to a larger one when the place where they lived became insufficient for their growing family. The others could not remember the reason. All those who ultimately bought a house, 15 out of 25, remembered both the date and the circumstances surrounding the move: for most it had happened in the late 1920's or mid-1930's and meant leaving North Beach or Old Potrero to go to the Outer Mission, where there were houses for sale.[84]

Moving was a new experience for most immigrants. In Italy most people spent all their adult lives in the same house, and some their entire lives. "Young men," the prefetto of Genoa noted, "do not necessarily move out of their father's house when they marry. Some do; and this is likely to be the only move in their lifetime, unless they are laborers and are forced to move again when they cannot afford the rent."[85] In Lucca it was not uncommon for young adults, especially in large families of sharecroppers, to remain with the parents after marriage. There were families that had lived in the same house for over a century.[86] In the south people moved more often.

Young adults did not stay with their parents after marriage, and landless laborers were sometimes forced to leave their rented dwellings to look for cheaper housing during depressions. Indeed, some peasants ended up living in caves, especially around the city of Cosenza.[87] In San Francisco immigrants from the south showed a greater tendency to move than those from the province of Genoa, and those from Lucca and Porcari moved the least.

Additional evidence available in Lucca, Porcari, Sestri Levante, and Genoa enables us to compare the geographical distribution and mobility of some San Francisco Italians with the geographical distribution and mobility of the same immigrants before they left their native communes. The records of Porcari are probably the most interesting. An examination of 85 of the families of individuals who eventually arrived in San Francisco revealed that 62 emigrants—that is, 73 percent—left from the house in which their family had been living since the late eighteenth or early nineteenth century.[88] In Lucca a slightly different pattern emerged. In 48 records on the families of emigrants to San Francisco, only 31 percent of the emigrants appear to have left from a house where the same family had lived since the early nineteenth century.[89] All the emigrants from Lucca, however, left from the house where they had been born.

In Sestri Levante and Lorsica it was difficult and sometimes impossible to find the records of the parents or grandparents of people who went to San Francisco. The reason is that in Lorsica and Sestri Levante a new record was created every time a person established a new family, whereas in Lucca and Porcari the same record was updated for several generations. But since most immigrants from Lorsica and Sestri Levante were single at the time of departure, it was possible to locate the records of their parents. Out of 62 records from Sestri Levante that I found, only seven emigrants had moved from the house where they were born.[90] A similar check of 45 families in Lorsica showed that only two emigrants, that is, less than 5 percent, had moved between the time of birth and emigration.[91] Unfortunately, no family records were available for the south.

It is often argued that geographical mobility is the hallmark of people living in modern, technological societies. Italians very early encountered this feature of American life. Of course, they moved within Italian settlements, but it was moving nonetheless. From the first days they learned that in the New World one's life is seldom spent in only one house.

In general, Italians in San Francisco lived near their work. For instance, by the late 1930's about 45 percent of the Italians engaged in farming lived in the southern section of Portola, another 35 percent in the southern section of Bayview, and 10 percent in Potrero. These areas were near the farms where the immigrants worked. Only 5 percent of the Italians who worked on farms lived in North Beach. Of the Italian fishermen, however, almost all lived near the bay: 72 percent lived in North Beach, in tracts A1, A3, and A4, and the rest in Hunters Point.

Immigrants with other work were not as concentrated in certain areas as farmers and fishermen, but some patterns can be discerned. About 45 percent of the immigrants engaged in manufacturing and mechanical work lived in Potrero and Portola, the industrial areas of the city. Those in trade and transportation were to be found in Portola (25 percent) and in tracts A3, A4, A5, and A6 of North Beach (32 percent). Immigrants engaged in domestic and personal services, almost half of the Italian working population in town, were to be found in all sections where Italians settled. They made up 48 percent of all Italians living in Richmond, 54 percent in the Mission, 35 percent in Bayview, 41 percent in Portola, 44 percent in Potrero, 55 percent in A5, and 47 percent in A1.[92] The Italian settlements in San Francisco were complex. They reflected the geographical distribution of the communities from which immigrants had come, and this maintained continuity with the past. Yet at the same time, the settlements responded to the demands of the new economic environment.

An important aspect of individual mobility within the basically stable immigrant settlement is seen from a comparison between immigrants who arrived earlier and those who arrived later. In our sample, a greater proportion of immigrants who arrived before the First World War lived outside North Beach by the 1930's than of the immigrants who arrived after the war. Of those who arrived before the war, 65 percent lived outside of North Beach by the 1930's, at the same time that almost 80 percent of those who arrived after the war still lived in North Beach. This difference shows once again that North Beach was where most immigrants went when they first arrived; moving to other areas was a subsequent step.

Those who moved out of North Beach commonly did so when they purchased a house in the Mission, Portola, or Richmond districts. An examination of a few blocks of census tracts A4 in North Beach and a heavily Italian neighborhood in the Mission reveals that by 1950 only 20 percent of the residents of A4 were homeowners, as against 70 percent in the Mission.[93] The immigrants who arrived before the First World War could save money for a down payment sooner than those who arrived in the postwar years. But little real estate was for sale in North Beach, where by the early 1910's a few Italian landlords controlled most of the available property.[94] Those who wanted to buy a house thus had to move to another district.

The movement of individuals and families within San Francisco, for the various reasons outlined, was unlike the pattern of mobility that had evolved in Italy. The Italians in San Francisco had to respond to new situations and, in different ways, learn the art of adapting in the New World.

The Children of the Immigrants

The settlements were the creation of immigrants; their children grew up there, but eventually left. The children began leaving in large numbers in the mid-1930's, when they came of age, and the movement lasted for about three decades. By the mid-1960's the still considerable number of Italians in North Beach were mostly old people. The younger generation had moved across San Francisco Bay to Oakland and Berkeley, or south along the peninsula, or north to Marin County. Others left northern California, following economic opportunities in the Los Angeles area or elsewhere in the United States.[95] The departure of the children obviously constituted a major change, but perhaps not as great as it looked.

Though the departure of Italians from the city became a mass movement by the mid-1930's, the pressure had been building for some time. Many of the immigrants' children grew up restless and rebellious, anxious to break out of the constricting world of their parents. In the records of the Italian Welfare Agency, the friction between immigrants and their children is probably the most discussed topic besides poverty. Social workers reported complaints of both parents and children. Parents almost invariably made the same points to judges, school principals, and social workers when their children got in trouble. The child had been properly raised, they said, and trouble started only when the child began to wander downtown or to associate with children of immigrants from other regions of Italy. Northern Italian parents, in particular, seem to have been unhappy about their children's associating with southern Italians.[96]

The growing children found the places where they were unknown more alluring than the close Italian settlements. To social workers and judges, juvenile offenders almost invariably said that life was boring in North Beach but exciting downtown. Sam Capelli, a young man arrested twice by the age of seventeen, told a social

8. Children at play, Telegraph Hill, 1889. In San Francisco, most of the Italian immigrants' children grew up in the Italian settlements of North Beach, Mission, and Potrero. But as adults they usually found the settlements too confining and moved to other sections of the city or spread throughout the Bay Area.

worker: "There is nothing more boring than a Sunday afternoon at North Beach. Life at home is even more boring. My father and uncle get together over the weekend and the topic of conversation is always life in the Old World. For me life begins outside North Beach."[97] Giacomo Covelli told the social worker who asked him why he had missed classes almost every other day for three months: "I do it because it is considered smart to do it. If you go to school every day you are considered a sissy. Besides, it is the only time when I can go downtown. I know that my parents would not let me go otherwise."[98]

The testimony in the records of the welfare agency, though important, must not be hastily extended to the entire Italian community, since it concerns only families with problems serious enough to need outside help. Confrontations between immigrants and their children, moreover, have to be seen as part of a broad intergenerational conflict that was not limited to Italians. It is important to notice, nevertheless, that this intergenerational conflict had to do with safe and unsafe places and with boring and exciting sections of San Francisco. The children were growing up with ideas of where they wanted to explore and where they felt safe that unsettled their parents.

The children were different from their parents; they had grown up in a different environment. Naturalization records of immigrants and marriage records of their children yield a profile of the children's lives. About 75 percent of the children of Italian immigrants were born in San Francisco, 15 percent in Italy, 6 percent elsewhere in California, and the rest in other states. The children of other immigrants were quite different: only 40 percent were born in San Francisco, another 8 percent in California, 10 percent in other states, and fully 42 percent in Europe.[99] This is consistent with what we have already seen, that non-Italian immigrants came to San Francisco less directly than Italians, and it also implies that Italian children were less likely to have known other countries than the children of other immigrants.

There were also differences among Italians. With the exception of the immigrants from Sestri Levante, all northern immigrant groups showed a higher percentage of children born in Italy than those from the south: 15 percent for Lorsica, 12 percent for Porcari, 20 percent for Lucca, and 13 percent for Genoa. These were children who either arrived with their parents or joined their father later, usually with their mother. Another difference was that 15 percent of the immigrants from Porcari and 12 percent of those from Lucca were born not in San Francisco, but in other parts of California. As Pietro Terzini told me, these were the children of families who went into farming in the San Joaquin Valley before moving to San Francisco.[100]

Almost all the children of the Italians grew up with their parents. The exceptions were a handful of children whose concerned parents sent them to live with their grandparents in Italy, especially if the grandparents owned land, when the depression came in 1929. Angelo De Martini, for instance, sent two of his three children back to Lorsica in 1932; they lived with their grandparents for three years.[101] Southerners were less likely to send their children to Italy during the depression. Southern parents gave many reasons for not sending their children back: the health of the grandparents, the age of the child, the cost of the trip. But social workers reported another important reason, that immigrants did not want people back in Italy to think they had been unsuccessful in America. Carmelo Rosario, for instance, when his wife was hospitalized with a nervous breakdown, rejected the suggestion that he send his four children to Cinisi. "Carmelo is a proud man," a social worker noted, "and will never allow his parents to know that he needs them."[102]

At the time most children of Italians married, they were still living in San Francisco with their parents. About 80 percent of the children were in that category; the rest had already moved out of their parents' house, and were living either in San Francisco or in other parts of northern California. Italian and Irish children seem to have been the least mobile among the large immigrant groups of the city. About 85 percent of the Irish children were living in San Francisco with their parents when they married, and the other 15 percent were still in the San Francisco Bay Area. The children of Russians and Germans were more mobile; about 40 percent of them had left the city by the time they married. Finally, only 30 percent of the children of British and Scandinavian immigrants were still in San Francisco when they married. As these figures indicate, the mobility of the children was remarkably similar to the mobility of their parents.[103]

Within the general Italian population, the children from the nine immigrant groups fall into two patterns. The highest degree of mobility was found among the children of immigrants from Lucca and Porcari: 15 percent of them had already moved out of the city when they married, and another 12 percent had reached southern California. The dispersion in the city of the Italian immigrants from Lucca and Porcari probably made it easier for their children to disperse. A considerable degree of mobility also existed among the Italo-Americans from the northern communities of Lorsica, Sestri Levante, and Genoa and the southern communities of Santa Flavia and Palermo. But almost all the children of the immigrants from Verbicaro and Trabia were still in San Francisco at the time of marriage.[104] Here too it is possible to draw a parallel between the types of enclaves the parents had established and the mobility of their children. The immigrants from Verbicaro and Trabia had established the most nucleated settlements, and their children showed the lowest degree of mobility. The immigrants from the other communities of the north and from Santa Flavia and Palermo created more than one settlement and were not as concentrated as those from Verbicaro and Trabia; and the children of the immigrants from those five communities dispersed much more readily. In sum, there is a direct correlation between the concentration or dispersion of the immigrants and the geographical mobility of their children.

One of the most intriguing changes in connection with children leaving their parents' home was that occurring between the immigrant and Italo-American generations from Lucca and Porcari. In Italy a good number of young men from Lucca and Porcari stayed in their parents' home even after marriage, albeit with some resentment of parental authority.[105] In San Francisco, on the other hand, many young men from these two groups moved away from their parents even before marriage.

The immigrants' background in Tuscany is perhaps important in understanding this break in tradition. Parental authority was strong in the province of Lucca, as many observed.[106] Often the deference children in this province showed their parents was related to the tradition of living with one's parents after marriage. Emigration, however, brought young people—married or single—financial independence and greater personal freedom. It is likely that the authority of the Italian parents in Italy was so strong that their children, the immigrants, did not dare to challenge it. Indeed, a large number of immigrants from these two communes returned to Italy for their marriage. The rebellion seems to have broken out in the following generation. San Francisco was a safe place to dispose of the deference that had conditioned the lives of the immigrants from Lucca and Porcari.

The immigrants tried to control the lives of their American-born children in the same way their parents in Italy had controlled their lives. But what worked with the immigrants, who by and large had well-established family attitudes by the time they arrived in San Francisco, did not work with the Italo-American generation. The authoritarianism of the immigrant parents simply did not make sense to children born in the United States. It belonged to another world.

Though marriage records confirm that most immigrants' children lived with their parents up to the time of their marriage, three years later many had not only moved out of the house, but had moved out of the city. It is assumed here that if the name of a male child who married in a given year was not in the San Francisco city directory three years later, that child had moved out of the city. A search in this way for all the names of children who married between 1938 and 1961 indicates that about 40 percent of the Italo-Americans moved out of the city within three years after marriage. Moreover, the group patterns already seen in the marriage records remain the same. The proportion of children of immigrants from Lucca and Porcari leaving the city was the highest, about 60 percent; that from Verbicaro and Trabia the lowest, 25 percent; and that from the other five groups somewhere in between, 40 percent. Both marriage records and city directories indicate that children from multiple settlements were more likely to move than those from nucleated settlements.[107]

The movement of Italo-American children out of San Francisco was of course shaped by many social forces. The year the children of the immigrants married was important. Those who married in the 1940's were less likely to be out of the city within three years than those who married in the 1950's—only 25 percent in the 1940's compared with almost 50 percent in the 1950's. Obviously the Italo-Americans were subject to many of the same impulses in the 1950's that produced a broad movement out of American cities. Many of the Italo-Americans who married in the 1950's, for instance, were financially better equipped to leave the city for the suburbs than those who had married in the previous decade.

Many who wanted to leave in the 1940's, besides, encountered a stronger opposition from their parents than those in the 1950's. In the 1970's, when I interviewed older Italians in San Francisco, they often expressed pride in the economic success of their children, who were then living outside the city. But some of these old Italians admitted that they had opposed their children's leaving. For instance, in 1952 Angelo Lucchetti disapproved of the plans of his two children Mario and Aldo, both recently married, to leave him alone in his Columbus Avenue grocery store and move to Oakland to open a liquor store.[108] The children confirmed that their parents had opposed their leaving the city; and those who had married in the 1940's generally recalled a stronger opposition. Arturo Vivante, for instance, said he could not count on financial help from his father, who was in a relatively good financial situation, when he moved to San Jose in 1948. Arturo's brother Vincent, however, met only mild resistance when he left San Francisco in 1955.[109]

The older children were generally far less likely to leave within three years than the younger ones. Only 20 percent of the firstborn left the city within the three years, as against 45 percent of the others. Again we can speculate on several possible explanations.

First, Italian parents traditionally counted on the support of the firstborn child in their senior years, and accordingly opposed the departure of the first child. Second, firstborn children were likely to marry before younger ones, and we have already seen that those who married in the 1940's were less likely to leave than those who married later. And third, younger children married at a time when their parents were likely to be more prosperous, and therefore better able to help them relocate out of San Francisco.

Another apparent influence was the occupation of the children's parents. There was a correlation in this area for non-Italians and Italians alike. Among non-Italians, those most likely to move were children of immigrants in the professions; next most likely came the children of immigrants in domestic and personal services; and finally came the children of immigrants in trade or transportation. For the nine Italian immigrant groups the picture is more complex, but some general patterns emerge. First, only 5 percent of the immigrants engaged in farming moved out of the city within the three years. Second, the children of fishermen are somewhat puzzling: only 8 percent of those from Sestri Levante, yet about 40 percent of those from Santa Flavia, moved. In the case of the Santa Flavia group, the children moved with their parents to Monterey, Martinez, or some smaller fishing town on the California coast. Third, only 16 percent of the children whose fathers were in trade or transportation moved within three years. A possible explanation for this—to be considered in the next chapter, on occupational patterns—is that the children followed their parents' line of work, and therefore found more opportunities in a large city like San Francisco than anywhere else in northern California. Fourth, those most likely to move out of the city were the children of immigrants in domestic and personal services, the lowest on the occupational scale. This group was perhaps least likely to be detained in the city by their parents' work. And fifth, the children of immigrants engaged in manufacturing were less likely to move than the previous group; 28 percent did so in the three years.

Finally, geographical mobility can be viewed in the light of the occupations of the children themselves. For the children of non-Italians the pattern is fairly clear. About 50 percent of the children who had a profession by the time they married and 40 percent of those in skilled crafts left the city within the first three years. Only 10 percent of those in trade and transportation and 25 percent of those in domestic and personal services did so. For the Italo-Americans the following pattern emerges. About 60 percent of those in skilled crafts left and 25 percent of those in trade and transportation; those in domestic and personal services were less likely to move. So few Italo-Americans were in the professions that no firm pattern can be established. In general, however, professional people seem to have been the most likely to move, and the children engaged in trade seem to have been the most likely to stay.

To summarize, proportionately more immigrants of other nationalities left San Francisco than Italians. Among the children of non-Italians, the most likely to move were those whose parents had not come to San Francisco directly from their native countries and those who had been born in places other than San Francisco. The differences among the Italo-Americans of the nine groups can be at least partially explained by the differences in their parents' lives. The children whose parents came from communes that established multiple settlements were more likely than the children of parents who lived in nucleated settlements, which seem to have acted as a negative force against geographical dispersion. The movement out of the Italian settlements did not occur suddenly; it started slowly in the 1930's and accelerated in the 1950's. Finally, children whose parents had skilled occupations and those children who themselves had skilled occupations by the time they married were more likely to leave San Francisco than the children of other immigrants.

The departure of the immigrants' children from the old settlements was the product of forces at work since the time immigrants arrived and established families. When the children left, they did not settle at random among other Americans. On the contrary, they built miniature pockets of Italo-Americans throughout the San Francisco Bay Area. For example, when Philip Cappello left San Francisco in 1947 to settle in San Bruno, a few miles to the south, he was the only Italian in the southwestern part of that town. By 1965 there were 25 Italo-American families within a few blocks of him.[110] Cappello started a process of chain migration in many ways resembling the one that had brought his parents and thousands of others from the old country.

Over the years, the children who moved to the suburbs developed a nostalgic feeling for the world of their fathers, occasionally returning to San Francisco to join in traditional family events like baptisms, weddings, funerals, and feasts of Italian patron saints. Italo-Americans typically attend mass on Sunday at their local church; but for baptisms, weddings, and funerals many return to San Francisco. As Ansano Camilli said: "We go back because our fathers were married there and we too were married there. We think that our children should be baptized there too."[111] Many Italo-Americans from the same town or region get together at least once a year, usually on the feast of the patron saint, for a dinner. Such an event provides the opportunity to keep alive a closeness that geographical separation threatens. Thus moving away from San Francisco has not caused the old settlement to disappear. The closeness survives, although in new forms.

The patterns of geographical mobility among the Italians are more complex than they first seemed. On the one hand, there was a great deal of mobility by individual immigrants. On the other hand, the departure of the children constituted neither a total immersion in American society nor a total break from the world of the immigrants. Indeed, the decline of the Italian settlement was more apparent than real. By the time it occurred, geographical proximity was no longer an indispensable requirement for group solidarity. This point is ordinarily overlooked in studies that correlate group cohesiveness with geographical proximity. In fact, by the 1950's it was within the ability of virtually everybody in the United States to move frequently from place to place. The old settlements, as a result, were transformed, not disposed of.

The most interesting and ironic sign of continuity between the generations is the similarity in the reactions of the Italian parents when their children decided to go to San Francisco and of the immigrants when their children left San Francisco. Carmelo Lo Muto described in 1976 how his parents had opposed his leaving Sicily in 1919 on the ground that there was enough work for eager young people in Sicily. Besides, they argued, he had to stay and help his aging parents. Sam Lo Muto, Carmelo's son, who was present at the interview, then stated that his father Carmelo had given him the same reasons and shown the same opposition when he wanted to leave North Beach for Oakland in 1951: there was enough work in San Francisco for any young man, and besides, he was the only son and should stay and take care of his aging parents. But parental opposition did not stop either Carmelo or Sam from leaving. And both parents benefited from their children's determination. Carmelo supported his father in Italy until his father died in 1931, and today Carmelo lives with his son in Oakland.

CHAPTER 6

From the Farm to the City

IN EARLY times San Francisco was depicted as a place where Italian immigrants could do the same work their fathers had done in Italy. Promotional literature claimed that Italians could profitably use their skills as farmers and fishermen in California, and several observers of the San Francisco Italian colony repeated the claim.[1] The 1887 survey by the Italian Geographic Society, for instance, found a large number of San Francisco Italians in farming and fishing.[2] Two decades later the Italian colony was described as "a successful group of farmers and fishermen."[3] A 1913 booklet by a San Francisco Italian and various writings by Americans seem concerned with little besides the success of San Francisco Italians in farming and fishing.[4]

Such evidence can be misleading. It is true that in the late nineteenth century a considerable number of San Francisco Italians were farmers, living in the Mission district and farming the land near the southern boundary of the city. And it is equally true that the Italians played a large role in the development of San Francisco's fishing industry. But farming and fishing provided jobs only for a small part of the group.[5] Most Italians who settled in San Francisco, and in other large American cities as well, had to switch from the farming and fishing they had done in Italy to other occupations.*

*In the United States only a few thousand Italians established farming colonies, like those of Dickinson and Bryan, Texas; Vineland and Hammonton, New Jersey; Independence, Louisiana; Daphne and Lambert, Alabama; and Tontitown, Arkansas. In South America, on the other hand, most Italians were farmers. See Foerster, *Italian Immigration of Our Times*, pp. 342–43; L. Villari, *Gli Stati Uniti*, pp. 255–63; Pecorini, "Italians," pp. 159–64; and *Bollettino dell'Emigrazione*, 18 (1908): 35–44.

In this chapter, in order to see those changes, I examine the occupational differences between Italian men and other male immigrants, and between the sons of Italians and those of other immigrants. I also explore similarities and differences among the nine groups of Italian immigrants that are the focus of this study, and among the three generations—Italian, immigrant, and Italo-American.

A caveat is in order. The occupational data I have used do not refer to the same stage in the working life of each of the three generations. For the immigrants' fathers, the data come from the birth records in Italy of the future immigrants; the parents in these records were typically 25 to 45 years old. For the immigrants, the data are derived from records of petition for naturalization, actual naturalization, and marriage, and from the city directories of San Francisco; this made it possible to see different stages of the working lives of the immigrants. For the immigrants' children, I used marriage records and city directories. Since the most complete data on the immigrants comes from the naturalization records, those have been used more than others. Thus the occupational distribution of the immigrants that I give is generally for an advanced stage of their working lives, and that of their children for the beginning, at the time of marriage.

In categorizing the occupations of the Italians, I did not use the common criteria of white- and blue-collar, unskilled, semiskilled, and skilled, since most by far were unskilled laborers. Instead, I adopted five main categories from the U.S. census of 1900 and added a sixth. These are:

1. Agriculture and food processing—including farmers, laborers, dairymen, gardeners, florists, lumbermen, and stock raisers
2. Professions—white-collar jobs involving long training or special talent
3. Domestic and personal services—unskilled workers, including janitors, laborers, servants, bootblacks, bartenders, waiters, and street workers
4. Trade and transportation—people involved in the sale of commodities, like wholesale and retail merchants, accountants, peddlers, packers, and shippers
5. Manufacturing and mechanical work—embracing all skilled workers involved in processing, like bakers, masons, blacksmiths, shoemakers, iron workers, and tailors
6. Fishing and fish processing

Though according to the census fishing and fish processing fell into

TABLE 5

Occupational Distribution of Italian Immigrants, Their Parents, and Other Immigrants

Occupation	Italians	Parents	Non-Italians	Greeks	German Jews	German non-Jews	Irish	Russians	British
Agriculture and food processing	4%	65%	2%	—	—	—	1%	2%	—
Professions	1	1	10	—	30%	18%	5	9	15%
Domestic and personal services	43	4	30	70%	12	15	44	27	24
Trade and transportation	25	5	15	20	13	22	24	21	21
Manufacturing and mechanical	22	10	42	10	45	45	25	40	40
Fishing and fish processing	6	15	1	—	—	—	—	—	—

SOURCE: For parents, birth records in Italian archives; for immigrants, records of petition for naturalization, naturalization records, and San Francisco city directories.

NOTE: Percentages in this table and others that follow do not always add up to 100 because of rounding.

the fifth category, I have made them into a sixth, since workers in these areas were a distinct group among San Francisco Italians.*

Italians and Other Immigrants

As Table 5 shows, less than one out of every ten Italian immigrants was engaged in either farming or fishing. Over 40 percent were in domestic and personal services and almost 50 percent were in either trade or manufacturing. Less than 1 percent were in professions. Among the immigrants' parents almost 65 percent were in farming, as landowners, sharecroppers, renters, laborers, or otherwise. Of the rest, 15 percent were in fishing and 10 percent were in manufacturing and mechanical work. This comparison shows sharp differences between the occupational patterns of the Italian and immigrant generations.

Immigrants from other nations generally had better jobs than Italians. The reader should keep in mind that the Italians were the last major group to arrive in San Francisco, which may have put them at a disadvantage in the competition for jobs. As the table indicates, non-Italian immigrants were even less likely to be farmers or fishermen in San Francisco. The contrast between Italians and other groups was the greatest in the professions and the manufacturing and mechanical jobs, that is, in white-collar and skilled occupations; about 50 percent or more of the non-Italian immigrants, except Greeks and Irish, worked in those areas. It would be useful to have some figures on the occupational distribution of the fathers of non-Italian immigrants; possibly the different occupations of Italian and non-Italian immigrants can be explained as a carry-over from their parents' work. The data at hand for non-Italian groups, however, only concern the immigrant generation. These data show, for instance, that 70 percent of the Greek immigrants had unskilled jobs, a much higher rate than for Italians. The Irish pattern of occupations was quite close to the Italian, the only difference being a noticeable representation of Irish in professions. The German Jews were the most successful group, with more than 75 percent in skilled occupations or professions, followed by the non-Jewish Germans, the British, and the Russians.[6]

*The people in domestic and personal services are unskilled workers, those in manufacturing and mechanical occupations are skilled workers, and those in trade and transportation can be either skilled workers, like merchants, or unskilled workers, like packers and shippers. The 1900 census uses the terms professions and professional people with a broader meaning than those terms have today.

Another difference between Italians and other immigrants was that Italians were less likely to change their occupation than other immigrants. Between petition for naturalization and naturalization—which varied from one to nine years—less than 6 percent of the Italians moved from one category to another. A breakdown by occupation reveals significant differences. Farmers and fishermen had the highest degree of occupational stability: 98 percent were in the same job at petition as at naturalization. Only 6 percent of the Italians in domestic services were in other occupations: 4 percent went into trade, 2 percent into manufacturing. Similarly, 6 percent moved out of trade and transportation: 3 percent into domestic and personal services and the other 3 percent into manufacturing. Of the 7 percent who moved out of manufacturing, most changed to domestic and personal services.

Among the other immigrant groups, by contrast, about 20 percent changed occupational category between petition and naturalization. The movement was most noticeable among immigrants in domestic and personal services: 24 percent of them moved to either manufacturing (17 percent), trade (6 percent), or agriculture (1 percent). But there was also another movement, apparently into less desirable jobs; of the 12 percent who left trade, half went into domestic services, and only a quarter into manufacturing; of the 13 percent who moved out of manufacturing, 7 percent went into domestic services.[7] An important factor in these differences in mobility between Italians and other immigrants may have been control over the San Francisco labor market by local labor unions, which openly discriminated against Italians in the 1900's and 1910's.[8] Italians may also have been less likely to seek new jobs because, as the 1930 survey on Italians in San Francisco suggested, they were generally more conservative than the other groups.[9]

The Influence of the Old World

Though most Italian immigrants entered jobs that were totally new to them—almost half into domestic and personal services—it is possible to see several links between their work in San Francisco and that of their fathers in Italy. First, the sons of fishermen were the most likely of all immigrants to stay in the same line of work in San Francisco. About 50 percent of the immigrant sons of fishermen remained in that business, 40 percent in fishing and 10 percent in fish processing. Second, over one-fourth of the immigrants whose fathers had been in trade in Italy stayed in trade in San Francisco.

Third, slightly less than one-fourth of the immigrants whose fathers were in manufacturing in Italy stayed in the same work in San Francisco.

In contrast to these three groups of immigrants, the children of Italian farmers naturally had little chance to be farmers in an urban setting: only 2 percent of the children of farmers remained in agriculture in San Francisco. Of the 98 percent who did not go into farming, their background in Italy appears significant in the kind of work they did get. It is perhaps not surprising that children of landowners ordinarily got better jobs than children of sharecroppers or renters, who in turn usually got better jobs than children of agricultural laborers.[10] Children whose fathers were illiterate tended to be in domestic and personal services, and those whose fathers were literate tended to be in manufacturing. Almost two-thirds of the Italians in domestic services had illiterate fathers, as against only a third of those in manufacturing. Finally, 58 percent of those in trade had literate fathers.

Another important variable is the time of the immigrants' first arrival in San Francisco. Although the occupational distribution outlined so far applies mainly to the 1930's, the immigrants in the sample arrived in the city any time between 1895 and 1924, except for the years of the First World War. Thus the sample groups together immigrants of different ages and, more important, immigrants who had lived in the city anywhere from ten to more than thirty years. Since time might be a factor in the process of adjustment in the new land, one might expect the immigrants who arrived earlier to have better jobs in the 1930's than those who arrived later.

The sample shows, however, that for both Italians and immigrants of other nationalities the opposite was true: a larger percentage of the immigrants who arrived at the turn of the century were in less skilled jobs in the 1930's than immigrants who arrived later. Of all the Italians who arrived in San Francisco between 1891 and 1900, almost two-thirds were in domestic and personal services in the 1930's, as against only about one-third of those who arrived from 1911 to 1920. Only 10 percent of those who came between 1891 and 1900 were in maufacturing in the 1930's, as against 30 percent of those who came between 1921 and 1930. Immigrants of other nationalities followed this pattern quite closely, although fewer non-Italians were in unskilled occupations. For instance, 10 percent of the non-Italians who arrived in the 1901–10 decade were in the professions in the 1930's, and 15 percent of those who arrived in the following decade. On the other hand, 40 percent from the

1901–10 decade were in domestic services in the 1930's, and only 20 percent of those who arrived between 1921 and 1930.*

It is likely that most immigrants who arrived at the turn of the century could only get jobs in domestic and personal services, whereas those who came later could shop for better jobs. A consular report of 1901 stressed that many Italian immigrants were unemployed or underemployed, and that the 1,500 newcomers each year could not count on the help of the relatively few well-established Italians.[11] In 1904 the Italian government issued a warning discouraging emigration to San Francisco, "since the opportunities available in the past in that area have now vanished."[12]

In the 1920's, on the other hand, opportunities for work apparently multiplied. As Salvatore Reina, a San Francisco Italian, described it: "In those years there was work for everybody. Newcomers were offered jobs on arrival that immigrants in previous decades had had to wait months and years for, if they were able to get them at all."[13] Two circumstances might help explain why the job market opened up in the 1920's. First, the end of free immigration eased the pressure on the job market, so that the immigrants who arrived in the early 1920's did not have to compete with other immigrants arriving after them. And second, some Italians had by then established themselves in business and could offer jobs to newcomers. This might have been out of genuine interest in the welfare of their compatriots or because the newcomers could be paid nonunion wages, as will be discussed later in connection with the San Francisco Italian economy.

The later immigrants, moreover, were more likely to be permanent immigrants than the earlier ones; this trend was clear after the war, but detectable as early as 1912.[14] The combination of confidence in the American economy after the recession of 1907, concern over the Italian economy, which was recovering at a much slower pace, and the disillusionment of returnees unsuccessful in Italy helped change the long-range plans of Italians. After the war the Italian consul reported that few, whether newcomers or old residents, were eager to return to Italy, "since they believe the Italian economic situation is desperate."[15] The immigrants at the turn of the century were satisfied with temporary seasonal employment as common laborers. The immigrants of the 1910's and 1920's

*Unfortunately, we do not have the data on the occupational distribution of San Francisco immigrants immediately after they arrived. Such data would be useful in order to compare the first jobs the immigrants of the 1891–1900 decade had with the first jobs of those who arrived after either 1910 or 1920, as well as the first jobs held by both groups with the jobs they had in the 1930's.

sought better, more permanent jobs, recognizing that they were likely to remain in San Francisco for a long time, and probably for the rest of their lives.[16]

A more important explanation for the difference in occupations of the two groups of immigrants is found in the immigrants' background. On the average, the earlier immigrants came from a lower socioeconomic class than the later ones. For example, almost three-fourths of the prewar immigrants had illiterate fathers, and eight out of ten came from families of farm laborers or sharecroppers. In contrast, four out of every ten postwar immigrants came from nonfarm families, and about half of the others were from the class of sharefarmers and landowners.

Even before the war the changing characteristics of the immigrants were noticed. An American pointed out in 1912 that the rapid turnover of Italians in the United States was slowing down, that newcomers were more likely to stay, and that the immigrants arriving after 1910 were generally better educated and with better skills than their predecessors.[17] The prefetto of Palermo related in 1913 that the emigration of mechanics and artisans as well as small landowners was increasing.[18] The consul in San Francisco wrote that the immigrants of the 1920's were more aggressive than their predecessors. "The new immigrants," he concluded, "are certainly better educated and more knowledgeable about employment and work than previous immigrants."[19] In sum, the occupational distribution of the San Francisco Italians was more influenced by the occupations that the immigrants and their fathers had had in Italy than by the length of the immigrants' residence in San Francisco.

The Children of the Immigrants

Between the children of the immigrants and their fathers, the occupational change was as great as it had been between the previous two generations. Nine out of ten in the Italo-American generation had a different occupation from that of their father, although sometimes it was in the same general field. For instance, both father and son might have been in trade, the father a grocery store clerk and the American-born son a grocery store owner or operator. The children of non-Italian immigrants were twice as likely to have the same job as their father had: about 20 percent fell in that category. A breakdown of this percentage by nationality shows that the children from the most successful immigrant groups were the most likely to follow their father's career: 30 percent of the children of German and British parents were in that category. The more successful

9. Above, Grant Avenue shop, 1911; below, the North Beach Cannery, 1908. The goal of most Italians who finally settled in San Francisco was to establish a business of their own. But the reality was that most of them had to settle for a salaried job. Although under quite different circumstances, the Italians in San Francisco kept doing what they had been doing in Italy for centuries: they worked for other people. The North Beach Cannery was the city's largest employer of Italians after the turn of the century.

TABLE 6

Occupational Distribution of Immigrant Generation

Occupation	Italians	Non-Italians
Agriculture and food processing	4%	1%
Professions	6	16
Domestic and personal services	15	17
Trade and transportation	35	15
Manufacturing and mechanical	35	50
Fishing and fish processing	6	1

SOURCE: Marriage records and San Francisco city directories.

immigrants, like the Germans and the British, undoubtedly provided better role models for their children than immigrants in domestic services. Moreover, the occupational status of Italian immigrants was so low that their children could go nowhere but up.

The occupational profiles of the Italo-Americans and the children of non-Italian immigrants (Table 6), when compared with the profiles of the immigrant generation, show the Italo-Americans moving up the socioeconomic ladder but still at a disadvantage. The proportion of Italians in the professions rose from 1 percent of the immigrant generation to 6 percent of the Italo-Americans; at the same time the other immigrants rose from 10 to 16 percent. A salient characteristic of the Italo-American generation was its move away from domestic and personal services, which fell from 43 to 15 percent between the generations, into trade and manufacturing, which rose from a total of 47 percent to a total of 70 percent. Thus the transition from the Italian immigrants to the American-born generation was marked by a shift from unskilled to skilled occupations.*

A clearer picture of the generational changes in the occupations of San Francisco Italians can be seen in Tables 7–9, which show the occupational distribution of the children of immigrants from each occupational category. For example, Table 8 shows that only one out of every four children of immigrant farmers remained in agriculture, the other three moving into trade, manufacturing, domestic and personal services, and the professions. On the other hand, two

*An important aspect of the occupational transition from the immigrants to their children was that the occupational differences between non-Italian immigrant groups almost disappeared in the next generation. For instance, the percentage of the Irish-Americans in domestic and personal services was not higher than that of the German-Americans—for both groups it was about 15 percent. In professions, Irish-Americans were not as heavily represented as Germans, British, and Russians; but the Irish rate was only slightly below the average.

TABLE 7

Occupational Distribution of Immigrant Generation by Father's Occupation

Father's occupation	Son's occupation: Agr. and food processing	Professions	Domestic and personal svcs.	Trade and transportation	Mfg. and mechan.	Fishing and fish processing
Agr. and food processing	2%	1%	49%	26%	19%	3%
Professions	7	15	31	15	31	—
Domestic and pers. svcs.	—	—	41	36	23	—
Trade and transportation	5	3	29	29	34	—
Mfg. and mechanical	6	3	38	28	23	1
Fishing and fish proc.	—	1	24	17	11	48

SOURCE: See Table 5.

TABLE 8

Occupational Distribution of Italo-American Generation by Father's Occupation

Father's occupation	Son's occupation: Agr. and food processing	Professions	Domestic and personal svcs.	Trade and transportation	Mfg. and mechan.	Fishing and fish processing
Agr. and food processing	25%	5%	15%	25%	30%	—
Professions	10	16	16	10	37	10%
Domestic and pers. svcs.	4	8	23	29	35	1
Trade and transportation	5	3	10	40	9	40
Mfg. and mechanical	2	16	15	17	51	11
Fishing and fish proc.	2	4	25	5	17	46

SOURCE: See Tables 5 and 6.

out of every four children of fishermen remained in fishing, fish processing, or fish distributing, the other two moving mostly into unskilled personal and domestic services or into manufacturing. Thus children of fishermen remained in fishing or related activities in large numbers, and most of those who left fishing took unskilled jobs. On the other hand, many children of farmers left farming for skilled occupations.

TABLE 9
Occupational Distribution of Italo-American Generation by Grandfather's Occupation

Grandfather's occupation	Grandson's occupation: Agr. and food processing	Profes-sions	Domestic and per-sonal svcs.	Trade and trans-portation	Mfg. and mechan.	Fishing and fish processing
Agr. and food processing	5%	8%	18%	30%	38%	1%
Professions	6	11	17	24	40	2
Domestic and pers. svcs.	4	8	16	31	40	1
Trade and transportation	5	9	16	28	42	1
Mfg. and mechanical	5	8	17	29	39	1
Fishing and fish proc.	4	3	22	27	32	11

SOURCE: See Tables 5 and 6.

Why this difference? It is likely that the children of farmers were forced to get other work as the expanding city of San Francisco took over farmland and as machines decreased the need for manpower. Farming was a complex and specialized activity, and the children of farmers were probably better equipped to handle skilled jobs than the children of fishermen.[20]

Table 8 also shows that the largest percentage of the children of the immigrants in domestic and personal services, 35 percent, moved into manufacturing. Another sizable group, 29.5 percent, became traders. Only 20 percent remained in the same occupational category, with smaller percentages moving into the professions and agriculture. One factor in the socioeconomic rise of the Italo-Americans was undoubtedly the arrival of many Mexicans and other Latin Americans in San Francisco, which pushed both Italo-Americans and the children of other immigrants up the scale. But better educational opportunities, the knowledge of English, and familiarity with the American environment since childhood also gave Italo-Americans clear advantages over their fathers.

The relatively large number of Italo-Americans in commerce deserves special attention. Some of these Italo-Americans were children of farmers who found fruit and vegetable brokerage more profitable than direct farming. Others were children of fishermen who found fish marketing more profitable than fishing, or who, as will be related in another chapter, were forced out of fishing by the competition of other Italian groups. A number of Italo-Americans inherited trading from their fathers and eventually discovered new opportunities in the expanding city of San Francisco. And a lack of industrial skills probably put Italo-Americans at a disadvantage in the San Francisco labor market.

Moreover, the Italians' intense individualism hardly prepared Italo-Americans for the discipline and regimentation of factory work. Italo-Americans wanted to be in business on their own, much as their fathers had wanted to become independent farmers in Italy. A small commercial enterprise like a fruit and vegetable stand or a grocery store, which could be started with modest savings, seems to have been particularly attractive to San Francisco Italians. In the move from Italy to San Francisco, the legacy of individualism was not lost.

To summarize, Italo-Americans showed a significant degree of occupational improvement over their fathers. Fewer of the children were in domestic and personal services, and more were in manufacturing and the professions. A higher proportion of Italo-Americans moved into trade and transportation than the children of other immigrants, who tended to move away from trade into manufacturing and the professions. The age difference between the two groups under examination should be noted: by the time of marriage the children of the immigrants in general had better jobs than their fathers had at the peak of their working lives. The transition from the Italian to the immigrant generation was characterized by a break with an agrarian past and a large concentration in unskilled occupations. The transition from the immigrant to the Italo-American generation was characterized by a high degree of concentration in manufacturing and commerce.

Table 9 shows occupational changes that occurred between the Italian generation and the Italo-American, skipping the intermediate generation of the immigrants. From this table we see, bearing in mind that most San Francisco immigrants had a background of farming or fishing, that about two out of three Italo-Americans whose grandfathers had been farmers were in trade and manufacturing. In two generations most Italians had made the transition from an agrarian environment to an urban-industrial one. Only one out of every ten grandchildren of Italian fishermen was in the same occupation in San Francisco; most had different jobs.

The San Francisco immigrants and their children, on the one hand, and the returnees and their children, on the other, achieved vastly different results. Most San Francisco Italians became urban unskilled or semiskilled workers. Their condition was in many ways worse than that of the returnees who became landowners. In the long run, however, permanent emigration, unlike return migration, offered a solution to the problem of poverty. Most San Francisco Italo-Americans became skilled workers, whereas the children of the returnees had to turn again to the old solution of emigration. This we saw demonstrated in the story of the Torrano family. One Torrano returned to live in Verbicaro; later, his children had to emigrate. But the sons of the Torranos in San Francisco, skilled urban workers, achieved economic security. The returnees, it seems, were more conservative, making choices well within their mental boundaries. The permanent immigrants, in contrast, were more adventurous, trying new solutions.

Sestri Levante and Santa Flavia

So far, this discussion of occupational change has treated Italians as a whole. As we have seen, however, Italians were far from being a homogeneous group. In the balance of this chapter we look at the differences among the nine groups of San Francisco Italians that we have been studying. For this analysis, the nine towns are separated into three clusters: first, Santa Flavia and Sestri Levante, which were fishing towns; second, Lorsica, Porcari, Trabia, and Verbicaro, where farming was the main activity; and third, Lucca, Genoa, and Palermo, which were large urban areas. Within each of these clusters the occupations of the immigrants can, as before, be compared with those of their fathers and sons.

Most of the immigrants from Santa Flavia and Sestri Levante were the children of fishermen—nine out of ten from Sestri and eight out of ten from Santa Flavia. Yet the occupational profiles of the two groups of immigrants in San Francisco were strikingly different. Almost 60 percent of the immigrants from Santa Flavia became fishermen in San Francisco, but only 15 percent of those from Sestri Levante. Most of the immigrants from Sestri went into trade and domestic and personal services, with 30 percent of them in each category.

The sample I took shows an additional difference between the two groups, according to the time of arrival of the immigrants. About 70 percent of the immigrants from each of the two towns arrived in San Francisco between 1901 and 1920. In the Sestri group, those who arrived between 1901 and 1910 were mainly in fishing and manufacturing in the mid-1930's, whereas those who arrived between 1911 and 1920 were mainly in domestic and personal services and in trade. A similar breakdown of the occupations of the immigrants from Santa Flavia, however, does not show any meaningful contrast.

It is possible that the immigrants from Santa Flavia tended to stay in fishing and those from Sestri to enter other occupations because the immigrants from each of the two towns came to San Francisco with a different purpose. In 1895 the mayor of Santa Flavia reported that cholera had brought the economy in the province of Palermo to a standstill. Fishermen were emigrating in large numbers, fearing a resurgence of the epidemic. These emigrants sought homes where they could continue doing what "their fathers and their fathers' fathers had done for centuries."[21] In Sestri Levante, on the other hand, the prefetto of Genoa wrote in 1904 that the fishermen were leaving for a different reason: "They are unable to sell their catch because of the poverty in this province. Some of them are leaving for South America, some for the United States. I have been told that most of these emigrants are not eager to become fishermen overseas. To them, fishing means poverty. And it is to escape poverty that they go."[22]

Interviews I had with old San Francisco Italians shed additional light on why the immigrants from Sestri gave up fishing and those from Santa Flavia did not: the immigrants from Sestri Levante were forced out of fishing by competition in San Francisco. The data for the 1930's used here do not reflect the occupational distribution in previous decades, when more immigrants from Sestri may have been in fishing. The son of a fisherman from Sestri told me that his father and two uncles, who came to San Francisco in 1912, worked at fishing only until 1919. "It was the competition in the business and the pressure from the Sicilians that forced my father and my uncles out. I also know that my father and my uncles were not exceptional in having to quit fishing because of pressure from the Sicilians."[23] A consular report noted that "Sicilian fishermen have been arriving in increasing numbers in the last five years. They have superior navigation skills; besides, their endurance when doing hard work is incredible. Unable to stand the competition from the Sicilians, many fishermen from the province of Genoa left fishing for other occupations."[24]

These changes that took place in San Francisco can also be viewed in relation to changes in Italy. Marriage records for the years 1882, 1892, 1902, 1912, and 1922, which include the occupations of the young men who married in those years, show the occupational structures of the two communities changing over time.[25] In Sestri Levante there was a substantial shift, accelerating after 1900, from farming and fishing into industrial occupations. In 1882 50 percent

10. Fisherman's Wharf, 1908. Italian fishermen, especially those from the south, found excellent opportunities to work at their trade in San Francisco. Their Old World boats and fishing techniques, combined with a distinctive lifestyle, made them a unique group in the then already cosmopolitan city.

of the men getting married there were farmers, 40 percent fishermen, and the rest in other occupations. Twenty years later only 20 percent were farmers; most of them had apparently moved into industry, since 20 percent were now industrial workers. The percentage of fishermen had not changed in those twenty years. By 1922, however, fishermen were down to 20 percent, and industrial workers had risen to 40 percent. Thus, between 1882 and 1922 there was a spectacular rise in the industrial sector, matched by a fall in the proportion of farmers and fishermen.

In Santa Flavia, in contrast, the occupational distribution was highly stable over the same period. The percentage of fishermen ranged from 60 to 65 percent of the total population in each of the decades from 1882 to 1922, and the percentage of farmers from 10 to 15 percent. In 1922 only 3 percent were industrial workers. These patterns of change in Italy were to a great extent repeated in America. Immigrants from Sestri were perhaps more accustomed to occupational change, those from Santa Flavia perhaps migrated with a more conservative outlook, since occupational change was minimal in their native community.

The differences between the two groups survived in several ways when their American-born children entered the labor market. First, the Santa Flavia group still tended to stay in fishing and the Sestri Levante group still tended to leave fishing. In the sample, in fact, none of the Italo-Americans from Sestri was a fisherman, whereas 35 percent of those from Santa Flavia were. Sicilians continued to dominate the San Francisco fishing industry. Second, the Italo-Americans from Sestri were among the most upwardly mobile of the Italian groups in San Francisco, with 90 percent in either manufacturing or trade. In the Santa Flavia group, on the other hand, 60 percent of the children were in either fishing or domestic and personal services. It is worth noticing that almost all the Italo-Americans from Santa Flavia in domestic services were children of fishermen. Those who left fishing, with few marketable skills, had to start at the bottom.

Thus, in three generations the immigrants from Sestri Levante made an almost total change from their traditional occupations: 90 percent of the fathers of the immigrants were fishermen in Italy, but not one of their grandchildren. At the same time, 90 percent of the Italo-Americans from Sestri were in trade and manufacturing, which very few of their grandfathers had pursued in Italy. In the Santa Flavia group, 80 percent of the fathers of the immigrants were fishermen, but only 35 percent of their grandchildren; those who had left fishing were likely to have menial jobs. In dealing with the assimilation of immigrants, historians have argued for some time about the relative importance of the attitudes immigrants brought from Europe and the impact of the American environment. Our sample suggests that the attitudes the immigrants brought from their native communities substantially influenced their response to American occupational opportunities.

Lorsica, Porcari, Verbicaro, and Trabia

Among San Francisco Italians, only about 15 percent were from fishing families. Most Italian immigrants—about 65 percent—came from a farming background, and from some Italian towns almost all immigrants were farmers. Slightly over 90 percent of the immigrants from Lorsica, Porcari, and Trabia were farmers, and about 85 percent of those from Verbicaro.

Most of the immigrants from these towns came to San Francisco after the turn of the century, mainly from 1907 to 1913 and from 1919 to 1923. In general, the northerners preceded the southerners. The immigrants from these four groups, moving from farms to a city, made probably the sharpest break with their Italian past in terms of occupation. By the mid-1930's very few were in farming; 5 percent from Porcari, 7 percent from Lorsica, 2 percent from Verbicaro, and none from Trabia.

These percentages, although small, indicate a noticeable difference between northerners and southerners, with the northerners more likely to remain in farming than the southerners. It will be recalled from Chapter 3 that the migrants who returned to the south were more committed to purchasing land and owning small farms than the returnees to the north, who were willing to open a business if land was not available. Moreover, we have seen how the returnees in the south often sought to buy specific tracts of land that had a special value for them, even when they could ill afford it. In San Francisco we see the opposite pattern: the southerners less likely to be in farming than the northerners.

What accounts for this difference? The time when the immigrants arrived may have been significant. Some northerners were already well established in San Francisco by the late 1860's, when land in and around San Francisco was inexpensive; but few of the immigrants who came after the turn of the century were able to buy land, as will be seen in Chapter 8. And as the consul wrote in 1906, "The northerners who own land hire almost exclusively northern labor."[26] This is an instance, possibly, of chain migration leading to a group occupational pattern.

Northerners came to have a virtual monopoly on farming, which excluded southerners. It is possible, besides, that southerners avoided buying land because they were more determined to return to Italy than northerners. Finally, land ownership did not seem as important in San Francisco as in Italy. As shown in Chapter 3, southerners bought land in Italy because land was the main source of economic security and social status in their small communes. In San Francisco, however, farming required cooperation and marketing skills that the individualistic southerners were unlikely to possess. And land ownership did not confer any special social status in San Francisco, at least no more than a job with a good income.

Apart from the north-south differences, the four groups each had distinctive occupational traits. Over half of the immigrants from Lorsica were scavengers, garbage collectors. We do not know how these immigrants got started in this business; but they soon controlled it. "The scavengers have created a true monopoly," the consul wrote in 1907. "There are 400 of them, all from the province of Genoa. If they need manpower and it is not available among the Genovesi from San Francisco, they send for someone in Italy."[27] The mayor of Lorsica told the prefetto of Genoa in 1909: "The emigrants leaving for San Francisco, if they have been summoned by a relative in San Francisco who is a scavenger, are very unlikely to return. I am told that the scavengers—all from Genoa province—have established themselves in a mutual aid society and take good care of each other."[28] This is another example of the impact of chain migration on the work a certain immigrant group did.

Apparently, Lorsicans who arrived in San Francisco after 1910 were unable to secure jobs as scavengers. In fact, more Lorsicans who settled in the city after that date were engaged in domestic and personal services in the 1930's. This reversal is surprising, since we have already seen that Italian immigrants of the postwar years generally had better jobs in the 1930's than immigrants who arrived before the war. Probably, most Lorsican immigrants arriving in San Francisco before 1910 had no problem in getting work as scavengers, since the trade was dominated by other Genoese, and did not move into other activities. But by the early 1910's the growing children of the Lorsica immigrants could supply the manpower the business needed. As a result, immigrants from Lorsica after the 1910's could find neither jobs as scavengers nor support from other Lorsicans in gaining other skilled or semiskilled work. The newcomers had to start on their own, at the bottom of the occupational ladder.

Slightly over 50 percent of the immigrants from Porcari were in domestic and personal services in the 1930's, and those who had arrived after 1910 had an advantage over the immigrants of the previous decade. Indeed, 65 percent of the immigrants who arrived between 1901 and 1910 were in this work in the 1930's, as against only 45 percent of those who arrived in the 1920's. Another 25 percent of the Porcari immigrants in the 1930's were in commerce, mostly with fruit and vegetable stands and grocery stores. And 20 percent were in manufacturing, two-thirds of them either shoemakers or cabinetmakers.

Most of the immigrants from Porcari who had businesses or crafts had arrived in San Francisco in the postwar years. They were able to establish themselves as small independent businessmen because they had left Italy with some capital after selling their land (or their share in the land if they were sharefarmers). "Before the war," the prefetto of Lucca wrote, "only rarely did emigrants sell the land. Now selling the land or one's share in the land is fairly common. It is likely that the emigrants who depart with some capital will not return, if they find success in the Americas."[29]

Of the four groups under consideration, the immigrants from Verbicaro occupied the lowest jobs: 80 percent were still in domestic and personal services in the mid-1930's, with the rest almost equally divided between commerce and manufacturing. The salient characteristic of this group is that by the mid-1930's almost 40 percent of them were bootblacks. Here too we do not know how the first immigrants from Verbicaro got started in shining shoes. As early as the beginning of this century they seem to have predominated in this work. The consul reported in 1908 that the immigrants from Verbicaro had "created a virtual monopoly" on shining shoes. "The Verbicarans are hard-working people, and prosperous. There are probably 2,000 of them in San Francisco, a large group of them in this line of activity."[30]

The figure of 2,000 is obviously exaggerated. In view of the number of departures from Verbicaro up to 1908 (see Table 4, Chapter 3) and the presence of other groups of Verbicarans in Buenos Aires, Rio de Janeiro, and New York, it is unlikely that there were more than 400 from Verbicaro in San Francisco at the time. The consul was seeking money from the Ministry of Foreign Affairs for the San Francisco Italian school and the Comitato di Soccorso e Patronato, an Italian employment agency, and this may explain the inflated figure. It is also doubtful that these immigrant bootblacks were very prosperous, especially as early as 1908. But with hard work, the Verbicaro immigrants were able to achieve, if not high status, at least a high standard of living compared with what they had known in Verbicaro. Their children, moreover, showed the greatest improvement over their fathers' occupations of any Italian immigrant group: 70 percent were in manufacturing and trade.

About six out of ten immigrants from Trabia were laborers, many of them janitors. On the whole, the Trabia group was at about the same level as the Verbicaro group, but without a single distinctive occupation. It should be noted, however, that 20 percent of the Trabia immigrants were in trade as peddlers.

In general, about half of the immigrants from these four medium-sized agrarian communities were in domestic and personal services, with Lorsica the only exception. Among all San Francisco Italians, by comparison, 40 percent were in that work. Immigrants in manufacturing and trade were less likely to be skilled workers or merchants than to be semiskilled workers, small traders, and peddlers. With the exception of immigrants from Lorsica, the immigrants of the post-1910 period had better jobs than the earlier immigrants. And immigrants from the north generally had better jobs than those from the south.

Despite the movement of almost all these immigrants from agricultural work into urban jobs, there was a continuity between the Italian and American experiences. This continuity can be seen by comparing the immigrants from the north and the south of Italy, and the immigrants who came before and after the First World War. In making these comparisons, I have correlated data in three areas. The first correlation is between land tenure in Italy among the immigrants' parents and the occupational distribution of the immigrants in San Francisco; the second is between the general occupational distribution in the Italian communes and the occupational distribution among the immigrants in San Francisco; and the third is between the literacy rates for the immigrants' fathers and the immigrants' occupations.

On the average, immigrants whose fathers were either landowners or sharefarmers had better jobs than immigrants whose fathers were renters or day laborers. This is true for each of the four groups, as well as for the four as a whole. In the 1880's in Lorsica about 75 percent of the heads of household were small landowners, and the other 25 percent renters or day laborers. In Porcari about 40 percent of the heads of household were sharefarmers, another 35 percent small owners, and the rest laborers working on a yearly contract.[31] In Verbicaro, for which census data are not available, perhaps 30 percent of the heads of household were very small landowners, and the other 70 percent day laborers.[32] And according to the prefetto of Cosenza, "Most landowners [in the Verbicaro region] have so little land that their condition is hardly better than that of the laborers."[33] Finally, in Trabia only about 20 percent of the heads of household owned land; most of the others were laborers working for a single local nobleman who owned 60 percent of the land in the commune.[34] The differing skills and financial resources associated with the varieties of land tenure may partly explain the differing occupations of northerners and southerners.*

*This correlation becomes clear when seen in the case of each commune. All the immigrants from Lorsica in domestic services had fathers who were either renters or laborers. The garbage collectors from Lorsica were almost all children of small landowners. And the few immigrants from Lorsica in manufacturing were children of the few Lorsicans who were either merchants, grocery store owners, or landowners. The

A second correlation is found between changes in the occupational distribution in Italy and the occupational distribution of the immigrants in San Francisco. Possibly, the immigrants from Lorsica and Porcari were likely to have better jobs than those from Trabia and Verbicaro because they came from a more dynamic social and economic environment. To test this hypothesis I used the marriage records for 1882, 1892, 1902, 1912, and 1922, as I did for Santa Flavia and Sestri Levante, in order to see how the occupational distribution in the four communes changed over time.

In Lorsica, one of the two northern communities, the percentage of working people who were farmers gradually declined, from 85 percent in 1882 to 70 percent in 1922. In the same period, the industrial workers increased from zero to 15 percent. The marriage records show that the jobs these industrial workers had were not in Lorsica, but in Sestri Levante, Chiavari, and other communes along the Ligurian coast.[35] In the other northern town, Capannori (which included Porcari until 1913), the farming population declined from 80 percent in 1882 to 60 percent in 1922. In Capannori, however, unlike Lorsica, most of those who left farming seem to have gone into trade, which rose 20 percent; industry rose by only 10 percent.[36] The location of Capannori helps explain this shift from agriculture to trade. Capannori was only five miles from Lucca, a city that almost doubled in population during the four decades. The growth of the city obviously provided opportunities for young people unable to find a job in farming but unwilling to emigrate. Regardless of the differences between Lorsica and Porcari, both were changing from an agrarian economy to a more diversified one.

Though the occupational profile of the two southern communes was similar to that of the two in the north, the change over time was different. In both Verbicaro and Trabia the occupational distribution in 1882 was about the same as in 1922. The farming population of Verbicaro was 85 percent of the total working population in 1882 and 87 percent in 1922; in Trabia it was 79 percent in 1882 and 75 percent in 1922.[37] As for industry, none of the men who married in Verbicaro was an industrial worker, and in Trabia only 2 percent were industrial workers in 1922. The mayor of Verbicaro reported in 1906: "There are no industries in this town. Young people who

---

immigrants from Porcari who ran grocery stores were mainly children of landowners or sharefarmers. About 80 percent of the immigrants from Trabia and Verbicaro who entered manufacturing and trade had fathers who owned land. Finally, the greatest majority of the immigrants from Verbicaro and Trabia in domestic and personal services were children of laborers.

cannot make a living off the land or do not want to be farmers have to leave permanently."[38]

A third correlation is that between the literacy rate of the fathers of the immigrants and the occupational distribution of the immigrants themselves. Immigrants whose fathers were illiterate were more likely to be in domestic and personal services than immigrants whose fathers were literate. In Lorsica the literacy rate was comparatively high; about half of the immigrants from Lorsica had literate fathers. But 70 percent of the immigrants from Lorsica in domestic services had illiterate fathers. The literacy rate was slightly lower in Porcari; in this case too the figures available for San Francisco indicate that the immigrants in domestic and personal services were likely to be children of illiterate fathers. In the two southwestern communities the literacy rate was much lower: 90 percent of the immigrants from them had illiterate fathers. In San Francisco all the immigrants from these two communities who were in domestic services had illiterate fathers.

When the immigrants' children entered the labor market, the differences among the four groups were still noticeable; and it was apparent that some groups had been more successful than others. As Table 10 shows, 40 percent of the Italo-Americans from Lorsica were in trade; many were scavengers. Half of these Italo-Americans from Lorsica in trade had fathers who were in trade themselves, and the other half were children of immigrants in domestic and personal services. But only 7 percent of the Italo-Americans from this group were in domestic and personal services; 10 percent were in farming, and 37 percent in manufacturing. Of the four groups of Italo-Americans, those from Porcari had the highest percentage in manufacturing, 55 percent; most were cabinetmakers, masons, ironworkers, and blacksmiths. Another 23 percent of the Italo-Americans from Porcari were in trade, most with fruit and vegetable businesses, grocery stores, or restaurants. Only 14 percent were in domestic services, 7 percent in professions, and 2 percent in farming.

The Italo-Americans from Verbicaro showed a remarkable improvement over their fathers: 45 percent of the Italo-Americans were in manufacturing, mostly as bakers, butchers, ironworkers, and machinists, and 25 percent were in trade. Only 18 percent were still unskilled and trapped in domestic and personal services. Most important, the Italo-Americans from Verbicaro showed a surprising presence in the professions: 12 percent of them were engineers, teachers, or lawyers. The Italo-Americans from Trabia, on the other hand, although better off than their fathers, were not as suc-

TABLE 10

Occupational Distribution of Sons of Immigrants from Four Towns

Occupation	Lorsica	Porcari	Verbicaro	Trabia
Agriculture and food processing	10%	2%	—	—
Professions	6	7	12%	4%
Domestic and personal services	7	14	18	45
Trade and transportation	40	23	25	27
Manufacturing and mechanical	37	55	45	24
Fishing and fish processing	—	—	—	—

SOURCE: See Table 5.

cessful as the Italo-Americans from Verbicaro. In fact, 45 percent of the Italo-Americans from Trabia were still in domestic and personal services, as janitors, street laborers, and servants. In addition, 24 percent were in manufacturing and 27 percent in trade and transportation. Only 4 percent of the Italo-Americans from this group entered the professions.

In general, most Italo-Americans from the four groups were either in manufacturing or trade: 77 percent of those from Lorsica, 78 percent from Porcari, 70 percent from Verbicaro, and 51 percent from Trabia. The occupational profile of the two northern groups remained better than that of the southern group from Trabia. But there was no longer a north-south dichotomy; the percentage of Italo-Americans from Verbicaro in trade and manufacturing was almost as high as that of the two northern groups. Moreover, Verbicaro had a clear superiority over the two northern groups in the professions. Statistical evidence does not explain why the Italo-Americans from Verbicaro were more successful than those from Trabia. Perhaps the modest financial success (but not social status) that the Verbicaro immigrants achieved as shoeshiners, which the consul noted in 1907, gave some advantage to their sons when they entered the labor market.

The occupational changes that occurred in the four groups of immigrants from agrarian communes can be explained, at least to a degree, by the immigrants' differing backgrounds in Italy in such areas as land tenure systems, occupational structures and changes, and literacy. In the transition from the immigrant to the Italo-American generation the differences among the four groups did not disappear. But a full explanation for the occupational changes remains elusive, as is demonstrated by the unexpectedly higher achievements of the Italo-Americans from Verbicaro than those from Trabia.

Lucca, Genoa, and Palermo

The immigrants from Lucca, Palermo, and Genoa had a more diverse occupational background than that of immigrants from rural areas. Between 20 and 25 percent of the immigrants from these cities had fathers in manufacturing. One out of ten immigrants from Genoa was the child of a merchant, and two out of ten from Palermo were fishermen.

Surprisingly, however, about 60 percent of these immigrants came from farming families. The birth records of the future emigrants show that most came from relatively small agricultural communities on the outskirts of the cities. In Genoa, as we have seen, a number of adjacent communities were incorporated into greater Genoa in 1881 (see Note to Table 1). Similarly, most immigrants from Lucca did not come from within the walls, but from the 79 surrounding villages that were part of the city. It is obvious that many areas, although classified as parts of a city by the census, were for all practical purposes rural towns like Lorsica and Trabia.[39]

The immigrants who came from the three cities before the First World War were very different from the postwar immigrants. Even more than other groups, the prewar immigrants from the cities were likely to be in domestic and personal services in the mid-1930's. Among the prewar immigrants from Lucca, 40 percent were in domestic services in the mid-1930's, as against only 20 percent of those who came after the war. The figures for Genoa and Palermo are similar. A breakdown of the sample shows that the prewar immigrants were more likely to be from the outskirts of the cities; the postwar immigrants tended to be from the cities proper, and to have fathers in trade or manufacturing. Thus in many ways the prewar immigrants from the three cities resembled those from the farming towns and had the same occupational problems in San Francisco. The postwar immigrants from the three cities, on the other hand, were virtually the only urbanites who came to San Francisco from Italy. Their fathers had city jobs, and they themselves were likely to be not only literate, but also skilled. Since most of them arrived with the intention of staying permanently in San Francisco, they may have brought along some capital as well, which would have helped them in getting started.

As Table 11 shows, a relatively high percentage of the immigrants from Genoa were in agriculture; most were truck farmers and florists, and some of these immigrants became large landowners

TABLE 11

Occupational Distribution of Immigrants from Three Cities

Occupation	Genoa	Lucca	Palermo
Agriculture and food processing	15%	4%	—
Professions	3	2	6%
Domestic and personal services	30	37	39
Trade and transportation	27	29	22
Manufacturing and mechanical	25	27	23
Fishing and fish processing	—	—	10

SOURCE: See Table 5.

around San Francisco. About half of the immigrants from the city of Genoa in trade and transportation, like many from Lorsica and elsewhere in the province, were garbage collectors, and most of the rest were salesmen or produce middlemen. As will be seen later, a number of these middlemen had started as sharefarmers and then became landowners, before moving into the more profitable business of produce brokerage. Some of the most successful San Francisco Italians were in this category. The New World provided these businessmen with the opportunity to build fortunes, but their background may have contributed to their success, for some were the children of merchants from Genoa.

The immigrants from Lucca, like those from Porcari, were not allowed to compete with the Genoese in truck farming; this helps explain the low percentage of immigrants from Lucca in farming. They were, however, allowed to join the Genoese in the distribution process. As the Italian consul reported in 1911: "Immigrants from Lucca are active in the retail produce business; their vegetable stands are to be found everywhere in the city."[40] Immigrants from Palermo had the highest percentage in the professions, most of whom were either musicians, performers, or teachers. Some of these artists and music teachers might have been political refugees who left Palermo after the Sicilian upheaval of late 1893.

Even among immigrants from cities, most workers were unskilled and, like most Italians in San Francisco, had to start at the bottom. There was, however, more diversity in the occupational distribution of the immigrants from cities. Almost all the professionals of the Italian immigrant generation came from these cities. But they were only a few. The absence of an educated professional elite was an important factor in the organizational problems the immigrants had until the second generation came of age.

TABLE 12

Occupational Distribution of Sons of Immigrants from Three Cities

Occupation	Genoa	Lucca	Palermo
Agriculture and food processing	10%	2%	—
Professions	20	15	10%
Domestic and personal services	5	27	25
Trade and transportation	35	32	30
Manufacturing and mechanical	30	24	30
Fishing and fish processing	—	—	5

SOURCE: See Table 6.

Table 12 shows that the children of the immigrants from the three cities moved into professions in relatively large numbers. Marriage records indicate that many were lawyers, dentists, or schoolteachers. A breakdown of the Italo-American professionals by father's occupation reveals that most second-generation professionals were children of immigrants in manufacturing. Among Italo-Americans from Genoa, 10 percent were still in farming. These were probably people living in the city but working for their fathers as truck farmers in the San Francisco area. The percentage of Italo-Americans from Lucca and Palermo in domestic and personal services was surprisingly high, especially compared with the Italo-Americans from other groups. Most of these workers were children of immigrants who had been in domestic and personal services, whose Italian fathers, in turn, had been landless farmers. In sum, even among the Italo-Americans from the three cities, the occupational differences survived, the Italo-Americans from Genoa showing the highest upward mobility.

The Italians in San Francisco, like most Italians who settled in the United States, had typically been farmers and fishermen in Italy. In America they generally became unskilled laborers, occupying a position somewhat below almost all other immigrant groups. Apart from discrimination, the main reasons for their condition were the combined handicaps of illiteracy, rural habits, and the lack of skills, along with the widely felt desire to return to Italy. The transition from Italy to San Francisco forced or facilitated a major break with the occupations the immigrants had been familiar with in Italy.

The immigrants who arrived before 1910 were generally less prepared to compete in an urban environment, and probably more committed to going back to Italy than the later immigrants. Possibly an important reason the post-1910 immigrants were less likely to return was that they had witnessed in Italy the general failure of return emigration to solve the problem of poverty. Almost all the immigrants, however, had to settle for jobs that were new to them. And the kind of work they got in San Francisco was not purely a function of the American labor market, but was also strongly related to the lives and circumstances of the immigrants and their parents in Italy.

CHAPTER 7

Immigrant Families

THIS CHAPTER deals with families that emigrated from Italy to San Francisco and families that were formed in San Francisco by immigrants who were single when they arrived. My main purpose is to show which family traditions San Francisco Italians were able to preserve and what changes in family life they were forced to make. In order to have a better understanding of Italian family life in San Francisco, I compare Italian families and families of immigrants of other nationalities. Finally, I explore whether there were differences in the way the family traditions of the nine groups discussed in previous chapters changed or survived in San Francisco.

The largest number of Italian immigrants were young people who arrived in the United States alone. Most of these young men were single. Of the few who were married, most did not take their wives along immediately; wives remained in Italy, to farm the land if the family had any. Only later, ordinarily when immigrants felt they could afford to support their families, did they ask their families to cross the Atlantic.[1] "It was a great pity," wrote Tony Cyriax, "so few men took their wives along. They went to America alone. Statistics say that one-third of the Italians take their wives, but this is not true in Campià. Of the 24 men of Campià in the United States [the town had two hundred people] only three had taken their wives to America with them. A sad story."[2]

Initially, on the average, male emigrants outnumbered females ten to one; but the ratio decreased over the years. Throughout the 1870's women made up 10 percent of all emigrants. In the 1880's the figure rose to 18 percent. The following decade over 20 percent of all emigrants were women; in 1893, for instance, when 230,000 people left Italy, about 50,000 were women. After 1910 the percentage of women continued to rise: 25 percent from 1911 to 1920, and 35 percent from 1921 to 1929.[3]

From these figures, showing an imbalance of four to one in favor of male emigrants, one might expect to find a similar imbalance in the Italian communities overseas. But that was not the case. In 1920, for instance, the sex ratio among San Francisco Italians was 164 men per 100 women.[4] And this was not the greatest imbalance among emigrant Italian communities. How do we explain the difference? The answer lies in the return migration and reemigration already discussed. The figures for male emigration were inflated because they indiscriminately included first-time emigrants and returnees going overseas for the second or third time. Return migration and reemigration by women, on the other hand, was uncommon. Women, the prefetto of Lucca reported, went overseas "to join their husband or to get married. Very few leave on their own for temporary emigration."[5] Thus, whereas men tended to be temporary emigrants, especially before 1910, most women emigrants were permanent, when men, after a series of temporary emigrations, decided to remain overseas permanently.*

Initially, then, San Francisco Italians were predominantly men. The Italian consuls in the 1860's and 1870's rarely mentioned families, and often dealt with problems arising from the separation of immigrants from their families.[6] The survey by the Italian Geographic Society in 1887 revealed that few Italians brought their families along, since they did not plan to settle in San Francisco.[7] The survey also pointed out problems encountered by those immigrants who brought their families to San Francisco: the children were reluctant to go when the parents decided to return to Italy. A survey taken in 1892 showed the sex ratio to be 83 percent men and 17 percent women.[8] The prefetto of Lucca reported on emigrants

*Unfortunately, the Italian Bureau of Statistics did not collect data on the marital status of emigrants. It did, however, compile statistics on whether emigrants left alone or in a family group. A family group was either the entire family or the father with one or more of his children. On the average, eight out of every ten emigrants departed alone, this ratio showing only small variations over the years. For instance, emigrants departing alone in 1908 and 1909 made up 81 and 79 percent of all emigrants; Italy [35], *Statistica 1908–9*, p. xv. See also RP, Cosenza 26.ix.1894, ASC; and RP, Lucca 7.v.1907. Giacosa reported (*Impressioni d'America*, p. 163) that almost the only Italians he met in America were men: "Of course, women and children were in Italy, because—it was clear—everybody counted on going back to Italy."

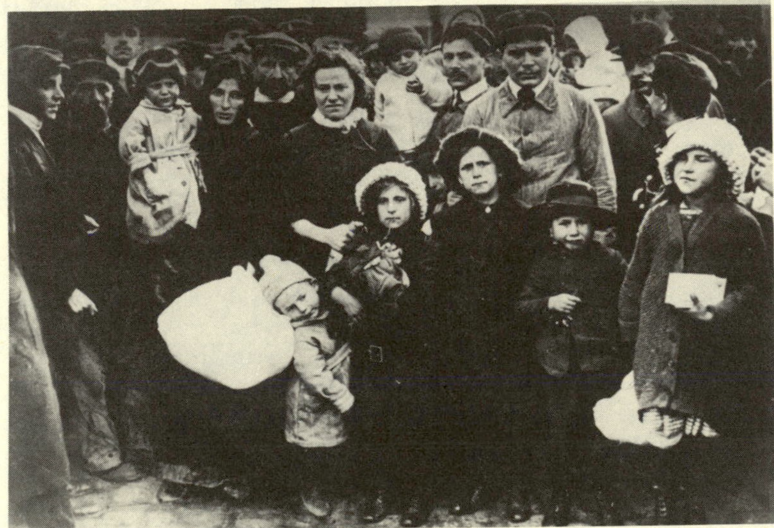

11. Above, emigration agency, Chiasso (Swiss-Italian border), early 1900's; below, families waiting to board ship, port of Genoa, ca. 1910. Almost all of the early Italian emigrants to the Americas were males. Until about 1910, even most of the married men who crossed the Atlantic departed alone, returning to Italy after a few years either to settle down there or to visit their families. The emigration of women and children increased substantially after that year. But this did not necessarily mean that the emigrants intended to settle permanently in the United States; it meant merely that they saw the advantage of having their families in America rather than returning to see them every few years.

leaving for California: "Although they plan to stay overseas for several years, emigrants do not take their families along. The trip is too expensive, and only a few intend to settle abroad permanently."[9] Thus, at least until the end of the nineteenth century, there were few Italian women in San Francisco.

Female emigration to San Francisco especially increased after 1910. A consular report in 1912 mentioned that women were arriving in growing numbers, "either to join their husband here, or because returnees come back to San Francisco with wives and children."[10] *L'Italia* observed in 1913 that the community was taking root, "mostly because Italians are sending for their wives and children."[11] The impact of female immigration showed up in the census: in 1930 the sex ratio had fallen to 133 males per 100 females.[12]

The Historiographical Problem

Historians differ on what impact immigration had on families, whether the families arrived together or were established in the New World. Earlier historians were likely to stress the negative impact that separation and relocation had on family life. Foerster, for instance, stated: "Emigration often took the place of a silent divorce court."[13] And Handlin, in his classic *The Uprooted*, discussed how immigrant families became unstable and fragmented.[14] In a study of Italians in New Haven, Irvin Child pointed to intergenerational conflict arising from immigration.[15]

Revisionist historians have been more positive, arguing that immigration did not disrupt families. Rudolf Vecoli, for instance, argued against Talcott Parsons's position that immigrant families became "mobile, detached, and nuclear"; Vecoli stressed that the southern extended family "did not disintegrate upon emigration," and that its stability helped immigrants adjust to city life.[16] Virginia Yans-McLaughlin concluded that families "made a relatively smooth transition from the Old World to the New," and that, although conflict occurred, there was no disorganization.[17] In Boston, Herbert Gans concluded, the Italians' "overriding goal was the survival of the nuclear family," and they were able by and large to maintain it intact.[18]

These conflicting interpretations were partly the result of two different approaches to social phenomena: some emphasized change and disruption, others stability and continuity. And there are other reasons as well. First, there is disagreement on the very composition of Italian families. Some contend that most Italian families were extended. And after movies like *The Godfather*, few would argue with this position.[19] Some, however, say they were nuclear.[20] The discrepancy is the result of two ways of determining who were the members of a family. For Leonard Covello, for instance, the family was "the social group which included all blood and in-law relatives up to the fourth degree"; for MacDonald it was the social group including only parents and children.*

Another reason for the difference between scholars has its source in popular mythology, which influences scholars too, and also in a less-than-accurate use of statistics. It is a myth that the typical southern Italian family was large and extended, at least at the time of mass emigration. Statistics and other records abundantly document that most southern Italian families were nuclear households, and that until 1936 southern households were smaller than northern households.[21]

Still another reason for the disagreement among immigration historians is the complex organization of Italian families. Constance Cronin, an American, found this complexity most discouraging in her effort to understand Italian emigration to Australia. Puzzled by contradictory statements she found in secondary sources, she went to Italy and concluded: "The basic cause of the entire problem is the intricacy of the Italian social organization, which is designed to keep things hidden, and has very effectively done so. The southern Italian skill at confusing the issue is nowhere better illustrated."[22]

The final reason I mention has to do with regional differences. Most immigration historians discuss Italian families in general, with occasional references to differences between the north and the south. In reality, there were profound differences in family structure and traditions between almost any two sections of the country. These differences were obviously the result of many circumstances, of which the land tenure system prevalent in each region was among the most important. Social scientists who charted the movement of Italian families from Italy to other countries were often insufficiently attentive to regional differences, and very likely to accept one regional type as the "typical" Italian family. Thus the differences in their conclusions.

*Certain expressions used in this chapter should be defined. *Nuclear family households* are formed by parents and children; *extended family households* include other relatives besides parents and children. *Extended families not in the same household* are formed by various related nuclear families that do not live under the same roof, but are considered by themselves and others as parts of an extended family. The so-called extended family of southern Italy, for instance, is generally in this third category.

Two Households

Before introducing statistics, I present two households, one from the north and one from the south, to give an immediate idea of regional differences and of the impact of emigration. These are the Arrighi family from Lucca and the Caffaro family from Sicily.

The Arrighis came from Tampagnano di Lunata, one of the 79 villages of Lucca. Angelo Arrighi came to America in 1906 at age sixteen, leaving a household of seventeen people. When his father Avertano and his uncle Rocco married—the father in 1877 and the uncle in 1880—they did not leave their father's house. From 1878 to 1900 Avertano had nine children; Angelo, the sixth, was born in 1890. Rocco had seven, born from 1880 to 1904. When the father of Avertano and Rocco died in 1889, Teresa, their mother, became head of the household, which she was until she died in 1903.[23] Three of Angelo's siblings died in infancy, two migrated to South America, one sister married in Italy, and another was married in America to a man from Tampagnano di Lunata. Angelo was 42 when he married in San Francisco; at that time, according to his naturalization records, he owned a small restaurant in the Old Potrero district.[24] His wife was a Scottish woman, born in Glasgow in 1903, who had arrived in San Francisco in 1913. Two children were born of that marriage: Elaine in 1933 and Mauro in 1935. Elaine pursued a career as a social worker and remained single.[25] Mauro had two sons and a daughter. Although he was nostalgic for the large household his father had described to him, he realized that he could not afford more than three children in America.[26]

The second family, the Caffaros, came from Trabia. Vincenzo Caffaro emigrated to San Francisco in 1899. Vincenzo's father, Carmine, born in 1841 and married in 1867, was a laborer and lived in a two-room house. Carmine had four children: the first two died in infancy, and the third married in Trabia in 1899. The fourth, Vincenzo, was born in Trabia in 1875 and married in San Francisco in 1903. His wife, Santina Sanfilippo, was born in Trabia in 1883 and arrived in San Francisco in 1902, probably joining Vincenzo to marry him. By 1931 Vincenzo and Santina had six living children.[27] In Italy the Arrighis were an extended family household, with three generations and in-laws in the same house. The Caffaros were a nuclear family household. In San Francisco both families were nuclear family households, and the southern Italian household was the larger of the two.

The Arrival of the Families

The Italian families in San Francisco can be classified in two groups: those formed in Italy, the members having arrived either together or at different times, and those formed in San Francisco by immigrants who arrived single.* Our sample shows that about 25 percent of the Italian families living in San Francisco in the 1930's were formed in Italy before the first departure of the head of the family; 75 percent were formed either in San Francisco by immigrants who arrived single or in Italy by returnees who later emigrated to San Francisco permanently. Few San Francisco Italian families were formed in other parts of the United States.[28]

There was a noticeable difference in marital status between Italians and immigrants of other nationalities. Over 40 percent of the non-Italians were married at first arrival. Moreover, there was a difference between northern and southern Italians, more northerners being married at first arrival.† These two differences suggest an inverse correlation between being married and return migration. Single immigrants were more likely to return than immigrants who were married at first arrival. And conversely, return migration was less common among those immigrant groups with large numbers married. As the prefetto of Cosenza wrote: "Almost all emigrants are single and return within three to five years to marry and settle down in the province. Unfortunately, this plan does not work out in most cases."[29] And the prefetto of Palermo: "Almost all emigrants are single and very young. Spending a few years overseas before marriage seems to have become almost a standard practice in many communities of this province."[30]

On the average, married non-Italians arrived in San Francisco nine years after marriage, and Italians four years after marriage. There were differences among Italian groups also. Immigrants from cities were more likely to arrive sooner after marriage than those from small agrarian communities or fishing villages. Immigrants

*The families established by immigrants who returned to Italy to marry and then came back to San Francisco are classified with the families established in San Francisco.

†For instance, naturalization records show that 29 percent of the immigrants from Sestri Levante, 26 percent from Lorsica, 25 percent from Porcari and Lucca, and 30 percent from Genoa were married. On the other hand, only 15 percent of the immigrants from Palermo, Santa Flavia, and Trabia, and 20 percent of those from Verbicaro, were married.

from Genoa and Palermo arrived about two years after marriage; those from Porcari, Lucca, Verbicaro, and Trabia four years after marriage; and those from Sestri Levante and Lorsica six years after marriage.

There was another difference between Italians and other immigrants: seven out of every ten non-Italians who were married at first arrival took their wives and children along, whereas only one out of four Italians did the same thing. These figures clearly show that most San Francisco Italians were either single or married men without families at first arrival; the immigrants arriving with their families were less than 10 percent of the total Italian immigrant population.[31]

The wives who did not arrive in San Francisco with their husbands usually came three to nine years later. On this score also there were differences between Italians and other immigrants. The wives of non-Italians were likely to join their husbands two to three years after the arrival of their husbands; wives of southern Italians about five years after; and wives of northern Italians six to seven years after.[32] Few emigrants-to-be—either Italians or others—departed immediately after marriage.

Married emigrants departing from large Italian cities typically left about two years after marriage; emigrants from smaller communities left after more than two years. It is possible that Italians living in cities had more information about employment opportunities overseas, and that they were more willing to uproot themselves from their communities than rural people. As for the striking difference between Italians and other immigrants in the number of years between marriage and emigration, the different goals of Italians and non-Italians provide a possible explanation. To most non-Italians, emigration implied permanent relocation overseas, and this was a momentous decision. But few Italians emigrated permanently the very first time they crossed the Atlantic. Thus it was easier for Italians to decide to leave, since their departure was to be only temporary.

We can offer several arguments to explain why married Italians were unlikely to take their wives along at first departure. Some married Italians considered first emigration exploratory, before reaching a final decision involving their families; some wanted to smooth the transition by preparing a place for wives and children; and some probably regarded emigration as only a temporary necessity in which their families should never get involved. Interviews with older San Francisco Italians show that most married Italians emigrated without their families either because they did not want to stay in San Francisco permanently or because they were uncertain about what to do. Angelo Marini, for instance, joined his father in San Francisco in 1922 with his mother and two sisters. His father had left the first time in 1919, intending to return to Italy "as most people did in those days, married or single." Another San Franciscan said his father sailed back and forth twice before asking his family to come.[33]

Some historians argue that financial considerations were what convinced Italians with wives and children in Italy to bring them to San Francisco. Few immigrants were able to take home the fortune they had hoped, and their wounded pride would not let them show up in their towns with only modest savings. The way out was to leave with the whole family. Moreover, inflation made it increasingly difficult to get established in Italy. Also, it was financially advantageous for immigrants to have their families join them and be put to work in the United States, rather than to leave them in Italy and return home periodically.[34]

Financial considerations, however, were not the only reasons that married immigrants asked their wives and children to join them. There was also a fear of what might happen to families in Italy. Many Italians cited the separation of families brought about by emigration as the cause of family and social problems. The prefetto of Palermo, for instance, reported that crimes of passion committed by returned husbands were increasing.[35] "Because of the separation of husbands and wives," another writer reported, "illegitimate children, child murders, and abortions are on the increase, as well as acts of vengeance committed by wronged husbands."[36] In Calabria sensational crimes were reported: wives who poisoned children they had had by other men before their husbands returned from America, and returnees who entered their native towns at night to stab wives and lovers.[37] As one writer put it: "Homecoming was often a tragedy, as if it had not been bad enough to go to America. . . . And homecoming was sometimes put off, and in the end abandoned, because of a tragedy which could not be faced."[38] Many married immigrants sent for their families out of fear of the consequences of a long separation.[39]

Two additional factors may help to explain why southerners sent for their families earlier than northerners. First, southerners were more sexually jealous, and the frequency and rapidity of family follow-up migration was prompted by suspicion and possessiveness.* And second, southerners were less culturally prepared to establish strong social relations outside the nuclear family household. Thus, for them, the reuniting of the family was more important than for northerners.[40]

Many married immigrants had children. Of all non-Italians who were married at the time of arrival in San Francisco, only about 10 percent had children; some arrived with their father and others remained in Europe. But about 25 percent of the northern Italian immigrants and 65 percent of the southerners had children at the time of first arrival. This difference between northerners and southerners is all the more striking if we recall that for southerners the time between marriage and emigration was shorter than for northerners. One might suspect that southern couples had children immediately after marriage and northern couples waited. But statistics do not support this hypothesis: in 1902, for instance, both in the north and in the south, about two-thirds of the newly married couples had their first child within a year.[41]

What we have seen shows that both in the north and in the south married men without children were more likely to emigrate than men with children. A general theory correlating family size and individual mobility explains why married men without children were more likely to emigrate. In modern societies, children are likely to be a hindrance to geographically and occupationally mobile people. Fertility rates, in fact, generally decline in urban and industrial environments.[42] It is impossible to determine, however, whether emigrants-to-be avoided having children because they were thinking about emigration, or whether it so happened that couples with no children were the more likely to emigrate when the opportunity arose.

Most immigrants who were single at first arrival eventually married. Some did not, however. In San Francisco about 40 percent of the non-Italians single at first arrival had not married by the time they were naturalized. For Italians, the percentage was about 15.†

*Meyriat, *La Calabrie*, p. 205. In 1909 the consul in San Francisco, noting that several southern Italians had sent for their families though they could ill afford it, remarked: "Northerners strongly disapprove of this irresponsible behavior. A number of southern families are supported by public charity, since their heads have no steady income." RC, SF 17.ii.1909.

†In the nation at large, the 1920 census showed only 25 percent of the foreign-born males age sixteen and older were not married. A possible reason for the higher percentage of unmarried immigrants in San Francisco was the shortage of marriage-

Family life seems to have been more important to Italians than to immigrants of other nationalities. Among Italian groups there were differences. Northerners were more likely to be single than southerners. About 20 percent of the immigrants from Lorsica and Sestri Levante and 15 percent of those from Porcari, Lucca, and Genoa were single at the time of naturalization; only 7 percent of the immigrants from the southern communities fell into this category. The correlation between marital status and occupational distribution shows that people in the professions and manufacturing were more likely to be single than those in domestic services.[43]

Italian censuses show that in Italy too there were more single adults in the north than in the south. In 1881, for instance, in the circondario of Paola (the area of Verbicaro) about 80 percent of the people in the age group 30–35 were married; and in the circondario of Palermo (the city of Palermo and Santa Flavia), 75 percent. On the other hand, the percentage declines to 70 in the circondario of Lucca, and to 65 in that of Chiavari (the area of Lorsica and Sestri Levante). The circondari of Chiavari and Paola each had about 6,500 people aged 30 to 35 in 1881; but there were slightly under 1,000 single people in Paola, and more than 1,500 in Chiavari.[44] Clearly, people were more likely to be married in the south than in the north, and this pattern persisted in San Francisco.

What about single women in San Francisco? Since the sex ratio was so unbalanced, we would expect few women to remain single, and statistics bear that out. In the United States in 1920 about 28 percent of the native-born-of-native-parents females fifteen years of age or older were single; this was true of only 14 percent of the foreign-born in the same age group.[45] In San Francisco, 8 percent of the northern Italian females fifteen years of age or older were single, and only 5 percent of the southern women.[46]

New Families in San Francisco

In San Francisco single Italian immigrants were very young, most between the ages of 16 and 25 at first arrival. There were noticeable

able females in the city. See *Immigrants and Their Children*, U.S. [18], p. 215. There was also a substantial difference between Italian immigrants and native-born-of-native-parents. About 35 percent of the native-born-of-native-parents aged sixteen and older were single in 1920, but only 15 percent of the Italians in the same age group. This difference between Italians and native-born-of-native-parents is even more surprising in view of the shortage of Italian women in America and the high percentage of Italian men marrying Italian women. The sex imbalance among Italians was the highest of any immigrant group in San Francisco; U.S. [9], 2:246.

differences between Italians and other immigrants. The mean age for non-Italians was 24, and that for Italians slightly over 20. There were also differences among non-Italians; for instance, about 35 percent of all British immigrants were over age 30 and less than 15 percent of Irish immigrants. Italians as a group were the youngest to arrive in San Francisco.

Single immigrants from the Italian south were likely to be younger than single immigrants from the north; 25 percent of the single southerners were under the age of 18.* How could southern Italian parents allow children to leave at such a young age? Social scientists have argued that in the south boys were trained to be independent at an early age as much as women were trained to be dependent; thus, the departure of a 17- or 18-year-old boy was socially acceptable. Interviews I had with San Francisco Italians revealed that some of the young immigrants arrived with relatives. An Italian from Trabia, for example, told me that he had come to San Francisco at 17 with a cousin a year younger, and both with a 35-year-old uncle.[47]

Three out of four immigrants who were single at first arrival married between 1911 and 1930, and most marriages occurred between 1920 and 1929. The 1920's were a relatively prosperous decade for the San Francisco Italians. The First World War increased job opportunities and lowered unemployment. Moreover, the war almost completely ended Italian immigration to San Francisco, which meant that from 6,000 to 10,000 potential Italian immigrants did not come. In addition, many young Italians left the United States and joined the Italian army, which also eased the pressure on the labor market. The postwar years were a time of social and economic dislocation in Italy. Many immigrants who were still undecided about whether to return to Italy decided to stay and get married. Finally, the National Origins Act of 1924 virtually ended Italian emigration to the United States, which permanently eliminated the pressure on the San Francisco labor market of one to two thousand new Italians each year. All these events made it easier for those Italians who had settled down in San Francisco to form their own families.

Marriage implies a degree of economic stability that immigrants

*About 40 percent of the immigrants from Genoa, Lorsica, Capannori, Sestri Levante, and Lucca were within the age bracket 21–25, as against only 25 percent from the southern communities. On the other hand, around 35 percent of the immigrants from the southern communes fell into the 16–20 bracket, but only 20 percent of the immigrants from the north.

generally did not have upon arrival. Our sample shows that only a small number of Italians married within the first three years of residence in San Francisco. Most of them married between four and ten years after arrival, with the greatest number between five and seven years. Our sample also reveals that whereas less than 10 percent of the immigrants who arrived from 1901 to 1910 married within the first three years of residence in San Francisco, slightly over 20 percent of those who arrived from 1911 to 1920 married within three years.[48]

In the discussion of occupational distribution in San Francisco, it was pointed out that the immigrants of the 1911–20 decade, unlike those of the 1900's, tended to be the children of landowners, or people engaged in manufacturing and trade, and of literate fathers. Thus the immigrants who arrived in the 1910's had economic and social advantages that probably brought them financial security sooner and allowed them to marry earlier. In addition, as we saw, the desire to return to Italy was stronger among immigrants arriving during the first decade of the century than among later ones.[49] Thus the earlier immigrants might have delayed marrying either because it would make returning to Italy more difficult or because they planned to marry in Italy.

By modern standards, San Francisco Italians married late. The mean age at marriage for men was 28, and for women 23. For both, however, the standard deviation was 7.5, which indicates that many immigrants married at a younger or older age. The difference between Italians and other immigrants was significant: non-Italians married at 31 years of age.[50] Italians arrived in San Francisco at a considerably younger age than other immigrants, and achieved financial security at a younger age.

Italian women were considerably younger than men at marriage. About 45 percent of the women were under 20 when they married. Southern women tended more than northern women to marry under the age of 20: 70 percent of the women from Trabia, 60 percent from Palermo and Verbicaro, and 50 percent from Santa Flavia, as against only 25 percent from Genoa and Lucca and 35 percent from Lorsica and Sestri Levante. For non-Italian women the mean age at marriage was slightly over 27 years. The striking difference between Italian women and other immigrant women was possibly the result of the unbalanced sex ratio among San Francisco Italians, which made Italian women much in demand.

In general, the age at which Italian men married was not affected by the immigrants' occupations. The mean age at marriage for men in agriculture, domestic services, trade, and manufacturing was about the same as that for the entire group. Only two groups married later: professionals, at age 31, and fishermen, at age 33. Professional people probably delayed marrying because of the demands of their careers. And fishermen were a group set apart from the Italian community, as will be seen; besides, there were few Italian women in the city, and fishermen showed the strongest tendency to marry Italian women. On the other hand, the Italian women's occupations affected the age at which they married. Housekeepers or women without an occupation married younger than women with an occupation. For example, women from Porcari married at 24; but those without an occupation were generally younger, and those in manufacturing and trade older. And among women from Santa Flavia the mean age at marriage was 20; but women without an occupation married at 19, and those with jobs married at 23.

If San Francisco Italian men of the 1920's seem to have married late, they nevertheless married at exactly the same age as men in Italy. In the early 1920's men in Italy married on the average at age 28, as in San Francisco. Marrying in one's late twenties had been common in Italy at least since the early 1880's.[51] In Italy women generally married at an older age than women in San Francisco; the mean age in Italy was between 24 and 25 years. And in Italy northern women married at a younger age than southern women. In 1922 women married between 23 and 24 years of age in the north and between 24 and 25 in the south, a pattern that also had not changed since the 1880's. Thus San Francisco Italian men married at about the same age as their contemporaries in Italy, whereas San Francisco women married considerably younger than those in Italy. Notwithstanding the obvious social dislocation caused by immigration, then, San Francisco Italian men did not delay entering marriage. But Italian women, who were greatly outnumbered by men in San Francisco, married at a younger age than in Italy.[52]

The reason that southern women in San Francisco married earlier than northern women may be that proportionally fewer women migrated from the south than from the north. In 1911, for instance, out of 6,000 emigrants leaving the province of Genoa, 25 percent were women. But out of 14,000 emigrants who left the province of Cosenza the same year, only 13 percent were women.[53] In 1911 in the circondario of Paola (the Verbicaro area) the sex ratio in the 30–35 age group was 65 women to 35 men, whereas in the circondario of Chiavari (Lorsica and Sestri Levante) the ratio was 55 to 45.[54] Thus southern women may have married younger in San Francisco because there were relatively fewer of them, and correspondingly more opportunities for marriage.

A Break with the Past

Of the San Francisco Italians who were single at first arrival, some married in San Francisco and others returned to Italy for their marriage. Young immigrants do not seem to have had a burning desire to marry in their native communes. "In the past," the mayor of Trabia wrote, "children whose marriage was opposed by their parents eloped; now they leave for the Americas."[55] The prefetto of Genoa reported that the emigrants to the United States were more likely to return to Italy for their wedding than those who went to South America. But, he added, "most do not return from either continent. The cost of the journey is not the only reason. The emigrants want to avoid parental control in marriage."[56] Both in the north and in the south, in fact, marriages were either prearranged or, in the more liberal places, at least had parental consent.[57] Few San Francisco Italians I spoke to were willing to discuss the circumstances of their marriage. Among those who were willing, however, an immigrant from Trabia related that his father had expected him to return to Italy to get married, and indeed threatened to disown him if he married in San Francisco. But the son, afraid that his father would force him to marry a woman not of his choosing, married in San Francisco.[58]

About one of every four Italians returned to his native town for marriage. Most of the others married in San Francisco, and a small number married elsewhere in the United States. Immigrants of other nationalities were quite different: only 2 percent returned to their native town, and about one-half married in other states of the union than California. The low percentage of non-Italians returning to Europe to marry shows that most of them had made a clear break with their past when they emigrated. Moreover, non-Italians were older than Italians on arrival and at marriage, and thus probably more independent. The fact that about half of the non-Italians married in other parts of the country before settling in San Francisco shows that they came to San Francisco, not in a process of chain migration directly from Europe, but in a series of moves, with San Francisco a stop, in the United States. In general, the marriage pattern of non-Italians indicates that they had weaker ties with the Old World than Italians did.

Among Italian regional groups southerners were less likely to return to Italy to marry than northerners. From 15 to 20 percent of the southern immigrants returned, whereas almost 30 percent of those from Lucca and Porcari and 35 percent of those from Lorsica and Sestri Levante returned. These are puzzling figures: as we saw earlier, return migration was generally greater among southerners than northerners. Lacking evidence, we can speculate about why southerners returned to Italy for marriage less than northerners.[59]

Family and cultural patterns may be important in explaining these differences. In the south, the constant competition to secure the best land available affected family relations, especially between fathers and sons. Young men coming of age competed to get land contracts as the only way to establish a family of their own, since southern children never remained with their parents after marriage. This competition created tension between parents and children; possibly parents used their authority to control the marriage of their children so as to minimize the potential competition from them. In the north, on the other hand, it was common for children to live and work with their parents after their marriage. Coming of age did not necessarily imply breaking away from one's parents and competing with one's father. Northerners, therefore, may have been more likely to return to Italy because for them marriage was less of a break with the family than in the south.

Following Tradition

It is well-established that of all national immigrant groups Italians showed the strongest tendency to marry within their own national group.* In addition, our San Francisco sample shows that almost 65 percent of the male immigrants from the nine Italian groups married Italian women from their own commune, with some differences between northerners and southerners. Endogamous marriages—that is, marriages within the group—were more common among southerners; from 65 to 70 percent of the immigrants from Trabia, Verbicaro, and Santa Flavia married women from their own town. Among northerners, about 50 percent of the immigrants from Sestri Levante, Lorsica, and Porcari married women

*In 1920, for instance, 97 percent of the married Italian men in the United States had Italian wives. The percentage of German men married within their group was 42, of Irish 62, and of immigrant men as a whole 79. Italian women were less likely to marry Italian men: 82 percent of the Italian women married Italian men. In the other groups, 70 percent of the Irish women and 21 percent of the Germans married men of their own nationality. *Immigrants and Their Children*, U.S. [18], pp. 234–35.

from their own town. Immigrants from the cities—Genoa, Palermo, and Lucca—were the least likely to marry women from the same city: less than 45 percent fell into this category. The other immigrants married women born in other parts of Italy, in San Francisco, or in other countries.[60]

Surprisingly, more Italian immigrants married American-born women than married Italian women from other regions. This was more common among southerners than northerners. About 15 percent of the immigrants from Palermo, Santa Flavia, Trabia, and Verbicaro and 10 percent of those from the five northern communities married American-born women.[61] These figures raise the question of whether it was easier for Italians to break down the barriers between them and the American society than those separating regional groups.

Most Italian men who married American-born women had arrived in San Francisco before age twenty or, if older, had come from the cities of Genoa and Palermo. For example, 10 percent of the immigrants from Lorsica in the sample married American-born women; all but three were under the age of nineteen at first arrival. About 11 percent of the immigrants from Sestri Levante married American-born women; all but one had arrived before age twenty. From Porcari, 13 percent of the immigrants married American women: 80 percent had arrived before age twenty. Fifteen percent of the immigrants from Lucca married American women, and 75 percent had arrived before age twenty. From Verbicaro, 17 percent married American women, and 95 percent had arrived before age twenty. With one exception, all the immigrants from Santa Flavia who married American women had arrived before the age of twenty. Genoa and Palermo were exceptions: only about 30 percent of the immigrants from Genoa and 15 percent of those from Palermo who married American women had arrived before age twenty. For the most part, then, it was the immigrants arriving after age twenty or coming from small agrarian communes who married Italian women from their own town.

The immigrants from other nations offer an interesting contrast. About 50 percent of the non-Italian immigrants who married either in San Francisco or elsewhere in the United States before settling in San Francisco married women of their own nationality; but only 5 percent married women from the same town. In fact, even immigrants who arrived in San Francisco as couples were likely to have been from different towns of the same country or from different European countries. Lyall William, for example, was born in Newcastle, England, in 1874, and lived in London until 1912, when he left for Canada. In 1925 he married Jane Wringly, an English woman born in Burnley in 1876, who had lived in Manchester until 1921 and then left for Canada. It was only in 1936 that the couple moved to San Francisco. Andrew Ivanoff was born in Toblosk, Russia, in 1898, left for the United States in 1923 from Tientsin, China, and was living in Seattle in 1925 when he petitioned to become an American citizen. The woman he married in San Francisco had been born in Harbin, China, of Russian parents in 1902, and had arrived in San Francisco in 1926 from Shanghai.[62]

Regardless of these differences between Italians and other immigrants, there was an important similarity. Even non-Italians who married American-born women were likely to have arrived in the United States before age twenty. About 20 percent of the Irish immigrants, for example, married American women, and three out of four had arrived in the United States before reaching age twenty. For both Italians and other immigrants, therefore, exogamous marriage seems to have been a function of age at first arrival.

San Francisco Italo-Americans, too, showed a strong tendency to marry within their ethnic group. From 50 to 60 percent of the Italo-American men married women of Italian parentage. A breakdown of these figures shows a pattern common to all groups, with minor variations. The percentage ranges from 55 to 60 percent for the Italo-Americans from Lorsica, Lucca, Verbicaro, Trabia, and Genoa; and from 50 to 55 percent for the other groups. About 20 percent of the Italo-Americans married women with California-born parents. The remainder married women with parents born either in other states or in foreign countries.[63]

Few Italo-Americans married women of non-Italian background; the highest percentage of immigrants in this category, 25 percent, was for Italo-Americans from Genoa, Palermo, and Lucca. Our sample also shows that second-generation Italians who married American or foreign-born women generally had one non-Italian parent. About 75 percent of the Italo-Americans from Genoa and Trabia, 70 percent of those from Lucca, and 60 to 70 percent of those from the other groups who married women of non-Italian background had at least one non-Italian parent. Second-generation immigrants of other nationalities showed a substantially higher tendency to marry outside their ethnic group: 75 percent of the British-Americans and German-Americans, and 60 percent of the Russian-Americans, fell into this category. A few Italo-Americans married women born in Italy. Surprisingly, Italo-Americans from Genoa and Palermo showed the highest rates of these marriages: 12 percent of those from Palermo and 10 percent of those from Genoa married Italian-born women.[64]

Thus more Italo-Americans married within their own ethnic group than second-generation ethnics of other nationalities. Moreover, fewer Italo-Americans with parents from small agrarian communes married outside the Italo-American group than those from cities. Many Italo-Americans of mixed parentage but with the one Italian parent from a large city like Genoa or Palermo married outside the Italian ethnic group or married an Italian-born woman.

In sum, our sample allows us to draw a profile of those Italo-Americans likely to marry women of non-Italian background and those likely to marry Italo-American women. The former were older, their fathers were either in trade or in manufacturing, and they themselves were either in the professions or in manufacturing. The latter were younger, their fathers were in domestic services and illiterate, and they themselves were either in domestic services or in trade. These distinctions apply to all nine groups. For instance, almost 80 percent of the Italo-Americans from Genoa who married women of non-Italian parentage had literate fathers in trade and manufacturing, and they themselves were either professional people or in manufacturing. Thus there was a direct correlation between socioeconomic status and the rate of exogamous marriage. Exogamous marriages occurred more frequently among Italo-Americans of higher socioeconomic status and with fathers from Italian cities.

Large Italian Families?

Demographers and historians generally accept the theory of demographic transition, which holds that there is an inverse correlation between urbanization and modernization on the one hand and family size on the other. Robert Wells, for instance, argues that "in an urban and industrial environment, children are no longer a benefit, but might be actually detrimental to parental aspiration, and hence fertility declines."[65] Most San Francisco Italians were from small agrarian communities, but were settled in an urban environment and working in nonfarming occupations. We might reasonably expect, therefore, to find a decline in the fertility of San Francisco Italian women and a smaller Italian family in San Francisco than in Italy.

High fertility rates among immigrants in the United States, and especially among Italians, were well publicized in the early twentieth century. The 1920 census showed that the general fertility rates for women from 14 to 49 years of age were 62 per 1,000 for native women and 92 per 1,000 for foreign-born women. The average foreign-born woman had more children than the American-born woman, 4 children each (3.4 alive) for the foreign-born and 3 (2.7 alive) for the American. Italian-born women had the highest number of children: 4.5 (3.8 alive).[66] San Francisco was no exception to the national trend. From the early 1900's, annual reports from the city Public Health Department give the different fertility rates of Italians, other immigrants, and American-born. In 1901, for instance, although Italians were only 6 percent of the city's population, they gave birth to 11 percent of the babies.[67] The 1930 census showed the median size of families with foreign-born heads to be 2.85, that of families with Italian heads 3.45.[68] In our sample the size for non-Italian immigrants is 2.7 and that for Italians 3.6.[69]

But the difference in fertility rates for foreign-born and American-born women was not as wide as the figures seem to indicate. General fertility rates can be misleading unless properly interpreted. The general fertility rate is the number of births occurring in a year per 1,000 women of child-bearing age, without taking into account whether those women are married or not. In a comparison between two groups, therefore, it makes a difference if one group has a substantially higher proportion of single women than another. Immigrant women in the United States were more likely to be married than American women: only 16 percent of the immigrant women were single, as opposed to 28 percent of the American women. And among immigrants, Italians had the lowest percentage of single women. In San Francisco, for instance, only about 6 percent of the Italian women from 14 to 49 years of age were single. Thus high fertility among foreign-born women was the result not so much of greater prolificacy as of the fact that relatively more of them were married.

The high family size reported for Italians is equally misleading. According to the 1930 census, each individual living on his own was a family—the so-called one-person family. Hence the average family size was low for those groups with a larger proportion of one-person families. For instance, in 1930 there were about 8,000 families with a German head and almost 13,000 with an Italian head in San Francisco. But both Germans and Italians had an equal number of one-person families, 1,400; that is, slightly over 10 percent of all Italian families and 17.5 percent of the German families. Obviously, the many one-person German families—and this was also the case with immigrants of other nationalities—lowered the median family size more than for the Italians, who had a smaller proportion of one-person families.

There were other circumstances, however, that affected the actual size of families. The decline in infant mortality among San Francisco Italians was certainly a major change from Italy. In 1920 the mortality rate for infants under the age of four was 174 per 1,000 in Italy and 95 per 1,000 in the United States.[70] In San Francisco, the 1900 census showed, 25 percent of the children of Italian immigrants died before leaving their families, compared with only 12 percent of the children of other immigrants. Apparently, the mortality rate was high among San Francisco Italians. But these figures should be put in perspective. From 1882 to 1922 the mortality rates were substantially higher in Italy than in San Francisco. In 1882 in the province of Cosenza 30 percent of the people who died were under a year old, 51 percent were under the age of five, and 57 percent were under the age of fifteen. In the provinces of Genoa and Lucca the mortality rate was only slightly lower: 25 percent under a year old, 47 percent under five, and 54 percent under fifteen.[71] Over the years, infant mortality did not decline significantly in Italy. In 1912, for instance, over 20 percent of the deaths occurring in the province of Genoa, 28 percent of those in Lucca, 45 percent in Cosenza, and 50 percent in Palermo were of infants under the age of four.[72]

As Table 13 shows, families formed in Italy were generally larger than those formed in the United States. Families formed in Italy averaged 3.3 children, those in San Francisco 2.5. This difference is not found among immigrants of other nationalities; in their case families formed in Europe and in the United States both averaged 1.7 children. As noted, Italians who were already married when they first migrated were generally older than single immigrants. Probably single immigrants who later married in San Francisco, being younger, adopted American standards in family matters more rapidly than Italians who had already started a family before they departed.

Our sample shows a correlation between literacy and family size. Illiterate immigrants who had married and had at least one child born in Italy had the most children in San Francisco, the average varying from 4.2 for Santa Flavia to 3.5 for Lorsica, Porcari, and Palermo. Illiterate immigrants who married in San Francisco had the second-largest number of children, 3.2 on the average. Literate

TABLE 13
Number of Children in 1930's in San Francisco Families Formed in Italy and in the United States

Place of origin	Family formed in: Italy	United States
Genoa	3.0	2.4
Lorsica	3.0	2.5
Sestri Levante	3.4	2.2
Lucca	2.1	2.1
Porcari	2.1	2.1
Verbicaro	3.5	2.7
Santa Flavia	5.2	3.2
Trabia	4.4	2.3
Palermo	6.0	2.4

SOURCE: Naturalization records.

immigrants who had married in Italy had fewer children than the previous two groups, an average of 2.6. Finally, literate immigrants who married in San Francisco had the smallest number of children, an average of 2.3, with a minimum of 2.0 for Porcari and a maximum of 3.6 for Trabia.[73] Thus literacy and illiteracy were more significant in determining the size of families than the time and place of marriage: illiterate immigrants—whether married in Italy or San Francisco—had larger families than literate immigrants. In addition, there was an inverse correlation between socioeconomic status and number of children. Fishermen had the largest families; immigrants in domestic and personal services had the second largest; those in the professions had the smallest families; and those in trade and manufacturing fell somewhere in between.[74]

Regional Differences

Table 14, comparing families in Italy and San Francisco, shows that in San Francisco northern families were considerably smaller than southern. Those from the north ranged from 3.5 for Lucca to 3.8 for Genoa and Lorsica. Those from the south varied from 4.4 for those from Verbicaro and Palermo to 5.2 for those from Trabia. In Italy in 1921, however, northern families were considerably larger than southern; the northern ranged from 4.5 in Genoa to 5.4 in Porcari, and the southern from 3.8 in Santa Flavia and Trabia to 4.6 in Palermo.[75]

A comparison of fertility and crude birthrates in the north and the south fails to explain why northern families in Italy were larger

TABLE 14

Size of Italian Families in Italy and San Francisco

Place of origin	Italy (1921)	San Francisco (1930's)
Genoa	4.5	3.8
Lorsica	4.2	3.8
Sestri Levante	4.5	3.7
Lucca	5.2	3.5
Porcari	5.4	3.6
Verbicaro	3.6	4.4
Santa Flavia	3.8	5.0
Trabia	3.8	5.2
Palermo	4.6	4.4

SOURCE: Italian census of 1921 and naturalization records.

than southern families in Italy. In the years 1900–1902 the general fertility rate for women from age 14 to 44 was 158 per 1,000 in northern Italy and 164 per 1,000 in the south; the gap was only 6 per 1,000 in favor of the south. Two decades later the gap was significantly wider, northern women having a general fertility of 126 per 1,000 and southerners 160.[76] We do not have general fertility rates for our nine communes. But the figures available for the nine communes show the crude birthrate declining in all nine, and more in the north than in the south.[77] It would be unwise, as we have seen, to assume a direct correlation between crude birthrate or general fertility rate on the one hand and family size on the other. But it is nonetheless surprising that families from the north were larger than families from the south.

A comparison of death rates in the north and the south again fails to explain why northern families were larger. In 1922, for example, the death rate was fifteen per 1,000 in the province of Genoa, sixteen in Lucca, seventeen in Palermo, and nineteen in Cosenza.[78] Thus death rates were slightly lower in the north than the south. But a difference of two or four per 1,000 hardly explains why northern families were substantially larger.

A more plausible explanation for this difference between north and south is found in the way the Italian census tallied not families but households. "By family," wrote the director of the 1871 Italian census, "we mean not the group of people related by bonds of marriage and blood—parents and children—but the domestic group, either occasional or stable, of all those people who eat at the same table, work the same tract of land, and assemble around the same fireplace."[79] The Italian censuses of 1861, 1871, and 1881 did not use "family," but rather "house," in tables describing households. And Italian writers on family life at the turn of the century used the word family indiscriminately to describe any sort of household. Coletti, for instance, discussing at length the difference between northern and southern families, and prefetti reporting on family problems, were actually describing households, not families.*

The households of the southwest were typically nuclear, though there were some extended family households, especially among middle-sized landowners.[80] In the north, by contrast, the extended household was the prevailing type, especially in Lucca; households included three generations and even relatives and in-laws. Children in the north did not necessarily leave home when they married, and even married brothers often lived in the same household after their father's death. In such cases, the widow or the oldest unmarried brother became the head of the household. Though the extended household prevailed in the northwest, there were, as in the south, exceptions; nuclear households were often found among laborers.[81]

The difference between northern and southern households was reported and analyzed as early as the 1870's and 1880's. In Tuscany: "Households with the advantage of sharefarming a large farm can afford to let children marry and remain in the paternal household. But if the farm is small the new couple has to find a new farm and a new sharefarming contract."[82] And in Cosenza: "The typical household is formed by parents and children under the age of twenty. When the children reach the age of twenty, they leave to serve in the army. Upon return, they marry and establish a separate household."[83]

Statistics on household composition are unfortunately available only for the four northern communes and not for the five southern ones. In Lorsica records from the 1860's until after the First World War show that 55 percent of the households were three-generation families and 65 percent had relatives and in-laws.[84] The 1881 census also shows about 50 percent of the households with three generations; less than 25 percent had only two generations, and the remaining households were either couples with no children or single people.[85] Households were only slightly different in Sestri Levante:

*That no distinction was made between family and household reflected a characteristic way of thinking in Italy at the time. The basic social unit was not the nuclear family, but the household, whose members shared a house and a common domestic economy. Blood, marriage, and emotional ties were not as central in Italian culture as they are in modern America.

about 40 percent were three-generational, and slightly over half had relatives or in-laws.[86]

As for Lucca and Porcari, I was able to locate the actual records of about half the immigrants to San Francisco from the two communes. Again we find evidence that northern households were mainly extended. About 40 percent of these immigrants came from households in which two or more married brothers lived in the same house, and about 65 percent had had in-laws or relatives in the house.[87] The Arrighi household from Tampagnano di Lunata, described at the beginning of this chapter on the basis of these records, was typical of the many extended households, from which San Francisco northerners came.

The land tenure system prevalent in each region goes far toward explaining the differences between northern and southern households. In Lucca, for instance, farmers typically worked under long-term contracts, often lasting for generations, and lived on farms that were large enough to require the labor of more than one man. The typical household of this area was composed of more than one nuclear family; that is, composed of several married men working the same tract of land. In Genoa landowners ordinarily did not own enough land to require the labor of more than the owner. But since farming was diversified and demanded a variety of skills, unmarried siblings or aging parents were an asset. Hence households were ordinarily three-generational, but never comprising two married brothers working the same tract of land.

In the south, sharecropping arrangements and other contracts by which landless farmers secured land were generally short-term and non-residential, and required only one adult male per allotment. Often one person had to have more than one contract. This system did not generate a spread of work over seasons, because southern agriculture was more or less monocultural. Tracts of land were often so small that landowners had to take sharecropping contracts to make ends meet. These landowners were not much better off than laborers.[88] And for neither landowners nor laborers was an extended family household feasible or desirable. Extended families were, to be sure, found in the southwest. But they served only as resources for the social network, not as a source of economic strength.

Italians commonly agreed that there was a correlation between land tenure and the composition and size of households. Coletti put it most clearly:

> Italian families are primarily a function of economic interests, and only secondarily of blood and marriage. Southern laborers who do not own land have

very small households. Aging parents are an economic burden, since most people do not own land. Southern households live on the uncertain income of one adult male, who can hardly afford to support his wife and children. On the other hand, small landowners in the north generally have larger households; aging relatives and parents can work in the fields or do chores around the house.[89]

San Francisco Families

In San Francisco, the records of the Italian Welfare Agency show that less than 10 percent of the Italian households were extended families in the years 1920–40, and that about 15 percent had one lodger or more.[90] Lodging was uncommon among Italians, at least in the 1930's. The 1930 census shows that there were 13,000 Italian households in San Francisco, of which 6.5 percent (about 850) had one lodger and an additional 2 percent had two or more lodgers.[91] Consular reports, other accounts, and interviews confirm that few Italians asked their parents to join them in San Francisco. Of 25 Italians I asked whether they had invited their parents, nineteen answered that they never had, three that they had and that the parents had come for a period of time and then returned, and three that their parents had joined them in San Francisco and remained.[92]

Thus we see that northern Italians in San Francisco did not reproduce in San Francisco the extended family households of the Italian northwest. Rather, almost all their households in San Francisco were nuclear families. The substantial decline in the size of northern households in the transition from Italy to San Francisco, as shown in Table 14, does not signify a drop in the general fertility rate of northern women, but simply a change from extended family households to nuclear family households.

Several factors can explain why southern nuclear family households were larger in San Francisco than in Italy. As already seen, infant mortality was significantly lower in San Francisco than in Italy. And the literacy rate for southerners was lower in San Francisco than in Italy. About 40 percent of the immigrants from Verbicaro and Santa Flavia and 45 percent of those from Trabia were illiterate at the time of marriage; but in Verbicaro itself in 1922 the rate was only 25 percent, and in Trabia and Santa Flavia about 30 percent.[93] Illiterate immigrants, as we saw, had more children than literate. In addition, the better nutrition and health care available in San Francisco raised the fecundity of southern women, and this might have increased their general fertility.

There was also a cultural reason why southern families were

larger in San Francisco than in Italy: extended family households enjoyed social prestige in southern Italy. As a southern writer remarked: "Only middle-sized landowners can afford large families."[94] Caputo wrote that to have a large family was the dream of every peasant, but that few could afford it.[95] Possibly the large families southerners raised in San Francisco, with its higher standard of living, were a delayed fulfillment of cultural aspirations common in the Italian southwest at the turn of the century.

The increased size of southern families in San Francisco brings into question the theory of a demographic transition when people move from a rural to an urban environment. And what happened with southerners in San Francisco, although uncommon, was not unique.[96] The theory should be qualified, since urbanization and industrialization do not necessarily bring about smaller nuclear families. The crucial point is not the transition from rural to urban life, but the way people perceive the transition. As sociologists have shown, almost all people who move from a rural to an urban setting consider a large family detrimental to personal aspirations.[97] But some may reach the opposite conclusion: since city jobs provide a higher income than farming, those to whom a large family is important can use their higher wages to raise a large family. When they move to the city, they take advantage of new opportunities to realize aspirations that remained from agrarian life.[98]

The Quality of Family Life

Social scientists who studied families in Italy at the time of mass emigration and more recently have generally seen Italian families as stable and bound together by strong emotional ties. In a controversial study, Edward Banfield argued that among southern Italians "adults hardly may be said to have an individuality apart from the family. They exist not as Egos but as parents."[99] Italians in Chicago established few social organizations, Nelli explained, because such organizations were not needed; "strong family ties ensured aid in time of need."[100] McLaughlin argued that among Italians in Buffalo, families "provided emotional, practical, and financial support during emigration and after."[101] Only a few have challenged this view of the close Italian family; one study, for instance, argued that defense mechanisms stemming from feelings of inadequacy were strong among southern Italians, and "insulated individuals within their own families."[102]

Regardless of how close Italian families might have been in Italy, some instability was bound to come out of a process involving the transatlantic migration of millions of people, some single and some married without families, and their adjustment to a different culture. Though some Italians went through separation and divorce in America, the rate was lower than for other immigrants. And there were clear regional variations. Our sample shows that the divorced and separated made up less than 1 percent of the northerners, whereas among southerners the rate was 9 percent for Verbicaro, 6 percent for Trabia and Santa Flavia, and 4 percent for Palermo. For immigrants of other nationalities the figures were much higher: overall about 20 percent either separated or divorced.

There is no direct evidence to explain why more southern families ended in divorce than northern. A plausible answer, however, comes from the socioeconomic structure of Italy. The southern society was one of individualism, which had its roots in the competition among farmers. That individualism magnified the importance of the nuclear family and made extra-familial relationships appear potentially dangerous. The family, and not the clan or the community, became the main refuge from a harsh society.

The family-centered culture of the south helps to explain the position of women. In a social context where the average southern man constantly felt powerless, the conquest and the possession of a woman gave a sense of authority. Many have observed that in the south a woman was appreciated by a man as an object under his total control; this attitude was at the heart of the sexual jealousy and the seclusion of women in southern Italy. As Jean Meyriat observed: "To possess a woman is the only way in which a man can exercise his power."[103] Emigration offered southern men a broad and unprecedented range of economic opportunities. Family life, the conquest and possession of a woman, and the role of father became less important. Moreover, it was easier to give vent to frustration in the New World than in Italy.

In the northwest, in contrast, the land tenure system based on small ownership and sharefarming created a less individualistic society. Extra-familial organizations offered men a variety of social situations in which to express themselves. Sexual jealousy and the seclusion of women were less common in the northwest; in fact, young single women were allowed to follow seasonal work as it shifted from district to district. Emigration certainly created some instability and tension in this society. But the impact was less because family life had not been all-important and other institutions offered alternative outlets.

Though family problems among Italians rarely ended in divorce or legal separation, practical separation was common. The usual reasons were heavy drinking, physical abuse of the wife, unwillingness to support a dependent wife and children, and insanity. Separation was not necessarily final; there were numerous cases of families reunited after a trial separation. In a sample of 300 families helped by the San Francisco Italian Welfare Agency in the 1920's and 1930's, 13 percent went through a period of separation, which in a few cases ended in divorce. The highest number of separations occurred in the early 1930's, the first years of the depression; and most followed a common pattern: loss of job or reduction in wages, heavy drinking and physical abuse of the wife and children, and finally—but less often—mental problems and institutionalization of the husband.[104]

12. North Beach family outing, Fourth of July, 1914. Most San Francisco families achieved a level of material success far beyond what they had known in Italy. Yet there were lingering doubts about the true value of the new economic prosperity. Many immigrants, looking backwards, idealized the picture of family life in Italy, and felt that emigration and life in America had undermined the closeness and stability of the family.

Two Italian novels on San Francisco themes, Paolo Pallavicini's *Tutto il Dolore, Tutto l'Amore* and Giovanni Pancrazi's *L'Etrusca all'Ovest*, deal with the problem of family instability. Pallavicini, a reporter for *L'Italia* in San Francisco, reached a large audience in the city with his novels, which were serialized in his newspaper. Pancrazi, who wrote in Italy, had lived in San Francisco around the turn of the century.[105] Both novels celebrate family life in Italy. A nostalgic tone emerges every time immigrants face the problems of life in San Francisco. "Family life in the native village," states one of Pancrazi's characters, "is the most cherished dream of those forced to leave their country because of need." And a character in Pallavicini's novel exclaims: "Only in Italy can family life exist in all its beauty."[106] Emigration broke that enchanted dream; but as the authors argue, there was a bright side to it, since emigration was an opportunity to save money to help one's family in Italy.[107]

That opportunity, however, carried a destructive potential: the seduction of making money for its own sake could lead immigrants to forget family obligations. Both novels argue that an unbridled commitment to financial success leads to family instability. In Pallavicini's novel, Velia, the wife of Andrea, a modest Italian merchant in San Francisco, leaves her husband for Albert, a successful New York stockbroker. Although Italian, Albert has cut himself off from everything Italian and changed his last name to Johnson. Velia follows Albert to New York; there she abandons her two children, who become street musicians. Andrea, a faithful husband, is determined to bring his family back together. After years of searching, in San Francisco, New Orleans, and New York, he finally encounters his children in New York and makes Velia aware of his presence. His arrival triggers powerful emotions in Albert, who commits suicide, and in Velia, who goes insane. Finally, Andrea returns to his native town in northern Italy with his children. There, at Christmas, he is reached by a penitent Velia, who dies on arriving at the threshold of the family house.

Pancrazi's historical novel, based on a real case, tells the story of Basile Ghiotto, a laborer from Corsagna in the province of Lucca who emigrated in the 1860's. Ghiotto comes to America with his brother-in-law Gino, who has already spent two years in Great Britain. When Gino dies in New York, the victim of an industrial accident, Ghiotto takes off for California. From that day, his family does not hear from him. But Jole, Ghiotto's oldest daughter, crosses the Atlantic in search of him. In the meantime, Ghiotto tries and fails in the mines of California, and then joins a fishing expedition to

Alaska. Jole meets her father in San Francisco as he returns. Ghiotto is sorry and promises to return to Italy after a period of time during which he and Jole will work to save money for the trip back and for the family. Jole finds work as a servant for a wealthy Canadian family in San Francisco, and Ghiotto joins other Italian fishermen.

As Jole keeps pressing her father to return, Ghiotto delays, hoping that some unforeseen event will allow him to stay. One day he is kidnapped from a bar on the Barbary Coast and forced to join another Alaska fishing expedition. Jole again meets him when he returns, now penniless and sick; he dies in a shack near the piers of San Francisco. Jole's perseverance is finally rewarded: the oldest son of the Canadian family marries her, and Jole's mother and sister join the young couple in San Francisco. According to the author, Ghiotto failed because money became more important to him than family life; Jole was rewarded because she was faithful to her family obligations.

Albert, Velia, and Ghiotto are not portrayed as villains. They are the victims of money, an almost irresistible attraction for former peasants raised in poverty. There is a pervasive sense of rural fatalism in both Pallavicini and Pancrazi: emigration is a necessity brought about by uncontrollable events, emigrants pursue economic opportunities almost without moral restraints, and in the end families break apart because of the consuming desire for money.[108] The two authors had a message for San Francisco Italians: curb your appetite for money or it will destroy your family; and settle in the country, away from the allurements of money and city ways.[109] Pallavicini devotes several pages to the contrast between country life and city life. He prefers the Santa Cruz Mountains in California to San Francisco.* The two novels pose a basic dilemma the San Francisco Italians faced: they went to the United States to make money, and money often seemed to bring problems. And the immigrants'

***Tutto il Dolore*, pp. 313–15. A recent booklet by a California Italian describes a visit he and his parents, then living in Newton, California, made to North Beach when he was twelve. His parents were puzzled by the changed attitudes of their San Francisco friends, one dying, toward family matters. "My parents were silent for a while, as we waited for the car. Then, inside the car, my father said: 'I cannot believe what money has done to him and to his family. He can talk only about money. Even his family is not important to him.' And my mother, to console him, replied: 'It is sickness. Everybody is sick in this city. This city destroys people and families alike.' " Gardella, *Reminiscences*, p. 54.

idealization of family life in Italy only sharpened their awareness of family problems in San Francisco.

Despite the immigrants' glowing memories, however, there is evidence that Italian family life was far from ideal, and that immigration did not create instability and family problems, but simply heightened them. Emigration, in fact, often seems to have offered married men an escape from family responsibilities, as can be seen in both Italy and San Francisco. Caputo, in a housing survey of Cosenza in 1908, found that a number of families had been abandoned by their heads, who had left either for overseas or for other regions of Italy. In 1903 the prefetto of Palermo lamented that an increasing number of emigrants in the United States had not written to their families in years.[110] This sort of abandonment had been occurring even before mass emigration to the Americas, as breadwinners migrated to other regions of Italy. But overseas migration broadened the possibilities for family abandonment. "Emigration," wrote Caputo, "has created opportunities not only for those who want to make money, but also for those who want to evade family responsibilities."*

Distant California provided an ideal place for such escape. In the 1860's and 1870's the Italian consul in San Francisco told how efforts to gather information on the whereabouts of Italians at the request of families often uncovered that immigrants had established new families. In 1864, for instance, Cerruti was asked to inquire about Carlo Caprile, an immigrant from Fontanabuona, province of Genoa, who had not written his wife since 1855. After several months an Italian from Newton, California, informed the consul that Caprile had an American wife and two children there.[111] Italian newspapers in San Francisco sometimes published lists of immigrants sought by Italian families and believed to be in northern California.[112] Articles in *L'Italia* at the turn of the century revealed a concern over married men abandoning their families in Italy and settling in San Francisco. In 1903 San Francisco Italians were reminded that "to forget wives and children in Italy is a terrible crime."[113]

*De Nobili wrote: "Emigration has contributed to the increase in the number of husbands abandoning wives and children and never being heard of again." A Calabrian lawyer told him: "It does not take great imagination to understand what happens to families in a province where about 50,000 wives do not live with the husband to whom they have been married for only a short time." Taruffi et al., *La Questione Agraria*, pp. 864, 866.

Desertion by husbands was not the only threat to the Italian family. A physician from Cosenza testified that infidelity was common among emigrants' wives who had been married only a few months or a few years.[114] In southern Italy, moreover, many young men married and left the same day, without having consummated their marriage. They expected, of course, to find a virgin when they returned. The reality did not match the expectations all the time. Cyriax wrote that in Campià "wives left behind invariably got into trouble: they were not to be trusted."[115] Apparently, this sort of disruption of families was more common in the south than in the north. There are, of course, no divorce statistics in Italy, since divorce was not legalized until 1976. But illegitimacy was twice as frequent in the south as in the north. In 1902, for instance, the illegitimacy rate was 28 per 1,000 newborns in the province of Genoa and 45 per 1,000 in Cosenza.[116] In 1912 the rate was 17 per 1,000 in Genoa and 33 per 1,000 in Cosenza.[117]

Contemporaries who regarded the family in Lucca and Genoa as more stable and united than that in the south generally ascribed this difference to the land tenure system in the north. As a Genoese wrote in the 1870's, "There is a closeness in our families, mostly because the members work the land together."[118] "The main reason for family stability," the mayor of Lorsica wrote, "is that the families jointly work the land they own or rent."[119] The prefetto of Lucca complained that family closeness was undermined by emigration. "There is a fundamental soundness in our families as long as they work the land together."[120] In Genoa the departure of one member of the family for America was usually resisted by others as a "threat to family stability."[121] And Carlo Mazzini noted that in Lucca "the authority of the father is still the foundation of family stability. Nothing happens without his consent. His authority is almost absolute, especially if he owns land."[122]

The picture of the southern family was rather different. The prefetto of Palermo reported that southern "families are not close. Poor economic conditions and the fact that people marry at a very young age are the usual explanations I hear for the lack of closeness. But I suspect another reason: most heads of families are laborers forced to be away from their families from sunrise to sunset. Families lack a center of interest, since most families do not own land."[123] "Love is a scarce commodity in many families," wrote a Sicilian. "There are fathers actively promoting the prostitution of their sons and daughters. Incest, prostitution, and illegitimacy have reached startling proportions in our society."[124] "Concubinage, adultery, and prostitution are common among peasants," wrote the prefetto of Palermo. "Wives and children are very independent of husbands and fathers, whose real control over their families is rather poor."*

From all this we see that the immigrants' concern about family life in San Francisco, and their placing of blame for the breakdown of the family on pressures created by immigration, were almost certainly exaggerated. To immigrants with golden memories of family life in Italy, family problems in San Francisco had to be attributed to the corrupting influence of America. But in reality family life was far from idyllic in Italy, especially in the south. And although immigration certainly brought new problems for families, its main effect was simply to heighten problems that already existed.

Social scientists have for a long time indulged in a depiction of Italian families as close and stable; this has become almost a stereotype. On the surface, southern families did indeed have all the signs of this: male possessiveness and jealousy, the seclusion of women, strong paternal authority. Family ties were only apparently strong, however, and this was largely because southerners had no other social outlet besides the family. In the south, as Meyriat said, the family was the social institution of last resort.

Emigration provided a set of circumstances and created a sequence of pressures under which the family isolated from broader social ties was bound to break. This message was illustrated by the movie *The Godfather, Part Two*: the family's attempt to keep unto itself and avoid interaction with the larger society ended in self-destruction, regardless of how strong the family ties seemed to be. Immigration, by opening up other social alternatives, revealed the inner weaknesses of the Italian family.

*Damiani, *Sicilia*, pp. 473–74. In the early 1880's a judge from Palermo who had served in several other Italian cities stated: "In no other region of Italy are families in worse condition than in Sicily. There is no love, no affection, no unity, no family life." Concerned people from the island voiced the opinion that the family as an institution was coming to an end (*ibid.*, pp. 369, 475).

CHAPTER 8

Italian Regionalism in San Francisco

THE conclusions reached in the three previous chapters were based on a twofold process of reduction: almost entirely statistical evidence was used; and the immigrants were treated as isolated individuals and groups, with little attention paid to social and economic institutions. These next two chapters use nonstatistical evidence and aim for a broader understanding of the Italian experience in San Francisco. As in previous chapters, the emphasis will be on the ambivalent attitudes of the immigrants, who tried to preserve their traditions in a new environment and at the same time had to be creative in coping with new problems.

In all the experience of the San Francisco Italians, probably the most pivotal period was 1941–43. One of the most revealing documents from those years is a report by a California legislative committee investigating anti-American activities.[1] The report, which included depositions from 35 leading San Francisco Italians, stated that the "spearhead of Fascist activities in California was found to be in San Francisco," and that of all Italian communities in the United States, only that of New York had been the target of more intense propaganda. The San Francisco Italians, the report said, turned to Fascism because American society had unfortunately allowed them to develop into a self-contained and almost self-sufficient ethnic enclave with only superficial ties to the United States.[2]

The committee recommended that leading Italians with strong ties to Fascism be removed from the city, and that Italians in general be made aware of the necessity of their giving their allegiance to the United States. Many followed the recommendation; a flood of Italian immigrants were naturalized between 1943 and 1945, more than in the entire preceding decade. The social transformatio celerated by the war, the defeat of Fascism in Italy, the progre departure from North Beach of the immigrants' children, and aging of the immigrants hastened the Americanization of Italians and brought to a conclusion a century-long historical process.

The period from 1848 to 1943 can be divided into two stages, the first characterized by regionalism, the second by nationalism. During the first stage, from 1848 until the turn of the century, regional loyalties shaped the immigrants' social and economic affairs. During the second stage, from 1916 until the Second World War, national interests emerged that made the old regional loyalties obsolete. Fascism, the most important ideology in this second period, reinforced the developing nationalism. The years from 1900 to 1916 were a time of transition, when social disorganization accompanied mass immigration.

Campanilismo and Regionalism

A number of historians have pointed out that immigrants from southern and eastern Europe who came to the United States at the turn of the century had primarily regional rather than national loyalties. It is possible to make a further distinction, between regionalism and *campanilismo.* Campanilismo is the sense of loyalty and attachment to the traditions of one's commune (literally to the local belltower), rather than to the entire region. Luigi Villari wrote at the turn of the century: "Each little town for many centuries led its own independent life, had its own policy, its own manners and customs, its own artistic development, its own parties, its own aristocracy, bourgeoisie, and working class, and each was a little world unto itself."[3]

The evidence we have already seen in our sample shows that campanilismo was transplanted to San Francisco by the largest groups of immigrants. For instance, almost 70 percent of the men who came from the nine communes married women from the same commune. Campanilismo also survived in the way immigrants settled in San Francisco, closely following the three patterns of geographical distribution common in Italy. Finally, campanilismo helped attract people from the same town into one line of work; the scavengers from Lorsica and the bootblacks from Verbicaro are the outstanding examples.

A larger question is whether campanilismo provided the basis for social and economic life in general. In San Francisco it is unlikely that this happened. "Italians in America," one historian wrote, "were no longer isolated from each other by mountain ranges. Here the barriers were only streets or paper-thin walls of tenement rooms."[4] To this we may add another consideration, that no group from one commune was large enough to create a viable social structure by itself. It is probable that none of the nine groups we are dealing with numbered over 300 families.[5] The evidence suggests this hypothesis: campanilismo provided the basis for personal interaction, whereas regionalism did so for social and economic activity. In the following pages we see how regionalism underlay the first Italian social and economic organizations in San Francisco.

Early Problems

A major problem early Italian immigrants faced was the lack of an educated or powerful group willing to provide leadership in community affairs. In the early 1850's two groups could have played this role: merchants and political refugees. The merchants were wealthy Italians who had left Milan or Genoa after the political turmoil of 1830 and 1848 and cautiously moved their capital to San Francisco. In 1856 Federico Biesta, the acting Sardinian consul in San Francisco (Italy was then still divided), reported that there were seventeen well-known Italian merchants in the city, but that they refused to associate with Italian laborers.[6] In 1864 the Italian consul lamented that most merchants were unwilling to provide leadership and cared only about their business interests.[7]

The political refugees were educated Italians who had left Milan or Genoa after 1830 and 1848. Some of them had lived in Great Britain before coming to the United States. They advocated the political unification of Italy under a republican government—thus they opposed the House of Savoy[8]—and in San Francisco their main concern remained Italian politics. Because of these refugees, Italian political events were hotly debated in San Francisco in the 1850's and 1860's.* The debate became more colorful after 1861, when an

*In November 1867, for instance, when the republicans in San Francisco found out that the king of Italy had sent troops against Garibaldi, who was trying to take Rome in order to make it the capital of the new nation, they organized an attack on the Italian consul and on the French colony, which supported the king of Italy. The consul reported: "The entire thing was orchestrated by two Italian outlaws whose names I will not even mention." The editor of the French newspaper *Le Courier de San Francisco*, a supporter of the king of Italy, was assaulted; the Italian consul barricaded himself in his office while a group of immigrants removed the Savoy coat of

Italian consul—representing the Italian crown—arrived in San Francisco.[9] There is no evidence that political refugees took any part in the organizing of the young community. The consul, not a neutral observer to be sure, commented in 1865: "Obviously, these gentlemen do not intend to stay in San Francisco. They have but one goal, the triumph of republicanism in Italy, after which they will return to Italy as heroes."[10]

The general lack of interest by merchants and political refugees in community organization was a clear indication of the distance between social classes in Italy. Luigi Villari noted that as late as the beginning of the twentieth century there was no communication between the aristocracy, the middle class, and the working people.[11] "The Italian middle class," Villari remarked, "is narrow-minded, more so even than the provincial aristocracy."[12] Businessmen—most were from the Piedmont and Lombardy regions—were well-traveled and curious about economic experiments abroad, but unconcerned about social problems. "Their ideas are limited to their occupation, and they have thought for little else."[13] This social cleavage, both in Italy and in San Francisco, helps explain the difficulties Italians had in immigration and return migration. Emigrants, receiving little guidance in making their decision to leave Italy or to return to their native community, had to rely on chain migration. And equally important, immigrants did not have the leadership of the few members of the middle class who migrated to the Americas. In this context, regional ties assumed a great importance for the mass of Italian immigrants.

A second problem the early San Francisco Italians had was their lack of experience with voluntary organizations. In the Europe of the restoration period following the Congress of Vienna, most governments did not allow voluntary organizations. By the late 1840's, however, networks of mutual aid societies and savings banks had been established in Germany and France. This did not occur in Italy, where freedom of association remained forbidden until the unification of the country.[14] The lack of experience with organizations in Italy had an effect in San Francisco; in 1865 Italians resisted the recruitment efforts of the recently founded Società Italiana di

---

arms from the front of his residence. On Sunday, November 17, while a group of Italian monarchists attended a mass at St. Francis's to show support for the king, the republicans rallied at Du Pont and Broadway to protest the repressive policies of the House of Savoy. See "Eventi Coloniali," *L'Eco della Patria*, 19.xi.1867. (A copy of this San Francisco newspaper can be found in Rome with the correspondence of the Italian consul; RC, SF 21.xi.1867.)

Mutua Beneficenza. The consul reported: "There is a deep distrust of any form of association among Italians. Whatever is organized is automatically suspect." But the Italians needed to organize in order to survive, the consul added.[15]

It was the French immigrants who taught Italians the basics of organization, in effect helping them overcome the two problems of lack of leadership and lack of experience. Throughout the 1850's, a decade of political understanding between France and Italy, the French consul in San Francisco protected the interests of the growing Italian colony; and other influential French people also took an active interest in the Italians.[16] The French seem to have shown Italians both the advantages of having mutual aid societies and the way to go about organizing them. Italians were invited to join the Società Francese di Risparmio e di Mutua Beneficenza (French Savings and Mutual Benefit Society, known by its Italian name as well as its French), which provided financial help in time of sickness and aided in the transfer of immigrants' savings to Europe. Common political interests cemented mutual loyalties, but language was a barrier. To overcome it, the activities of the Società Francese were published in both languages, and the editor of the French newspaper *Le Phare* allowed Italians to buy space in his publication. Some understanding between the two groups seems to have survived even when political events in Europe strained relations between them in San Francisco.[17]

The Mutual Aid Societies

Eventually, Italians established their own societies, though with little success at first. The first Italian society in San Francisco was founded in response to a social problem that became pressing after 1855: sick and impoverished Italians who, after failing in the California mines, sought refuge in the city.[18] As the merchant Nicola Larco wrote,[19] Italians were unwilling even to take care of their own relatives when they got sick: "There are cases of immigrants unwilling to take care of sick brothers."[20] To deal with the problem, Larco founded the Società Italiana di Mutua Beneficenza in 1858. Few Italian immigrants joined the society; only about 15 percent were members by 1865, when the colony already numbered a thousand.[21] With such limited membership, the society could not cope with the problem of the sick ex-miners. The Italian consul had to repatriate many of them, using government funds or charity tickets paid for with money collected in the community.[22]

Ten years after its founding, however, the Società Italiana was booming. It had over a thousand members in 1868 and was contemplating building an Italian hospital in San Francisco.[23] An 1865 consular report suggests a twofold explanation for the change. First, the society began to prosper when it changed its original purpose—probably in 1862—and provided its members with free medical assistance and a decent burial. And second, the society became more regional in its orientation. Larco's Società Italiana had failed because it tried to be a national organization, open to all Italians, at a time when the immigrants did not share a common national identity. Now, membership was restricted to immigrants from Liguria—the two provinces of Genoa and Porto Maurizio. No doubt this helped attract new members. Consul Cerruti wrote: "Immigrants feel comfortable only with people of their region, and refuse to associate with Italians from other regions. Immigrants from Liguria and Tuscany regard each other as people from foreign countries."[24] Indeed, Liguria and Tuscany were independent states until the late 1860's; immigrants who came to San Francisco before then regarded themselves as Ligurians, Tuscans, or Venetians, not as Italians.*

Other societies San Francisco Italians established before the end of the nineteenth century continued to reflect the strong regional loyalty of the immigrants. Most of these societies grouped people from the same region. For example, immigrants from the province of Lucca established the Società di Mutuo Soccorso dei Cavalleggeri di Lucca in 1874; Calabrians founded the Società dei Carabinieri Italiani in 1890; Sicilians started the Società Meridionale at about the same time; Piedmontese founded the Società Piemontese in 1891.[25] The list of San Francisco Italian societies prepared in the late 1890's by the Italian government reads like a survey of the regions of Italy.

With time, these regional groups tended to splinter into various organizations. In some cases the new societies were the outcome of conflict within existing societies. For instance, when in 1868 a group of Genoese did not approve of the way the Società di Mutua Beneficenza had handled the construction of the Italian hospital, they left the organization and formed the Compagnia Garibaldina, a mutual aid society that eventually became the wealthiest in San Francisco.[26]

*The official records of the Italian states, which reported the destination of emigrants, reflect this division of the country. Emigration from Tuscany to Liguria, for instance, is listed as international emigration, along with emigration to France and to the United States.

In 1890 it had 600 members, was capitalized at over $50,000, and operated on a yearly budget of $20,000.[27]

In other cases groups with common economic interests formed new societies. In 1879, for instance, scavengers from the province of Genoa established the Compagnia Carreggiatori. In 1872 truck farmers—also either Genoese or Milanese—established the Società degli Agricoltori e Giardinieri to promote their interests, and fishermen founded the Società dei Pescatori.[28] The bylaws of the societies did not discriminate on the basis of regional origin, but the practice of requiring each applicant to be sponsored by two members maintained the regional character. As the consul noted, "New immigrants are not allowed to join any societies they choose, but only those of their own region."[29]

13. Members of the Scavenger's Protection Association marching in a funeral procession, 1910. By the time this group marched along Columbus Avenue, the role of such mutual aid societies was declining; the problems of mass immigration were more than they could cope with. In the preceding half century, however, they had provided social identity, important services, and a certain degree of security to Italian regional groups.

The division of the Ligurians into several groups was most probably brought about by economic rivalries. But local rivalries of Italian origin played an important role too. Apparently, there was friction between the Ligurians from the coast and those from the hinterland. The consul reported: "Ligurians in general are aggressive in fostering their economic interests. Those from the city of Genoa and the large communities of the coast like Chiavari and Sestri Levante have carried with them the native prejudice that the immigrants from Fontanabuona [a valley in the hinterland] are primitive people."[30] Luigi Villari, among others, noted how "local jealousies are often found to exist between towns separated by a few miles from each other."[31] One of the outstanding rivalries in Italy, for example, was that between Siena and Florence. The battle of Montaperti of 1260, in which the Florentines established their hegemony in Tuscany, was still a popular topic of conversation in the late nineteenth century. It gave the Sienese a pretext for blaming their problems on the hostile attitude of the Florentines. Such local differences were not easily forgotten, even under the pressures of the New World.

It was only in the late 1880's that the immigrants founded societies open to all Italians regardless of regional origin. Some societies were founded by freemasons, like the Loggia Mazzini (1890), the Loggia Volta (1892), and the Loggia Aurora (1897). Others were founded by veterans of the Italian army, like the Veterani e Reduci dell'Esercito (1887) and the Società Indipendente di Mutua Beneficenza (1893). The establishment of these societies, however, did not signal that San Francisco Italians were abandoning regionalism. The societies, in fact, had few members. With the exception of the Loggia Galileo, which had about 250 members, all these societies had fewer than 100 members in 1897: the Veterani e Reduci dell'Esercito had 50; the Indipendente, 61; the Loggia Aurora, 59; and the Loggia Mazzini, 60.[32] According to a consular report of 1893, "Only Italians who served in the army or are better educated choose to belong to societies not restricted to one regional group."[33]

Military service in Italy was a major factor in ending the regionalism of San Francisco Italians. Most of the immigrants fell into one of two groups: men who arrived before age twenty and had to return to Italy for military service; and men who arrived shortly after their tour of duty in the army. Most of those younger than twenty seem to have returned to Italy for their military service and then come to San Francisco again.[34] Thus the lives of most San Francisco Italians were touched in some way by military service. Villari wrote: "Military service helps to weld the union between the different provinces even more firmly, and to break down the barriers of narrow-minded regionalism and particularism."[35]

The mutual aid societies provided free medical assistance, unemployment compensation, and burial. And they did more. They also became the center of social life for immigrants, establishing recreational centers from the outset. Since most immigrants were then either single men or married men without families, they spent the time after work and on the weekends with friends. The more affluent societies invested large sums of money in their centers. The Compagnia Garibaldina and the Compagnia dei Bersaglieri, for instance, took great pride in their halls in the 400 block of Broadway, and other societies could rent the halls for their annual celebrations.[36]

The organizing of social activities was another purpose of the societies. Several societies affected Italian army uniforms, and drilled their members in military arts. These weekly drills entertained Italians and non-Italians alike.[37] The members of the Compagnia Garibaldina would parade down Broadway in their red shirts, reminiscent of Garibaldi's soldiers. The drills of the Compagnia dei Bersaglieri attracted large audiences, since its members wore the uniform that Italians associated with a popular hero of Italian independence—Luciano Lamarmora.*

Societies also became informal placement agencies. Well-established immigrants owning a grocery store or some other independent business, growers in need of fieldworkers, and vegetable wholesalers were expected to help find jobs for newcomers. "As soon as new immigrants arrive," the consul reported, "they join a regional society, and usually they get their first job through the society."[38] New immigrants were urged to join their regional societies as the best way to find a job.[39]

The societies also promoted literacy and education. The bylaws of most societies urged members to attend classes if they were illiterate, and required the expulsion of members who did not send their children to school.[40] Societies were less successful in this area than in others, however. The largest and richest societies, like the Società

*An Italian visitor reported his impressions: "San Francisco Italians have formed their societies, two of which are also military organizations: the *Bersaglieri* and the *Garibaldini*. They turn out with great pomp on special occasions and national celebrations. The Garibaldini especially are very wealthy and have built a magnificent hall for balls and reunions." See Böhme, "Vigna Dal Ferro's 'Un Viaggio,' " p. 158.

Italiana di Mutua Beneficenza and the Compagnia Garibaldina, offered night classes in English for adults and after-school Italian classes for the immigrants' children. But these and similar operations were short-lived.[41]

Although the Italian societies throve on regionalism, their stated goals were to transcend regionalism. The Compagnia Garibaldina, in its statutes, solemnly proclaimed its dedication to "the union and fellowship of the entire working class in order to unite all workers into one family."[42] Mutual aid societies in Italy offered similar declarations. In Porcari, for instance, the mutual aid society declared that the unity of the working class had to go beyond barriers of race and creed, which was a rather liberal stand for the late nineteenth century.[43] In Lorsica one of the society's goals was to teach its members to regard the interests of the working class as more important than those of any one group.[44] Such proclamations, though testifying to a general awareness of current social thought, found little practical application either in Italy or in San Francisco. San Francisco Italians did not show a great ability to achieve goals when the cooperation of all regional groups was required.

Beyond Regionalism?

The most obvious example of this inability was the failure to support an Italian hospital in the city. The success of the French community in building its hospital encouraged the Italians to start one of their own. In late 1865 the officers of the Società Italiana di Mutua Beneficenza launched the idea, arguing that an Italian hospital would save the community thousands of dollars in payments to hospitals, would be a source of national pride, and would eventually break down regional barriers.[45] Promoted in newspapers that reached Italians all over northern California, like *La Parola*, *La Voce del Popolo*, and *L'Eco della Patria*, the idea gathered support not only in San Francisco, but in such places as Sacramento and Virginia City, Nevada.[46] For a while it seemed that all the immigrants were rallying behind the project. Larco and Cerruti were unanimously elected to head the construction commission, and over 400 Italians were present for the ground breaking in 1868. *La Voce del Popolo* predicted that the future would be "safe and bright"—the Italians of San Francisco finally had a "national institution" able to make them feel "at home even in the United States."[47]

Despite these auspicious beginnings, within a few years several groups had withdrawn their support. The first withdrew for political reasons. In 1868 Cerruti took up a collection to help the cause of Italian unification. Immigrants with republican sympathies objected, both because they opposed the unification of Italy under the king and because they considered the collection a drain on the already limited resources of northern California Italians. An editorial in *La Voce del Popolo* saw "a pervasive conspiracy to undo the best efforts of this colony. The conspiracy has been going on secretly for some time; but it is now out in the open. It was orchestrated by the official leaders of the colony, for whom double-talk and hypocrisy are the rule."[48] By the end of 1868 several hundred Italians had ceased to support the project.[49]

Another group withdrew during the winter of 1868–69, objecting to the construction committee's decision to increase the monthly contribution of each immigrant by 25 cents. Some apparently intended to return to Italy and had second thoughts about investing in a project that might not benefit them.[50] By the late spring of 1869, *La Voce del Popolo* reported that the project no longer enjoyed the support of most Italians: "Cooperation among immigrants from different regions seems to be impossible."[51] With the support of the remaining members of the Società Italiana di Mutua Beneficenza, the building was eventually completed, but by 1871 the society had defaulted on the mortgage. The financial backing of the Italian-Swiss colony prevented an immediate shutdown. But in 1876 the hospital went bankrupt and the building was auctioned off.[52]

Unwelcome Outsiders

Catholic priests and various Italian consuls also made attempts to unite the San Francisco Italians. To Italians, the priests represented the only large and long-standing public institution of a nonregional character. The consuls, acting on behalf of the new Italian government, tried to bring about a sense of national loyalty in San Francisco. Neither the priests nor the consuls achieved any great success.

The Catholic Church began to take a special interest in the Italians of San Francisco in the 1860's. At that time Italians worshiped with Spanish and Portuguese immigrants at St. Francis's church, where a Chinese priest ministered to them all. In 1884 Bishop Patrick Riordan assigned an Italian priest to San Francisco and allowed the construction of an Italian national church. The Italian Salesian Fathers took over the guidance of the city's Italians in 1897. San Francisco Italians and their clergy came into conflict over questions of saints and processions. Each regional society had its own patron saint, whose statue was kept in the meeting hall. Every year the society celebrated the feast of the patron saint. The highlight of the celebration was a procession, usually on a Sunday afternoon. The consul reported in 1892 that there was a procession almost every Sunday in North Beach, since some societies "honored several patron saints to cater to the demands of immigrants from different towns of the same region."[53]

San Franciscans seem to have enjoyed going to North Beach to watch the Italian parades. The city's predominantly Irish clergy, however, strongly disapproved of these "devotions of pagan Mediterraneans."[54] Possibly at the order of the bishop, or possibly simply to enforce orthodoxy and increase clerical control over the plethora of societies, Italian priests exhorted immigrants to bring the statues of the saints to the churches, to reduce the number of processions, and to join church organizations like the Holy Name Society. The societies responded by no longer inviting the clergy to the processions.[55] Eventually, after 1900, the societies surrendered the statues and joined church organizations, but by that time both the saints and the processions had lost their importance. Up until the end of the century, saints and processions helped immigrants to maintain and express their regional loyalties.[56]

Italians reacted even more strongly to the repeated efforts of Italian consuls to organize them into supraregional groups. One of the consul's main tasks was to neutralize the republican propaganda of political refugees. In 1863 Cerruti complained that this was impossible since "most Genovesi share the republican views of the political refugees."[57] In 1866 the consul invited immigrants to join the Consorzio Nazionale, a society that collected money in order to promote the unification of Italy under the House of Savoy. To this end the consul also started a newspaper, *L'Eco della Patria*, subsidized by the Italian government. Some Italians in the city and the surrounding region responded to the appeal, and in 1867 the consul sent Prince Eugenio Savoia of Carignano in Rome a golden spike as a contribution to the cause of national unity.[58]

But the consul's success did not last long. In 1868 a group of Genoese organized the Associazione Nazionale Italiana, which openly promoted republicanism. Using the association's newspaper, *La Voce del Popolo*, the group founded a school for Genoese children, organized lectures on social and political topics, and opened a recreational center. The school lasted only two years; but the other activities prospered. In 1871 the consul complained that his Consorzio Nazionale "had no funds to compete with the powerful Genovesi."[59]

The consul's efforts to convince the growing Italian business community to join the Italian Chamber of Commerce were equally unsuccessful. In the early 1880's the consul had criticized as unpatriotic the reluctance of the most successful Italians to do business with Italy. In 1885, when he started the chamber, about seventy Italians joined. But membership declined, and in 1894 there were fewer than fifty members. The *Rivista Commerciale*, the monthly publication of the chamber, survived on its own for only five years; after 1890 an annual grant from the Italian government sustained it.[60] The consul also failed in an attempt to control the school that the Società Operaia, another Genoese association, had opened in 1884. When the school was in trouble in 1885, the consul offered to pay one-third of the school's expenses in exchange for the right to name teachers and select textbooks. The offer was accepted, enrollment immediately declined, and by 1893 the school was on the verge of closing.[61]

The consul also tried to pool the resources of the various mutual aid societies in order to provide assistance to all Italians regardless of regional origin, but in this he also failed. In 1865, in *La Parola*, the consul announced the founding of the Associazione Italiana di Beneficenza to "help the poor of the colony, prevent pauperism, and do away with mendicancy."[62] Until 1870, when the society became inactive, it never had more than 50 members; most immigrants continued to seek solutions to their problems in regional societies. In 1887 the consul revived the pan-Italian society and gave it a new name, Comitato di Soccorso e Beneficenza. Once again he appealed to all Italians, and a committee was set up to solicit donations from the various mutual aid societies. A survey in 1889 suggested that the Comitato did not enjoy the confidence and support of the immigrants.[63]

Throughout the 1890's the Comitato was virtually inoperative, since it could not handle the problems created by mass immigration and the ensuing poverty. In the early 1900's the Italian Commissariato dell'Emigrazione—a bureau of the Ministry of Foreign Affairs in Rome created in 1901 to coordinate all services for Italians abroad—decided to fund the Comitato, but this did not increase its effectiveness. Vice-Consul Gerolamo Ricciardi noted that among the Italians the Comitato was "as suspect as anything else emanating from the national government," and that "Italians prefer to organize in regional groups."[64] The Comitato was dissolved in 1916, when the Italians themselves established their first large supraregional society,[65] one that received the support of virtually all San Francisco Italians.

There were several underlying reasons why Italians rejected these would-be organizers from outside. Let us begin with the resistance to the clergy. Italian immigrants, although practicing a popular Catholicism that found its most fervent expression in processions, were generally unfamiliar with the official teachings and rituals of the Catholic Church. Most San Francisco Italians at the time were young men who, as Villari noted, had never attended church in Italy: "The great majority of men never go to church at all."[66] It is likely that the distance from their families and the lack of social pressure in San Francisco to conform to basic religious requirements increased the disaffection of these young men from the official church.

Moreover, immigrants who were in any way familiar with Italian political events since 1848 were probably antagonized by the political interference of the Vatican. Anticlericalism was particularly strong in the Italian northwest, where the Ligurians came from.[67] The activities of Catholic priests in San Francisco could easily be seen as further attempts by the official church to mix in political matters. Finally, Italian priests working among San Francisco Italians could not allow immigrants to express their popular religion as freely as they had done in Italy. The leadership of the San Francisco Catholic Church—and most other dioceses in the United States—was in the hands of Irish clergy, who had little sympathy for Italian religious folklore.

The reasons for the rejection of the consuls were more complex. Basically, immigrants distrusted official government representatives. As Villari put it, "The lower classes regard the government with a feeling of distrust and suspicion, engendered by former misrule; to them it is merely an instrument to collect taxes."[68] Italian consuls reported time and again that this feeling of distrust was common among immigrants. Besides, many immigrants blamed the Italian government for the poverty that had forced them out of Italy. Some had lost their small property because of taxes. According to two British observers at the turn of the century, "It is on the small farms and properties that direct taxes fall heaviest."[69] Nor did landless Italians escape the burden of taxation; in the 1890's the income tax in Italy was higher than in any other large European country except Spain.[70] To many immigrants, the consul symbolized past oppression. A mixture of distrust of government and memories of past oppression, then, worked against any appeal to supraregional loyalty.

The Italian Press

The activities of the societies, and especially their strongly regional character, are best seen in the bulletins and newspapers they put out in the early years in San Francisco. The use of the press to promote group cohesion was not something Italians had been familiar with in Italy. French immigrants showed Italians how the press could reach immigrants scattered throughout the city and the surrounding territory.[71] In fact, the first Italian news appeared in the French paper *Le Phare* in 1852. Soon Italians started their own independent bulletins, initially the work of political refugees who were among the few Italians in San Francisco with writing ability. It took almost forty years before San Francisco Italians would outgrow their commitment to regionalism in the press and support newspapers serving the entire Italian community. Thus the press closely reflected the more general phenomenon of regionalism.[72]

Ultimately, Italians settled on two daily papers that served the whole community; but before that time virtually every regional society had tried to publish a bulletin. These periodicals were short-lived, mostly because of financial problems and the lack of editorial skills. Their financial support came partly from the societies and partly from the classified advertising section, which often occupied half the space in the bulletins. But the funds of the societies were limited; most of the money collected in dues and at social events was disbursed to care for sick members.[73] Because of low circulation, advertising revenues seldom offset printing costs, despite the many advertisers: produce dealers, grocery store operators, importers of Italian goods, steamship agents, immigration agencies, liquor dealers, physicians, and practitioners of popular medicine.[74] In the 1870's, it should be recalled, there were only about 2,000 Italians in San Francisco, many of them illiterate. Editors with an adequate knowledge of the Italian language were in short supply, and in any case the work was only part-time and poorly paid; the societies' newspapers often had to call for volunteers to work on them.[75] Because of these problems, the bulletins normally survived only a few months, or at best a few years.[76]

In the early 1850's San Francisco Italians took their first steps in publishing by buying space in *La Crónica*, a Spanish bulletin, and *Le Phare*. By 1865 Federico Biesta, the correspondent of a New York

Italian newspaper, had started what seems to have been the first Italian newspaper in San Francisco, *L'Eco della Patria.* But that newspaper died the same year when Biesta left on a geological expedition to Death Valley.[77] The second newspaper lasted longer. Founded in 1862 by Agostino Spivalo and Roberto Angarani, who had had success in the pastry business, *La Parola* was a monarchist weekly. When the two editors put the paper up for sale in 1864, Consul Cerruti bought it to "make it the official publication of the San Francisco Italians."[78] Biesta, who had fled to British Columbia because of insolvency, was offered the editorship. After some Italian businessmen bailed him out, Biesta assumed his duties and changed the paper's name to *L'Eco della Patria*, a nostalgic reminder of the paper he had put out in 1855.[79]

The conflict between Italian consuls and the republican Genoese led to the founding of additional newspapers. In 1868 the Genoese started *La Voce del Popolo*, which engaged in endless political debates with the monarchist *Eco della Patria.* The conflicting views of the two newspapers seem to have polarized San Francisco Italians from 1868 to 1872, when *L'Eco della Patria* was bought out by its competitor. In 1875 Consul Domenico Barrili launched another monarchist newspaper, *La Scintilla Italiana*, to "foster respect for the traditions of the country and the House of Savoy."[80] But the rebellious republicans of *La Voce del Popolo* bought out the new competitor within a year. The consul sadly reported: "From now on the future of the colony will only be downward. There is no newspaper representing the views of the Italian government."[81]

Most of the San Francisco bulletins and newspapers, however, had no avowed political purpose. They were almost exclusively the mouthpieces of the societies, especially in the early days. Biesta, after his second unfortunate experience as editor of *L'Eco della Patria*, started two independent newspapers, hoping to serve the interests of several small societies by advertising their social events. But both the *Italian-American News* and *La Patria* lasted only a few months. Again Biesta's monarchist sympathies probably limited the appeal of his paper severely.[82] Other newspapers published in San Francisco in the 1870's and 1880's were *L'Elvezia*, serving the Italian-Swiss colony, *L'Unità Nazionale*, *L'Eco della Razza Latina*, *L'Emigrante*, *La Vespa*, *La Terra*, *La Verità*, *L'Unione*, *La Tribuna*, and *La Colonia Italo-Svizzera.* None was still in existence in 1890.[83]

Soon enough, Italians from different regional groups realized that no single group had the financial resources and editorial skills to sustain a regional newspaper. With this in mind, immigrants came to support the two dailies that eventually served the entire Italian community. This pattern, however, was solidly established only in the late nineteenth century; by that time *L'Italia* had become the evening paper and *La Voce del Popolo* the morning one.

Initially linked to the Associazione Nazionale Italiana, *La Voce del Popolo* in time broadened its coverage to other societies. This newspaper advocated republicanism in Italy, the assimilation of Italians in American society, and the interests of labor over those of management.[84] *L'Italia* was started as a weekly in 1887 by the society La Lega dei Mille. Within five years it turned into a daily, and later it achieved the widest circulation of any Italian newspaper on the West Coast. Although it labeled itself "an independent Republican newspaper," *L'Italia* catered to a more conservative audience. It supported the House of Savoy in Italy and the Republican Party in the United States, opposed the Americanization of Italians, and promoted the interests of management rather than labor.[85] Regardless of the social orientation of the two newspapers, the important fact was that by the turn of the century the Italian immigrant press had overcome the regionalism that had prevailed since the early days.

Regionalism in the Economy

Regionalism also played an important role in the early economic activity of Italians in San Francisco. As in the case of the mutual aid societies, the Genoese were the most conspicuous group. By the late 1860's, a sizable group of Genoese—probably 150—were truck farmers. They shared their rather modest economic success with immigrants of other nationalities, but were adamantly opposed to any other Italian group that tried to compete with them.[86] A decade later another group of Genoese had established themselves in fishing, firmly resisting attempts by other Italians to break their control.[87] Obviously, this attitude of the Genoese led to interregional conflicts, and these were more bitter and persistent than any of the other conflicts stemming from regional traditions, dialects, and mutual aid societies.

By and large, the Genoese were able to maintain their control, which explains a good deal in the development of the San Francisco Italian economy in the twentieth century. The most successful Italian bankers and businessmen were either Genoese or of Genoese parentage. But the challenge by other regional groups was not a complete failure. Both in farming and in fishing, immigrants from other regions forced the Genoese to compromise, or at least to allow others into ancillary activities.

The conflict between Genoese farmers and fishermen and other Italian groups is an important chapter in the long story of regionalism in San Francisco. Until 1860 few Italians around San Francisco were farmers or fishermen. Before 1848 most were adventurers.[88] One of these adventurers, for example, was Giovanni Battista Leandri, a northern Italian who joined the cattle aristocracy of Spanish California by investing capital he brought from Italy and by marrying into a prominent Spanish family.[89] In 1849 other adventurers arrived from South America, heading for the gold country. The federal census of 1850 counted about 300 Italians in or around San Francisco: almost 200 in the mines, 50 in commerce, 40 in domestic services, and less than 10 in farming. Two years later the California census showed that the Italian population had doubled. Of about 600 Italians, 300 were in the mines, 100 in trade, 25 in farming, and the remainder in unspecified activities.[90]

Gold attracted others besides adventurers. San Francisco drew investors and merchants from Italy who foresaw favorable opportunities in an expanding urban area. Moreover, social and political instability in Italy suggested to businessmen that it was safer to sell and invest elsewhere; Genoa and Milan were, after all, among the European capitals affected in the revolutionary year 1848. Some of these Italian businessmen commanded considerable capital. Larco, for instance, was able to buy a shipping company doing business with Mexico. Others dealt in domestic and imported goods or owned and operated hotels.[91] One of the first reports we have on the economic conditions of the San Francisco Italians, written in 1856 by Federico Biesta, the acting Sardinian consul, names seventeen such investors and merchants.

Biesta did not mention regional conflict. "The Italians," he wrote, "are strong, industrious, and accustomed to suffering and hard work. Immigrants take care of their own interests without taking part in the regrettable disorders that the San Franciscans seem to indulge in." Immigrants were also prosperous, according to Biesta, and there was no small town in northern California "where Italian business is not represented, just as there is no mining district where Italian miners are not known for their energy and hard work."[92] Biesta was probably exaggerating the prosperity of the Italians; a few years later the first Italian consul in San Francisco, Giovanni Battista Cerruti, painted a picture of poverty and desperation.[93]

Only in the early 1860's did consular reports mention an increasing presence of Italians in farming.[94] In 1863, for instance, "several Italians who had come to join other adventurers in the gold country took up farming when their dreams of becoming rich in the gold country vanished."[95] A few years later Italians were entrenched in farming: "Although there are six or seven well-known Italian merchant houses in the city, most Italians are either farmers or fishermen." The farmers, the consul added, were thriftier than the fishermen and generally more successful. Farming did not produce fortunes overnight, but "some farmers have made enough money in a decade to go home and enjoy the rest of their lives in Italy."[96]

Italian truck farmers were successful because there was little commercial farming in the San Francisco area in the early 1850's; most ranches grew only enough for their own needs. When the rapid growth of San Francisco created a demand for vegetables, Italians, together with Mexicans, Spaniards, and Chinese, took up growing them in the foothills of the Sierras or in the sand hills around San Francisco.[97] Truck farming expanded rapidly: in 1850 its production was valued at $75,000; by the early 1860's it was over $1 million. By the late 1860's production had reached almost one-third of the value of livestock production, which at that time was the most profitable business in northern California.[98]

As Italian immigration increased in the 1860's, friction developed between the Genoese and other groups. The consul wrote in 1868: "Most farmers are from Genoa. They are efficient and well organized; and more important, they intend to exercise a monopoly in their own business."[99] A few years later the Genoese were in conflict with the Luccans, the second group to arrive in San Francisco: "The Genovesi do not intend to share their advantages with other Italians. If manpower is needed in farming, the Genovesi will send for a relative or friend in Italy, and will not offer the job to an Italian from another region."[100] In 1869 *La Voce del Popolo* supported the Genoese's attitude: "New immigrants arrive in the city almost every month. It is advisable for newcomers to look for jobs elsewhere than in farming; the market seems to be saturated."[101] As late as 1903, *L'Italia* wrote: "The practice of starting a business in competition with one that is doing well or the determination of a regional group to enter a line of work already controlled by another group is likely to ruin both groups and both activities, and to create unnecessary confusion."[102]

Most of the early farms were small, averaging between ten and fifteen acres: a few were large farms of 250 acres. Since almost no immigrant arrived with the capital to buy land, tenant farming was the most common form of tenure at first. Partnership was the typical business arrangement among Italian farmers, both because of the shortage of capital and because Italians did not want to live alone two or three miles outside the city.[103] Even on small plots as many as six men would join together to clear the land and build a shelter; there they lived until they could afford individual dwellings.[104]

Few Italians, it seems, bought land around San Francisco. A report by the California Immigration Commission on Italian vegetable growers in San Francisco County said: "Few Italians have purchased the land they till, for, lying near the city, it has a great speculative value, and when purchased the investment is too large for profitable farming. Hence the majority of the farmers are tenants. Moreover, they usually farm in groups of partners, numbering from two to eleven."[105]

Some of the possible reasons why Italians did not buy land are suggested by the response of the San Francisco Italians to an agricultural project in the late 1880's. Andrea Sbarboro, an Italian businessman who had made a fortune in the grocery business and in mutual loan associations, decided to apply his expertise to solving the problem of unemployment among Italians in San Francisco.[106] Since most immigrants had been farmers in Italy, he planned to resettle them on the land by forming a cooperative farming association. Sbarboro and a group of associates agreed to pay $10,000 down on 1,500 acres of land in Sonoma County, 90 miles north of San Francisco. They would pay off the $15,000 balance at $1,000 a month out of the subscription income. The bylaws of the association stated that preference for employment would be given to Italians and Italian-speaking Swiss who were citizens of the United States or who had first papers. Wages were set at $35 a month, plus room and board. In addition, every worker was to pay $5.00 of his monthly wages for five shares of the colony stock. In this way each subscriber would build his equity in the land, and ultimately would be an independent farmer.[107]

Not a single Italian joined Sbarbaro's association. There were several reasons for this failure. Sbarboro explained that Italians rejected the plan because they were generally unwilling to join corporate ventures; and besides, since most of them still intended to return to Italy, they were unwilling to invest in land.[108] The legal status of most immigrants was another obstacle. No figures are available on how many Italians had become American citizens or had taken out first papers by the late 1880's, but a consular report of the late 1870's suggests that very few qualified for Sbarboro's plan:

"Only a handful of immigrants give up their allegiance to the motherland."[109] In 1904 a representative of the Italian government recorded how the secretary of the Italian Chamber of Commerce in San Francisco explained the immigrants' tendency not to buy land: "The land is expensive and new immigrants can purchase only if they enter into financial partnership with other immigrants. But they are diffident toward one another. This attitude has prevented them from becoming landowners since the early days of Italian settlement. And most of them want immediate profits so as to be able to return as soon as possible. Thus they rent."[110] It is also likely that many Italians did not join Sbarboro's colony simply because they preferred to remain in the city.

In 1874 the Genoese established the San Francisco and San Mateo Ranchers' Association. Its purpose, the bylaws stated, was "to establish and maintain a vegetable and produce market in San Francisco; to buy and sell, lease and release all real estate [that] may be required for this purpose; and to do all things necessary to compute maintenance and success in the same."[111] Before 1874 marketing techniques were rather primitive. Vegetables were taken to San Francisco in handcarts or horsedrawn wagons by the growers themselves, unloaded, and set on the sidewalk of Sansome Street—the center of the vegetable market—for public display. Prices fluctuated, but the generally rising demand made it impossible for growers both to farm the land and to ride to the city two or three times a week to supervise the sale of the produce. Increasing congestion on Sansome Street and unsold loads of vegetables left to rot on the sidewalk only compounded marketing problems.[112]

Ostensibly, the association was founded to solve these problems. But there was another unexpressed goal: to reaffirm the quasi-monopoly of the Genoese, who controlled the produce business but were willing to accept the Luccans as subordinate partners.[113] A year later the consul reported: "The immigrants from Lucca tried several times to become growers, but met the strong opposition of the Genoese. After the creation of the association last year, the Luccans act as distributors to the consumers, either by working at the Colombo market or by peddling the produce through the streets of San Francisco."[114]

The new Colombo market, completed in 1876, was a large structure divided into stalls that faced the streets; members of the association could rent the stalls. An Italian visitor reported his impressions after a day at the market: "The society of the gardeners has built a large market. In the morning it is a handsome sight to see the coming

14. Columbus Avenue sausage factory, 1926. Regionalism shaped the San Francisco Italian economy. Two groups dominated the food industry. The Genoese started out as truck farmers. Some advanced to become fruit and vegetable commissioners, and the most resourceful became suppliers of canned goods to the national market. The Luccans started as fruit and vegetable peddlers for the Genoese, and later became independent owners and operators of grocery stores.

and going of the two-horse wagons with the names of the owners on the side."[115] By the early 1880's it was the center of the produce industry in San Francisco.[116] The market was already controlled by the Genoese: their dialect dominated the activities at the market until 5:00 A.M., when the Florentine dialect took over. At that hour Luccans began distributing the produce, and the Genoese went back to their farms.[117] Some Luccans peddled the produce in the streets of San Francisco from pushcarts; others supplied fruit and vegetable stands throughout the city. In 1881 there were about a hundred of these stands, most owned by Luccans. The cooperation between

Genoese and Luccans proved profitable to both groups. Eventually, the Genoese established food-processing corporations, some of which became national conglomerates. The Luccan vegetable stands became grocery stores, retail outlets for domestic and imported goods, and restaurants.[118]

As the produce business expanded into a multimillion-dollar operation, a group of brokers emerged who specialized in marketing produce. Called commission dealers, or commissioners, they bought the farmers' produce in advance, freeing the farmers from the burden of selling their crops. Many commissioners solicited business from growers with salesmen or by mail; others solicited personally, sometimes gaining a reputation for integrity in this way.[119] Initially, relations were difficult between growers and commissioners. Regional rivalry often made growers wary of commissioners, who were likely to be from the city of Genoa. Many growers came from smaller communities of the province, and carried to the New World the suspicion that city people were out to cheat them.[120]

Working relations improved when commissioners began to act as moneylenders, advancing short-term cash to farmers for land improvements. Some commissioners established themselves financially in a rather short time, and could lend thousands of dollars at a time. The origins of the banking system of the San Francisco Italians are to be found in these loans and in the confidence they generated between commissioners and growers. Lorenzo Scatena, for instance, was one of the commissioners who worked hard at gaining the growers' confidence by extending loans. His stepson Amadeo P. Giannini, about whom more will be said, spent his after-school hours writing letters to growers in the Santa Clara Valley on the reliability of his stepfather's house, in search of consignments.[121]

The Fishermen

Regionalism played a major role in the growth of the fishing industry too. In this activity compromise was even more difficult than in the produce business. The Genoese came to fishing at a later date than to farming. Chinese started fishing in the Sacramento and San Joaquin rivers during the gold rush, and dominated the industry until the 1880's. Only three Italian fishermen worked out of San Francisco in 1852, according to the California census.[122] By 1870, of the 353 fishermen of San Francisco, 86 were Italians. Most of the Italian fishermen were from the coastal towns near Genoa; in San Francisco they kept their boats in a basin at the foot of Vallejo

Street, in North Beach.[123] In their new habitat, they did not alter their customs: fishing methods were imported from Italy, as well as the *paranzella*, a small trawling net, and the *felucca*, a fishing boat that later formed the backbone of the San Francisco fishing fleet.[124] By the late 1880's the Genoese dominated the industry. An American writer of the 1930's attributed their success to superior ability: "Italian fishermen follow the fish as instinctively as a gull trails a scavenger ship. They seem to be particularly fitted for the task of fishermen."[125] Superior ability was not the only reason for the success. Violence and intimidation also helped establish a quasi-monopoly, in a city where anti-Chinese sentiment made these tactics safe and useful ways to achieve economic success.[126]

The strategy used by the Genoese for dominating farming was less successful in fishing. Though they managed to keep the Luccans out of the fishing industry, the Sicilians succeeded in breaking the monopoly in the 1890's.[127] Stronger physical endurance and superior skills, which have already been noted, played no small part in the Sicilian success. An American reported this concession made by a San Francisco Genoese fisherman in 1906: "At night, when [Sicilians] are not fishing, they curl up in front of their boats. They have a skin like a green turtle and never take cold."[128] Initially, the Genoese hired Sicilian labor, hoping to be able to control them as they had done with the Luccans. Soon enough the laborers became independent fishermen.[129]

Attempts by the Genoese to defend their monopoly sparked some of the most violent conflicts in the history of the Italians in San Francisco. The *San Francisco Chronicle* reported: "Boats were sunk, nets have been cut, and sometimes owners too have been cut. Launches have gone to sea and neither launches nor owners have been seen again."[130] But the Sicilians were there to stay. In 1913 a San Francisco Italian reported that both Genoese and Sicilians were entrenched in the fishing industry.[131] But even in 1913 the Genoese had the upper hand. They controlled the more capital-intensive operations such as tuna fishing and deep-sea fishing, and the Sicilians were confined to small operations and inshore fishing.[132]

The competition between Genoese and Sicilians had other victims: the losers often had to leave the city if they were to remain fishermen. The immigrants from Isola delle Femmine illustrate this point. Isola delle Femmine was a town of about 5,000 people on a small island a few miles from Palermo. In early 1890 a few people from the town came to San Francisco. Fishermen in Italy, they became fishermen in San Francisco too.[133] But by late 1898 almost all the fishermen from Isola had left the city and settled in the coal mining town of Black Diamond, later called Pittsburg, at the confluence of the Sacramento and San Joaquin rivers.[134] Possibly it was the concerted efforts of the Genoese and the other Sicilians that had forced them out. *La Voce del Popolo* reported: "Newly arrived fishermen should abide by the regulations of the [fishermen's mutual aid] association or they should find other places to fish."[135] These fishermen from San Francisco, in Black Diamond, were joined by other immigrants from Isola delle Femmine; by 1903, 3,000 people had migrated to Black Diamond from Isola delle Femmine.[136] Other fishing communities in California, like Martinez, Santa Cruz, and Monterey, had similar beginnings.[137]

The conflict between the Sicilian fishermen from Isola and other Sicilian fishermen is one indication that campanilismo was stronger than regionalism among fishermen. By the early 1910's Sicilian fishermen were divided into a number of competing groups, each typically consisting of people from one town, specializing in one type of fishing, and following the leadership of one man.[138] Some of these groups were the Crab Fishermen's Association, the Western California Fish Company, the Paladini Company, the International Fish Company, and the Borzone Fish Company. The Crab Fishermen's Association, for instance, gained a monopoly in the crab market. Antonio Farina, the lord of the association, determined the number of crabs that would enter the market each day, set the price, devised ways to keep the surplus crabs alive, and directed the group's battle with the Fish Commission. His youthful deputies, as the *San Francisco Call* put it, liked to flash guns in the face of fishermen as much as fishermen liked to defy the law.[139] Achille Paladini ruled another association. He was nicknamed the Fish King, and not only controlled his trust, but established three independent companies, allegedly in order to evade an indictment for monopolistic practices.[140]

In 1910 a United States Senate investigation found that some of these companies were indeed monopolies. In the case of Paladini, the hearings revealed that captains of vessels were instructed to turn in only a given amount of fish each day, and ship the rest off to a glue factory. The superintendent of the factory testified that in 1909 he received from the Paladini and Western companies 100 tons of fresh fish. Joseph Catania, an independent dealer, was threatened by Paladini's men when he sold fish for less than the price set by Paladini. There was no need for a second warning. In another instance, when Catania and some associates attempted to go into business on their own, prices fell so low that they were forced to close down. The following day prices were back to normal.[141]

With few exceptions, Italian fishermen, because of their clannishness and their internal fights, did not enjoy a good press in San Francisco. As early as 1863 an Italian described them as antisocial and unwilling to cooperate among themselves. And he added: "They could make good money; but they are not as thrifty as farmers."[142] After the turn of the century, Consul Ricciardi deplored their endless quarreling, when "cooperation could yield much better profits."[143] San Franciscans sometimes took a more positive view of them; one wrote: "They are hardy, frugal, temperate. They are generous and kind to each other, keen in business, and they are not easily cheated in business by dealers."[144] In 1906, however, another San Franciscan asserted that their clannishness had separated them from society more than any other immigrant group. "As a class they have fallen behind the other members of the industrial community in their general level of intelligence and progressiveness."[145]

Regardless of the reputation of the Italian fishermen, they provided 90 percent of the fish consumed in the city and controlled 80 percent of the fishing industry in California. Some 3,500 Italians were directly involved in fishing in California. Two-thirds of them lived in North Beach, the others in Black Diamond, Collinsville, Martinez, Santa Cruz, Monterey, and smaller places. In 1910 the San Francisco Fisherman's Wharf had a fleet of some 700 fishing craft, operating mostly in the bay and off the coast. The average daily catch per vessel was eleven to twelve tons, six to be consumed fresh, the remainder processed for shipment. Besides those who fished in California, about 1,000 Italians left San Francisco every year for six to nine months to join fishing expeditions to Alaska.[146]

A striking difference between the Italian farmers and fishermen in San Francisco was that farmers organized in regional groups, whereas fishermen often formed groups based on campanilismo. Thus some fishermen adhered to a more traditional form of social organization than farmers. Undoubtedly, working conditions had a lot to do with the survival of campanilismo among fishermen: fishermen seldom came in contact with other Italians. As a survey in 1930 noted: "A commercial fisherman associates only with other fishermen, and their families have little in common with the world outside their villages."[147] Fishermen proved that in San Francisco a group could isolate itself almost totally from the larger society, recreating patterns of economic and social organization almost entirely from the Old World.

The Decline of Regionalism

By the mid-1890's Italians in San Francisco were expressing concern about problems caused by the increasing influx of their countrymen. One writer offered a multiple complaint: that more immigrants were arriving than the community could absorb, that there was a rapid turnover of immigrants and returnees, and that newcomers were unwilling to join mutual aid societies. "It is not unlikely," he concluded, "that we will become like the Italian colonies in New York and Chicago."[148] Many San Francisco Italians, we should recall, thought the city had avoided the overcrowding, unemployment, and crime that blighted Italian areas in eastern cities.

The new immigrants themselves also expressed a feeling of discomfort and restlessness. When in 1896 Pietro Gori, a noted Italian anarchist, came to San Francisco and spoke at Columbus Hall in North Beach, a large crowd of Italians turned out to listen to him. Cesare Crespi, the editor of *Il Messaggero*, covering the speech and noticing how the Italians seemed sympathetic to anarchism, wrote about the California paradise turning into "hardships and endless humiliations" for most immigrants. Throughout 1896 and 1897 Crespi continued to comment on the "restlessness of those who came to find El Dorado in California and ended up regretting that they had ever left the true, beautiful, and loving Italy."[149] The San Francisco Italian press often wrote of the immigrants' restlessness. *La Voce del Popolo* complained that "the newcomers are not willing to take the advice of those who have been in this city for many years."[150] The consul summarized the signs of discomfort: "Our colony is growing fast, it is badly divided, and it seems to have lost its sense of purpose."[151] Similar observations dotted consular reports and newspaper articles throughout the 1890's.

What was happening? The economic distress and mass unemployment that affected the United States from the winter of 1893 to 1898 certainly explain some of the dissatisfaction of the San Francisco Italians. And there seem to have been two other basic problems: an increasing tension between old and new Italians, and the inability of the mutual aid societies to cope with new problems. In other words, regionalism was showing its limitations, and Italians were finding out that they had few skills with which to bring about new solutions. This period of uncertainty and search lasted until 1916, a year that is not arbitrarily chosen as the beginning of a new stage in the history of the San Francisco Italians.

The first signs of distress appeared when it became clear that regional societies were unable to meet certain pressing social needs. Regional societies served immigrants from a given region. But what about those immigrants who were too few to establish their own society? They were on their own, and usually ended up with the worst jobs. In 1870 the consul pointed out that of 1,600 Italians, only 250 were in farming and fishing, and a few others in trade and transportation; and most of these were from the provinces of Genoa and Lucca. But "there are 600 to 700 immigrants who are bootblacks, servants, waiters, and laborers, or are unemployed. They cannot count on the support of the mutual aid societies, since they are from regions that are not well represented here."[152] Most of these immigrants had come to the city on their own, without an invitation from relatives or friends, and often in response to promotions engineered by California immigration societies.*

The problems created by new immigrants who could not join regional societies increased in the late 1870's and the 1880's with the arrival of several hundred unskilled Italian laborers forced out of the mines of Nevada by the drop in the price of silver. They were from a variety of regions in Italy, and in San Francisco they found neither friends nor mutual aid societies to help them find jobs.[153] Older immigrants expressed resentment that some of these newcomers became beggars in San Francisco.[154] By the late 1880's there were, as the consul noted, two classes of Italians in the city: those who had come by chain migration, and those who had come on their own.[155]

The situation became unmanageable immediately after the turn of the century, as a result of a sudden and artificial increase in the number of yearly arrivals. In the tense atmosphere of labor disputes in San Francisco at the time, two groups had a vested interest in the creation of a large pool of immigrant labor: American businessmen and Italian immigrant entrepreneurs. The Americans had realized that the city's isolated geographical position worked against them, since labor could not easily be imported from other cities to break strikes. Italian immigrant labor was the answer. The San Francisco

*To supply cheap manpower for the city transportation system and for industry, some leading San Francisco entrepreneurs created three immigration agencies in the 1860's: the Immigration Union of California, the Immigration Association of California, and the State Board of Immigration. The good performance of early Italian immigrants as workers, and especially as farmers, convinced the members of the three associations that an increased supply of Italian labor was desirable. See Alexander Bell, *Arguments*, pp. 3–4; and California Immigration Union, *All About California*, pp. 53–54.

unions, for their part, systematically excluded Italians from membership. To bring more Italians, in 1902 a group of San Francisco entrepreneurs, merchants, and real estate agents organized the California Promotion Committee; by 1908 it had 3,000 members.[156] Promotional material was printed in several languages and agents were dispatched to the cities of the East Coast and Europe. Some Italian businessmen in San Francisco had similar interests: since they could not pay local union wages, a large supply of Italian immigrants seemed a solution to their need for cheap labor.[157]

Other circumstances in 1903 and 1904 combined to push up the number of yearly arrivals. The exceptionally good harvest of 1903 allowed Italian growers to hire all of the unemployed Italians, plus some Chinese and Japanese. *L'Italia* criticized Italian growers for hiring non-Italian labor and urged San Francisco Italians to send for relatives and friends, since "the future is promising and there is plenty of work in San Francisco."[158] The boom of 1903 did not last. Newcomers were offered jobs as pickers in 1904, then "they became idle for months, going into debt, moving in and out of the city in search of work, fighting local unions, and finally causing concern among local officials."[159]

The Italian government, alerted to these problems by the consul, made a survey of the San Francisco labor situation in order to see whether emigration to San Francisco should be discouraged. Adolfo Rossi, who conducted the survey, wrote an extensive report of his visit to San Francisco. He began by asking leading San Francisco Italians about the labor situation in the city and whether immigration from Italy should be encouraged or discouraged. Some Italians argued that San Francisco still had opportunities for strong, honest, and hardworking immigrants. Among those taking this position were Andrea Sbarboro, founder of the Italian-American bank, Marco Fontana, president of the California Fruit Canners' Association, and James Fugazi, owner of the White Line Travel Agency and founder of the Fugazi People's Bank. Italians taking the opposite position were Carlo Dondero, the secretary of the Italian Chamber of Commerce, Teodoro Bacigalupi, director of the Italian school of San Francisco, and the physician Paolo De Vecchi. They argued that immigrants could get jobs for three to four months a year as pickers, but then they were either unemployed or underemployed; labor unions made it impossible for them to get permanent jobs.[160]

In the end, Rossi concluded that emigration to San Francisco had to be discouraged. This recommendation was accepted by the Italian government and communicated to all Italians.[161] But warnings had no practical effect. Mass migration to San Francisco continued until 1924, creating what the Associated Charities of the city called the "Italian problem." The city's charities and the Italian mutual aid societies were unable to cope with the problems created by the arrival of so many Italians.[162]

Another source of tension was the leadership and indeed the purpose of the societies themselves. Competition for positions of leadership was one problem. The original officers of the mutual aid societies were Italians who were better educated or wealthier than most other immigrants.* Over the years these leaders were challenged by immigrants who had arrived as poor as anybody else, but who, with hard work and good fortune, had prospered. *La Voce del Popolo* reported on several stormy meetings of the Compagnia Garibaldina. "There are Italians," a news item of 1887 said, "who assume they can control the society because they have money."† As early as 1868 the Italian consul reported friction between officers of associations and wealthy immigrants. In the Società Italiana di Mutua Beneficenza, he said, certain merchants were trying to take control.[163] Thus an important change was taking place as the societies slowly moved away from their Italian origins and took root in the New World. Achievements in America were being advanced as better qualifications for leadership than social status brought from Italy.

The very purpose of the associations came into question as the more powerful societies started to act as loan associations, lending money to help immigrants to establish businesses. As the immigrants' economic activity expanded, some tried to do away with the original purpose of the societies, mutual assistance. In 1885, for instance, *La Voce del Popolo* reported that at a meeting of the Compagnia Garibaldina several members proposed that the association be made into a savings and loan association, to transmit money to families in Italy and to speculate in real estate.[164]

By the mid-1890's, with increased immigration and the internal

*The consul reported in 1882: "Mutual aid societies usually select as their officers immigrants who had some experience in dealing with people in Italy. Ex-schoolteachers, ex-employees of the Italian government, or simply immigrants arriving with some capital are the people the societies rely on." RC, SF 17.ii.1882.

†*VP*, 17.ii.1887. Though we do not have the minutes of the societies' meetings, San Francisco Italian newspapers, especially *La Voce del Popolo* and *L'Italia*, regularly reported decisions made at meetings and occasionally commented on the activities of the societies.

development of the colony, the Italians had outgrown the formula of the mutual aid societies. Immigrants from less-represented regions did not enjoy the protection of a society. Mass immigration almost paralyzed existing societies. Competition for positions of leadership and the emergence of new goals showed that Italians were changing and that imaginative new solutions had to be sought. But the immigrants were hardly prepared to do that. The years from the mid-1890's to 1916 were a period of groping for new solutions.

At this point I want to draw some general conclusions about the regionalism of the San Francisco Italians up to the late nineteenth century. In both their social and their economic life, regionalism was the basis of interaction: it kept immigrants from the same region together and it created competition among regional groups. Although regionalism may appear to have been a legacy of an agrarian past and a manifestation of particularism, it was for most immigrants actually a step toward a rather broad concept of social organization. Regionalism demanded the sacrifice of companilismo and the ability to compromise local differences in order to achieve communal goals. In view of Italian intraregional rivalries, as described by Luigi Villari and others, regionalism was probably not an easy goal to achieve. Regional societies were not solely a nostalgic recreation of the past. Equally, they were designed to respond creatively to the challenges of the present. As we have seen, there is no necessary dichotomy between preserving the past and adapting to change; both were vital to San Francisco Italians. But regionalism could not provide the solution to all community problems. It worked for large regional groups that came to San Francisco by chain migration; but it could not work for immigrants who came on their own and did not find large numbers of immigrants from their region.

One could argue that Italians would have been better off had they abandoned regionalism and merged with American society upon landing in San Francisco. This argument has the seduction of all the things that are too logical. Human beings, as creatures of emotion and tradition, do not usually change according to the rules of logic; they do not like to, nor are they able to, take more than one step at a time. Tradition and continuity are important forces, and probably are most important to people who, because of circumstances, have to undergo accelerated change. The preservation of tradition does not prevent change; rather it makes it possible. It is likely that the most radical change is brought about by people who try to preserve some cherished traditions—real or only in the mind—in the face of events that seem to challenge those traditions.

Probably, Italian regional groups could not have merged with American society in the late nineteenth century even if they had wanted to. The assimilation of immigrant groups in a national culture presupposes the existence of a national culture. The question is whether there was a nationally integrated American culture into which Italian regional groups could assimilate. A number of historians have demonstrated that the national integration of western societies occurred mostly in the late nineteenth and early twentieth centuries—Eugen Weber, for instance, shows this to have been the case in France.

The United States was different, of course. It did not have the burden of long-established traditions and regional loyalties. But it had analogous problems. The country was by and large a composite of immigrant and ethnic groups that only tenuously shared in a national culture. The First World War both revealed the depth of the ethnic differences in the United States and stimulated the nationalization of ethnic cultures. I suspect that the immigrants who arrived in the United States before the war saw America more as a collection of immigrant and ethnic groups than as a national culture. The commitment of Italians to regionalism should be seen in this context.

CHAPTER 9

From Regionalism to Nationalism

In October 1916 a handful of Italian businessmen, encouraged by certain California Progressives, established the Italian Welfare Agency, the first large nonregional Italian organization in San Francisco.* The agency was started as an answer to social problems that regional societies had been unable to handle. From the distance of over half a century, the founding of the agency appears as a milestone in the history of the San Francisco Italians. It marked the end of regionalism and the final acceptance of nationalism as the basis for social organization. The agency was not, of course, founded in a vacuum, nor was it the result of transitory concerns. It was the outcome of changes that had been occurring since early in the century, and of dynamics that had been at work since the day the first Italian immigrants settled in San Francisco.

Despite many studies, historians are far from a consensus on these dynamics. Some argue that the transition from regionalism to nationalism occurred because Italians from different regions shared the same districts in American cities. Paul McBride, for instance, holds that immigrants were forced to go beyond regionalism in the same way that they had been forced to abandon campanilismo: daily interaction in the Italian enclaves created common interests, first

*The Comitato di Soccorso e Patronato was also an organization open to all Italians, and it was established at a much earlier date. But the Comitato was set up by the Italian consul and to a great extent was supported by the Italian government; and it never had more than 100 members. The other societies that were opened to all Italians regardless of regional origin, like the masonic lodges and the veterans' associations, were also small organizations.

regional and later national.[1] Others argue that discrimination cemented group solidarity among Italians. As one historian put it: "The stresses of assimilation and the pressures of American society isolated them, burdened them with a destructive and pervasive sense of inferiority, and filled them with bitter resentment against the United States."[2] Two social scientists link the disappearance of regionalism to the passing of the first generation: "There is a limit on how much ethnicity the first generation can pass on to the second. Provincialism was deeply rooted in memories and customs that could take root only in the feudal isolation of Italy."[3]

A sociologist sees the church as playing the key role in the weakening of regionalism; but this is hard to accept, since as we saw, Italians had little contact with the church and were strongly anticlerical.[4] One historian argues that labor unions broke down the provincial allegiance and peasant fatalism, and persuaded Italians that collective organization could work.[5] Whatever the case in the United States in general, this did not happen in San Francisco, where Italians were systematically excluded from the unions. Other historians emphasized the role of Fascism in breaking down regional loyalties.[6] This is an important issue, and it will be dealt with later. Finally, still other historians stress the ethnic press and political leadership as agents of Italian social integration.[7]

These explanations have a common element, all seeing the transition as the product of forces that the Italians did not control—like the physical environment, prejudice, the fading away of memories, the Catholic Church, the unions, Fascism, the ethnic press, and political leaders. In this chapter, however, we see that the decline of Italian regionalism in San Francisco was mainly due to the immigrants' economic success. Regionalism became a hindrance to economic growth, and Italian national interests became paramount. Moreover, the slow but steady improvement of the material condition of most immigrants, especially after the First World War, progressively decreased the desire to return to Italy, and return migration indeed slowed down. This decline in the rate of return migration also contributed to the decline of regionalism.

An external, secondary impulse that helped in this transformation was the ideology of Italian nationalism. Nationalism spread throughout Italy early in the twentieth century, and some Italian nationalists, like Enrico Corradini, established a link between it and Italian emigration. This not only provided a major social issue by which to spread the new ideology among the impoverished masses in Italy, but also stimulated the dissemination of the new ideology among Italians abroad.[8] Most Italians in San Francisco and elsewhere in the United States readily embraced the new ideology.[9] The First World War and its favorable conclusion for Italy greatly stimulated nationalism both in Italy and among Italians abroad. And finally, Italian nationalism reached a peak with Fascism. San Francisco Italians probably responded to Fascism more enthusiastically than any other Italian community in the United States.

Expanding Economic Activity

As we have seen, until the end of the nineteenth century the economic activity of Italian immigrants was largely confined within regional groups. The way Italian growers set up their operations is the best illustration of this. The growers were from the province of Genoa, and they established a regional association to protect their interests. If labor was needed, it was recruited among immigrants also from Genoa. The capital for land improvements or other needs was provided initially by regional associations and later by commissioners. Competition from other groups was either eliminated or kept under control, by formal or informal arrangements. The goal of the growers was the control of the produce market of the city and the surrounding territory. In sum, it was a regional economy, consisting of a single regional group confined within a regional market.

By the late 1890's this pattern was changing, mostly because of certain immigrants who saw regionalism as an obstacle to the expansion of their businesses. The goal of energetic entrepreneurs was mass production, in order to compete not in regional markets but in the national market. Mass production required amounts of capital that neither regional associations nor even the entire Italian population in San Francisco could supply. And it required large numbers of workers. These entrepreneurs, therefore, were not concerned about the regional origins of the labor they hired. In fact, they came to regard regionalism as a problem. Regionalism, they felt, created an endless turnover among workers and undermined work discipline. Indeed, at the turn of the century the movement back and forth from Italy to the United States was probably more intense than in the 1880's. Entrepreneurs considered regional loyalty one of the major reasons why Italians kept going home. Thus eliminating regionalism was a way to stabilize the work force.

All these tendencies are illustrated by the career of the Italian businessman Marco Fontana and the growth of the Del Monte Corporation. Fontana, the son of a marble cutter, was born in

Cerisola, near Genoa, in 1849. In 1860 his family moved to New York, and in 1867 he left New York by himself to try his luck in the mines of California. Soon disillusioned, he moved to San Francisco, where he worked as a clerk for A. Galli and Company, fruit commission merchants. In the early 1870's he bought the G. Ginocchio firm, a commission house, and a few months later he tried fruit growing with another Italian, but both ventures failed.[10] Fontana's early career evolved within the boundaries of the Genoese group.

But he was more daring than most of his fellow commissioners. Fontana realized that the local market was limited, and that the largest markets were the cities of the east. Shipping fresh produce was expensive, however; and besides, it was necessary to provide eastern cities even during the winter months. Canning was the solution. An apparently insurmountable obstable to competing in the national market was the need for large capital, which was not available within Italian regional groups. Fontana, with his own limited resources and help from the Compagnia Garibaldina, moved into canning twice, and failed both times. Finally, in 1891, two non-Italians, L. S. Goldstein, a financier with strong banking connections, and William Fries, an entrepreneur, provided the capital for the establishment of M. J. Fontana and Company.[11]

Another obstacle was the possibility of unrestricted competition among Italian regional groups. Fontana feared that the market would be disrupted if too many canneries were started in California. To solve this problem he created a syndicate in 1899, the California Fruit Canners' Association, which eventually controlled most of the California output. The shortage of capital continued to be a problem, but one that newly created Italian banks helped to solve.[12] In 1899 Fontana joined the board of directors of the Italian-American Bank, which became one of his chief backers—from 1900 to 1913 he borrowed $250,000. Indirectly, Italian immigrants working in the canneries became the financial backers of Fontana, since most of the immigrant cannery workers in San Francisco deposited their savings in the Italian-American Bank.[13] In 1916, to consolidate his control over the canning industry in California, Fontana formed the California Packing Corporation by merging four large packing companies that had interests throughout the United States. The new firm, popularly known as Del Monte, became the largest seller of canned produce in the country.

Mass production required a large work force; and since Fontana was unwilling to hire American labor at union wages, Italians entered his canneries en masse. Clearly, he could not follow the practice of hiring exclusively Genoese labor. Fontana centered his operations in San Francisco, where he could count on an almost limitless supply of cheap Italian labor from virtually all regions of Italy. In 1913 the California Fruit Canners' Association operated the world's largest cannery in North Beach. It had a capacity of 24 million cans a year, about one-seventh of the state total, and most of the more than 1,000 workers were Italians.[14] Women made up a large part of the labor force in Fontana's San Francisco canneries. A survey in the early 1910's found about 400 Italian women, most of them from the north, receiving 60 to 70 cents for a thirteen-hour-day in the North Beach cannery.[15] When Fontana expanded his operations to other places in California, such as San Jose, San Leandro, Hanford, and Los Angeles, Italian immigrants provided most of the labor. Regional discrimination was not significant in hiring. As an Italian visitor noted, "One can hear almost every Italian dialect in the canneries of North Beach."[16]

Marco Fontana was an outstanding example of the entrepreneurial activity that contributed to the breakdown of regionalism. By the early 1910's there were about a half-dozen San Francisco Italians whose success approached Fontana's. Together, these entrepreneurs changed the character of the San Francisco Italian economy, and indeed the character of the San Francisco Italian community.

Domenico Ghirardelli was one of these entrepreneurs. He too was a Genoese, born at Rapallo in 1817. Like Fontana, Ghirardelli had initially come to San Francisco seeking gold. But whereas Fontana immigrated by way of New York, Ghirardelli came from Lima, Peru, where he had gone from Rapallo in 1837. He too was quickly disillusioned; his adventure in mining lasted only a month. After that he made a living manufacturing and selling chocolate to San Franciscans and to the people of mining towns. By the 1890's Ghirardelli's chocolate business was on its way to becoming an empire. The Italian-American Bank provided the capital for expansion, and Italian immigrants provided the manpower in the factories, which were located in North Beach.[17]

Giuseppe Di Giorgio was another of these entrepreneurs. One of the very few Sicilians in this club of Genoese, he entered San Francisco only after establishing himself in the markets of the East Coast. The Di Giorgio family had migrated to New York in 1888, and Giuseppe had initially ventured into the fruit commission business in New York and Baltimore, where he established several produce auction firms; these had the function of securing markets for both small and large producers.[18] In a visit to California in 1910, Di Giorgio purchased the Earl Fruit Company, a produce marketing and shipping firm founded in the 1880's. He also purchased 1,000 acres of land in Kern County, and progressively increased the acreage to 10,000. By 1922 Di Giorgio was the largest fruit grower in the nation. This growth was accomplished with the aid of loans from the Italian-American Bank, of which he became the president in 1922, and with Italian labor recruited in San Francisco and throughout California.[19]

The Italian-Swiss Colony company and the Western Fish Corporation came into existence only because their founders sat on the board of directors of the Italian-American Bank. The Petri Italian-American Cigar Company, the P. Grassi Travertine Company, the White Line Travel Agency, and the International Fish Company were all firms that borrowed from the Italian-American Bank, the Columbus Italian Bank, the People's Italian Bank, and the Bank of Italy. All had nationwide markets, and all relied on Italian manpower. Andrea Sbarboro's speculation in real estate, especially in North Beach, originated and developed within the Italian-American Bank. Expanding commission houses, such as A. Galli and Company, the G. B. Lavaggi and B. Barbieri Company, the Lelio, Paolucci, and Casanova Company, and the Lorenzo Scatena Company, all did business with the Columbus Italian Bank, the oldest Italian bank of San Francisco, before becoming clients of the Bank of Italy, which bought up its Italian competitors. Amadeo P. Giannini himself was a borrower from the Italian-American Bank, and held stock in it, while he was a commissioner.[20]

By 1910 the days of the modest Italian businessman selling produce on Sansome Street or peddling vegetables through the streets of San Francisco were only a memory. The San Francisco Italian economy had changed. Italian banks had supplanted the mutual aid societies and vegetable commissioners as a source of capital. The determination to compete in the national market had replaced the more modest goal of previous years, to compete in the Northern California market. The old practice of hiring only people from one region had yielded to the hiring of all Italians regardless of regional origin. The goal was no longer to save a little and return to Italy to enjoy it. Rather, Italians wanted to compete at the national level with prominent U.S. businessmen. The days of regionalism, of nostalgia for the old country, and of limited financial goals were over.

The Italian Banks

The creation of the Italian banks was probably the most important step in the growth of the Italian economy in San Francisco and the decline of regionalism. The informal beginnings of the banking system are to be found in the loans extended to growers by commissioners. Consular reports and newspaper articles suggest that this was a widespread practice. In 1889 the consul reported that "farming, especially for those who want to buy land, requires a considerable amount of capital. New immigrants who want to become farmers, as well as old immigrants who want to improve their land, can obtain loans from commissioners."[21] *La Voce del Popolo* notified "Italian immigrants who live out of the city that some commissioners are willing to extend loans to growers interested in selling in the San Francisco market."[22]

Travel agents and regional mutual aid societies also acted as informal bankers, although in a different way. The immigrants deposited their savings with them and relied on them to transfer money to their families in Italy; and the agents and societies made small loans to clients or members who wanted to go into business.[23] But obviously neither commissioners nor mutual aid societies could make loans for major enterprises.

Theoretically, two avenues for raising capital were then available to Italian entrepreneurs. They could borrow from American banks, or they could adopt the corporate form of ownership. American banks were generally unwilling to lend to Italians; according to *L'Italia*, "American banks seem to have serious misgivings about the reliability of Italians in financial matters."[24] And corporate ownership seems to have been particularly unpalatable to most Italians. As early as the 1860's, Consul Cerruti reported that immigrants were generally suspicious of each other, and only rarely entered into financial partnerships.[25] Sbarboro, in 1887, remarked that immigrants were "most unwilling to enter into partnerships with others or to join in any financial venture where they had to share ownership with others."[26] Italians did form a few small corporations. But as the consul reported, "If immigrants enter into partnership with other Italians, it is ordinarily with brothers or close relatives."[27]

The establishment of the first Italian bank in San Francisco, by James P. Fugazi, stimulated the creation of three other banks between 1899 and 1906. Fugazi, an immigrant from Milan, started the White Line Travel Agency in San Francisco in 1876. It handled most of the tickets for immigrants returning to Italy from San Francisco, and also tickets San Francisco Italians purchased for relatives planning to come to America. The agency offered other services too. Since Fugazi was one of the very few Italians to own a safe, some immigrants deposited their savings with him; and some who sent their savings to Italy used Fugazi's connections with other Italian travel agencies and banks.[28] These transactions reached a volume large enough to justify the hiring of a full-time clerk, and eventually, in 1893, the Columbus Savings and Loan Society was chartered.[29] Before then, Italians brave enough to trust banks had used a French bank located in North Beach. In the depression of 1889, that bank failed, with the resultant loss of both the savings and the trust of Italian depositors. But by 1901 the savings deposited with the Fugazi bank amounted to $1.5 million.[30]

The second Italian bank was started in 1899 by Sbarboro, the Genoese known among San Franciscans as the dean of Italian financiers.[31] Unlike Columbus Savings and Loan, which came about almost as an afterthought, the new bank, called the Italian-American Bank, resulted from experiments Sbarboro had been conducting since the late 1880's. After success as an importer and distributor of foreign goods in San Francisco in the 1870's and early 1880's, Sbarboro became increasingly interested in the social aspects of Italian immigration. He became convinced that the solution to the persistent problem of unemployment among Italians lay in cooperation. His first test of this idea was the foundation of what became the Italian-Swiss colony; in this endeavor his idealism suffered a major blow.

He did not give up, however. Throughout the 1890's he promoted the founding of savings and loan associations in San Francisco and Alameda counties. The bank he finally created in 1899, with an initial capital of $750,000, quickly became the largest Italian bank in the city. When in 1901 the Italian government granted the Banco di Napoli the franchise for all Italy to handle emigrants' savings, the Italian-American Bank was chosen as the correspondent for Italians on the West Coast. By 1913 the deposits in the Italian-American Bank amounted to $4 million, and the loans to over $5 million.[32]

In 1906 a third bank came into existence, the Italian People's Bank. Its purpose was to extend loans to Italians who needed to rebuild their houses and businesses after the earthquake. James Fugazi once again promoted the idea. Within a few weeks, some 400 stockholders had subscribed a capital of about $200,000.[33]

Although established both as commercial and savings institutions, the Columbus Savings and Loan Society and the Italian-American Bank catered more to entrepreneurs than to ordinary immigrants. There were two reasons for this. First, many immigrants did not trust banks. "For every immigrant who deposits his savings with the Italian-American Bank," the consul remarked, "there are seven who keep their savings at home or with their mutual aid society."[34] And some Italians preferred American banks, regarding Italian bankers as less reliable. Although Italians in San Francisco had been spared the tragedies of those in several other American cities, where local Italian bankers had either disappeared with the money or gone bankrupt, they were suspicious nonetheless of bankers of their own nationality.[35] Second, bankers in turn did not trust immigrants, especially southerners. Ordinary immigrants were not considered reliable borrowers; though both banks welcomed their savings, the banks seldom made loans to them.[36]

Amadeo P. Giannini played an important role in bridging the gap between banks and immigrants, by reorienting the immigrants away from the mutual aid societies and toward the banks, and by breaking down regional barriers. If Sbarboro helped Italian businessmen overcome their narrow regionalism, Giannini did the same for the average immigrant. Giannini was aware that the main economic potential of unskilled immigrants was in their numbers—a bank could prosper by attracting their savings, regardless of how small, and by making loans to them. Giannini was also aware that the immigrants' main concern was to save; his task was to convince them to trust banks more than mutual aid societies.

Giannini urged the Italian-American Bank to do business with the average immigrant, and opposed the brokerage business conducted by members of the bank's board with bank money. For taking these positions, Giannini was censured, and accordingly he resigned. A few months later he founded the Bank of Italy, with an initial capital of $300,000.[37] Lorenzo Scatena, one of the most energetic Italian merchants, became the president, and Giannini became vice-president and general manager. By 1913 deposits amounted to $12 million.[38]

To counter the immigrant's suspicion of banks, Giannini embarked on a massive publicity campaign. In the fall and winter of 1904, eye-catching advertisements appeared in newspapers like *L'Italia* or were posted and distributed in virtually every street of North Beach, Potrero, Mission, and Portola. One of the fliers read: "One dollar is not much, but it is worth saving. With one dollar you can open a savings account that could become the beginning of your fortune. If at this moment you have one dollar that you may either spend thoughtlessly or put in a safe place, come to the bank and deposit it." Another read: "It is not easy to save money. But if you do, it is safer to put it in a bank than to hide it under a mattress where thieves can steal it and fire can destroy it." The consul re-

15. Andrea Sbarboro, Marco J. Fontana, and A. P. Giannini, architects of the San Francisco Italian economy. Sbarboro (above, left), the dean of the Italian financiers, started out as an importer of foreign goods, then promoted the founding of savings and loan associations among San Francisco Italians. He was also the prime mover behind the creation of the Italian-Swiss colony. In 1899 he founded the Italian-American Bank. Fontana (above, right) had the vision to see the potential in producing canned vegetables and fruit for the national market; his Del Monte Corporation has become a giant in the field. Fontana and Giannini, founder of the Bank of Italy (now the Bank of America), were prominent in the struggle to break the hold of regionalism in the San Francisco Italian community.

ported: "In the last few months A. P. Giannini, one of the leading bankers, has been trying to convince immigrants to deposit their savings with him. Immigrants are skeptical of banks and bankers, and generally refuse to deposit money with people they do not know personally. A few Italians to whom I talked argued that if they deposit the money with the bank, they might not get it back when they return."[39]

By the end of 1904 Giannini realized that his campaign had had only limited success. The immigrants, it seemed, had to be personally reassured, and told what a bank could do for them. Giannini and his associates, therefore, began soliciting new accounts by visiting Italians at home and by appearing at North Beach social events, at Fisherman's Wharf, at the Colombo market, and at other places where Italians congregated. The personal approach succeeded; by 1910 the bank was opening 1,500 new accounts annually, many from Italian immigrants.

Giannini set up branch offices wherever a large group of Italians were settled. As early as 1904 he opened the first branch, in the Mission district; the second was in the Italian section of Oakland. Other branches soon opened elsewhere in California: Santa Barbara, Stockton, Los Angeles. In 1910 the Bank of Italy moved to San Jose, Giannini's birthplace and his old stamping ground when a commissioner. By the mid-1920's the Bank of Italy was present in almost all the important urban areas of California. *L'Italia* commented: "Most immigrants were unfamiliar with banks when they arrived. But Giannini's idea was to make the bank a part of every Italian neighborhood, something Italians could see and learn to trust, and an institution serving all of them regardless of regional origin."[40] Consul Daneo wrote: "The Bank of Italy is becoming the strongest and the most popular among Italians. Part of its appeal is that branches are created wherever there are large groups of Italians. Besides, Giannini has been able to convince Italians that the Bank of Italy is the bank of all Italians."[41]

An obstacle to gaining the immigrants' trust was the near-total control of the bank by northern Italians, mostly Genoese. The members of the board of directors of Columbus Savings, the Italian-American Bank, and the Italian People's Bank were also all northern Italian. Giannini perceived that southern Italians were unlikely to respond to his appeal. In 1912 Giannini wrote: "The secret of our success is to appeal to all Italians. There are 15,000 in San Francisco now, without counting their children, a third from the south. They all want to save, and in this regard there is no difference between northerners and southerners. Our bank can teach and help them to do it if we are able to break the barriers of suspicion and regionalism."[42] *L'Italia* expressed the same idea: "The Bank of Italy was not established for the benefit of one regional group, but for all Italians."[43]

Giannini was aware that most immigrants still cherished the idea of returning to Italy. As long as that idea was alive, immigrants were unlikely to develop a strong commitment to the San Francisco Italian colony or to go beyond regionalism. But Giannini probably guessed that many immigrants would ultimately stay. To those who said their goal was to buy land in Italy, Giannini countered: "Why can't the goal that includes yourself, your family, and your land in Italy become instead yourself, your family, your job, and your savings account in San Francisco?"[44] This argument did not engage the sympathies of the Italian consul, who commented: "There are bankers who would rather have immigrants stay than save and return. They often try to convince immigrants that it is in their best interest to stay, that life is better in the United States than in Italy, and that a piece of land is not the best security for the future; this reduces the immigrants' attachment to the motherland."[45]

By the 1920's the strong regionalism of the 1890's was, if not dead, at least moribund. The Bank of Italy had become "the national institution of the Italians of California," as *L'Italia* put it.[46] One by one, the Bank of Italy purchased all the other Italian banks. The last to go was the Italian-American Bank, in 1926. Sbarboro realized that the days of the small bank had come to an end, and that the Bank of Italy had captured most of the Italian market in California. The following year Giannini created the Calitalo Investment Corporation, a holding company that offered "the Italians of California a new and homogeneous way to invest their savings."[47]

The way in which *L'Italia* promoted the Bank of Italy is another sign of how San Francisco Italians were progressively thinking more in national than in regional terms by the late 1920's. To patronize the Bank of Italy, immigrants were told, was both an economic and a patriotic act. "Italians are asked to support those institutions that promote the Italian name abroad. The Bank of Italy is that institution for the Italians of California."[48] This rhetoric mirrored the attitude of the community; when the bank building failed to display the Italian flag on Italian national holidays, immigrants complained. One Italian wrote to the editor of *L'Italia*: "You have to do it. After all, it is the symbol of our national unity."[49]

The problem regionalism posed for Italian businessmen in San

Francisco was not greatly different from the problems other American entrepreneurs confronted. For both, the goal of organizing the economy and increasing production would not be served by a laboring class divided into groups. As Robert E. Park and Herbert A. Miller wrote in 1921, the main problem America had to face was that of "homogenizing the life of the immigrants with our own by breaking down national differences."[50] Italian entrepreneurs, within their own world, faced a similar challenge: to homogenize regional differences into one Italian community.

Emigration and Nationalism

The rise of Italian nationalism in the early twentieth century was a complex phenomenon that had an important impact on immigrants. Unlike any other nationalistic movement in Europe in the early twentieth century, Italian nationalism made a direct connection between nationalism and emigration.

Mario Morasso, who laid the groundwork for the new Italian nationalism, developed the two basic ideas: a glorification of imperialism, and a theory of the productive bourgeoisie. According to Morasso, civilization was not evolving toward democracy, but toward a system based on force and violence—among nations competing for markets, and among men competing for the control of resources in technologically oriented societies. Krupp and Morgan were the "new men," who understood and exercised power. Morasso was pessimistic about the competitiveness of Latins in imperialistic conflict. Italy, he thought, had one advantage, the fertility of its people, which qualified the nation to be, along with England, one of the world's greatest colonizers.[51]

It was Enrico Corradini, the most prominent Italian nationalist of those years, who linked nationalism to emigration, by expanding on Morasso's ideas on the fertility of the Latin race and its implications. Lecture trips to South America and the United States gave Corradini a firsthand acquaintance with the consequences of mass emigration, and convinced him that emigration was the great social issue of the time. Nationalists, he felt, could use that issue to spread their ideas.

Corradini argued that every poor Italian peasant deserved to remain and work in Italy. But since that was not possible, everyone at least deserved to live in a colonial extension of Italy. Corradini summed up this rationale for expansion in a slogan: "The imperialism of the poor." Unfortunately, Italy had little chance of gaining rich colonial extensions in competition with the more powerful nations of Europe. This realization offered Corradini a basis for combining revolutionary syndicalism with nationalism. The fate of Italian emigrants, he argued, was merely a reflection of the larger and universal exploitation of the poor nations by the rich ones. The exploitation of peasants by landlords in Italy was, in the light of international events, less important than the exploitation of Italy by other nations. The conclusion was logical. Italians should forget their class differences and subordinate class goals to national goals. Moreover, internal conflict had to be redirected outward in the form of expansion or war.[52]

Corradini's linking of revolutionary syndicalism and nationalism had several implications for Italian emigration. First, emigrants were part of a national community whose exploitation by richer nations was a reminder that only national solidarity—not class conflict—could restore the greatness of Italy. It was not important, according to the nationalists, that class differences in Italy gave rise to emigration; the key point was that the international exploitation of Italy made every Italian a potential emigrant. Second, emigrants, as part of the national community, could not be allowed to drift away, lose their national identity, forget their language, or abandon their determination to return home. Third, since Italy had no formal colonies, Italians had to live among foreign people.

Therefore, the large Italian settlements in North and South America had to be considered informal extensions of Italy, and to be kept as close as possible to the motherland. As the argument went, Italians as a race did not have a great future in North America, since Italians were ill-equipped to compete with the Anglo-Saxon race.* As a consequence, Italy's colonial expansion depended not on the power to compete with other European nations, but on keeping the allegiance of her citizens living abroad. As an Italian journalist put it in 1910: "Emigration can be a way to national prosperity and a peaceful avenue to colonial expansion. If Italy will take advantage of emigration, it will rise in economic and political power."[53]

The nationalist movement prompted the creation of national organizations aimed at fostering a deeper sense of national identity among Italians abroad. Organizations that already existed, like the Associazione Nazionale, founded in 1887, and the Opera di Assistenza, founded in 1900, responded to the nationalist ideas. Old

*They had a great future, however, in Latin America, which, without being Italian territory, could become a great Italian country. See King and Okey, *Italy Today*, pp. 314–21.

and new organizations were invited to join the Italica Gens, a federation of all agencies concerned with Italians living abroad. The federation's journal, *Italica Gens*, founded in 1910, observed that most Italians abroad showed little national loyalty because regional loyalty was more important for them. The federation pointed to the mutual aid societies as the main forces keeping regionalism alive; moreover, the most successful Italians tended to leave regional groups and identify with the nation where they lived, which deprived the less successful immigrants of a much-needed leadership.[54] The conclusion was that in order to overcome regionalism and prevent the defection of the most influential immigrants, "history and the opinion of the experts in matters of emigration advise us that the solution is to be found in the creation of Italian schools abroad, which is the first priority of the federation."[55]

In support of these goals, the Italica Gens promoted the founding of secretariats in the larger Italian communities of Europe and the Americas. A secretariat was a center that provided Italians with social services and worked for the establishment of Italian schools. In 1910 there were already five secretariats in San Francisco: two on Dupont Street, one on Stockton, another on Clay, and the last at the Jesuit College, now the University of San Francisco. The Italian communities of New York and Chicago also had five.[56] In 1914 the Italian consul in San Francisco wrote: "The secretariats are slowly replacing the mutual aid societies and breaking down regionalism. Unfortunately, the interest in the Italian school is not as widespread as it should be. In addition, the school has financial problems. But there is no doubt that it is fulfilling a great need."[57] In the prewar years, it seems, the shift from regionalism to nationalism picked up momentum, for as late as 1912 the consul had concluded: "Our colony has not yet developed a collective social awareness. We are still at the stage of social regionalism."[58]

It should be noted that Americans helped and encouraged San Francisco Italians to abandon regionalism. California Progressives like Hiram Johnson, Simon Lubin, George Bell, and James Mullenbach were opposed to the concentration of immigrants in cities, hoping to prevent the apparently insoluble problems seen in eastern cities. With rumors abounding that the opening of the Panama Canal would substantially increase immigration to California, these Californians argued that it was in the best interests of the state to discipline the movement of immigrants. Of all the nationalities the Progressives were concerned about, Italians were first, because of their numbers and their fierce regionalism. The California Progressives thus tried to combat regionalism by advocating the creation of national organizations for San Francisco Italians—that is, organizations for all Italians. And they tried, although unsuccessfully, to foster cooperation between Italians, immigrants of other nationalities, and city agencies like the Associated Charities.[59]

The Italian Welfare Agency

A good illustration of how economic expansion, nationalism, and the pressure of California Progressives contributed to the decline of regionalism and the rise of national organizations is provided by the events surrounding the establishment of the Italian Welfare Agency. This agency came into being in 1916, when Italy was involved in the world war and nationalism ran high both in Italy and among San Francisco Italians. The story begins, however, in December 1913, when a disagreement between Italian farm workers and Italian growers ended in a series of riots that terrorized the towns of Maryland and Wheatland, northeast of San Francisco. After the riots the workers moved to San Francisco, where they spent the winter waiting for the new season. The national news coverage of the events and the growing alarm of San Franciscans prompted a federal investigation, which detected both the influence of the Industrial Workers of the World among Italian farm workers and a number of irregularities in the way growers dealt with immigrants. The investigation also revealed that the state of California had neglected to carry out certain labor laws.[60]

The recommendations of the Federal Commission on Industrial Relations reached Governor Johnson at about the same time as those of his own commission. In 1912 he had appointed a team of social workers and social scientists to study California labor. Their report warned that the already-pressing problems of immigrant labor would worsen after the opening of the Panama Canal.[61] Katharine Felton, a social worker and the executive director of the Associated Charities of San Francisco, called the governor's attention to the condition of Italians in the city, and asked him to exercise leadership before the situation became unmanageable.[62]

In 1914, following the proposals of both studies, Johnson recommended to the California Legislature the creation of a commission with the power to regulate relations between immigrant labor and management, to inspect the working conditions of farm workers, and to enforce federal and state labor legislation. The state had been negligent long enough, he said. "In the latter part of 1913, a condition which perhaps in some degree had existed for several years, but which in its unorganized and unmassed state had attracted little public attention, became a burning problem. We cannot let it become worse than what it is."[63] The California Legislature accepted the recommendation and created the California Commission on Immigration and Housing.[64]

The first task the five members of the commission set themselves was a detailed study of immigrant labor in California, with special attention to San Francisco and the surrounding region. It was not true, the members argued, that immigrants were a threat to society. They had become a threat only when abused by management, and management had frequently ignored its obligations. But the core of the problem was the lack of organization among the immigrants. It was true, the commission concluded, that there were some regional Italian groups. But by and large they were inefficient, because they pursued parochial goals without coordination between the groups. The report noted: "As to interaction among groups and agencies, social workers at times express wonder that with all the talk about cooperation and coordination a complete fusion has not yet taken place."[65] Simply stated, the goals of the commission were two: first, to organize the Italian immigrants along national lines; and second, to have the activities of the national organization coordinated by the commission.

The members of the commission must have been aware that Italians, long divided into regional societies, would be reluctant to convert to the new faith. Lubin told Katharine Felton that "Italians are not one but many groups; besides they are almost totally isolated from the larger society."[66] But Lubin also pointed out that there were prominent Italian businessmen in San Francisco who enjoyed social respect and knew the techniques of organization. They could use their prestige and knowledge to bring the dispersed and inefficient regional organizations together. Felton communicated the plans of the commission to a select group of Italian businessmen and bankers in September 1916. It was perplexing, she said, that "such a rich colony as the Italians are unwilling to take care of their social problems."[67]

Many defended the regional societies that already existed. The secretary of the Comitato di Soccorso e Patronato stated that it had been "the first institution established for the assistance of Italians in San Francisco, and ought to be enlarged and consolidated."[68] The consul also tried to save the Comitato; he wrote to Lubin that it was "a branch of the Italian government and a glory of the Italian colony in San Francisco."[69] And *La Voce del Popolo* protested that "the mutual aid societies have been doing and are still doing a valuable and probably irreplaceable service."[70]

But the members of the commission and the Italians were not swayed by such pressure. On October 15, 1916, at an open meeting, a group of about fifteen Italian businessmen and bankers put Felton's program into effect. Because a "deep mistrust of the Comitato di Soccorso e Patronato made it impossible to reorganize its services," and because regional societies were incapable of coping with the problems created by mass immigration, they were setting up the Italian Welfare Agency, to serve all Italians regardless of region or origin.[71] Marco Fontana and Domenico Ghirardelli were elected president and vice-president of the organization. T. Bacigalupi, president of the Columbus Savings and Loan Society, Amadeo P. Giannini, Andrea Sbarboro, and F. N. Belgrano, president of the Italian People's Bank, were elected to the board of directors. After making personal contributions of $300 to $500 each, the directors appealed for broad support: "All Italians are asked to contribute. It is our intention to tax every member of the colony who has an independent business an annual sum for the support of the social services the Italian community needs."[72]

The San Francisco Italian newspapers responded to the appeal enthusiastically. "A great step has been taken," said *L'Italia*; "the will of the colony has been followed, and its real needs have been acknowledged. Now all Italians, regardless of their regional origin, will follow their leaders in this common project."[73] The following day another appeal was made: "Fishermen, grocers, scavengers, artisans, fruit commissioners, and all Italians regardless of regional origin or occupation—and especially those who feel they do not belong in the colony—will be asked to join, to act, and to give. The agency is the new national institution where the masses of unskilled Italian workers will find a social purpose and a way to help themselves and those less fortunate."[74]

Located in the heart of North Beach, the agency offered important social services: help in finding work, financial support in time of need, medical assistance, referral to other agencies for special services, and legal advice. Immigrants hampered by language and a lack of familiarity with the American system sought agency help in dealing with the courts, the hospitals, the police, and the schools. From 1916 to the present—the agency is still in operation—thousands of families have received some sort of aid from the agency.

An important detail must be added to this story. At the end of

1916, at a meeting at the St. Francis Hotel in San Francisco, the California Commission and the Associated Charities of San Francisco expressed a desire for closer cooperation with the new Italian agency.[75] The Italians thanked these organizations, but went their own way. In late 1918 Felton expressed disappointment that the effort to bring Italians into "a larger and city-wide super-organization" had been practically ignored, and that there was no sign that the Italians were willing to cooperate.[76]

The Italian Welfare Agency was the creation of a small group of successful businessmen, supported by the local Italian press. But how widespread was the support for the new organization? This is not a simple question to answer, since we do not have public opinion surveys for the San Francisco Italians of the time. But the changing editorial policies of the two major San Francisco Italian newspapers from 1900 to 1920 throw some light on the matter, if we assume that major changes in editorial policy reflect, at least to a degree, changes in the attitudes of readers.

As we saw, *L'Italia* and *La Voce del Popolo* started out as bulletins of particular regional societies, and in time covered the activities of other societies as well. Up to 1910 the two newspapers were clearly no more than the combined bulletins of several regional societies, rather than the press of an ethnic community enjoying some sort of internal cohesion. The first page reported in detail the different activities of regional societies. There was only one annual event that engaged the interest of all societies, the Columbus Day parade.[77]

Beginning around 1910, the format of the newspapers changed. The front page covered problems and activities common to the Italian colony at large. The societies were covered less extensively, and ordinarily on the inside pages. And the papers expressed disapproval of conflicts that arose between regional societies. We can notice a similar change in the few descriptive accounts of San Francisco Italians that we have for those years. Those written before the First World War typically dwelt on regional differences.[78] But by the 1920's and 1930's writers had become concerned with the accomplishments of the San Francisco Italians as a national group. Regional differences are seldom mentioned.[79]

The events of 1916 reflected important changes among the Italians of San Francisco. They were now willing to think of themselves as one group, with common interests and goals. Regional identity did not disappear; but it was superseded as the basis of social organization. The action taken in 1916 encouraged the centralization of leadership in the hands of a business elite—people who had made their fortune in San Francisco rather than Italy, and whose main concern was not to return to Italy, but to expand their economic interests in the United States.

This was all part of a trend that picked up momentum, especially in the late 1920's and the 1930's with the advent of Fascism in Italy. There was an increasing awareness of a common national identity. Economic activity expanded beyond regional boundaries, supraregional organizations were created, and regionalism was progressively confined to less consequential areas of social interaction. But the tacit refusal of the Italian Welfare Agency to cooperate with the Associated Charities and the California Commission was a sign that the Italians were still either unwilling or unable to close the gap between themselves and the larger American society.

Fascism

There was an irony in the immigrants' conversion to Fascism. As Massimo Salvadori, an anti-Fascist émigré in the United States, put it: "In Italy they had never been Italians; but in America they became nationalists, and to that extent they were Fascists."[80] The immigrants' nationalism had little impact on the history of Italian nationalism; but it was a significant step in the social history of the immigrants.[81] Throughout the 1920's, Fascist propaganda, emphasizing themes calculated to create a feeling of solidarity between Italy and the immigrants, was left undisturbed both by Americans and by anti-Fascist Italians. Arthur Livingstone, an American expert on Italian affairs, wrote in 1927 that "on the scale of the whole American scene Fascism, like London, is really nothing." He pointed out, however, that Fascism was important for those immigrants "who have found their homesickness roused to self-consciousness by the spectacle of a vibrant Italy and seek formal recognition from Mussolini as individuals who have done credit to their country by successful lives abroad."[82]

In the 1930's refugees arriving from Europe tried to expose the incompatibility of American democracy and Fascism. They denounced discrimination against Italians as the root of the immigrants' alienation and of their receptivity to Mussolini's nationalism. Carlo Sforza, for instance, wrote: "You cannot make a good citizen out of a man who is intellectually and culturally impoverished by being cut off from the only past he had."[83] And Gaetano Salvemini, in probably the best analysis of the influence of Fascism on Italians in the United States, argued that Fascism was accepted because it played on "the inferiority complex and reactions against real or imaginary injustices."[84] Interest in this topic died with the Second World War, which spurred the assimilation of Italo-Americans. The recalling of the Fascist era, moreover, was not good policy for Italy at a time when Italy needed massive American assistance.[85]

The interest in Fascism and its impact on immigrants revived during the 1950's and 1960's for several reasons. A number of anti-Fascist exiles wrote memoirs that raised questions about the impact of Fascism both in Italy and among emigrants.[86] Scholarly studies of Fascism and anti-Fascism attracted wide attention.[87] And an increased interest in immigration and ethnic history led historians to reexamine the impact of Fascism on the Italian-American experience.[88]

Of the several American publications on this topic, John P. Diggins's is probably the most extensive and informed. His interpretation adds little to Salvemini's. Diggins wrote:

> Fascist propaganda provided the fertilizer, but American society had planted the seed. Pressures both external and internal left Italian-Americans ripe for Fascism. A nascent inferiority complex, a nostalgic nationalism, and a fear for family solidarity and community produced a quiet, collective anxiety. Inasmuch as Fascism was an answer to those psychic questions, the Italian American reaction to it was more a socially conditioned reflex than a politically conscious response.[89]

Diggins's and Salvemini's interpretation is problematic. It is difficult to obtain evidence about a state of mind, and statements in this area can only be tentative. Also, both authors seem to imply that external pressures, and discrimination above all, forced Italians into isolation and made them receptive to Fascism.

This assumes, however, that Italians both wanted to be part of American society and were conscious of discrimination against them. The evidence on Italians in San Francisco hardly bears out these assumptions. In general, Italians showed little desire to assimilate into American society, even before the advent of Fascism, and they showed little awareness of discrimination.

The attitude of Italians toward naturalization is one measure of their lack of interest in becoming a part of American society. Naturalization was unpopular with Italians from the earliest days. Consular reports in the 1860's and 1870's proudly reported that few immigrants had severed their ties from the motherland and become American citizens.[90] When in 1868 *La Voce del Popolo* urged Italians to naturalize in order to have the right to vote, it met a negative response.[91] Sbarboro's cooperative farming venture failed partly because applicants had to be either American citizens or immigrants with first papers, and few Italians qualified. The 1910 census showed that about 70 percent of all Italians in California were still aliens, as against 15 percent who were Americans and 5 percent who had first papers (10 percent did not state).[92] By 1920 only 30 percent of the Italians in San Francisco had become American citizens, compared with about 70 percent of the Germans, 76 percent of the Irish, and 65 percent of the Russians. Ten years later 44 percent of the Italian-born males living in San Francisco were American citizens; that is, 7,000 out of 16,000. Among females the percentage was even lower, only 31 percent.[93]

It is more difficult to measure the perception Italians had of discrimination. There was discrimination to be sure, but to what extent were Italians aware of it? Though the argument here is obviously negative, there is little evidence in *La Voce del Popolo* and *L'Italia* to suggest an awareness by Italians of what the non-Italian press or San Franciscans in general thought about them. And many Italians lived in relative isolation, coming in contact with American society only rarely, as the survey of the 1930's pointed out.[94]

It seems more plausible, therefore, that the reasons Fascism became popular in San Francisco lay within the Italian community. By the 1930's the Italians in San Francisco had achieved a level of success that in their eyes was probably as spectacular as the success the returnees of several decades before had seen in themselves. The rate of home ownership illustrates the material success of Italians. By 1930, 47 percent of the Italians of the city—or about 6,000 families—owned their own house. The rate for the city as a whole was 41 percent, and among immigrant groups, only the Irish, with 57 percent, were higher than the Italians.[95]

Immigrants needed formal recognition for their achievements, as Livingstone pointed out, and traditionally Italians had found it within their regional groups.[96] By the 1920's and 1930's, however, the regional groups had been undermined by economic and social developments. To replace their regional orientation, San Francisco Italians might in theory have established themselves as a semiautonomous national community; they had common social and economic interests. But they lacked a supraregional or national ideology. As Massimo Salvadori put it, the immigrants had never been Italians when they were in Italy—that is, they had never felt part of the nation. Fascism, therefore, provided a set of ideas that enabled immigrants to endow their common experience with a global meaning, to give formal recognition to individual efforts, and to advance the organization of the colony along supraregional lines.

Renzo De Felice's interpretation of Fascism suggests points of convergence between Fascism in Italy and Fascism in San Francisco. According to De Felice, Fascism found its most ardent supporters among the Italian middle class, which, after the world war, underwent a profound crisis. The middle class had to confront "a society in the process of rapid transformation, best represented by the growing strength of the proletariat and of the upper bourgeoisie." The middle class felt caught in between, without "adequate instruments for collective bargaining and in a situation of steady loss of social and economic status."[97] Thus Fascism represented an effort to create a vital space for the middle class by curbing, at the same time, the inordinate power of both the proletariat and the upper class. Fascism was the coming of age of the middle class under adverse circumstances.

The situation in America, of course, was different, but there were similarities. In San Francisco too the most ardent supporters of Fascism were Italians, and also some Italo-Americans who had achieved middle-class status. The leading Italians who were interned during the Second World War were lawyers, doctors, businessmen, and newspaper editors. Why did they support Fascism, when their education and their success seemingly qualified them to be full members of American society? They may have felt themselves of uncertain status, caught between two groups. On the one hand, they could not, or would not, identify with middle-class Americans, perhaps because of prejudice and personal insecurity. On the other hand, they had separated themselves from the mass of ordinary immigrants by achieving economic or professional success. These middle-class immigrants needed to be different both from the middle-class Americans and from the average San Francisco Italian. Fascism provided an identity.

Support for Fascism, of course, was strong among most San Francisco Italians, regardless of social class. But it is likely that working-class Italians in San Francisco were coopted into supporting Fascism by middle-class Italians in the same way as Italians in Italy. Recall that Corradini asked Italians to forget their class differences in favor of national goals. That argument certainly provided middle-class San Francisco Italians with a device to reinforce their power within the Italian community. Moreover, even many working-class Italians had achieved a success that was in their own eyes very great, however American society viewed it. Thus the adherence of these Italians to Fascism was related to the high estimation they had of their success in San Francisco and the low recognition they were accorded by the host society. This explains why support for Fascism was probably stronger in San Francisco than in Italy. In sum, for both the average Italian immigrant and the middle-class San Francisco Italian, Fascism seemed to offer stability and social recognition.

A number of occurrences in the 1920's and 1930's illustrate these general points. The Italian press of San Francisco, for one thing, was rather selective in reporting Fascist ideas. Two themes were often sounded, especially in *L'Italia*, which became the most vocal Fascist publication in San Francisco. First, immigrants were told that Italy had not forgotten them, but, on the contrary, considered them most important, both because their achievements had demonstrated Italian strength and because the power they had achieved with hard work was a "prophesy of further expansion by the Latin race."[98] And second, these achievements had been possible because immigrants had set aside regional animosity; emigration was not the result of poverty, but of the "exuberant expansion of a great race, destined to conquer the world again."[99] To many immigrants, perhaps, such talk gave a higher meaning to their economic success.

The rise of supraregional goals resulted in new organizations, centered around Fugazi Hall, a building in the heart of North Beach. The Italian Legion, the After Work Club, the After School Club, and the Union Sport Club were all recreational youth groups of Fascist inspiration. The Fascio Umberto Nobile and the Dante Alighieri Society met every month at the Fugazi Hall, where the Dante society had its library. The Cenacolo Club, a social organization for prominent businessmen and professionals of Italian birth or parentage; the Ex-Combattenti Society, a federated, nationwide Italian version of the American Legion, with headquarters in New York; the Sons of Italy, the largest Italian organization in the United States and probably the only nationwide Italian organization before the First World War—all these greatly expanded their membership among San Francisco Italians in the 1930's. Even the San Francisco Italian Chamber of Commerce was revitalized, and its publication, *La Rassegna Commerciale*, revamped.[100]

Riding the crest of nationalism, the Italian press also greatly expanded its circulation in the 1930's. The two major newspapers reached a wide audience. In 1931 *L'Italia* had almost 10,000 subscriptions in the city and 4,000 in the surrounding region; ten years earlier its entire circulation had been 6,000. *La Voce del Popolo* had almost 7,000 subscribers in San Francisco, and 3,000 more in Northern California; ten years before the total had been 5,000. *L'Unione*, a Catholic weekly established in 1919 by James Bacigalupi and Sylvester Andriano, had an initial circulation of 2,000 copies; it reached 5,000 copies in the early 1930's. *Il Leone*, the newspaper of the Sons of Italy, reached a circulation of about 1,000 copies. *La Critica*, a weekly founded in 1891 by Carlo Mancini, turned anti-Fascist in the 1920's and soon disappeared. Only one anti-Fascist newspaper survived through the 1930's, *Il Corriere del Popolo*. Founded in 1911 by two brothers, Mameli and Pierino Pedretti, it turned anti-Fascist in the 1930's, mainly under the editorship of Carmelo Zito, the best-known maverick writer the San Francisco Italian colony ever produced. Three Italian radio programs were also started in the 1930's, all openly Fascist.[101]

Even the Italian schools enjoyed a few years of success, with increased support from Italians. Starting in the mid-1920's, the Italian Language School expanded from Fugazi Hall, establishing five branches in the city. Operational costs were met with large contributions from the Italian government, which, besides paying the teachers, sent textbooks from Italy. The school's curriculum was under the control of the Italian consul, who used the schools to promote Fascist ideas. For example, the third-year reader used by Italo-American children read: "You, little children, are forced to be away from your country; but remember that when you love a country, the country is always within you. Remember that your country is Italy; you will think of it every time you see the three colors. Italy and its hero [Mussolini] must make your heart thrill."[102]

Italians denied being anti-democratic or anti-American. The Italian Chamber of Commerce, the Italian-American Society, the Cenacolo Club, the Transamerica Corporation, and the Bank of Italy rejected accusations by the Daughters of the American Revolution, the Elks, the American Legion, and other patriotic societies that Italians in San Francisco were undermining American democracy. From the arguments presented in *L'Italia*, it is clear that the Italians and the Americans were speaking different languages. Americans were concerned with the implications of a group of immigrants' being loyal to a foreign totalitarian government; but Italians were supporting Fascism for the sense of identity it gave them. In 1937, for instance, there was strong criticism of the Italian school for cultivating undemocratic ideas among young children who would be adult members of American society. The Italians' rebuttal

16. Italo-American children arriving in Genoa for summer camp, 1930's. Mussolini took various measures to extend his influence among Italians living abroad, including the organization of summer camps expressly for the children of Italian immigrants. San Francisco Italians responded positively to Fascism because it recognized the importance of their achievements in the United States, and because it provided a bond with Italy of a sort that they had never had, even before departing.

did not mention the political implications at all: "All we want to do through our schools is to defend our country of origin from attacks and false accusations by people of bad faith. Our determination is to make known the progress that our country has made under Fascism."[103]

The growing uneasiness of American society toward Italians was brought to national attention in 1937 in a Senate speech by William Borah of Idaho. Borah declared that "no one can be a loyal American citizen who advocates Fascism." Ettore Patrizi, the editor of *L'Italia*, responded: "I am deeply convinced that of all social and political reforms since the time of the French Revolution, Fascism has been the most beneficial for every social class. . . . The real problem with Americans is that they have never taken the trouble to understand Fascism. Even the most intelligent Americans seem to have problems in understanding the true nature of Fascism." Borah's reply, reported by most newspapers in the nation, pointed out that Italian leaders had isolated Italian communities from the mainstream of American life by promoting Fascism, and cited San Francisco Italians as an outstanding example.[104]

What happened in 1943 was mentioned at the beginning of the previous chapter. According to the committee investigating Fascism in San Francisco, Italians had built their identity around Fascism. Depositions from 35 witnesses placed the Italian consulate at the center of Fascist propaganda operations. The major Italian-American newspapers openly supported Fascism, and *La Rassegna Commerciale* was registered with the State Department as foreign government propaganda. Amadeo P. Giannini was blamed for allowing his picture in that journal to be framed by the coat of arms of the House of Savoy and the fasces of Mussolini.

Fugazi Hall was described as the meeting place of Italian Fascists on the West Coast. The Italian Legion, the After Work Club, the After School Club, the Union Sport Club, the Cenacolo Club, the lodges of the Sons of Italy, and the Italian Chamber of Commerce were all described as organizations promoting Fascism. The Italian Language school and the textbooks it used became the central target of the commission's investigation. The three radio programs were also censured. To the California Legislature the commission reported: "It was with some pardonable gratification that the committee viewed the order from General De Witt's headquarters removing Andriano, Patrizi, and Turco, plus many others from the area comprising the Western Defense Command for the duration of the war." The leaders who were not so removed were publicly discredited, and most organizations either died or found it virtually impossible to operate.[105]

The war brought to an abrupt end a train of events that had started in 1916 with the founding of the Italian Welfare Agency. In those 25 years Italians in San Francisco had transcended regionalism, developed a sense of national identity that came to have its inspiration in Fascism, and by and large evaded the issue of Americanization. Only during the war did American society force Italians to come to terms with the fact of over half a century of living in San Francisco: it was time Italians gave their loyalty to the country where they had spent almost all their lives.[106]

For Italians, nationalism was a necessary step in the process of assimilation into American society. In modern societies an individual or a group must in some measure transcend particularism and localism and relate to a variety of groups and other individuals. Italian immigrants brought to San Francisco a culture rooted in localism, and their introduction to American society occurred by stages. The first stage saw the decline of campanilismo and the rise of regionalism; the second, the decline of regionalism and the rise of nationalism. Paradoxical as it might sound, Fascism contributed to the assimilation of Italians in America by helping them discover a common national identity.

The transition from regionalism to nationalism occurred mostly because of dynamics that the immigrants themselves generated. Outside stimuli, like Italian nationalism and Fascism, provided timely ideologies and increased the tempo of change. But it was the drive for material success that in the end made immigrants feel a national identity. Italians did not necessarily welcome the change; indeed, there was a good deal of questioning. But it is clear that Italians in San Francisco wanted success—material success—enough to let go of regionalism when regionalism did not serve their interests. The mental journey that San Francisco Italians made in a century changed their social universe almost totally. They started out with campanilismo and ended with Americanization, which made them a part of a multiethnic and almost infinitely diverse society.

The Americanization of Italian immigrants should be seen as a chapter in the larger story of declining regional cultures under the impact of modernization, but with a difference. For most people in western societies, the transition was from a regional culture within a geographical territory to the dominant national culture of the same territory. For instance, the southern French peasants were absorbed into the national French culture, the culture of Paris. For Italians, and others in the United States, the process was more complex. They went from a regional culture of a certain geographical area to an altogether new and unrelated national culture. And the important point is that Italian-Americans did not move directly from campanilismo to Americanism; first came Italian nationalism, and then the American national culture. Immigrants from the Italian provinces had to discover that they were Italians before they could become Americans.

CHAPTER 10

The Immigrant Experience

TWO questions have been emphasized in this study of the San Francisco Italians: whether change or continuity predominated in the transition the immigrants made from the Old World to the New, and whether regional differences survived in the United States. The two questions are interrelated. The disappearance of regional differences in the New World would direct our attention to change; the survival of regional differences would show continuity.

In the last 30 years the answers historians have given to the two questions have gone through two phases. Earlier historians emphasized change, contrasting the premodern, agrarian societies the emigrants left and the modern, industrialized American society in which they settled. Accordingly, the immigrants' experience was described as a process of uprooting and alienation: the loss of a familiar world, and the bewilderment induced by a new and threatening environment. In the end, however, the process, painful though it was, proved worthwhile, for the new American man that emerged from the ordeal of immigration was unquestionably better suited to the modern world than his European grandfather.

Recent historians have emphasized continuity. The transition from Europe to America was certainly a break with the past, and it did indeed lead to the slow and painful disappearance of cherished traditions and the assumption of new attitudes. But the immigrants, according to this view, were able to preserve the core of the old culture even as they made superficial changes in order to function in the new society. Recent events seem to corroborate this interpretation. How could the resurgence of ethnic awareness in the 1960's and 1970's have occurred if ethnic differences had disappeared?[1]

The historians of change, as we may call them, focus on structures; they argue that changes in structures necessarily bring about changes in individuals. Both the Marxist and the structural-functional schools share this assumption. Marxist historians, for instance, argue that if we understand how structures change, we understand how individuals change, too, since individual lives are simply epiphenomena of larger social configurations. The historians of change have made an invaluable contribution to the study of immigration. By showing the difference between European and American conditions, they have underlined both the deep sense of loss immigrants felt for the world they left behind and their long-lasting alienation from a new society that they could not understand.

My analysis does not disprove these conclusions. On the contrary, my study of return migration reveals that structural changes in the immigrants' lives and personal alienation were probably more pervasive than we had assumed, and not only in the United States. When Italians returned to Italy, they witnessed additional changes and felt a different and more disturbing kind of alienation. The towns and villages were not the same as those they had left: much had changed in the few years they had been gone. Returnees painfully recognized that they no longer had a place they could call their own. They were aliens both in the United States and in Italy.

And yet the approach of the historians of change, however valid, does not fully explain the experience of the Italians in Italy and San Francisco. These historians overlook powerful continuities between the Italian and American experiences. For instance, the assumption that individuals respond in predictable ways to structural changes is not supported by our sample, which shows that poverty in Italy elicited not one response but several. In some regions the peasants refused to leave, organized, and fought for better contracts and working conditions. In other regions peasants left for a while, then returned to buy land and build a house with money made in America. And in Sardinia peasants simply acquiesced in their poverty. The structural-functional school argues that if there are two regions of differing prosperity, people will move from the poorer to the richer. In reality, however, different levels of economic development may determine only whether or not moving makes sense economically. The final decision to go or to stay is made by individuals not for economic reasons but for sociocultural reasons, reasons that may be rooted in local economic conditions but are not solely a function of them.

Our sample also casts doubt on the notion of demographic transition. The historians of change argue that the transition from a rural to an urban environment increases individualism and reduces the size of families because of the pressures of urban life. As we have seen, however, there is not necessarily an inverse correlation between urbanization and family size. Indeed, we found that southern Italians increased the size of their families when they moved from an agrarian to an urban setting. A large family was probably not in their best economic interest, but it was important to them for other reasons.

The historians of change also fail to recognize the complexity of the societies emigrants came from. My research shows that in the late nineteenth century Italy was far from being the stagnant, premodern agrarian society portrayed by the historians of change. On the contrary, Italy was undergoing change as a result of the radicalization of peasants' goals, which were land ownership in the small-property areas and better contracts and working conditions in the areas of large estates. The socioeconomic dynamics of Italy were, of course, different from those the immigrants encountered in the New World. But attentive study shows many important similarities between the two societies.

The historians of change de-emphasize the role of regionalism among Italians in the United States: the experience of immigration, they argue, dissolved the regionalism that peasants had commonly felt before they left for America. Our sample, however, shows persistent regional differences permeating the whole immigrant experience: the settlements the Italians created, the work they did, the families they raised, and the goals they set for themselves. Moreover, regional differences continue to show up when their children come of age.

Finally, the historians of change have played down the active role of the immigrants themselves, preferring to see them simply as products of their environment. But the story of the San Francisco Italians shows that individuals and socioeconomic structures can move in different and even opposite directions. For instance, whereas the historians of change see Italian migration to San Francisco as the logical response of people seeking better economic opportunity, most immigrants, as we have seen, intended to return to Italy at the earliest opportunity. In the end, to be sure, events proved the returnees ill-advised; few indeed realized their goal of the good life in Italy, and many returned permanently to the United States. But the original determination of millions to return to Italy suggests that historians have to look at immigration not only structurally but also from within, through the eyes of the immigrants themselves.

The historians of continuity, as we may call the other school, reacting to these narrow structural and environmental explanations, argue the need to reintroduce the immigrants into the study of immigration.[2] They argue, among other things, that in modern societies structures are likely to change at a faster pace than individuals. Despite being subjected to major structural changes, Italian immigrants had little trouble concentrating on what the French historian Pierre Bourdieu called "the essentials of life": the striving for material betterment and the preservation of traditions. To be sure, material betterment required personal adjustments, but immigrants were skillful in choosing the paths of least resistance. Immigrants accepted changes, but only those changes least disruptive of their traditions or those that allowed them to recreate the old way of life in the New World.

My research too stresses continuity. I see the emigrants' departure for America as caused not by an impossible situation in Italy, but by the determination to bring about changes at home: to make it possible for people like themselves to own land and to preserve an agrarian way of life. Moreover, the emigrants had a sufficient idea of what was happening in their society to permit them to discriminate among three basic options: to emigrate temporarily; to stay, organize, and fight; and to accept the situation and make the best of it.

In general, the study of Italians in San Francisco supports the argument of continuity. Immigrants adjusted with only minimum disruption. To be sure, resettling in America was a major break with the past, but Italian settlements in San Francisco were essentially miniatures of settlements in Italy. Farming, of course, was virtually impossible in or around San Francisco, and immigrant farmers were forced into other work. Yet our examination of the occupational transition from Italy to San Francisco reveals that obvious changes masked elements of continuity.

The history of Italian families in San Francisco is complex. Seemingly major structural changes occurred, among them the substantial decline in the size of northwestern families and the increase in the size of southwestern families. But in reality, northwestern families were smaller simply because the extended-family households of northern Italy could not be duplicated in San Francisco; and the southwestern families were larger because southwesterners took advantage of their new prosperity to fulfill their long-standing aspiration of raising larger families.

The persistence of regional differences among immigrants and their children is the strongest argument in favor of continuity. Regional differences are apparent not only in the immigrants' settlements, their jobs, and their families, but also in their social and economic institutions. Even the transition from regionalism to nationalism, also apparently a major change, occurred without a break from regional traditions. The immigrants embraced nationalism only after their interests had enlarged to the point where regional and national interests coincided, only when they perceived nationalism as serving all the purposes previously served by regionalism and new ones as well.

The historians of continuity saw immigrants as people in control of their own destiny, intelligent and alert, fighting to preserve their personal identities and cultural traditions. And most important, winning: successfully preserving and celebrating their heritage while at the same time making superficial adjustments to placate the host society. Impressed by polls in the past decade that have described a society hungry for identity, the historians of continuity have recounted the successful fight of European "tribes" against the impersonal and homogenizing forces of American society.

This new profile also has its problems. There were in the end, as the historians of change assert, structures that limited the range of choices peasants and immigrants could make, and also non-structural changes that affected immigrants' lives. For Italians, the most unexpected force for change was the failure of return migration. In personal terms, their experience in the United States made them too sophisticated to tolerate the Italy they had left. In structural terms, small-scale capitalism in Italy could not survive in competition with the large-scale capitalism of the United States and northern Europe. Most Italian returnees never suspected that their old world was coming to an end, let alone that by temporarily emigrating to the United States they were hastening that end. It is doubtful whether Italian emigrants would ever have crossed the Atlantic had they foreseen the impossibility of returning to live in their native land.

Italian emigrants can be seen as people who were ready, whether from desperation or adventurousness, to try new strategies to achieve traditional goals. Ironically, inevitably, the strategy of temporary emigration changed the very goals they wanted to achieve.

Things were not as simple as they had thought. The drive for material success put a premium on change; the attachment to tradition made them resist it. Neither goal could be pursued except at the other's expense.

Their experience, I believe, was not greatly different from our own. We too live with ambivalence and contradiction. We strive for a better life, only to find that the changes it entails are not always welcome. Like the immigrants, we seek to achieve success without paying too high a social and personal price; and in the end, successful or not, we find that our deepest concern is with the "essentials of life" that we feel we have lost. Like the immigrants, we have essayed the impossible task of changing our status for the better while holding all else constant; and like them we have succeeded only in accelerating the pace of the change we dread. If anything, our strong commitment to continuity often seems to be the very spring of change.

Notes

Notes

Complete authors' names, titles, and publication data for works cited in short form are given in the Bibliography, pp. 323–38. I have used the following abbreviations in the citations:

ACC	Archives of the Commune of Capannori
ACG	Archives of the City of Genoa
ACHD	Archives of the California Health Department, Sacramento
ACL	Archives of the Commune of Lorsica
ACLU	Archives of the City of Lucca
ACP	Archives of the City of Palermo
ACSF	Archives of the Commune of Santa Flavia
ACSL	Archives of the Commune of Sestri Levante
ACT	Archives of the Commune of Trabia
ACV	Archives of the Commune of Verbicaro
AIWA	Archives of the Italian Welfare Agency, San Francisco
ASC	Archives of State in Cosenza
ASG	Archives of State in Genoa
ASL	Archives of State in Lucca
ASP	Archives of State in Palermo
BR	Birth Records
CM	Correspondence of Mayors with the Prefetto
DR	Death Records
FF	Foglio di Famiglia (Family Record)
MR	Marriage Records
NR	Naturalization Records, Federal Archives, San Bruno, Calif.
PN	Petition for Naturalization, Federal Archives, San Bruno, Calif.
RC	Report of the Consul, in Diplomatic and Consular Correspondence, Archives of the Ministry of Foreign Affairs, Rome
RM	Reports of the Mayor, in Correspondence of Mayors with the Prefetto
RP	Reports of the Prefetto, in Gabinetto della Prefettura
SF	San Francisco
VP	*La Voce del Popolo*

Chapter 1

1. Ferenczi, pp. 356–84; Italy [11], pp. 66–67.
2. Foerster, p. 324.
3. Schuyler, p. 481.
4. Italy [35], *Statistica 1908–9,* p. xxii.
5. Willcox, 2: 112–13.
6. For an interesting discussion of the temporary nature of Italian emigration, see Taruffi et al., pp. 726–30.
7. See Yans-McLaughlin, Briggs, Nelli, Bianco, Barton, and Kessner.
8. This is a translation of the Italian *comune,* or municipality. For a fuller explanation of the term commune, as well as town, village, and others, see ch. 2, p. 29.
9. FF, ASC.
10. Interview with Franco Torrano, SF, May 1975.
11. RP, Cosenza 12.v.1886, ASC.
12. RP, Cosenza, 21.ix.1896, ASC.
13. RP, Cosenza 14.xii.1877, ASC.
14. RM, Verbicaro 2.iv.1887, ASC.
15. RP, Cosenza 7.iv.1896, ASC.
16. RP, Cosenza 2.iv.1887, ASC.
17. RP, Cosenza 4.viii.1889, ASC.
18. RP, Cosenza 7.v.1893, ASC.
19. Ricciardi, p. 248.
20. Interview with Franco Torrano, SF, May 1975. The account that follows is based on this interview, unless otherwise noted.
21. MR and DR, ACV.
22. Interview with Rosa Torrano (Nunzio's wife), Verbicaro, Sept. 1975.
23. Cyriax, p. 257.
24. MR, ACHD.
25. NR.
26. Interview with Sam Torrano, South San Francisco, May 1975.
27. MR, ACHD.
28. Sam Torrano interview.
29. MR, ACHD.
30. Interview with Angelo Torrano, Burlingame, Calif., May 1975.
31. MR, ACHD.
32. Angelo Torrano interview.
33. MR, ACHD.
34. NR.
35. MR, ACHD.
36. Angelo Torrano interview.
37. MR, ACHD.
38. Interview with Jonathan Torrano, San Mateo, Calif., May 1975.
39. Livi-Bacci, p. 98.
40. Puzo, p. 48.
41. Handlin, p. 4.
42. Yans-McLaughlin, p. xx.
43. Briggs, p. xx.
44. Passi, p. 99.
45. L. Villari, *Italian Life,* p. 2.

Chapter 2

1. C. Hall.
2. Italy [35], *Statistica 1884–85,* p. 146.
3. RP, Genoa 3.vi.1882, ASG; RM, Verbicaro 21.ix.1892, ASC. Italian newspapermen and other writers liked to describe San Francisco as "the Italian city of the west," cloaked in gold and mystery; the mystique survived for years. See Rinaudo, p. 29.
4. Adams, p. 2.
5. Paul, pp. 185–87, 240–62.
6. Hill, pp. 63–68.
7. Gordon, pp. 97–111.
8. *Ibid.,* pp. 102–4.
9. *Ibid.,* pp. 104–9.
10. *Ibid.,* p. 111.
11. Caughey, p. 214.
12. Young, p. 489.
13. U.S. [22], pp. 411–13; U.S. [20], pp. 94–95.
14. U.S. [21], pp. 538–39.
15. U.S. [16], pp. 138–39; U.S. [6], p. 1227; U.S. [22], pp. 411–13.
16. U.S. [17], pp. 12–13.
17. U.S. [5], p. 726.
18. U.S. [18], pp. 373–75.
19. *VP,* 12.v.1867.
20. *L'Italia,* 17.xii.1891 and 2.iii.1895.
21. Nelli, p. 23.
22. RC, New York 17.v.1867, 7.iv.1869, and 13.xii.1882.
23. RC, New Orleans 16.ix.1873.
24. Giacosa, pp. 161–97.
25. Palmer, p. 354.
26. Mangano, *Sons of Italy,* pp. 39–68.
27. The death records I used, covering the years 1913 to 1939 and filled out by the Italian clergy of the national church of Saints Peter and Paul in San Francisco, specify the native province and town of each immigrant whose funeral took place in that church. In a random sample of 25 percent of the 9,000 records, 65 percent of the Italians had come from the provinces of the north. The 1,600 naturalization papers are for Italians who became American citizens in the Superior Court of San Francisco between 1919 and 1945 and who were living in the city at the time of naturalization. Of these, 68 percent were northerners.
28. RC, SF 6.vi.1869. The newspapers of the mutual aid societies of the city sometimes listed the names of new immigrants or new members of the organizations, also giving their province of origin; for the 1860's and 1870's almost all were from the north. On this see *VP,* 3.v.1867; and *La Parola,* 7.x.1865.
29. Società Geografica Italiana, p. 87. See also C. Dondero, p. 9. Consular reports and accounts by visitors published in Italian journals often reported that among the Italian colonies San Francisco stood out because of its northern characteristics. See for example *Bollettino dell'Emigrazione,* 5 (1902): 45; and Rinaudo, pp. 29–30.
30. Italy [16], pp. 187, 193, 196, 208.

31. De Mauro, p. 127.
32. Fortunato, *Il Mezzogiorno,* 2: 67–70.
33. L. Villari, *Italian Life,* p. 2.
34. Mangano, *Sons of Italy,* p. 41.
35. Italy [7], p. 517. The most extensive documentation of these regional differences is found in the survey on agriculture and the peasants that was supervised by Senator Stefano Jacini and published in thirteen volumes in the 1880's. The four volumes used here are those by Bertani, Mazzini, Branca, and Damiani.
36. RP, Genoa 27.v.1869, ASG.
37. *Ibid.,* 17.xii.1888, ASG.
38. RP, Lucca 2.v.1879; Teodoro Fraetti to the prefetto of Lucca, 4.iv.1885, CM, ASL.
39. Maggiore-Perni, pp. 211–15.
40. RP, Palermo 7.vi.1892, ASP.
41. Battaglia, p. 7.
42. Italy [31], *Popolazione 1882,* p. xxix.
43. Italy [31], *Popolazione 1902,* p. xxi.
44. Italy [31], *Popolazione 1919–23,* p. lxvi.
45. Italy [28], pp. 177–78.
46. Italy [26], 1: 241.
47. Italy [29], pp. 65–66.
48. Italy [26], 1: 241.
49. Italy [27], pp. 75–84.
50. Italy [26], 1: 240.
51. Italy [30], pp. 69–70.
52. Italy [26], 1: 240.
53. Jacini, p. 7.
54. Moss, p. 152.
55. Coletti, *La Popolazione,* p. 127.
56. Angelo Piccini to director of the Agricultural Committee of Lucca, Borgo a Mozzano, 7.vi.1887, CM, ASL.
57. Rosario Donati to the prefetto of Palermo, 15.ix.1892, CM, ASP.
58. Bertani, p. 327; Mazzini, p. 521; Branca, p. xxxv. A survey commissioned by the Italian Parliament in the early 1900's to investigate whether any progress had been made in the southern provinces since the time of the Jacini survey concluded that the conditions were about the same as in the 1870's, and that the few changes that had occurred were due to returnees from America. For this see Italy [8], pp. 86–119.
59. Moss, pp. 151–52.
60. RC, SF 13.v.1886.
61. RM, Lorsica 21.v.1891, ASG. In 1976 I asked twenty San Francisco Italians how they had come to San Francisco; fourteen answered that they had been called by a member of their immediate family or a close friend, and nine had come with prepaid tickets.
62. J. S. and L. D. MacDonald, "Chain Migration," pp. 82–85.
63. Riis, p. 19.
64. Huganir, p. 273.
65. Child, p. 79.
66. Sangree, p. 1.
67. Coulter, pp. 10–13; Briggs, p. 70.
68. It will be useful to keep in mind the chronological sequence of the three generations. The Italian generation was born roughly between 1845 and 1885,

the immigrants between 1875 and 1905, and the Italo-Americans between 1905 and 1940.

69. RP, Cosenza 2.v.1891, ASC.

70. J. S. MacDonald, "Italy's Rural Social Structures," pp. 437–56; "Agricultural Organization," pp. 61–75.

71. For an interesting discussion of the direct correlation between emigration rate and altitude in Cosenza province, see Taruffi, pp. 710–16, 755.

72. Falbo, "Stato," pp. 311–33, and *California and Overland Diaries,* pp. 61–69.

73. Camera di Commercio di Genova, p. 46.

74. RP, Genoa 21.ix.1871, ASG.

75. RC, Antwerp 8.ii.1871.

76. Sereni, p. 465.

77. De Stefani, pp. xxxiv–xxxv.

78. *La Voce del Serchio,* 8.viii.1880.

79. Cesare Sardi to the prefetto of Lucca, July 1882, CM, ASL.

80. RC, SF 18.ix.1887.

81. *VP,* 3.xii.1889.

82. RP, Cosenza 3.i.1879, ASC.

83. *Ibid.,* 7.iii.1882.

84. *Ibid.,* 7.iii.1871.

85. RP, Palermo 3.iii.1892, ASP.

86. *Ibid.,* 27.ii.1878.

87. RC, SF 11.v.1891.

Chapter 3

1. Briggs, pp. 1–68; Yans-McLaughlin, pp. 17–71; Barton, pp. 27–47; Bell, p. 180.

2. Carpi, *Dell'Emigrazione,* pp. 3–27, and *Delle Colonie*; Matteuzzi; Virgilio.

3. Italy [35], *Statistica,* 1912–13, p. x.

4. Italy [11], pp. 65–66.

5. RP, Lucca 7.v.1887, ASL; RM, Capannori 17.ix.1889, ASL.

6. RP, Cosenza 1.xii.1894, ASC.

7. RM, Santa Flavia 11.i.1897, ASP; RP, Palermo 27.x.1898, ASP; RP, Lucca 7.ix.1889, ASL.

8. RP, Genoa 7.v.1884, ASG.

9. Carlo Mazzini to the prefetto of Lucca, 7.v.1888, ASL.

10. Jerome, p. 202.

11. Isaacs, p. 167; Eisenstadt, pp. 241–45; W. Moore, p. 196; Lorenzoni, pp. 278–95.

12. The articles were later published in one volume; see *Lettere Meridionali* (Florence, 1878), p. 44.

13. Sonnino, "Le Condizioni," p. 157.

14. *Ibid.,* p. 158; Sonnino, *La Sicilia,* p. 127; Franchetti, *Condizioni Economiche,* p. 327.

15. Fortunato, *Pagine,* pp. 305–6; Bonansea, pp. 23–24.

16. Bertani, p. 125; Negri, p. 39; Pasquali, pp. 20–25; Mazzini, pp. 474–89.

17. Sonnino, "Le Condizioni," p. 157; Caputo, *L'Abitazione,* pp. 1–13. See also Edward Camphousen (U.S. consul in Naples) to Secretary of State, Naples, 9.vii.1886.

18. Phillip Carroll to Secretary of State, Palermo, 14.vii.1886. See also Damiani, pp. 450–54.

19. Italy [16], *Censimento,* 1881, pp. 186–87; for a detailed description of housing in Cosenza province, see Taruffi, pp. 762–69. Interesting accounts of housing in Calabria today are in Angarano, pp. 17–26, and Blasutti, pp. 1–24.

20. Samogyi, pp. 844–55.

21. Sonnino, "Le Condizioni," p. 147. Concerning the province of Lucca, Carlo Mazzini (pp. 503–4) reported: "There are entire communities, especially in the mountains, where the people live on chestnut flour for months." See also Pasquali, p. 126.

22. P. Villari, *Lettere Meridionali,* p. 137.

23. RP, Genoa 29.ix.1887, ASG. See also the reports of the prefetto published in the *Bollettino di Notizie Agrarie*, 69 (1887): 1945–62; 14 (1888): 597–84; 45 (1888): 1373; 68 (1888): 2135; 19 (1889): 1163; 9 (1890): 314; 58 (1890): 1092; 42 (1891): 635; and 2 (1892): 129. Mauro Camilli, the director of the agricultural committee of Chiavari, province of Genoa, wrote: "Our peasants have always been poor. But now poverty means starvation, and the peasants are forced to leave." Camilli to the prefetto of Genoa, 7.vi.1881, CM, ASG. On the province of Lucca see *Bollettino di Notizie Agrarie,* 69 (1887): 1975; 59 (1893): 567; 10 (1894): 359; and 30 (1895): 623. Count Cesare Sardi wrote: "The unrelenting depression is like a blind force driving people out of their communities. Apparently, there is little that anybody can do to change the situation." Sardi to the prefetto of Lucca, 2.v.1893, CM, ASL. After a crop failure in the fall of 1890, the mayor of Capannori wrote: "Survival is the problem. The average family seems to be unable to face the winter. Emigration is not an alternative. It is a necessity." RM, Capannori, 7.x.1890, ASL.

24. RP, Cosenza 3.ix.1885, ASC.

25. *Bollettino di Notizie Agrarie,* 69 (1887): 1957; 14 (1888): 589; 45 (1888): 1381–82; 68 (1888): 2143; 1 (1889): 12; 44 (1899): 1151; 59 (1889): 1668; 9 (1890): 324; 25 (1891): 1285–87; 44 (1891): 751; 28 (1892): 362; 15 (1893): 541.

26. RP, Cosenza 27.x.1894, ASC.

27. RP, Palermo 18.ix.1888, ASP.

28. *Bollettino di Notizie Agrarie,* 14 (1888): 589; 52 (1888): 1957; 45 (1888): 1383; 68 (1888): 2143; 1 (1889): 12; 44 (1889): 1151; 59 (1889): 1669; 9 (1890): 324; 58 (1890): 1101; 30 (1891): 4; 42 (1892): 640–41; 5 (1892): 321; 5 (1893): 141; 59 (1893): 573.

29. RM, Santa Flavia, 1.v.1895, ASP.

30. Mangano, "Threatened Depopulation," p. 1329.

31. RM, Lorsica 7.iv.1889, ASG.

32. RP, Palermo 15.xii.1896, ASP.

33. A. Rossi, "Vantaggi e Svantaggi," p. 12.

34. RP, Palermo 7.iv.1896, ASP. Similar observations were made in other provinces: RP, Genoa 26.ix.1887, ASG; RP, Lucca 13.xiii.1889, ASL.

35. Corsini, p. 27.

36. RP, Genoa 17.xii.1885, ASG; RM, Lorsica 28.ix.1884, ASG. See also Italy [35], *Statistica,* 1884–85, p. 149.

37. Italy [35], *Statistica,* 1884–85, p. 161; RP, Lucca 27.ix.1888, ASL.

38. Taruffi et al., pp. 827–35; Caputo, "Di Alcune Questioni," pp. 1175–76; Italy [35], *Statistica,* 1884–85, pp. 169–70; RP, Cosenza 23.iv.1891, ASC; RP, Palermo 3.vi.1884, ASP.

39. RP, Cosenza 23.x.1891, ASC.

40. J. S. MacDonald, "Agricultural Organization," p. 62.

41. Italy [35], *Statistica,* 1880–81, p. 56; Marenco, p. 32.

42. Italy [35], *Statistica,* 1882, pp. 41–42.

43. Pasquali, pp. 34–35; Italy [35], *Statistica,* 1912–13, p. x.

44. Taruffi et al., p. 708; Italy [35], *Statistica,* 1904–5, pp. 83–85.

45. Italy [35], *Statistica,* 1902–3, pp. 66–69.

46. Sonnino, "Le Condizioni," p. 149.

47. Taruffi, pp. xxxix, 789.

48. Mazzini, p. 532.

49. Sonnino, *I Contadini.*

50. Maggiore-Perni, p. 161.

51. Coletti, "Dell'Emigrazione," pp. 3, 142; J. S. MacDonald, "Agricultural Organization," p. 62.

52. *Bollettino dell'Emigrazione*, 7 (1904): 17.

53. Foerster, pp. 7–29; Coletti, "Esame Critico," pp. 330–57.

54. *Bollettino dell'Emigrazione*, 9 (1907): 26; J. S. and L. D. MacDonald, "Urbanization," pp. 433–48.

55. J. S. MacDonald, "Agricultural Organization," p. 63. According to an estimate of MacDonald's based on emigrants departing from Naples, 28 percent of those who left in 1910–11, 30 percent in 1911–12, and 25 percent in 1912–13 had prepaid tickets.

56. Italy [35], *Statistica,* 1908–9, p. xxii.

57. *Ibid.,* 1911–12, p. xxi.

58. *Ibid.,* 1908–9, p. xxiii.

59. *Ibid.,* 1911–12, p. xxi.

60. Italy [11], pp. 66–67.

61. *Ibid.*

62. Kessner, p. 29.

63. M. Hall, pp. 116–40; Meritani, *passim.*

64. Borrie, p. 81.

65. Foerster, p. 428. See also Boccardo, pp. 22–36, and Nitti, pp. 775–76.

66. P. Hall, p. 78.

67. *Ibid.,* pp. 78, 80.

68. Corinaldi, p. 5.

69. Giacosa, p. 163.

70. Ferroni, p. 1.

71. RC, New York 7.v.1882; Boston 2.v.1882; New Orleans 13.i.1879.

72. Foerster, p. 324.

73. Willcox, 1: 206. On British returnees see Shepperson; on Greek returnees see Saloutos.

74. Caroli, pp. 5–22.

75. Beneduce, p. 96.

76. L. Rossi, pp. 35, 38, 40.

77. Italy [35], *Statistica,* 1878, pp. 37–38.

78. *Ibid.,* 1880–81, pp. 9–10.

79. D. O. Fletcher to Secretary of State, Genoa, 26.ix.1888; Marenco, p. 157.

80. RP, Genoa 7.v.1897, ASG.

81. De Stefani, p. xliii; Italy [35], *Statistica,* 1878, p. 39.

82. *Ibid.,* 1880–81, p. 36.

83. *Ibid.,* 1882, pp. 42, 61, 66; RP, Lucca 13.v.1897, ASL; J. S. and L. D. MacDonald, "Urbanization," pp. 438–40; J. S. MacDonald, "Chain Migration," pp. 85, 88.

84. Italy [35], *Statistica,* 1880–81, p. 51.

85. Taruffi et al., p. 698.

86. Italy [7], p. 737.

87. Caputo, *Inchiesta,* pp. 12–38.

88. Italy [35], *Statistica,* 1882, p. 66.

89. Italy [11], p. 67.

90. Italy [35], *Statistica,* 1886, pp. 88–89.

91. *Ibid.,* 1902–3, pp. 68–69.

92. Necco, "Il Problema," pp. 432–75; Spagnoli, pp. 8–55; Izzo, "Per la Storia," pp. 449–59.

93. RP, Genoa 7.v.1889, ASG; Palermo 17.ix.1892, ASP; Lucca 10.iii.-1895, ASL.

94. This according to two registers, covering the years 1888 and 1889, in the town archives. These list the names of those who left Sestri Levante either for other communes of the Liguria region or for international destinations, and those who immigrated into Sestri; "Registro di Emigrazione per l'Anno 1888" and "Registro di Emigrazione per l'Anno 1889," ACSL.

95. Jones, pp. 200–201; De Conde, pp. 77–97.

96. RM, Lorsica 19.v.1893, ASG.

97. RP, Lucca 21.ix.1896, ASL.

98. L. Rossi, *Relazione,* p. 45.

99. RM, Santa Flavia 12.iii.1898, ASP.

100. RP, Cosenza 24.iii.1898, ASC.

101. Branca, pp. xlix–xlx.

102. Izzo, *Agricoltura,* p. 11.

103. Blandini, p. 1.

104. *Ibid.,* pp. 3–6.

105. Italy [10], p. 372.

106. *Ibid.*

107. RP, Palermo 21.v.1904, ASP.

108. J. S. MacDonald, "Agricultural Organization," pp. 61–75.

109. G. Luzzatto, *L'Economia,* pp. 36–39; Bertozzi, p. 40.

110. J. S. MacDonald, "Institutional Economics," p. 113; Giorgetti, pp. 746–58; De Marco, pp. 490–91.

111. Giorgetti, pp. 745–59; Zangheri, pp. 761–808; J. S. MacDonald, "Agricultural Organization," pp. 61–75.

112. Medici, pp. 33–34.

113. De Marco, p. 490.

114. G. Luzzatto, *L'Economia,* p. 139.

115. Italy [9], pp. 221, 228–29.

116. G. Luzzatto, *L'Economia,* p. 139.

117. *Ibid.,* p. 141.

118. *Ibid.,* p. 142.

119. J. S. MacDonald, "Agricultural Organization," pp. 65–74.

120. On this important topic the reader can usefully consult Zangheri; Preti, pp. 352–63; Gui; and Caracciolo, pp. 157–65.

121. Massari, p. 15.

122. *Atti Parlamentari: Camera dei Deputati,* 30.i.1883, p. 992.

123. Pestalozza, pp. 120–21.

124. Società degli Agricoltori Italiani, pp. 16–18.

125. Italy [8], pp. 86–87.

126. Coletti, "Dell'Emigrazione," pp. 3, 141; Coletti, "Le Associazioni Agrarie," pp. 575–96.

127. Taruffi, pp. xxxix, 789; Italy [8], pp. 685–91.

128. Camera di Commercio di Genova, p. 45.

129. RP, Genoa 16.ii.1887, ASG.

130. *Ibid.,* 29.xi.1893.

131. Mazzini, p. 401.

132. RP, Lucca 22.i.1887, ASL.

133. De Marco, pp. 491–93.

134. Branca, pp. xlix–xlx.

135. Blandini, p. 1.

136. Renda, *Il Movimento,* p. 67.

137. RP, Palermo 27.v.1891, ASP.

138. Coletti, *La Popolazione Rurale,* p. 125.

139. *Ibid.*

140. Italy [8], p. 102.

141. A. Rossi, "Vantaggi e Svantaggi," p. 48. See also RP, Lucca 3.ii.1893, ASL; and Bertani, pp. 126–27.

142. Coletti, *La Popolazione Rurale,* pp. 124–27.

143. Italy [35], *Statistica,* 1876, p. iii.

144. J. S. MacDonald, "Chain Migration," p. 85, and "Agricultural Organization," pp. 65–68.

145. Marenco, p. 99.

146. *Cenni sulla Provincia di Chiavari,* p. 7.

147. Felloni, *Popolazione,* p. 173.

148. RP, Genoa 19.xii.1874, ASG.

149. RP, Lucca 7.iv.1874, ASL.

150. Paolucci, p. 75.

151. RP, Lucca 23.viii.1885. See also Eugenio Lazzareschi, "L'Emigrazione Lucchese in Corsica," *La Nazione,* 15.xii.1938.

152. RP, Cosenza 7.v.1874, ASC.

153. Renato Santilli to the prefetto of Cosenza, 7.iii.1887, ASC; De Nobili, "Appunti," pp. 401–4; B. O. Duncan to Secretary of State, Naples, 10.vii.1883.

154. Italy [35], *Statistica,* 1884–85, pp. 175–79; Renda, *L'Emigrazione,* pp. 24–43; RP, Palermo 4.iv.1875, ASP.

155. Weber, p. 281.

Chapter 4

1. A. Rossi, "Vantaggi e Svantaggi," p. 39.
2. Italy [8], p. 39.
3. *Ibid.,* pp. 113–14.
4. Cerase, p. 120; Renda, *Il Movimento,* p. 19; Cinanni, pp. 222–29.
5. P. Villari, "L'Emigrazione," pp. 55–56.
6. Franchetti, *Mezzogiorno,* p. 230.
7. De Luca, p. 73; Cerase, pp. 96–100.
8. Jones, pp. 192–94.
9. Coletti, "Dell'Emigrazione Italiana," p. 372; Ziino, pp. 13–14.
10. P. Villari, "L'Emigrazione," p. 59.
11. Cagli, p. 6.
12. Coletti, "Dell'Emigrazione Italiana," p. 3.
13. Salvemini, *Il Movimento Socialista,* p. 424.
14. *Ibid.*
15. Bodio, p. 79.
16. P. Villari, "L'Emigrazione," p. 87.
17. Carpi, *Delle Colonie,* p. 65.
18. RP, Cosenza 23.iv.1878, ASC.
19. *Ibid.,* 15.xii.1905.
20. Interview with Franco Ciccotti, Verbicaro, Sept. 1975. See also Mangano, "Toritto and San Demetrio," p. 170. On the impact of American savings on housing in the Calabria region, see Italy [7], pp. 504–5.
21. RP, Cosenza 3.iii.1901, ASC.
22. L. Villari, *Gli Stati Uniti,* p. 93; Preziosi, p. 77.
23. Carpi, *Dell'Emigrazione Italiana,* p. 133. A more complete source is the table published by the *Bollettino dell'Emigrazione,* 14 (1905): 107, which, however, reported only the money arriving in Italy through the Banco di Napoli, the bank authorized for that purpose by the Italian government in 1901. See also Balletta.
24. Italy [2], p. xxxv.
25. *Bollettino dell'Emigrazione,* 18 (1910): 38.
26. Von Borosini, p. 793.
27. *Bollettino dell'Emigrazione,* 18 (1910): 38.
28. Marenco, p. 157.
29. RP, Genoa 2.v.1897, ASG.
30. De Stefani, p. xxxiv.
31. Pasquali, p. 60; RP, Lucca 17.xii.1903, ASL.
32. Von Borosini, p. 792. The deposits in the local post offices grew rapidly. In 1876 they amounted to 23,000 lire, ten years later 2 million, in 1898 7 million, and in 1904 16 million. In the early 1900's there were 200,000 lire deposited in the post office of Gerace Marina and 800,000 in that of Serra. See Taruffi et al., p. 853.
33. RP, Cosenza 3.ix.1893, ASC.

34. RP, Palermo 22.v.1891, ASP; *Bollettino dell'Emigrazione,* 18 (1910): 381.

35. Mangano, "Ci Manca," p. 18.

36. Jacini, p. 13.

37. RP, Genoa 9.ix.1879, ASG; RP, Lucca 3.i.1883, ASL; RP, Cosenza 17.ix.1894, ASC.

38. Blandini, p. 1.

39. RP, Cosenza 28.xii.1889, ASC; Rosario Catturi to the prefetto of Palermo, 3.v.1907, ASP.

40. Agostino Bertani to the prefetto of Genoa, 28.v.1885, ASG.

41. Taruffi et al., p. 875.

42. *Ibid.,* pp. 845, 873.

43. Mangano, "Ci Manca," p. 18.

44. Caputo, *Di Alcune,* p. 14.

45. *Bollettino dell'Emigrazione,* 18 (1910): 47.

46. Von Borosini, p. 792.

47. Vöchting, p. 236. All quotations from this book are from the Italian edition, approved by the author.

48. The price of wheat declined from 39 lire per quintal in 1874 to 20 in 1894; the price of wine from 80 lire per hectoliter in 1877 to 35 in 1894; the price of olive oil from 172 lire per hectoliter in 1878 to 109 lire in 1894. On declining prices see Italy [4], 1895, pp. 512, 514; Felloni, *I Prezzi,* pp. 15–17; Bandettini, pp. 13–17; and *Petino,* Appendix.

49. Blandini, p. 2; Italy [9], p. 113; RP, Cosenza 16.x.1906, ASC.

50. RP, Lucca 21.xii.1907, ASL.

51. Massimo Cattani to the prefetto of Genoa, 2.ii.1891, ASG.

52. Vöchting, p. 325.

53. Italy [1], p. 126.

54. Lorenzoni, p. 221.

55. Vöchting, p. 326.

56. RP, Cosenza 21.ii.1907, ASC.

57. RP, Palermo 15.x.1905, ASP. On this topic see also Rossi-Doria, p. 237.

58. Italy [18], pp. 46–101; Italy [21], pp. 82–483; Italy [37], p. 148; Italy [38], p. 194; Italy [36], p. 166; Italy [39], p. 376.

59. Italy [9], pp. 89–92; De Marco, pp. 483–513; Taruffi et al., pp. 779–85.

60. *Ibid.,* pp. 781–83; Caputo, *Di Alcune Questioni,* p. 13.

61. RP, Genoa 17.iii.1879, ASG.

62. Mazzini, pp. 373–75, 405–10; Bertani, pp. 125–28.

63. Mazzini, pp. 452–62.

64. De Marco, pp. 485–86.

65. RP, Palermo 16.iv.1912, ASP.

66. Cyriax, pp. 77–78.

67. Capuana, p. 24.

68. Gilkey, "United States," p. 25; see also Gilkey, "The Effect of Emigration," *passim.*

69. Von Borosini, pp. 792–93.
70. *Bollettino dell'Emigrazione,* 11 (1907): 219.
71. Taruffi et al., pp. 877–78.
72. RC, SF 7.v.1867.
73. RC, Boston 29.ix.1891.
74. RP, Cosenza 12.ii.1891, ASC.
75. RP, Palermo 3.iii.1896, ASP. In a study of return migration in the south up to 1910, Sartorius concluded that 40 to 50 percent of the emigrants from the south returned, but that only a few successfully established themselves there ("Die Suditalienische," pp. 183–86).
76. Vöchting, p. 23.
77. Sartorius, *Die Sizilienische,* p. 108.
78. A. Rossi, "Vantaggi e Svantaggi," p. 68.
79. Vöchting, p. 236.
80. *Ibid.*
81. Italy [7], pp. 138, 206.
82. RP, Cosenza 14.ii.1902, ASC; Palermo 2.v.1903, ASP.
83. RP, Cosenza 27.v.1909, ASC.
84. RP, Palermo 19.ix.1909, ASP. The mayor of Trabia wrote in 1911: "Second departures are often the result of blunders returnees made in overestimating what they could do with their savings." RM, Trabia 19.ix.1911, ASP.
85. RP, Genoa 4.xii.1904, ASG. See also Italy [7], p. 596. Carlo Toti, a 34-year-old peasant from Calabria, had been in the United States twice, and like many others had bought land. "But I do not have enough to make a living out of it. To make ends meet I have to hire myself out, exactly as I did before going to the United States. This is not what I expected." *Ibid.,* pp. 100–101.
86. Cyriax, p. 83.
87. RP, Palermo 3.v.1909, ASP.
88. Gramsci, p. 330.
89. Vöchting, p. 240. In an extensive study of the development of capitalism in Italy in the late nineteenth century, one Italian historian argued that the increase in small properties and the political rhetoric the government used to promote return migration masked an elaborate plan to drain the savings of the returnees in order to support the expanding industries of the north. See Candeloro, p. 214.
90. Gramsci, p. 362. See also Salvemini, "La Deviazione," p. 330.
91. Bertani, p. 427.
92. Mazzini, p. 529.
93. Archbishop of Palermo Michele Celesia to the Sacred Congregation of the Bishops, Palermo, 6.ix.1881, Archivio Segreto Vaticano, Vatican City.
94. "L'Emigrato Italiano," *La Civiltà Cattolica,* 48 (1887): 878–923.
95. Bertani, pp. vii–xii.
96. Carmelo Sanfilippo to the prefetto of Cosenza, 2.v.1892, ASC.
97. Italy [7], p. 137. The prefetto of Palermo reported: "Signs of social deference are important among Sicilians. But returnees are daring to the point of denying the traditional signs of deference peasants have always paid to landowners." RP, Palermo 7.v.1905, ASP.

98. Mangano, "Ci Manca," p. 16.
99. Caputo, "Di Alcune Questioni," p. 1176.
100. Italy [41], p. 795.
101. Bertani, p. 106; Mazzini, p. 526.
102. Italy [23], pp. 103–4.
103. Taruffi et al., pp. xxxv, 802.
104. Italy [23], pp. 85–86, 146–47. Educated people in the south expressed time and again their frustration at the adverse response to their efforts. An itinerant teacher in the province of Cosenza wrote to the prefetto: "Experience has taught me that these people consider the educated their natural enemy." Camillo Bettini to the prefetto of Cosenza, 2.i.1879, ASC.
105. *Bollettino dell'Emigrazione,* 18 (1910): 50.
106. *Ibid.,* 12 (1909): 126.
107. Italy [7], p. 96.
108. Taruffi et al., p. 804.
109. Italy [4], 1905–7, pp. 262–65.
110. Jones, p. 269.
111. RP, Palermo 7.xi.1909, ASP.
112. Italy [7], p. 136.
113. Mangano, "Toritto and San Demetrio," p. 172.
114. Italy [9], p. 366.
115. Italy [40], p. xv. See also Italy [5], and Italy [6]. For a study of the mutual aid societies among the peasants, see Valenti.
116. Franceschini, p. 516.
117. Candeloro, pp. 215–25.
118. Italy [5], p. vi.
119. Minuti.
120. Franceschini, p. 517.
121. Società di Mutuo Soccorso del Paese di Porcari, p. 2.
122. Bocci, p. 325.
123. Caputo, *Di Alcune Questioni,* pp. 6–7; De Nobili, "L'Emigrazione," p. 10.
124. Italy [5], pp. 418–19.
125. RP, Genoa 7.iii.1887, ASG; Palermo 2.v.1887, ASP.
126. Società degli Agricoltori Italiani, pp. 16–18. The reports of the prefetto of Lucca are informative on this subject, pointing out that although militancy was widespread in the neighboring provinces of Pistoia, Arezzo, and Florence, in Lucca there was almost none. RP, Lucca 17.ix.1904 and 10.ii.1907, ASL.
127. Moss, p. 157.
128. J. S. and L. D. MacDonald, "Institutional," pp. 114–17, and "Agricultural Organization," pp. 65–68.
129. Caputo, "Di Alcune Questioni," pp. 1165–66. Two physicians from Lagonegro, a town in the province of Cosenza, reported that returnees had come back "with a previously unknown interest, developed in the United States, in joining and establishing societies." Italy [7], pp. 569–70.
130. Italy [7], p. 571.
131. RP, Lucca 4.ix.1895, ASL.

132. RP, Genoa 17.ix.1894, ASG.

133. Moss, p. 147.

134. Foerster, p. 428.

135. Caputo, *Di Alcune Questioni,* p. 4.

136. Cyriax, p. 9.

137. Gilkey, "United States," p. 25; Foerster, p. 430.

138. Foerster, p. 428.

139. RP, Palermo 17.ix.1901, ASP.

140. Gilkey, "United States," p. 25.

141. Italy [7], pp. 100–101. Salvatore Cecchitani, another returnee from the same province, argued: "Those who have been in America and have savored it will never be able to settle here and stay put. Sooner or later they will feel the urge to go again. They cannot make up their minds whether to stay here or to go forever." *Ibid.,* pp. 106–7.

142. RP, Palermo 24.v.1906, ASP.

143. Bernardy, *Italia Randagia,* pp. 229–30.

144. RP, Cosenza 16.ix.1894, ASC.

145. Italy [10], p. 368.

146. *Ibid.*

147. Interviews, SF, Nov.–Dec. 1976. Carmelo Spotino, a returnee who lived in Trabia in 1975, told me (Oct. 1975) he kept delaying his return for so long that his wife left him and went to South America to live with relatives who had settled in Brazil.

148. Foerster, p. 429.

149. RP, Palermo 21.v.1907, ASP.

150. Italy [7], p. 106.

151. Caputo, "Di Alcune Questioni," p. 256; RP, Palermo 3.v.1902, ASP.

152. Foerster, p. 430. A few San Francisco Italians told me that experiences of this sort were what prompted their final departure. Carmelo Tracci, for instance, bought 20 acres of land after three trips to the United States. But he was not accepted as a gentleman in his town, since he had formerly been a day laborer; so he left for good. Interview, SF, Dec. 1976.

153. Gilkey, "United States," p. 32. See also Scalise and Sulpizi.

154. Scalise, p. 93; Taruffi et al., p. 872.

155. Mangano, "Toritto and San Demetrio," p. 171.

156. Taruffi et al., p. 872.

157. Foerster, p. 430.

158. Koht, p. 161.

159. E. Rossi, p. 3–37; De Vincenzi.

160. Italy [4], 1895, p. 512.

161. *Ibid.,* 1905–7, p. 558.

162. *Ibid.,* 1895, p. 513.

163. Felloni, *I Prezzi,* pp. 15–25; Bandettini, pp. 13–24; Petino, Appendix.

164. G. Luzzatto, "Gli Anni," p. 424.

165. Necco, "La Curva," pp. 63–68.

166. Italy [3], pp. 1–185.
167. *Ibid.,* pp. 157–58.
168. *Ibid.,* p. 24.
169. Camera di Commercio di Genova, p. 45.
170. RP, Lucca 29.v.1875, ASL; Cosenza 3.ix.1876, ASC.
171. G. Luzzatto, "Gli Anni," p. 420.
172. The fullest documentation for these years is found in the *Bollettino di Notizie Agrarie,* published by the Ministry of Agriculture, which contained excerpts from the quarterly reports of the prefetti.
173. RP, Genoa 7.v.1884, ASG; Lucca 21.ix.1882, ASL; Cosenza 7.xii.1884, ASC.
174. Michels, p. 69.
175. Vöchting, p. 239.
176. Weber, p. 486.
177. Piore, pp. 115–16.
178. Tapinos; Bohning, pp. 28–32.

Chapter 5

1. Marazzi, p. 475.
2. "L'Ospedale Italiano," *VP*, 12.xi.1866. The very word Italians used for their community, *colonia,* was indicative of their attitude; a colony was a temporary settlement created by people who would return to the mother country.
3. RC, SF 12.iv.1868.
4. Società Geografica Italiana, p. 121. Another Italian who participated in the survey said: "There is no doubt that our emigration is essentially temporary. Italians cannot forget their families, and sooner or later they return to their villages." *Ibid.,* p. 122.
5. C. Dondero, p. 9.
6. RM, Capannori 7.v.1903, ASL. See also RM, Sestri Levante 6.ix.1904, ASG; and RP, Genoa 26.ii.1910, ASG.
7. RM, Verbicaro 7.v.1908, ASC.
8. RC, SF 24.ix.1911.
9. RP, Palermo 23.iii.1913, ASP. In the fall of 1975 I asked seven returnees from San Francisco—two in Santa Flavia and five in Sestri Levante—whether they had ever regretted not returning to San Francisco. Three answered that they had been in Italy in 1924 when the Johnson Act was passed and thus had had no opportunity to return to America; two said they had come to regret it, especially after the Second World War; and two said they were happy with their decision to stay in Italy.
10. Interviews, SF, Nov.–Dec. 1976.
11. RC, SF 7.v.1867. See also R. Dondero, pp. 35, 39, 41.
12. Scanlan, p. 327.
13. Norris, pp. 314–17.
14. Asbury, p. 87; Lloyd, p. 78; Hittel, pp. 311–12.
15. R. Dondero, p. 35.
16. P. Hall, pp. 85–95.
17. Foerster, p. 329.
18. Nelli, p. 24.

19. Kessner, pp. 128–29.

20. Barton, pp. 54–59; Briggs, pp. 118–19; Yans-McLaughlin, pp. 116–17.

21. Lieberson, p. 127.

22. Chudacoff, pp. 73–93.

23. Handlin, pp. 129–51.

24. Warner, pp. 173–87; Chudacoff, pp. 84–93; Nelli, p. 25.

25. Briggs, p. 119.

26. Cressey, p. 61.

27. Kessner, pp. 157–60.

28. Yans-McLaughlin, p. 78.

29. Thernstrom, pp. 85, 198–99.

30. Kessner, p. 159.

31. Peixotto, p. 80; Thompson, pp. 604–7; D. Moore, pp. 376–77. The area was popularly known as the "Italian shanties" in the 1880's, and in 1893 the area was described as the "shambling barracks of the poor." Hogan, p. 64.

32. Böhme, p. 158.

33. Palmer, p. 221; R. Dondero, p. 61.

34. Filippi, p. 181.

35. U.S. [1], p. 610. Some census tracts, however, were more densely Italian. Census tract 289, for instance, bounded by Mason, Francisco, Stockton, and Greenwich streets, was 75 percent Italian; tract 283, bounded by Montgomery and Kearny, was 65 percent Italian; and other neighboring tracts, such as 286, 287, and 294, had percentages of Italians ranging from 40 to 60. Computation based on a random sample of 10 percent of the original census schedules of San Francisco for the year 1900, in Federal Archive, San Bruno.

36. U.S. [4], p. 186.

37. U.S. [7], p. 43.

38. NR.

39. Patrizi, p. 43.

40. RC, SF 3.v.1913.

41. Lubin to Johnson, SF 3.v.1914, Papers of the California Commission on Immigration and Housing, Bancroft Library, Univ. of California, Berkeley. In 1929 the newspaper *L'Italia* expressed satisfaction that the Italians of San Francisco had avoided the problem of crime "common among the Italians of other cities in the east." The paper claimed that the high crime rate there was due to the Italians' having segregated themselves from American society. *L'Italia*, 21.iv.1929. We might rightly be skeptical of the self-praise of San Francisco Italians; non-Italians, like Lubin, however, made similar observations.

42. U.S. [3], p. 189.

43. U.S. [5], p. 43.

44. U.S. [15], pp. 7–12.

45. RP, Genoa 7.v.1891, ASG; Palermo 19.ix.1895, ASP.

46. Società Geografica Italiana, p. 186; RC, SF 7.ii.1901.

47. "Problems of New Immigrants," Reports, AIWA.

48. RC, SF 13.xii.1871. "Housing for Italians," Reports, AIWA. Social workers seeking apartments for needy Italians found the lowest rents in North Beach. Family Files: K1, K2, K3, and K4; AIWA. The archives of the Italian Welfare Agency have about 500 files of families that applied for relief from

1916 to the present. (A few files go back to 1909; these were opened by the Comitato di Soccorso e Patronato, which was superseded by the Italian Welfare Agency.) Because many of the people involved are still alive, permission to use the files was granted only on condition that the confidentiality of the people be protected. Accordingly, all names used in reference to these files have been changed, and the files are identified only by a K followed by a sequence number.

49. Interview, SF, Oct. 1976. Donato Santucci told me in May 1976 that after living for six months in an apartment in Mission he had decided to move to North Beach because of the lower rents.

50. U.S. [14], p. 5.

51. Ihlder, p. 161.

52. Griffith, p. 18. See also Devine, p. 608.

53. U.S. [14], p. 5.

54. Lubin to Johnson, 29.ix.1924, Papers of the California Commission on Immigration and Housing.

55. Alice Griffith to Lubin, 17.x.1916, *ibid.*

56. Interview, SF, May 1975.

57. Some stories from naturalization records illustrate this point. Peter Kunz was born in Poppeland, Germany, in 1898. Before coming to the United States in 1923 he was living in Heidelberg. He worked for three years in Chicago before settling in San Francisco in 1926. Karl Hey, born in 1884 in Dorrenbach, Germany, was living in Paris in 1922, when he left for the United States at age 36. Michael Hogan was living in Castle Island, Ireland, when in 1914, at age 19, he left for the United States. He had been born in Tralee, Ireland. Isabella Gough was a nurse in Vancouver, Canada, when she left for San Francisco in 1919 at age 44; she had been born in Belfast, Ireland. Joseph Almazoff, born in Panza, Russia, was living in Harbin, Manchuria, in 1910, when he left for the United States. Franz Klingler was born in Wintherthur, Switzerland, in 1879 and was living in Zurich when he left for the United States in 1924. In 1925, when he applied for naturalization, he was a bookkeeper in Salt Lake City. In 1930, when he actually became a citizen, he was a banker in San Francisco. Nicolai Kaido was born in Vladivostok, Russia, in 1901, and lived in Harbin, before entering the United States. He applied for naturalization in 1923 in Los Angeles, and became an American citizen in San Francisco in 1930.

58. RC, SF 7.v.1868; Società Geografica Italiana, p. 169.

59. "I Nuovi Arrivati," *L'Italia*, 23.x.1903. In 1912 G. Gamboni Mazzitelli, the executive secretary of the Comitato di Soccorso e Patronato, wrote that newcomers were ordinarily people who joined relatives and settled with them for a while or returnees coming back to America. Mazzitelli to Lubin, 7.v.1912, Papers of the California Commission on Immigration and Housing. Some immigrants arrived at the invitation of relatives, and then were left without assistance. Rosario Benedetto, for instance, came in 1920, invited by a married brother who died in an industrial accident while Rosario was en route. The widow had to vacate the apartment where Rosario had hoped to stay for a

while, and Rosario had to seek assistance. K4, AIWA. Antonio Lorrano arrived in 1922, invited by a brother. But the two quarreled, and Antonio's relatives living in San Francisco refused to help him; so he too applied for relief. K5, AIWA.

60. RC, SF 7.iv.1887. See also J. S. and L. D. MacDonald, "Chain Migration," pp. 85–86.

61. Andrew Rolle, however, asserts that "California's Italians experienced little discrimination" (Rolle, p. 259).

62. Powell, p. 98; for a similar view see Dessery. An early specimen of anti-Italian prejudice may be found in *Alta California*, 7.iii.1851. See also Crespi, "Il Miraggio," p. 2.

63. Bonardelli, pp. 447–48; RC, SF 11.ix.1912. Vice-consul Giulio Ricciardi wrote: "Skilled laborers are all unionized. Some trades, like the plumbers, are almost feudal institutions where only workers' children are usually admitted. Only a few Italians who have been here for over fifteen years and have been successful are admitted to the unions. Even Italians who arrive here from other cities of the east are not accepted by the unions, regardless of the fact that some of them carry membership cards from unions in the east." Ricciardi, p. 247.

64. AIWA, K6, K7, and K8. Older Italians still remember with bitterness the discrimination they suffered when they moved out of Italian neighborhoods and their decision to return to Italian settlements. Antonio Muzzi, from Lucca, for instance, found that he was so unwelcome in Richmond in 1936 that after six months he was back in Potrero where he had initially settled. Carlo De Maestri had his rent raised so high two months after he moved into an apartment in the Sunset district that he was forced to go back to North Beach. Interviews, SF, Oct. 1976.

65. *L'Italia*, 3.v.1902; *VP*, 7.vi.1902.

66. *L'Italia*, 10.ix.1902. For a similar opinion, set down in the 1930's, see Pallavicini, p. 187. This novel was first published as a serial in *L'Italia.* In 1975 a number of Italians, when I asked why they had lived all their lives in North Beach, answered that they had felt their families would be safer there than anywhere else. One said: "I could not allow my children to associate with Americans, who have no sense of family and only care about money."

67. RC, SF 6.xi.1903.

68. Mangano, *Sons of Italy*, pp. 41–47; Williams, p. 9.

69. Dessery, p. 26.

70. "The Italians of San Francisco are still a community within a community, almost untouched by the outside world and coming in contact with it only when business demands it." Radin, 1: 59. This statement is probably too strong; but it conveys an idea that was popular in San Francisco for a long time.

71. Patrizi, p. 43.

72. R. Dondero, p. 41.

73. Barton, p. 58.

74. "Registro d'Emigrazione per gli Anni 1889–90," ACL.

75. NR for this and following data.

76. Italy [12], pp. 166–67; Italy [37], pp. 10–11.

77. Italy [12], pp. 181–85; Italy [38], pp. 31–37.

78. Italy [12], pp. 127, 251; Italy [36], p. 24; Italy [39], p. 44.

79. The family of Aldo Puccinelli, for instance, moved eight times between 1930 and 1942, usually within the central area of North Beach. The family was at 310 Santa Clara in 1930, 402 Broadway in 1932, 1233 Kearny in 1934, 526 Broadway in 1935, 127 Fresno in 1937, and 1449 Powell in 1939; K9, AIWA. Angelo Facchini, an immigrant who arrived in San Francisco in 1917, changed address eight times between 1932 and 1941, when he was committed to Laguna Honda Hospital; K10, AIWA. The evidence from the files of the Italian Welfare Agency should be taken with the qualification that it does not represent the experience of Italians at large, since the agency dealt with families that were particularly poor. Older Italians, however, confirm that there was great mobility within the settlements. In 1976 I asked 25 Italians how many times they had moved before settling down permanently. Nine said four times, seven three times, four twice, and five once. Nineteen of them said they had stayed for a week or longer with relatives. Angelo Concetti, for example, stayed for three months with an uncle at 513 Green Street after he arrived in San Francisco in 1913. His first residence was at 623 Green Street, for one year; then, at the end of 1914, he moved to 973 Vallejo; and finally, in 1924, he made a down payment on a house on Amazon Avenue.

80. K11, AIWA. Carmelo Cavalli moved into a two-room apartment in 1922 with his wife and three children. Four more children were born between 1922 and 1930, which forced Carmelo to look for a larger place, even though he could ill afford one with his wages as a janitor. K12, AIWA.

81. K13, AIWA.

82. K14, AIWA.

83. K15, AIWA. The reaction of the Genoese was so strong largely because Franco had eight children. After 15 months Franco moved back where he had lived before. In a letter to a social worker he explained: "The Genovesi seem to think that they own the city, because they arrived first in San Francisco. They are worse than the Americans." SF, 7.v.1938, K15, AIWA.

84. Interviews, SF, Nov.–Dec. 1976.

85. RP, Genoa 17.v.1879, ASG. See also Bertani, p. 529; and Marenco, p. 27.

86. Mazzini, p. 522.

87. RP, Cosenza 21.x.1887, ASC. The president of the Chamber of Commerce of Palermo remarked: "To own a house is still a privilege for the people of these towns. But even those who rent do not like to move; if they can afford it, they remain in the same house they are renting when they get married." Rosario Bazzilli to the prefetto of Palermo, 7.v.1902, CM, ASP.

88. FF, ACL. Santo Azzolini, when he left Porcari in 1911, was living with his parents and grandparents in the same house where the great-grandparents had lived in the 1770's. FF (Valentino Azzolini), ACC.

89. FF, ACLU.

90. FF, ACSL.

91. FF, ACL.

92. NR. If we focus on the immigrants from a specific community, we discover the same pattern. For example, over half the immigrants from Santa Flavia became fishermen in San Francisco. About 75 percent of these fishermen lived in tracts A1, A3, and A4, the part of North Beach adjacent to Fishermen's Wharf. About half of the immigrants from Sestri Levante became fishermen in San Francisco too; they also settled in A1, A3, and A4, although they lived a few blocks west of the fishermen from Santa Flavia. About one third of the immigrants from Lorsica went into trade and transportation, and of these, 30 percent settled in A3 and 45 percent in the southern section of the Portola district. A sizable number of the immigrants from Lorsica went into farming, and 75 percent of these lived in the Portola district.

93. U.S. [15], pp. 3–4.

94. Griffith to Lubin, 3.iii.1916, Papers of the California Commission on Immigration and Housing.

95. Scherini.

96. Two examples will illustrate these general statements. When James Corelli, a young man of 15, was arrested for stealing tools from a construction site, his mother Assunta asked the social worker to tell the judge that her son had gotten out of hand in the past year when he had started frequenting the downtown area. "We cannot have any control over him when he is out of our neighborhood," she said. Fernando Turati, the father of a 16-year-old boy arrested with other friends for vandalism, told the judge his son's troubles had started when he had joined the Sicilian gang led by the Duranto and Lucia boys. K16, AIWA.

97. K17, AIWA.

98. K18, AIWA. Frank Sereni, a young man who was eventually killed at 19 while resisting arrest, told a judge who asked him why he was embarrassing his family with his behavior, that he had asked his father to let him go away. The young man concluded: "My friends are Americans and I want to live like them." K19, AIWA.

99. NR. There were considerable differences among non-Italian immigrant groups. Only 13 percent of the children of British immigrants were born in San Francisco; 9 percent more were born in California, and another 9 percent elsewhere in the United States. But 27 percent were born in Canada, a few in New Zealand, and the rest in Great Britain. In contrast, about 55 percent of the children of Irish immigrants were born in San Francisco; another 8 percent were born elsewhere in California, 9 percent in Canada, and the other 28 percent in Ireland. Of Russians, 31 percent were born in San Francisco, about 50 percent in Russia, and 15 percent in China. Finally, 61 percent of the German immigrants' children were born in San Francisco, 10 percent in other states, and the rest in Germany.

100. Interview, SF, Oct. 1976.

101. K20, AIWA. Deliso Santucci told me that both he and his mother had gone back to Sestri Levante in 1932. For some time his father had also contem-

plated going back to Italy, where he owned some land. But in 1937 he decided to remain in San Francisco, and his wife and son returned. Riccardo Puccini spent six years in Lucca, from 1932 to 1938, with his grandparents, and returned to San Francisco only when his grandmother died and the aging grandfather could not take care of him. Interviews, SF, Dec. 1976.

102. K21, AIWA.

103. MR, ACHD.

104. *Ibid.*

105. Mazzini, p. 509.

106. RP, Lucca 21.ii.1907, ASL.

107. City directories of San Francisco from 1941 to 1965 for this and following data.

108. Interview, SF, Oct. 1976.

109. *Ibid.*, May 1976.

110. Interview with Philip Cappello, San Bruno, May 1976.

111. Interview, Burlingame, Oct. 1976.

Chapter 6

1. C. Hall, pp. 3–17. In the 1860's, Acting Consul P. A. Abbate reported, most San Francisco Italians were either farmers or fishermen, with farming the more lucrative and prestigious occupation (Abbate, pp. 3–18).

2. Società Geografica Italiana, pp. 121–22.

3. RC, SF 2.ii.1907. Consul Lambertenghi also noted the founding of the four major Italo-American banks between 1899 and 1906. The consul's assessment of the conditions of the San Francisco Italians was popularized in Italy by Luigi Villari in his widely read and discussed *Gli Stati Uniti.*

4. Patrizi, *Gli Italiani*, pp. 46–60. See also Fisk, pp. 383–93; Pecorini, pp. 389–90; and Peixotto, pp. 75–84. More recent examples are Paoli, pp. 78–116, and Nicosia.

5. Foerster, pp. 342–43.

6. Although these occupational categories are different from those ordinarily used by historians, the findings seem to confirm other data from Boston, Cleveland, and New York. See Thernstrom, pp. 111–44; Barton, pp. 91–116; and Kessner, pp. 44–70.

7. This intragenerational mobility was characteristic of all non-Italians. Among the Irish, for instance, between petition and naturalization 25 percent of those in domestic occupations left that category, 15 percent going into trade and the other 10 percent into manufacturing. But there was also a movement downward: about 18 percent left manufacturing, most going into domestic services. Germans showed similar rates of intragenerational mobility, but mostly upward. The Russians and the English were closer to the German pattern than to the Irish.

8. Bonardelli, pp. 488–89; Ricciardi, pp. 245–47. Even Italians who had been union members in eastern cities of the United States were denied admission to the San Francisco unions when they moved there.

9. Radin, 1: 26–37.

10. Some figures will illustrate this point. Of the children of landowners, 35

percent went into manufacturing in San Francisco, and only 29 percent into domestic and personal services. About 47 percent of the children of sharecroppers and tenants were in domestic services, and only 24 percent in manufacturing. Finally, 83 percent of the children of day laborers were in domestic services.

11. RC, SF 2.iv.1901.

12. Ravaioli, pp. 40–44.

13. Interview, SF, Sept. 1976.

14. Von Borosini, pp. 791–93.

15. RC, SF 17.ix.1921.

16. J. S. MacDonald, "Urbanization," p. 441.

17. Von Borosini, p. 792.

18. RP, Palermo 7.iii.1913, ASP.

19. RC, SF 27.ix.1920.

20. RC, SF 7.x.1924.

21. RM, Santa Flavia 17.v.1895, ASP.

22. RP, Genoa 19.ix.1904, ASG.

23. Interview, SF, Nov. 1976.

24. RC, SF 3.v.1912; Fisk, p. 390.

25. For Sestri Levante, I used a sample of 30 percent of the marriage records for those years; for Santa Flavia, I used all the records, since Santa Flavia was a relatively small commune.

26. RC, SF 12.v.1906.

27. Ricciardi, p. 248.

28. RM, Lorsica 7.ix.1909, ASG.

29. RP, Lucca 3.v.1921, ASL.

30. Ricciardi, p. 248.

31. Based on the census of 1881; manuscripts in the archives of the communes of Lorsica and Capannori.

32. Estimate based on description in RP, Cosenza 29.ix.1887 and 3.i.1893, ASC.

33. RP, Cosenza 23.iii.1889.

34. Loncao, p. 27.

35. Based on all marriage records in Lorsica for 1882, 1892, 1902, 1912, and 1922.

36. Based on 20 percent of the marriage records for the same years.

37. Statistics based on 50 percent of the marriage records of each commune in the same years.

38. RM, Verbicaro 17.x.1906, ASC.

39. The birth records of the future emigrants, which include the part of town where the parents lived, show that 74 percent of the immigrants to San Francisco from Genoa, 69 percent of those from Palermo, and 50 percent of those from Lucca came from the villages around the cities.

40. RC, SF 7.ii.1911.

Chapter 7

1. Italy [8], p. 109; J. S. and L. D. MacDonald, "Chain Migration," p. 85.

2. Cyriax, p. 218.

3. Italy [35], *Statistica*, 1908–9, p. xiii; Von Borosini, p. 782. For an interesting statistical discussion of emigration by sex in the province of Cosenza, see Taruffi et al., pp. 726–29.

4. U.S. [5], p. 754.
5. RP, Lucca 1.xii.1909, ASL.
6. RC, SF 3.v.1865; see also A. Rossi, "Per la Tutela," pp. 113–21.
7. Società Geografica Italiana, p. 233.
8. Italy [42], p. 477.
9. RP, Lucca 17.ii.1887, ASL.
10. RC, SF 17.v.1912.
11. *L'Italia*, 23.iv.1913.
12. U.S. [9], p. 246.
13. Foerster, p. 441.
14. Handlin, pp. 203–30.
15. Child, pp. 76–117.
16. Vecoli, p. 409.
17. Yans-McLaughlin, p. 19.
18. Gans, p. 210. See also J. S. MacDonald, "Migration from Italy," p. 97, which reaches a similar conclusion with respect to Italian immigration in Australia.
19. Vecoli, p. 14; Covello, p. 149; Yans-McLaughlin, pp. 30–31; Day, p. 162.
20. Gans, p. 210; J. S. MacDonald, "Migration from Italy," p. 97.
21. Yans-McLaughlin argues (p. 30) that southern Italian families were larger than northern families at the time of mass emigration. According to her, Italian statistics show that in the periods 1881–85 and 1896–1900, crude birthrates were 40.5 and 38.5 per 1,000 in the south, and only 35 and 33.3 per 1,000 in the north. It is inaccurate, however, to conclude that families were larger in the south simply because crude birthrates were higher. The crucial factors in assessing family size are mortality rate, the correlation between the crude birthrate and the marriage rate, and a clear understanding of the difference between families, households, nuclear family households, and extended family households. Crude birthrates by themselves tell us very little about family and household structures, and are likely to be misleading.

Italian census data show that northern households were considerably larger than southern households. In 1861, for instance, the average size of northern households was 4.9, and southern 4.4. Fifty years later the northern households were still larger, 4.8 to 4.1. In 1921 the ratio was 4.6 to 4.1. Only in 1936 were north and south the same, at 4.3. After the Second World War southern households became larger than northern; in 1951, for instance, it was 4.2 to 3.8. See Italy [41], *Un Secolo di Statistiche Storiche*, p. 29. Moreover, the number of births per nuclear family was higher in the north than in the south. The average in 1882 was 4.61 for Liguria, 4.90 for Lombardy, and 5.13 for Veneto, three regions of the north. In the south the average was 3.94 in Abbruzzi, 4.39 in Calabria, and 4.65 in Sicily. Italy [31], *Movimento*, 1882, p. xxvii. Other evidence confirms that southern households were smaller. A survey early in the century concluded: "The agrarian system of the south cannot support large families. In Italy the large families are to be found in the north." Italy [10], p. 465. See also Coletti, *La Popolazione*, p. 126; and RP, Palermo 21.i.1907, ASP.

22. Cronin, p. 30.
23. FF, ACL; BR, ACL.
24. MR, ACDH.
25. Interview, SF, Nov. 1975.
26. Interview, SF, Dec. 1976.
27. NR; MR, ACHD.

28. The high percentage of single men in San Francisco casts doubt on MacDonald's model of the Italian emigrant as a married man departing alone. Among Italians in the United States, MacDonald wrote, "were many married men, but very few were accompanied by their wives and children on their first voyage." J. S. and L. D. MacDonald, "Chain Migration," p. 85. This might have been the case in other Italian communities in the United States; but it does not apply to San Francisco. The large percentage of single people among first-time emigrants means that returnees generally were not married men going back to their wives, but single young men returning to their parents' families. The high percentage of single immigrants might explain, at least to a degree, the intensity of return migration and reemigration: single young men could leave their Italian communities without major problems, since they had no family responsibilities.

29. RP, Cosenza 7.v.1908, ASC.

30. RP, Palermo 13.xii.1911, ASP. The discrepancy between MacDonald's model of married men emigrating alone and later being joined by their families, and our sample showing San Francisco immigrants to have been mainly single at first arrival, can probably be reconciled. Our sample is derived from families living in San Francisco in the 1930's. It is likely that many married immigrants returned permanently to Italy, either without ever asking their families to come to San Francisco or after spending several years with their families in San Francisco and in the end deciding to resettle in Italy. These immigrants, being in Italy in the 1930's, do not show up in our sample. Moreover, single immigrants were probably more likely to settle in San Francisco after a series of emigrations and returns, since they had no family ties in Italy except their parents' family. And married immigrants were more likely to be older than single immigrants, and thus less able to adjust to the new society. Finally, it is possible that married immigrants were concerned about the impact of the new society on their wives and children. In short, the percentage of married men who arrived in San Francisco was probably higher than our sample shows. If that was the case, the married immigrants were more likely to return permanently to Italy, and the single immigrants more likely, after a series of emigrations and returns, to settle permanently in San Francisco.

31. NR.

32. NR.

33. Interviews, SF, Jan. 1976.

34. J. S. MacDonald, "Chain Migration," p. 89.

35. RP, Palermo 14.xii.1907, ASP.

36. Von Borosini, p. 792.

37. Taruffi et al., p. 862. A local magistrate noticed: "Millions of lire arrive every year from the United States. But our families are the losers, regardless of how much money we receive. Family instability has reached unprecedented proportions because of emigration." *Ibid.,* p. 866.

38. Cyriax, pp. 218–19.

39. Caputo, *Di Alcune Questioni*, p. 10. I interviewed twelve San Francisco Italians in 1976 on the reasons they had sent for their families. Some were old

and their recollections were poor. Seven explained that they had sent for their families because they were making good money and were concerned about the effect of their long absence on their families. Most also said that even when they sent for their families they were still convinced that they would return to Italy.

40. Edward Banfield (*Moral Basis*, p. 85) argues that in the Italian south of the 1950's there were no meaningful social relationships outside the nuclear family household; he called this attitude "amoral familism." Others argue similarly for southern society at the time of mass emigration, as we saw in connection with land ownership and social structure; see J. S. MacDonald, "Institutional Economics," p. 115. Since the competition to secure favorable agricultural contracts was fierce, setting laborers and sharecroppers against each other, the family became the prime social group in a highly individualistic and competitive society. Thus many southerners in San Francisco sent for their wives because family life provided their only meaningful social relationships.

41. Italy [31], *Popolazione*, 1902, p. xxxix.

42. Harr, pp. 99–114.

43. NR.

44. Italy [15], pp. 307, 337, 355, 413. Other data show that the rates of people marrying in a given year in the provinces of Palermo and Cosenza were higher than in Lucca and Genoa. In 1882, for instance, the rate was 6.9 per 1,000 in Genoa and 7.7 per 1,000 in Lucca; in the province of Cosenza it was 8.3 and in Palermo 8.5. Italy [31], *Popolazione*, 1882, p. x. Three decades later the rates were about the same: 6.9 in Genoa, 7.8 in Lucca, 8.3 in Cosenza, and 8.4 in Palermo. *Ibid.*, 1912, p. xviii. Computations made directly from marriage records of the nine communes show a north-south contrast too. From 1880 to 1920 marriage rates in the communes of Lorsica and Sestri Levante varied between 6.5 and 7.5 per 1,000, and in Capannori and Lucca from 7.5 to 8. In the south the rates ranged from 9.5 to 10.5 in Verbicaro, Trabia, Santa Flavia, and Palermo.

45. U.S. [18], p. 212. These figures refer to the country as a whole.

46. NR.

47. Bertani, p. 528; Mazzini, pp. 521–22; interviews, SF, Dec. 1975.

48. NR.

49. Von Borosini, p. 782; Williams, pp. 73–90.

50. Only 8 percent of the male immigrants from Porcari married before age 20; 10 percent married between 21 and 23, 25 percent between 24 and 26, almost 30 percent between 27 and 30, and the rest after 30. Of the males from Palermo, 10 percent married before their twentieth birthday, about 15 percent between 21 and 23, 20 percent between 24 and 26, and 30 percent between 27 and 30. Less than 2 percent of the non-Italians married before age 20, 9 percent between 21 and 23, 15 percent between 24 and 26, 25 percent between 27 and 31, and 45 percent over 31. NR.

51. The mean age for Lorsica was 29 in 1882, 1892, and 1902, and 28.5 in 1912 and 1922. Sestri Levante, Capannori, Lucca, and Genoa followed that pattern closely. In the south, the mean age in Santa Flavia was 27.5 in 1882

and 1892, and 28.5 in 1902, 1912, and 1922. Other southern communes were about the same. Besides marriage records, see RP, Genoa 7.v.1897; and RP, Cosenza 2.ix.1909.

52. U.S. [9], p. 754.

53. Italy [35], *Statistica*, 1910–11, pp. 86–87.

54. Italy [23], pp. 353, 376.

55. RM, Trabia 3.x.1907, ASP.

56. RP, Genoa 7.ii.1909, ASG.

57. Williams, pp. 73–106.

58. Interview, SF, Nov. 1976.

59. RP, Palermo 23.x.1906, ASP; RP, Cosenza 4.iv.1911, ASC.

60. NR. Our sample seems to run against the findings of historians who argue that most Italian immigrants did not marry women from their own town, but only from their own region. Briggs, for instance, shows that over half the Italian marriages in Cleveland, Utica, and Rochester were between people from different towns (p. 86). The high rates of endogamous marriages found in our nine groups are probably not typical of Italians in general. The San Francisco groups were relatively large and had been established largely by chain emigration. And frequent new arrivals, at least until 1924, kept alive the ties between the groups in San Francisco.

61. NR.

62. NR.

63. MR, ACHD.

64. NR.

65. Wells, p. 518; see also Harr, pp. 99–114.

66. U.S. [18], p. 184.

67. *Report of the Department of Public Health* (San Francisco, 1910), p. 33.

68. U.S. [19], p. 180.

69. NR.

70. U.S. [19], p. 186.

71. Italy [31], *Popolazione*, 1882, pp. 230–33.

72. *Ibid.*, 1912, pp. 75–76.

73. NR.

74. NR.

75. Italy [41], p. 124. In 1921, it might be objected, a large number of southern Italian men were abroad, and this could account for the smaller families in the south, since fewer people from the north were abroad, and many who were, especially if in South America, had their families with them. The Italian census figures, however, were based not on actual residents in 1921, but on all legal residents of Italy, even those living abroad. As seen earlier, at least 80 percent of all Italian emigrants kept their legal residence in Italy. Thus most of the Italians who were abroad in 1921 were counted in the computation of family size.

76. *Ibid.*, p. 98.

77. In 1882, for instance, the crude birthrate was 32 per 1,000 in Lorsica and Sestri Levante, 35 in Porcari and Lucca, 39 in Verbicaro, and 38 in Santa Flavia and Trabia. Italy [31], *Popolazione*, 1882, p. xxxiv. By 1912 the rates had dropped to 24 per 1,000 in the province of Genoa, 29 in Porcari, 35 in

Verbicaro, and 33 in Trabia and Santa Flavia. *Ibid.,* 1912, p. xxxiii. In 1922 the rate was under 20 in the province of Genoa, 26 in Lucca, and 29 in the two southern provinces. *Ibid.,* 1919–23, p. lxxii.

78. Italy [31], *Popolazione*, 1919–23, p. cvi.

79. Italy [12], p. vi.

80. Italy [10], p. 465; Italy [7], p. 588; RP, Palermo 23.i.1901, ASP; RP, Cosenza 17.v.1902, ASC; Taruffi et al., pp. 96–97.

81. Mazzini, pp. 521–22; see also Coletti, *La Popolazione Rurale*, p. 125.

82. Mazzini, p. 522.

83. Branca, p. 119.

84. Sample of 20 percent of the FF of the town of Lorsica, archives of the commune of Lorsica.

85. Data from a 10 percent sample of the census returns of 1881, archives of the commune of Lorsica.

86. Data from a 5 percent sample of the FF of the commune of Sestri Levante, in the town archives.

87. Data from 100 FF of the city of Lucca and 85 FF of the commune of Porcari; local archives.

88. Branca, pp. 118–19.

89. Coletti, *La Popolazione Rurale*, p. 126, and *Economia Rurale.* Cf. Taruffi et al., pp. 96–97; Italy [10], p. 465; and RP, Cosenza 23.i.1907, ASC.

90. AIWA.

91. U.S. [19], p. 14.

92. Interviews, SF, Dec. 1975.

93. MR in ACHD, ACV, ACT, ACSF.

94. Pitrè, 13: 127, 213.

95. Caputo, "Di Alcune Questioni," p. 342.

96. Wrigley, pp. 179–84.

97. Harr, pp. 99–114.

98. The evidence presented here casts doubt on a commonly held assumption, that in the Italian south the extended family household was the rule. Probably, this assumption comes mainly from the classical model of agrarian societies. Besides this, however, many American writers on Italy have relied on Williams, *South Italian Folkways*, a handbook for social workers, schoolteachers, and physicians who had to deal with Italian immigrants. Her main source, in turn, was the 25 volumes on southern Italian folklore published by the Sicilian Giuseppe Pitrè, *Biblioteca delle Tradizioni Popolari Siciliane.* Pitrè used popular refrains to map the social reality of Sicilian families. For instance, he quoted the Sicilian proverb "He who obeys father and mother will live happily and prosper" to show that Sicilian families were stable and close. On marriage, he reported that "marriage takes place at an early age, with the bride as young as fourteen and the groom one or two years older." (Pitrè, 25: 83.) As we saw, the Italian census disproves that. Possibly Pitrè was expressing a longing of Sicilians for the extended family household, which in the south was the exception, not the rule.

99. Banfield, p. 107.

100. Nelli, p. 170.

101. Yans-McLaughlin, p. 21.

102. Cronin, p. 26; cf. Anfossi et al, p. 200.

103. Meyriat, p. 205.

104. AIWA. A family history illustrates this sequence. Problems in the Casale family started in Nov. 1931, when Fernando's wages as a laborer at the Southern Pacific Railroad were cut from $4.00 to $3.25 a day. The family had four children and lived in a three-room flat on the 300 block of Green Street, for which they paid $20.00 a month. After the wage cut, the family was unable to pay the grocery bills at the Anastasia grocery store. A social worker noted: "Fernando is a proud man and does not want anyone to know that he cannot provide for his family." Between 1931 and 1935 two more children were born, and the family had to look for another apartment; from 1935 to 1939 the family moved once a year.

In 1935 Fernando began to drink heavily. The children created additional stress. Carlo, the oldest, got in trouble with the law. When he was arrested for stealing, the family was so embarrassed that it moved. Marcello, the third child, developed epilepsy in 1936. Fernando's wife Rosa's health also deteriorated, and the next year she was committed to the Sonoma State Hospital. In late 1939 the Visiting Nurse Association of North Beach telephoned the Italian Welfare Agency that Rosa "was having difficulties with her husband, who was beating her and neglecting his family." The social worker found that Fernando "stayed out until late, had increased his drinking, and gave Rosa only a few dollars a week, while before he gave her the entire paycheck." The children were one by one placed in foster homes. Finally, Fernando and Rosa separated. Their last argument occurred when Fernando discovered that Rosa was using birth control, as suggested by a nurse at the North Beach clinic. K22, AIWA.

105. Paolo Pallavicini's other novels include *L'Amante delle Tre Croci, Per le Vie del Mondo, La Casa del Peccato,* and *La Terra del Sogno*. The novel of his that I discuss, and that of Giovanni Pancrazi, were chosen for their bearing on family life.

106. Pancrazi, p. 343; Pallavicini, p. 359.

107. The idealization of the old country, and especially of family life, played a major role in the perceptions of the immigrants and their children. Possibly, such an idealization explains some historical interpretations, like that in Handlin's *The Uprooted.*

108. Pallavicini, pp. 142, 298; Pancrazi, pp. 321–33.

109. Pallavicini, pp. 252, 302, 313–15.

110. Caputo, *L'Abitazione*, p. 27; RP, Palermo 3.v.1903, ASP.

111. RC, SF 2.iii.1865.

112. *VP,* 7.v.1887; *La Parola*, 16.iii.1865; *L'Eco della Patria*, 13.xi.1867.

113. *L'Italia*, 21.ix.1903.

114. Taruffi et al., p. 864.

115. Cyriax, pp. 218–19, seems to put all the blame for infidelity on wives. It should be noted that the writer was an unmarried woman.

116. Italy [31], *Popolazione*, 1902, pp. xxxiv–xxxv.

117. Italy [31], *Popolazione*, 1912, pp. xlii–xliii.

118. Bertani, p. 523.

119. RM, Lorsica 7.v.1893, ASG.

120. RP, Lucca 29.xii.1897, ASL.

121. Bertani, p. 528.

122. Mazzini, pp. 521–22.

123. Damiani, p. 368.

124. *Ibid.,* p. 358.

Chapter 8

1. California State Legislature, pp. 281–321.

2. *Ibid.,* p. 230.

3. L. Villari, *Italian Life*, pp. 9–10. Among recent historians of Italian immigration to the United States, only Briggs deals with the difference between regionalism and campanilismo. Campanilismo, he says, hardly influenced Italians in Cleveland, Rochester, and Utica; regionalism, however, was strong enough to prevent Italians from forming nationally integrated organizations for a long time. Regionalism, in Briggs's view, replaced campanilismo because distinctive communal traditions could not be maintained in Italian enclaves where immigrants from various communes lived and closely interacted. Italians, unlike Poles and Slovaks, were not strongly nationalistic, Briggs concludes, because their culture and national identity were not threatened in Europe. The assumption is that immigrants from countries threatened by more powerful nations were more likely to put aside regional differences and unite in support of their motherland. See Briggs, pp. 86, 161–62.

4. McBride, p. 273.

5. RC, SF 27.ix.1896.

6. Falbo, "Stato di California," p. 321.

7. RC, SF 7.v.1864.

8. RC, SF 27.ix.1867.

9. RC, SF 7.xii.1871.

10. RC, SF 1.v.1865.

11. L. Villari, *Italian Life*, pp. 21–28.

12. *Ibid.,* p. 35.

13. *Ibid.,* p. 43.

14. King, pp. 193–214; Franceschini, p. 509.

15. RC, SF 25.vi.1865.

16. *Ibid.* 19.v.1867.

17. Società Francese, pp. 2–11; "La Società Italiana di Mutua Beneficenza, L'Ospedale e la Società Francese," *VP*, 13.viii.1868; RC, SF 2.vi.1863.

18. Abbate, p. 9.

19. Larco was the only Italian merchant I have discovered who was active in the community affairs of the early Italian colony. He wrote to the Italian government a number of times; his memorandums are kept in the archives of

the Ministry of Foreign Affairs in Rome, together with the correspondence from the San Francisco consul.

20. Larco to the Sardinian Minister of Foreign Affairs in Turin, SF 3.v.1857, with RC. All the correspondence from San Francisco to the Sardinian minister in Turin and the Italian Minister of Foreign Affairs in Florence before 1870, when Rome became the capital of Italy, is now in the archives of the Ministry of Foreign Affairs in Rome.

21. RC, SF 25.vi.1865. See also "La Società Italiana di Mutua Beneficenza," *VP*, 5.iii.1869; "I Nostri Problemi," *VP*, 20.iii.1869; and "Le Attività della Società," *VP*, 3.vii.1868.

22. In 1865 Consul Cerruti requested funds from the Italian government to pay for the repatriation of Daniele Cochi, who had arrived in California from Florence in 1849 at age twelve. Cochi had made some money in mining, but then lost his sight. As long as his money lasted, relatives in Sacramento took care of him. The consul concluded: "He is blind and sick. The friends from the old days have disappeared, and the Società Italiana di Mutua Beneficenza does not have the funds to help him. Immigrants are unwilling to take care of less fortunate Italians." RC, SF 3.iii.1865. Luigi Bidoni from Venice was another for whom the consul asked government assistance. Bidoni had also made money as a miner; but after being wounded during a robbery near Sacramento, he exhausted his savings for medical care. Unable to provide for himself, he went to the Italian consul, who requested funds from Rome, but concluded: "I have already promoted too many collections among Italians to repatriate ex-miners. Immigrants are beginning to resent my appeals." RC, SF 21.i.1866. See also "Ospedale Italiano," *VP*, 12.ix.1868.

23. "Società Italiana di Mutua Beneficenza," *VP*, 14.vii.1868.

24. RC, SF 7.v.1865; see also 2.xii.1864.

25. *Bollettino del Ministero degli Affari Esteri*, 1898, pp. 344–45.

26. "Ospedale Italiano," *VP*, 12.ix.1868.

27. *Bollettino del Ministero degli Affari Esteri*, 1898, p. 344.

28. *Ibid.*, pp. 344–45.

29. RC, SF 24.ii.1879.

30. *Ibid.*, 19.v.1872.

31. L. Villari, *Italian Life*, p. 10.

32. *Bollettino del Ministero degli Affari Esteri*, 1898, pp. 344–45.

33. RC, SF 29.v.1893.

34. *Ibid.*, 17.ix.1874; Cyriax, p. 262.

35. L. Villari, *Italian Life*, p. 175.

36. Marazzi, p. 480; "Parata del Quattro Luglio," *VP*, 7.v.1868. See also the booklet *Statuti della Compagnia dei Bersaglieri Italiani Indipendenti* (San Francisco, 1879), pp. 14–17.

37. *VP*, 4.i.1868, and 13.viii.1868.

38. RC, SF 17.v.1879.

39. "Per i Nuovi Arrivati," *VP*, 23.ix.1876.

40. For this see the bylaws of the Compagnia Garibaldina in *Società Italiana di Mutuo Soccorso della Compagnia Garibaldina* (San Francisco, 1868), p. 9.

41. Marazzi, p. 429; De Medici, pp. 59–60; "La Scuola Italiana," *VP,* 22.viii.1868; "Società Italiana di Beneficenza," *VP,* 4.vii.1868.
42. *Società . . . della Compagnia Garibaldina*, p. 3.
43. *Statuti della Società di Mutuo Soccorso di Porcari*, p. 2.
44. *Statuti della Società di Mutuo Soccorso di Lorsica*, p. 3.
45. "La Società Italiana di Mutua Beneficenza e l'Ospedale Italiano," *VP,* 13.viii.1868.
46. "Ospedale Italiano," *VP,* 5.ii.1869; "Prestito per l'Ospedale Italiano," *VP,* 5.iii.1869; "La Società Italiana di Mutua Beneficenza," *VP,* 5.xii.1868; "Finalmente Sta per Andare in Esecuzione il Progetto," *VP,* 12.ix.1868.
47. "Cose Locali," *VP,* 11.xi.1868; Casper, p. 28.
48. "Società Italiana di Mutua Beneficenza," *VP,* 8.vii.1868.
49. "Il Futuro," *VP,* 13.xii.1868.
50. "Relazione del Comitato del Prestito," *VP,* 5.iii.1869.
51. "L'Ospedale Italiano," *VP,* 2.vi.1869.
52. Dore, pp. 18–19.
53. RC, SF 23.x.1892; see also *VP,* 11.iv.1872; 3.v.1872; and 17.vi.1872.
54. RC, SF 23.x.1892.
55. RC, SF 13.x.1892.
56. On regionalism in religion see Crespi, *San Francisco*, p. 63; Frangini, pp. 11–15; R. Dondero, p. 109; and Fisk, p. 390.
57. RC, SF 12.ix.1863, and 2.v.1864.
58. *Ibid.,* 4.ix.1867.
59. RC, SF 3.xii.1871. See also "Circolo Italiano," *VP,* 4.i.1868; "Federazione per l'Educazione," *VP,* 7.i.1868; "L'Associazione Nazionale Italiana," *VP,* 16.vii.1868; and "Inaugurazione del Nuovo Locale dell'Associazione Nazionale Italiana," *VP,* 31.xii.1868.
60. Callegaris, pp. 1–13; C. Dondero, *Relazione.*
61. Marazzi, p. 479; Naselli, p. 226.
62. "Associazione Nazionale di Beneficenza," *La Parola*, 2.v.1865.
63. RC, SF 2.v.1889.
64. *Ibid.,* 29.vii.1906.
65. "Il Comitato di Soccorso," *L'Era Democratica*, 36 (1922): 13–14; "Comitato di Soccorso e Patronato per Emigrati," *La Rassegna Commerciale*, 24 (1906): 6; "Il Comitato di Soccorso," *Il Topo*, 1 (1904): 4; Shinn, pp. 535–47; Serra, pp. 52–53.
66. L. Villari, *Italian Life*, p. 152.
67. *Ibid.,* p. 153.
68. *Ibid.,* p. 145.
69. King and Okey, p. 140.
70. *Ibid.,* p. 138.
71. RC, SF 7.v.1863.
72. Daggert, p. 11.
73. *Resoconto*, pp. 5–9. See also RC, SF 19.x.1885; and *VP,* 7.iii.1869. The publication of bulletins was not as pressing a need as the immediate care of immigrants facing major personal or family problems.
74. See for example *La Parola*, 7.v.1865.
75. *Ibid.,* 7.vi.1865.

76. RC, SF 17.xii.1879.
77. Falbo, "Stato di California," pp. 312–13; Wheast, p. 206.
78. RC, SF 2.viii.1865.
79. RC, SF 17.x.1865; 29.xii.1865; 9.iii.1866; 27.v.1866.
80. *La Scintilla Italiana*, 21.ix.1875.
81. RC, SF 3.ix.1879.
82. RC, SF 13.ii.1881.
83. Gregory, pp. 34, 52, 56.
84. *VP*, 3.v.1879; 14.vi.1884; 21.iv.1893.
85. *L'Italia*, 23.iii.1894 and 3.i.1896.
86. "I Giardinieri di Genova," *VP*, 3.xii.1869.
87. RC, SF 17.ii.1877.
88. At that time the financial control of the region was in the hands of Spanish and Mexican rancheros, although most of the trade was controlled by Americans.
89. R. Dondero, p. 101; C. Dondero, *Relazione*, p. 9.
90. Palmer, p. 394.
91. RC, SF 7.xi.1867.
92. Falbo, "Stato di California," pp. 331–33. At the time there was no Italian consul, there being no Italian government. The Kingdom of Sardinia was made up of the three regions of Piedmont, Liguria, and Sardinia.
93. RC, SF 3.ix.1865. Biesta had a vested interest in portraying a united and prosperous Italian colony. He concluded his report with the suggestion that such a community needed a permanent official representative such as the French and Germans had. Out of devotion to the King of Sardinia, he was willing to assume such a post. Abbate, p. 34.
94. RC, SF 7.xii.1864, 9.xi.1865.
95. RC, SF 27.ix.1863.
96. RC, SF 24.x.1866.
97. R. Dondero, p. 101; C. Dondero, *Relazione*, p. 9.
98. Palmer, pp. 213–24; Nicosia, p. 13.
99. RC, SF 27.ix.1868.
100. RC, SF 27.iii.1872.
101. "Nuovi Arrivati," *VP*, 29.x.1869.
102. *L'Italia*, 3.xii.1903.
103. RC, SF 17.xi.1869.
104. Palmer, pp. 220–21.
105. U.S. [22], p. 466. R. Dondero (p. 35) says that most immigrants purchased land after working as tenants for several years; but he gives no figures and no evidence for this statement.
106. The source for this story is the "Life of Andrea Sbarboro: Reminiscences of an Italian-American Pioneer," an unpublished manuscript written in 1911 and now at the Bancroft Library, Univ. of California, Berkeley.
107. R. Dondero, pp. 47–51; Frangini, pp. 78–81; Naselli, pp. 228–29; Perret.

108. Sbarboro to the president of the Italian Geographic Society, SF, 18.i.1889, in Società Geografica Italiana, p. 86.

109. RC, SF 17.iii.1878.

110. A. Rossi, "Per la Tutela," p. 121.

111. "Articles of Incorporation of the San Francisco and San Mateo Ranchers' Association" (typewritten), in California Historical Society, SF.

112. Patrizi, p. 37.

113. *VP,* 29.ix.1874.

114. RC, SF 28.x.1975.

115. Dal Ferro, p. 123; Böhme, pp. 149–62.

116. RC, SF 7.vi.1882.

117. *Ibid.*

118. Jackson, p. 18; "The Colombo Market," *The Morning Call*, 3.iii.-1887.

119. Crespi, *San Francisco*, p. 7.

120. RC, SF 4.vi.1884.

121. James, p. 7; Dana, p. 31; Bonardelli, p. 487.

122. Palmer, p. 394.

123. RC, SF 11.x.1870.

124. U.S. Commission of Fisheries, *Report of the Commissioner for 1888* (Washington, D.C., 1892), p. 127; Palmer, p. 181; Abbate, p. 8; Bonardelli, pp. 493–94.

125. Radin, 1: 27.

126. RC, SF 3.v.1893.

127. Consular reports from the 1880's and 1890's and newspapers from the 1900's and 1910's document the occurrence of violence, first between Genoese and Luccans, and later between Genoese and Sicilians. An 1882 report stated: "Some Luccans have tried to become fishermen on their own. But the opposition of the Genoese has discouraged them; violence has been used on both sides. Now the Luccans have settled down and become fishmongers for the Genoese." RC, SF 1.v.1882.

128. Fisk, pp. 390–91. Consul Naselli wrote: "Sicilians are undoubtedly the best fishermen; no other group is superior to them in navigational skills." RC, SF 7.x.1907.

129. RC, SF 7.iv.1894.

130. *San Francisco Chronicle*, 8.ix.1907.

131. Patrizi, p. 49.

132. R. Dondero, p. 73.

133. The prefetto of Palermo wrote: "The fishermen of this province tend to remain fishermen even when they emigrate. It is worth reporting that all the emigrants from Isola delle Femmine go to San Francisco to fish." RP, Palermo 12.xi.1895, ASP.

134. "La Società di Mutua Beneficenza dei Pescatori," *VP,* 12.xi.1898.

135. *VP,* 12.ix.1898.

136. Patrizi, pp. 38–39.

137. R. Dondero, p. 73.

138. RC, SF 3.xi.1907.

139. "Deputies Accused of Prosecuting Crab Fishermen," *San Francisco Call*, 20.iv.1913; London, pp. 177–78.

140. "Merritt Pool Mixes Up War on Paladini," *San Francisco Chronicle*, 22.vi.1918; "Achille Paladini of the Fish Nets," *Pacific Marine Review*, 1925, pp. 40–41.

141. "Fisheries Move on Fish Trusts," *San Francisco Examiner*, 26.viii.-1915; "San Francisco Fish Companies Pool Their Equipment," "Fish Companies of the Bay District Will Pool Catch," and "Paladini Admits Fish Dumping," *ibid.*, 21.vi.1918.

142. Abbate, p. 8.

143. RC, SF 3.v.1907.

144. "The Fishermen of San Francisco," *San Francisco Chronicle*, 16.x.-1883.

145. Fisk, p. 384.

146. U.S. [22], pp. 402–5.

147. Radin, 1: 60.

148. C. Dondero, *Relazione*, p. 12.

149. Crespi, "Il Miraggio," p. 1.

150. *VP*, 31.x.1892. A few years later a writer in *L'Italia* (5.i.1896) warned that the colony was growing too fast.

151. RC, SF 18.ix.1898.

152. RC, SF 3.v.1870.

153. RC, SF 7.iv.1892.

154. *VP*, 14.iii.1889.

155. Ricciardi, p. 248. The survey by the Italian Geographic Society reached the same conclusion: immigrants in mutual aid societies generally had steady jobs, and the others had temporary jobs as unskilled laborers. Società Geografica Italiana, p. 121.

156. Ricciardi, pp. 248–51.

157. Rinaudo, p. 43.

158. *L'Italia*, 29.ix.1903.

159. A. Rossi, "Per la Tutela," pp. 104–36; Rossati, pp. 66–79.

160. A. Rossi, "Per la Tutela," pp. 113–17.

161. Ravaioli, pp. 40–44; Des Planches, pp. 374–425. The advice was repeated year after year in Italian publications dealing with emigration to the United States. In 1911, for instance, the journal *Italica Gens* discouraged emigration to San Francisco "since the favorable conditions of years ago have disappeared." Bonardelli, p. 494–95.

162. Gamboni Mazzitelli to James D. Phelan, SF 3.vii.1913; Phelan Papers, Bancroft Library, Univ. of Calif., Berkeley; Consul Francesco Daneo to Simon Lubin, SF 17.ii.1913, Papers of the California Commission on Immigration and Housing, *ibid.*

163. RC, SF 11.iii.1868. A consular report of 1882 stated: "To be an officer in one's regional society is an aspiration of all Italians, especially those who have made money." RC, SF 12.vi.1882.

164. "La Compagnia Garibaldina," *VP*, 18.ix.1885. The consul thus reported on the status of the associations: "The better-organized associations are financial as well as social organizations. As financial institutions, they keep the

savings of their members. They also loan money to members who want to start an independent business and transmit savings to Italy, and a few invest in real estate. But disagreements over how best to invest have created problems. It has happened more than once that leading businessmen have left their regional society over this issue." RC, SF 21.vi.1891.

Chapter 9

1. McBride, p. 273.
2. Cannistraro, p. 58.
3. Fishman and Nahirny, pp. 311–26.
4. Tomasi.
5. Fenton, pp. 3–12.
6. Diggins, pp. 79–81; De Medici, pp. 5–25.
7. McBride, p. 179.
8. De Grand, pp. 16–23.
9. "I Segretariati dell'Italica Gens nei Paesi Transoceanici," *Italica Gens*, 1 (Feb. 1910): 17–19.
10. *L'Italia*, 20.x.1922; Palmer, pp. 241–42.
11. *A Biographical Sketch of Marco Fontana* (New York, 1909), p. 3.
12. Palmer, p. 243.
13. *Del Monte Shield*, 7.x.1926, p. 7.
14. *San Francisco Call*, 5.v.1913; U.S. [22], p. 253.
15. Rinaudo, pp. 31–36; Bernardy, "Sulle Condizioni," pp. 140–44; "L'Emigrazione," pp. 3–209.
16. Rinaudo, p. 35.
17. On Ghirardelli's career see the five handwritten pages containing notes taken by an unidentified person during a conversation with him in 1887, in Bancroft Library, Univ. of California, Berkeley.
18. "Joseph Di Giorgio," *Fortune*, 34 (Aug. 1946): 96.
19. Palmer, pp. 237–38.
20. Giovinco, pp. 195–218; Byington, pp. 279–81; "Le Banche Italiane di San Francisco," *VP*, 4.vii.1918; R. Dondero, pp. 52–53.
21. RC, SF 2.v.1889.
22. *VP*, 15.ix.1883; Società Geografica Italiana, p. 174.
23. RC, SF 13.xii.1885.
24. *L'Italia*, 24.ix.1893. The consul wrote: "Immigrants who need credit can hardly rely on local American banks." RC, SF 21.ii.1895.
25. RC, SF 7.v.1872.
26. Andrea Sbarboro to the president of the Italian Geographic Society, SF, 18.1.1889, in Società Geografica Italiana, p. 86.
27. RC, SF 7.v.1897; R. Dondero, p. 70.
28. The mayor of Lorsica wrote: "Our emigrants in San Francisco use the White Line Travel Agency to transmit their savings to their families via the Banco di Chiavari. Others, of course, rely on returnees to carry their savings." RM, Lorsica 21.ii.1892, ACL.
29. "Gli Italiani in California," *Bollettino dell'Emigrazione*, 5 (1902): 51.

30. R. Dondero, pp. 52–53; see also "Gli Italiani in California," p. 51.

31. Frangini, p. 33.

32. *Ibid.,* pp. 33–36; "Gli Italiani in California," pp. 51–52.

33. Frangini, pp. 22–23; R. Dondero, p. 53.

34. RC, SF 3.v.1901.

35. "Gli Italiani in California," p. 52.

36. Thus the consul: "Unless an immigrant has established a solid reputation as a businessman, it is hard for him to get a loan from these two banks. If he is from the south, his chances are practically nil." RC, SF 3.v.1901.

37. James, p. 234; *VP,* 17.x.1924; Frangini, pp. 22–23, 39–49; Giovinco, pp. 195–218.

38. Frangini, pp. 39–43.

39. RC, SF 15.iii.1905.

40. *L'Italia,* 12.x.1912.

41. RC, SF 9.v.1912.

42. A. P. Giannini to A. Paganini, SF 7.v.1912, archives of the Bank of America, SF.

43. *L'Italia,* 19.ix.1914.

44. *Ibid.,* 7.xii.1909.

45. RC, SF 7.iii.1911.

46. *L'Italia,* 14.xii.1926.

47. Tuoni, p. 51.

48. *L'Italia,* 21.iv.1927.

49. *Ibid.,* 7.x.1931.

50. Park, p. 13.

51. Morasso, pp. 13–15, 32; De Grand, pp. 11–12.

52. Corradini, pp. 51–75; Solimani, pp. 459–86.

53. "Italica Gens," *Italica Gens,* 1 (Feb. 1910): 5.

54. Venerosi, pp. 297–98, 300.

55. "Programma della Federazione," *Italica Gens,* 1 (Feb. 1910): 8.

56. *Ibid.,* pp. 18–19.

57. RC, SF 18.x.1914.

58. "Un Banchetto Patriottico," *L'Italia,* 12.x.1912.

59. Hiram Johnson to Simon Lubin, Sacramento, 20.viii.1912; George Bell to Lubin, SF 3.viii.1915; James Mullenbach to D. Bartlett, SF 8.ix.1912; Grace Abbott to Robert Lynch, Chicago, 22.i.1913. All letters in Papers of the California Commission on Immigration and Housing, Bancroft Library, Univ. of Calif., Berkeley (hereafter cited as CCIH). See also Agresti.

60. On the riots see C. H. Palmer (member of the Federal Commission on Industrial Relations) to Lubin, Washington, D.C., 10.i.1914. On the activities of the IWW, see F. J. Cunningham to Lubin, Sacramento, 12.ii.1914. On the infiltration of the IWW among Italian immigrants, see the article "Una Ingiuria Fatta ad Uno è una Ingiuria Fatta a Tutti," *Il Lavoratore Industriale,* 1.v.1912. All in CCIH Papers.

61. The original nine-page typed report, sent to Governor Johnson by Lubin on March 1, 1913, is in CCIH Papers. See also Olin, pp. 305–15.

62. Felton, pp. 350–58.

63. CCIH Papers, p. 12.

64. Parker, pp. 56–59; see also Wood.

65. California Commission on Immigration and Housing, *Bulletin,* 1 (Sept. 1920): 3–5.

66. Lubin to Katharine Felton, Sacramento, 18.v.1917. CCIH Papers.
67. *L'Italia*, 17.ix.1916.
68. Gamboni Mazzitelli to Lynch, SF 28.i.1913. CCIH Papers.
69. Consul Daneo to Lubin, SF 24.ix.1916. CCIH Papers.
70. *VP*, 2.x.1916.
71. "The Italian Board of Relief," *L'Italia*, 16.x.1916; "La Nuova Istituzione della Colonia Italiana," *ibid.*, 23.x.1916.
72. "Il Comitato di Soccorso e la Sua Riorganizzazione," *ibid.*, 10.xi.1916.
73. "È un Fatto Compiuto," *ibid.*
74. "Appello per il Nuovo Comitato di Soccorso," *ibid.*, 11.xi.1916.
75. "Il Nuovo Comitato di Soccorso all'Opera," *ibid.*, 16.xii.1916.
76. Felton to Lubin, SF, 13.xii.1918. CCIH Papers.
77. *L'Italia*, 17.x.1904; Venerosi, p. 300.
78. C. Dondero, *Relazione*, pp. 11–17; Patrizi, pp. 34–37.
79. Frangini, p. 9; Tuoni, p. 17.
80. Salvadori, p. 163.
81. Cannistraro, pp. 51–66.
82. Livingstone, p. 750.
83. Sforza, p. 125.
84. Salvemini, *Italian Fascist*, pp. 6–7.
85. Cannistraro, p. 55.
86. Sturzo, pp. 388–91; Garoschi, pp. 219–24; Borghi.
87. De Felice, *Interpretation*; see also Delzell and the multivolume biography of Mussolini by De Felice.
88. Cassels, pp. 707–12.
89. Diggins, pp. 80–81.
90. RC, SF 12.ix.1896, 4.v.1873.
91. "Il Club Unionista," *VP*, 19.ix.1868 and 23.ix.1868.
92. U.S. [8], p. 1075.
93. U.S. [9], p. 476.
94. Radin, 1: 38–69.
95. U.S. [19], p. 136.
96. Livingstone, p. 750.
97. De Felice, *Interpretation*, p. 177.
98. "Biografia di Mussolini," *L'Italia*, 26.xi.1936.
99. *Ibid.*, 14.iii.1932 and 9.ix.1935.
100. California State Legislature, pp. 282–321; "Sons of Italy: Fascist," *Il Corriere del Popolo*, 22.vii.1937; "Anti-Fascismo," *ibid.*, 5.viii.1937; "La Federazione delle Società Italiane," *ibid.*, 5.viii.1937; "Analisi del Fascismo," *ibid.*, 22.vii.1937; "Fascisti ed Anti-Fascisti," *ibid.*, 17.vi.1937.
101. California State Legislature, pp. 285, 291, 296–97; De Medici, pp. 15–61.
102. California State Legislature, pp. 314–19; "Contro Mussolini," *Il Corriere del Popolo*, 7.iii.1937; "Federazione Italo-Americana Anti-Fascista," *ibid.*, 4.iv.1935.
103. *Monterey Peninsula Herald*, 18.viii.1937.
104. "Patrizi Traditore di Due Bandiere," *Il Corriere del Popolo*, 18.v.-1937; "America Against Fascism," *ibid.*, 16.vi.1938; "Cultura Popolare," *ibid.*, 16.vii.1938; "Fascismo ed Italianità," *ibid.*, 23.vi.1938; "The Philosophy of Fascism," *ibid.*, 23.vi.1938.

105. California State Legislature, pp. 285–88; "Il Nuovo Console Fascista," *Il Corriere del Popolo*, 25.i.1935.

106. "Il Problema degli Italiani non Naturalizzati," *Il Corriere degli Italiani*, 2.viii.1942; "Compromessi con il Fascismo," *ibid.*, 4.xi.1943.

Chapter 10

1. On the resurgence of ethnicity in the United States and throughout the world, see Glazer and Moynihan.

2. These historians are among the many social and behavioral scientists who have argued that academics neglect individuals and overemphasize structures. As early as the 1950's Ernest R. Hilgard and Daniel Lerner called for the reintroduction of the individual into social analysis; see Hilgard and Lerner, p. 16. More recently, Peter Gay (p. 7) lamented the tendency of historians to emphasize and even quantify what he called the world of realities and to underestimate the world of perceptions. Cf. Homans, p. 817.

Bibliographical Essay

Bibliographical Essay

Complete authors' names, titles, and facts of publication, when not given here, may be found in the Bibliography.

1. Personal Records

Several kinds of records, referred to throughout the book, were used to narrow the focus of my research to nine communes in Italy and nine immigrant groups in San Francisco, and to describe the three generations that are the special topic of this study. A set of 9,000 death records, covering the years 1907–39, is central to Chapters 5, 6, and 7. These records are from the archives of the Italian national parish of Saints Peter and Paul in San Francisco. A computer analysis of 25 percent of those records revealed that over half of the Italians in San Francisco came from four Italian provinces, and that nine communes in those provinces were more heavily represented than any others.

The most useful source of information was 2,000 records of both petition for naturalization and naturalization itself, consulted in the archives of the Superior Court in San Francisco. (In 1976 they were moved to the Federal Archives in San Bruno, California.) These records list both the birthplace of the immigrant and the place of residence in Italy at the time of departure for the United States. I used as many naturalization records for the nine communes as I could find, ending up with 1,418 records, as follows:

Lucca	250	Lorsica	150	Trabia	133
Porcari	193	S. Levante	146	Sta. Flavia	130
Verbicaro	183	Genoa	135	Palermo	98

The naturalization records also allowed me to establish two control samples. One was a random sample of 250 Italians naturalized in San Francisco between 1919 and 1945; the other was a random sample of 400 immigrants of other nationalities naturalized in San Francisco over the same period of time. The reader might keep these numbers in mind, since the comparisons I make in the chapters are ordinarily expressed in percentages.

The naturalization records were ordinarily filed with the corresponding petitions for naturalization. The time that passed between the petition and the actual naturalization varied from a few months to several years. In the case of the Italians, about 80 percent of the naturalization records had a corresponding record of petition; for other nationalities the records were 90 percent complete. This double set of records—petition and actual naturalization—allowed me to analyze changes in the lives of the immigrants between the two dates.

The naturalization records offered the possibility of linking the immigrants to their parents in Italy. Each record of naturalization had both the birthplace and the date of birth of the immigrant. With these, I could search for the birth records of the immigrants in their native Italian communes. These birth records, obviously, provided information not about the future emigrants, but about their parents. Of the 1,418 birth records I looked for, I was able to find 1,020. I was most successful in the small communes; in Verbicaro and Lorsica I found all the birth records. I found about 90 percent in Trabia, Sestri Levante, and Porcari; 85 percent in Santa Flavia; and from 60 to 70 percent in the cities of Lucca, Genoa, and Palermo. A possible explanation for this difference between small communes and large cities is that a good number of immigrants who declared that they had been born in Genoa or Palermo had actually been born in a small commune in the province, not in the city itself.

The naturalization records also yielded information on the children of the immigrants, the Italo-American generation: the names of the children of each immigrant, their birthplaces and birthdates, and their residence at the time the parent became an American citizen. About 3,500 children appear in the naturalization records I used. I examined a random sample of 1,000 of them: 85 from each of the nine groups from the nine Italian communes, 85 from the control sample of Italians, and 150 from the immigrants of other nationalities.

To learn about the lives of the immigrants' children, I asked the Health Department of the State of California to look up marriage records for the 1,000 names. Of course, no records were found for those who never married, died very young, or moved out of the state before marrying. The Health Department provided photocopies of the 800 marriage records they found. In some cases identical names caused a problem. But since marriage and naturalization records list the parents of the subject, all but two cases of confused identity could be solved.

Of these three sets of records—birth records in Italy for the immigrants' parents, naturalization records in San Francisco for Italians and other immigrants, and marriage records in Sacramento for the immigrants' children—the third is the smallest and the second is the most important. In this study I often refer to the records, but I have kept tables to a minimum for readability.

2. Statistical Sources

Statistics of all sorts on Italian emigration are in the 29 volumes published from 1876 to 1925 by the Ministero di Agricoltura, Industria, e Commercio (MAIC), Direzione Generale della Statistica (DGS), under the general title

Statistica dell'Emigrazione Italiana all'Estero. For a useful compendium of the 29 volumes, see Commissariato Generale dell'Emigrazione, *Annuario Statistico dell'Emigrazione Italiana dal 1876 al 1925* (Rome, 1926).

There are no comprehensive statistics on departures from Italy before 1876. The most reliable data are found in Jacopo Virgilio, *Dell'Emigrazione Italiana all'Estero nei Suoi Rapporti coll'Agricoltura, coll'Industria, e col Commercio* (Florence, 1871); *Delle Colonie e dell'Emigrazione Italiana all'Estero sotto l'Aspetto dell'Industria, Commercio, ed Agricoltura, e con Trattazione di Importanti Questioni Sociali* (Milan, 1874); *Statistica Illustrata dell'-Emigrazione all'Estero nel Triennio 1874–1876 nei Suoi Rapporti con i Problemi Economico-Sociali* (Rome, 1978); and Giovanni Florenzano, *Dell'-Emigrazione Italiana in America Comparata alle Altre Emigrazioni Europee* (Naples, 1874). At the time of the second and third national censuses, the DGS surveyed Italians living abroad: *Censimento degli Italiani all'Estero al 31 Dicembre 1871* (Rome, 1874), and *Censimento degli Italiani all'Estero al 31 Dicembre 1881* (Rome, 1884). The 1871 census relies on reports by Italian consuls, and the 1881 census on data provided by foreign governments. Both publications, taken before mass emigration began, are important sources on the early stages of Italian communities abroad.

Private agencies also gathered data on Italian emigration. Società Geografica Italiana, *Statistica dell'Emigrazione Italiana all'Estero al 1881, Confrontata con Quella degli Anni Precedenti e coll'Emigrazione Avvenuta da Altri Stati* (Rome, 1882); and *Memorie della Società Geografica Italiana*, vol. 4, compare emigration from Italy and other European countries and elaborate on official data. For an analysis of the socioeconomic conditions in some provinces with high emigration rates, see Giulio Del Vecchio, *Sull'Emigrazione Permanente Italiana nei Paesi Stranieri, Avvenuta nel Dodicennio 1876–1887* (Bologna, 1892).

The best analysis of emigration statistics, government and private, is in Coletti, "Esame Critico" and "Dell'Emigrazione Italiana." Foerster, *Italian Emigration*, is still the best analysis in English. Livi-Bacci, in *L'Immigrazione e l'Assimilazione*, is critical of Italian statistics; he uses American statistics to argue that the rate of returnees was higher than either Italian or American statistics show. For a discussion of the techniques used by the DGS to gather data, see Istituto Centrale di Statistica, "Le Rilevazioni Statistiche in Italia dal 1861 al 1951: Statistiche Demografiche e Sociali," *Annali di Statistica*, 8th ser., 89 (1957), and "Le Rilevazioni Statistiche in Italia dal 1861 al 1956," *ibid.*, 88 (1960).

The student of Italian emigration should be familiar with the decennial Italian national censuses, Italy [12]-[26]. The first, in 1861, is incomplete, since several regions were not yet part of the nation. The second, in 1871, was published in three volumes; the 1881 and 1901 censuses were published in four volumes, the 1911 census in six, and the 1921 census in as many volumes as the regions of Italy. (There was no census in 1891.) Another important source on emigration is a series of annual publications of the DGS, beginning in 1861, on vital statistics, Italy [31]. These report birth, marriage, and death rates by province and region, with occasional tables on literacy at the time of marriage. The vital statistics are broken down by age group, sex, and occupation. In this study I used the vital statistics for the years immediately following each national census.

3. Return Migration

There is no comprehensive study of return migration from the United States. The best short summary is Gilkey, "United States and Italy"; for a more detailed account see Gilkey, "Effect of Emigration." The parliamentary report on conditions in southern Italy (Italy [8], pp. 86–119) contains a detailed account of the social and economic impact of return migration. Ettore Marenghi, the author of the report, argued that return migration was the only hope for social and economic renewal in Calabria. Antonio Mangano, a naturalized American who made several visits to Italy, reported to Americans on the impact of emigration and return migration in the south in five articles that appeared in *Charities and the Commons* in 1908.

Caroli, *Italian Repatriation*, is a collection of statistics on returnees, with much data from the *Bollettino dell'Emigrazione.* Rossi, *Relazione*, and Beneduce, "Saggio," are two extensive studies on repatriation, but limited to the years 1909–10. Francesco Cerase, *L'Emigrazione di Ritorno* (Rome, 1971), is a sociological study of return migration from the United States after the Second World War. Finally, Von Borosini, "Home-Coming Italians," is a very brief summary of return migration from the American point of view.

By far the best study on the buying and selling of land in Italy and on the impact of American savings from 1890 to 1925 is Friedrich Vöchting, *Die Italienische Sudfrage* (Berlin, 1951). Michels, *L'Imperialismo Italiano*, discusses return migration only up to 1910, but is impressive in its treatment of the economic problems of return migration. For a positive assessment, written when return migration had just started, see G. Bonsignori, *L'America in Italia; Ossia la Resurrezione delle Terre e dei Villaggi* (Brescia, 1898). Joseph Lopreato, *Peasants No More: Social Class and Social Change in an Undeveloped Society* (San Francisco, 1967), is an unconvincing sociological study arguing that return migration had a substantial impact in modernizing the Italian south. Cerase, *Sotto il Dominio*, elaborates on the economic dependency of the south on the north, and argues that return migration could not change the south because the savings of the returnees were drained for the benefit of northern industries.

Italian liberals discussed at length what they saw as the potential social benefits of return migration, mainly for the south. Pasquale Villari, "L'Emigrazione Italiana," and L. Franchetti, *Mezzogiorno e Colonie*, are representative of this position. Guido Dorso, *La Rivoluzione Meridionale* (Turin, 1925), on the other hand, is a strong indictment of the Italian government for abandoning the agrarian south in favor of the industrial north. Antonio Gramsci, "Il Mezzogiorno e la Rivoluzione Socialista," in Rosario Villari, ed., *Il Sud nella Storia d'Italia* (Bari, 1961), written in 1926, argues that the unification of the country was a conservative event made possible by the alliance between the large landowners of the south and the industrial entrepreneurs of the north, an alliance that return migration could not break.

4. The Province of Genoa

A good introduction to the economy of the province after 1800 is Giulio Giacchero, *Genova e la Liguria nell'Età Contemporanea: Un Secolo e Mezzo di Vita Economica*, 2 vols. (Genoa, 1963). Giacomo Conissoli, *Geografia della Provincia di Genova in generale e del Circondario di Chiavari in Particolare* (Chiavari, 1888), has much information on Lorsica and Sestri Levante. A lucid account that brings together demography, economics, and emigration is Felloni, *Popolazione e Sviluppo*, which unfortunately covers only the nineteenth century. For well-informed studies on demographic change and the impact of overseas emigration, see Alberto Ferrantini, *Variazioni della Popolazione nel Piemonte, Valle d'Aosta, e Liguria dal 1848 al 1948* (Turin, 1952), and Achille Necco, "Il Problema della Popolazione in Italia."

Any study of the peasants should begin with Bertani, *Atti della Giunta*, which examines in depth the general condition of agriculture and the peasants, and also reveals differences within the province. A good supplement to Bertani is Camera di Commercio di Genova, *Condizioni Economiche*, a small volume with data for the 1850's. The interesting point is that it exposes the dangers inherent in the increasing division of land. Equally useful is Giovanni Molfino, *Relazione al Nono Congresso dei Consorzi Agrari della Zona Ligure in Genova al 1883* (Genoa, 1884). For a discussion of the impact of return migration, see Giovanni Celesia, *Sulla Liguria del 1912: Dati e Confronti* (Genoa, 1912). Giuseppe Arieti, *Consorzio Agrario Cooperativo per il Circondario di Chiavari: L'Opera Svolta dal 1907 al 1913* (Chiavari, 1914), deals with farmers' cooperatives in the area of Chiavari, where Lorsica and Sestri Levante are located. On efforts made to modernize the local agriculture, see Arieti, *Relazione della Cattedra Ambulante di Agricoltura per il Circondario di Chiavari* (Chiavari, 1910). Finally, Giovanni Adami, *Cenni sulla Città di Sestri Levante* (Chiavari, 1893), deals with changes occurring in Sestri in the early 1890's.

On industrial and commercial developments, besides the volume by Giacchero, the Camera di Commercio di Genova, *Relazione sul Commercio e l'Industria della Provincia di Genova al 4 Gennaio 1864* (Turin, 1864), is useful, although limited in scope. Giovanni Battista Brignardello, *I Merletti nel Circondario di Chiavari* (Florence, 1873), describes the cottage industries in the area of Sestri Levante and Lorsica. The first reliable source on industry in the province is Italy [28]. Italy [26], *Censimento degli Opifici e delle Imprese Industriali*, the first national industrial census, allows us to compare Genoa with other provinces.

There is no comprehensive study of emigration from, or return migration to, this province. The Bertani and Felloni works have sections on emigration, and most publications of the late nineteenth and early twentieth centuries touch on the topic. An account of Genoese emigration that summarizes provincial statistics and compares them with national statistics is Marenco, *L'Emigrazione Ligure.*

5. The Province of Lucca

For a general introduction to the history of the province, see E. Lazzareschi, *Lucca nella Storia, nell'Arte, nell'Industria* (Lucca, 1941). For two useful accounts written at the time of mass emigration, see A. Carina, *Notizie Storiche sul Contado Lucchese* (Lucca, 1872), and Vittorio Sacchi, *Lucca e la Sua Provincia* (Rome, 1893). Raffaello Uccelli, *Contributo alla Bibliografia della Toscana* (Florence, 1922), is a useful bibliography for the years 1861–1921. The most comprehensive work on demographic changes is Pier Francesco Bandettini, *La Popolazione della Toscana dal 1810 al 1959* (Florence, 1961). Equally useful, although confined to the nineteenth century, is Giotto Dainelli, "L'Aumento della Popolazione in Toscana nel Secolo Decimonono," *Memorie Geografiche: Monografia No. 19* (Florence, 1912), and Anna Maria Cozzolini, *Le Variazioni della Popolazione di Toscana dal 1911 al 1951* (Pisa, 1958).

The study of agriculture and peasants should begin with Orlando Orlandini, *Il Progresso dell'Agricoltura in Toscana* (Florence, 1860), and Francesco Inghirani, *Compendio Storico dell'Agricoltura della Toscana dai Suoi Principi a Tutto l'Anno 1880* (Rome, 1880), two accounts of the process of agricultural modernization in Tuscany. Incidentally, the agriculture of the region was considered the best in the nation in the 1870's. The most detailed account, which deals with every aspect of agriculture from credit to crops to markets, is Mazzini, *Atti della Giunta*, which is supplemented by Mazzini's *La Toscana Agricola* (Florence, 1884). Carlo Signorini, *L'Agricoltura ed i Lavoranti della Terra in Toscana* (Arezzo, 1906), updates Mazzini and discusses cooperative societies and militant organizations. Fortunato Bonnuccelli, *Le Condizioni Agricole della Provincia di Lucca* (Pescia, 1907), deals with declining local production, overpopulation, and the competition from American farm products. On peasant unrest in the province, see Agostino Gori, *Il Presente Momento della Mezzadria in Toscana* (Florence, 1906), and Gian Francesco Guerrazzi, *Per la Nostra Terra: Agitazioni Coloniche in Toscana* (Rome, 1919).

The most reliable account of industries in the province is Italy [29]. Italy [26], *Censimento degli Opifici e delle Imprese*, is a useful follow-up of the 1900 survey. The Camera di Commercio of Lucca published several reports on local industries. Particularly important are the 1908 publication *Statistiche Industriali e Commerciali della Provincia di Lucca al 1907* (Lucca, 1908) and the 1915 publication *Andamento dell'Industria e del Commercio nel Distretto, Anni 1910–1914* (Lucca, 1915). Camera di Commercio e di Arti di Lucca, *I Lavori della Camera e le Condizioni Economiche della Provincia di Lucca, 1905–1906* (Pescia, 1907), lists the achievements of Luccans abroad.

There are two monographs on emigration from the province. Michele Lo Sacco, *La Garfagnana nei Suoi Aspetti Generali ed in Rapporto al Problema dell'Emigrazione* (Gubbio, 1931), discusses internal and international migrations from the mountain communities of the Garfagnana district. Pasquali, *L'Emigrazione*, is one of the best accounts of emigration from an Italian province; it treats the conditions that prompted emigration, the impact of the exodus, and the changes brought about by American savings and the returnees. Guido Marcelli, *L'Emigrazione e le Condizioni dell'Agricoltura in Toscana* (Arezzo, 1910), compares the provinces of the Tuscany region. Also informative is R. Dalla Volta, "L'Emigrazione in Toscana," *Rivista d'Emigrazione*, 1 (1908). The Società di Patronato per gli Emigranti della Provincia di Lucca e della Garfagnana, a local organization that provided information on job opportunities abroad and advice to returnees eager to invest their savings, put out an important series of annual reports on the destination, occupation, and age of the emigrants, especially women and children. The Biblioteca Nazionale of Lucca has the reports for 1908–21, and also literature on local mutual aid societies and other cooperative organizations. For example, see the *Regolamento Interno della Società di Porcari* (Pescia, 1891), and the *Statuto della Società di Mutua Associazione sul Bestiame Bovino di Porcari* (Lucca, 1909).

6. The Province of Cosenza

Leopoldo Lupinacci, *Calabria: Studi di Politica ed Economia* (Reggio Calabria, 1889), is a general introduction. For a more detailed account, by the economist who supervised the sale of public land in the province, see Blandini, *Inchiesta*. Angarano, *Vita Tradizionale*, is an excellent study of regional folklore. Lucio Gambi, "Dinamica degli Insediamenti Urbani in Calabria dal 1861 al 1951," in *Atti del Secondo Congresso Storico Calabrese* (Naples, 1961), deals with demographic changes, and specifically explores the depopulation of the mountain communities. For a more detailed demographic study, see Giorgio Mortara, "Basilicata e Calabria secondo le Statistiche Demografiche," *Giornale degli Economisti e Rivista di Statistica*, 74 (1910): 435–51, 461–73, 656–79.

Izzo's *Agricoltura e Classi Rurali* is the most comprehensive study of Calabria. His *La Popolazione Calabrese nel Secolo Decimonono: Demografia ed Economia* (Naples, 1965) is more restricted in scope, but contains demographic analysis not found in *Agricoltura e Classi Rurali*. Franchetti, *Condizioni Economiche ed Amministrative*, was the first in-depth study of the Italian south—Calabria included—and remains one of the best. Branca, *Atti della Giunta*, is as valuable a source on the south as the Mazzini and Bertani volumes are for the north. Another useful study is De Marco, "Considerazioni." Raffaele Casca, "Le Transformazioni Agrarie in Calabria dopo l'Unità," in *Atti del Congresso Storico Calabrese* (Rome, 1957), carries the analysis of the provincial agrarian economy into the twentieth century.

Between 1905 and 1920 Agostino Caputo published several works on the economy and emigration. His *Di Alcune Questioni Economiche* is probably the best analysis of the economic problems of the region at the turn of the century. Equally important is his housing census of the city of Cosenza; see *L'Abitazione in una Città di Provincia*.

Emigration from Calabria and return migration received wide attention in Italy early in the twentieth century. Taruffi, *La Questione Agraria*, is a 900-page report, by three northern Italians, of a 1907 survey of Calabria. The authors discuss agriculture, emigration, and the impact of return migration. De Nobili, "Appunti sull'Emigrazione," is an interesting essay on how middle-sized landholders lost their land and status in competition with returnees. Scalise, *L'Emigrazione*, is one of the best studies of emigration from Calabria, written by a native son. Adolfo Rossi, "Vantaggi e Svantaggi," based on a visit by the author to the poorest areas of Cosenza province, describes the ambivalent feelings of the returnees toward permanent emigration and life in Calabria.

E. Misefari, *Le Lotte Contadine in Calabria nel Periodo 1914–1922* (Milan, 1972), is a recent scholarly work on the few militant organizations that were established in Calabria around the time of the First World War. Giovanni Bonacci, *La Calabria e l'Emigrazione* (Rome, 1908), discusses the mountain communities. For another general account of emigration, see Camera di Commercio di Reggio Calabria, *L'Emigrazione in Calabria* (Reggio Calabria, 1907). Caputo wrote several essays on the impact of return migration: "Di Alcune Questioni," deals specifically with the province of Cosenza, and his book of the same title, *Di Alcune Questioni*, also covers the other two Calabrian provinces, Catanzaro and Reggio Calabria. For the impact of mass emigration on laborers' wages and for greater detail on the intensity of return migration, see Caputo, *Inchiesta*. De Nobili, "L'Emigrazione in Calabria," discusses the increasing instability of family life because of emigration, comparing families in this province with those of northern provinces. For local industries see Italy [27].

7. The Province of Palermo

A good bibliography on Sicily is Santi Correnti, *Fondamenti Teorici e Orientamenti Bibliografici della Storia della Sicilia* (Catania, 1972). Francesco Brancato, *Storia della Sicilia Post-Unificazione*, pt. 1, *La Sicilia nel Primo Ventennio del Regno d'Italia* (Bologna, 1956), is an introduction to the history of Sicily in the first twenty years after unification. Rosario Romeo, *Il Risorgimento in Sicilia* (Bari, 1950), and Francesco Romano, *Momenti del Risorgimento in Sicilia* (Messina, 1953), argue that political unification failed to bring about expected social reforms, especially in Sicily. Finally, Maggiore-Perni, *Delle Condizioni Economiche*, shows how the annexation of Sicily to Italy had a negative impact on the island's economy.

For a comprehensive account of demographic changes, see Spagnoli, "Lo Sviluppo della Popolazione." Equally useful, for the years it covers, is Elio Floridia, *La Distribuzione della Popolazione in Sicilia: Variazioni e Tendenze del Cinquantennio 1911–1961* (Rome, 1964). A. Di San Giuliano, *Le Condizioni Presenti della Sicilia* (Milan, 1894), and Bonansea, *L'Agricoltura in Sicilia*, deal with the economic dependency of the island on the Italian northern provinces. Maggiore-Perni, *La Popolazione di Sicilia e di Palermo nel Secolo XIX* (Palermo, 1897), discusses demographic changes.

The Giunta per l'Inchiesta sulle Condizioni della Sicilia, *Relazione della Giunta per l'Inchiesta sulle Condizioni della Sicilia del 1876* (Rome, 1963), is a government report arguing that the unrest of the 1870's had political, not social, origins. On the other hand, Sonnino and Franchetti, *La Sicilia nel 1876*, show that the unrest of the 1870's stemmed from the inequitable distribution of land on the island. Damiani, *Atti della Giunta*, is the basic source on agriculture and the peasantry in the 1870's. Salvatore La Rosa, *Aspetti Principali dello Sviluppo Agricolo in Sicilia dal 1861 al 1965* (Palermo, 1967), deals with a century and a half of agricultural development. The large Inchiesta Parlamentare volumes on Sicily, Italy [9] and [10], based on an early-twentieth-century government survey, discuss both the agrarian economy of the island and the impact of return migration.

For an introduction to mutual aid societies among peasants, see Giuseppe Vaccaro-Russo, *La Cooperazione nell'Agricoltura Siciliana* (Palermo, 1902). Francesco Palmigiano, *Cronaca delle Società Operaie dal 1860 al 1890* (Palermo, 1891), deals with mutual aid societies among industrial workers and how they affected peasant unionism. The best account on peasant unionism from a leftist perspective is Renda, *Il Movimento Contadino*. Peasant unrest became open rebellion—the most violent in Italy in the second half of the nineteenth century—in 1893 with the *rivolta dei Fasci Siciliani*. The most complete account of the ideology, goals, and accomplishments of the rebellion is Francesco S. Romano, *Storia dei Fasci Siciliani* (Bari, 1959). The best source on industry in Palermo province is Italy [30]; for an update see Tommaso Mercadante, *Storia delle Industrie della Provincia di Palermo* (Palermo, 1913).

There are no monographs on Sicilian emigration and return migration that compare with those on Calabria. Luigi Arcuri Di Marco, *L'Emigrazione Siciliana all'Estero nel Cinquantennio 1876–1925* (Palermo, 1949), although three decades old, remains a good source. Giovanni Battista Raja, *Il Fenomeno Emigratorio Siciliano con Speciale Riguardo al Quinquennio 1902–1906* (Palermo, 1908), is also good, but limited in time span. Renda, *L'Emigrazione*, is a collection of statistics with little elaboration.

8. The Four Provinces and the Nine Communes

The most extensive and detailed sources on the four provinces and the nine communes dealt with in this study are in the Archivi di Stato of Genoa, Lucca, Cosenza, and Palermo, and in the Archivi Comunali of Genoa, Lucca, Sestri Levante, Lorsica, and Capannori. The state archives keep two particularly important sets of correspondence: that of the provincial prefetti with the Minister of the Interior in Rome, and that between the prefetti and the mayors. The quarterly reports sent from the prefetti to the minister, based on quarterly statements by the mayors to the prefetti, contain information on the social and economic conditions in each province. Both the mayors and the prefetti dealt extensively with emigration, return migration, and their impact on their provinces and communes. The most interesting material from the reports by the prefetti was published in the government journals *Bollettino di Notizie*

Agrarie, Annali dell'Agricoltura, and *Bollettino Ufficiale del Ministero di Agricoltura, Industria, e Commercio.*

The Archivi Comunali keep records on virtually all facets of community life, organized in fourteen categories. Category 12 has material on agriculture, industry, and commerce, including farm production by quarter, peasant conditions, cooperative societies, credit, fluctuations in farm prices, and new industries. Category 11 has vital statistics, lists of Italians who died overseas, population registers, censuses, and data on housing, internal and international migration, and societies established for the protection of emigrants.

In addition, the five communal archives of the northern communes hold family records—Fogli di Famiglia (FF)—with data on households from the early nineteenth century to the end of the First World War. These records are the best source on family structure in Italy at the time of mass emigration. Finally, four of the five northern communes—Genoa is the exception—have the original census returns of 1881, and Lorsica also has those of 1911. Unfortunately, the Archivi Comunali of the four southern communes contain only birth, marriage, and death records.

9. Agriculture and Peasants

The study of the Italian peasantry should begin with Stefano Jacini, *La Proprietà Fondiaria e le Popolazioni Agricole in Lombardia* (Milan, 1854), the first scientific survey in modern Italy. Franchetti, *Le Condizioni Economiche*, is equally important for the south. Pasquale Villari, *Lettere Meridionali*, a collection of articles originally published in the Milan newspaper *L'Opinione*, had a great impact on Italian public opinion.

For the decades of mass emigration, there are three basic sources. The first is the thirteen volumes published in Rome between 1880 and 1885 with the general title *Atti della Giunta per la Inchièsta Agraria e sulle Condizioni della Classe Agricola*, as the final reports of a government-sponsored survey. C. Bertagnolli, *L'Economia dell'Agricoltura in Italia e la Sua Transformazione secondo i Dati dell'Inchièsta Agraria* (Rome, 1886), sums up the most important data of the thirteen volumes. The very useful introduction to the survey is Jacini, *Atti della Giunta.*

The second basic source is eight volumes published in 1909–11 under the general title *Inchièsta Parlamentare sulle Condizioni dei Contadini nelle Province Meridionali e nella Sicilia.* These also report the findings of a government-commissioned survey, this one seeking to discover whether any significant change had occurred in the economy and society of the south since the earlier survey.

The third source is the bulletins and publications of the MAIC on agriculture. MAIC, Direzione Generale dell'Agricoltura, *Relazione Intorno alle Condizioni dell'Agricoltura in Italia*, 4 vols. (Rome, 1876), the first national survey on agriculture, was based on information from local chambers of commerce. The same agency's *Notizie Intorno alle Condizioni dell'Agricoltura negli Anni 1878–1879*, 3 vols. (Rome, 1881–82), has a section on 300 family budgets. From 1879 to 1896 the MAIC published the bimonthly *Bollettino di Notizie Agrarie*, which featured reports from the prefetti, agricultural committees, and chambers of commerce. The Ministry of the Interior published sporadically the *Annali dell'Agricoltura*, 2d ser., from 1878 to 1911. The 269 volumes contain extensive reports on agriculture in the provinces. From 1901 to 1907 the MAIC, Direzione Generale dell'Agricoltura, issued the 31 volumes of the *Bollettino Ufficiale del Ministero di Agricoltura, Industria, e Commercio*, also a source of agricultural data. Another useful publication is the *Annuario Statistico Italiano*, Italy [4], which gives statistics on agricultural output by region and province.

The literature on agriculture and peasants, though sizable, is not all equally good or relevant. Coletti, *La Popolazione Rurale*, is a perceptive essay on the peasant psychology, especially on the reluctance to embrace change. Ghino Valenti, *L'Italia Agricola dal 1861 al 1911* (Milan, 1911), and "L'Italia Agricola dalla Costituzione del Regno allo Scoppio della Guerra Europea," in *L'Italia Agricola ed il Suo Avvenire* (Rome, 1919), are two excellent studies of Italian agriculture. E. Levi, *Le Condizioni dell'Agricoltura, le Sue Forme, e le Sue Funzioni in Italia* (Turin, 1887), and Negri, *Sulle Condizioni*, are two useful accounts of the condition of the peasantry. A. Agnelli, *Il Problema Economico della Disoccupazione Agricola: Cause e Rimedi* (Milan, 1906), discusses peasant unemployment and outlines remedies. Finally, Pier Ludovico Occhini, *La Crisi Agraria in Italia* (Florence, 1921), deals directly with the prolonged agricultural depression of the late nineteenth century, and indirectly with peasant responses to economic pressures.

10. Housing and Diet

There are many studies of peasant living conditions. Italo Giglioli, *Malessere Agrario ed Alimentare in Italia* (Portici, 1903), is the most extensive treatment of diet, with comparisons between Italian and other European peasants. Also useful are Guido Baldaccini, *Il Vitto del Contadino e la Condizione del Podere* (Foligno, 1892), and Diomede Carito, *Un Capitolo sull'Alimentazione* (Naples, 1896). Two other publications widely acclaimed when first published are Cesare Lombroso, *Sulla Pellagra e sulle Condizioni della Proprietà Fondiaria e della Classe Agricola in Italia* (Rome, 1882), and Luigi Bodio, *Condizioni dell'Alimentazione dei Contadini in Varie Zone d'Italia* (Rome, 1879). Angelo Celli, *Sull'Alimentazione del Proletariato in Italia* (Rome, 1894), and Antonio Marro, *La Razione Alimentare dell'Alienato Povero* (Rome, 1888), deal with conditions in the south. A brilliant survey is Samogyi, "L'Alimentazione nell'Italia."

The basic source on housing is the 1881 census, Italy [16], which reveals the differences between north and south, within each section, and between urban and rural communities. A useful addition is DGS, *Risultato della Inchièsta sulle Condizioni Igieniche e Sanitarie nei Comuni del Regno*, pt. 2, *Notizie per Ciascun Comune* (Rome, 1886). A local study that in some ways diverges from the national statistics is Caputo, *L'Abitazione*.

11. Cooperative Societies and Militant Organizations

Government publications are the basic source on farmers' cooperatives; see Italy [5] and [6]. Another useful source on the People's Banks is Direzione Generale del Credito, della Previdenza, e delle Assicurazioni Sociali, *Statistica delle Banche Popolari, Decennio 1899–1908* (Rome, 1911). The best study on cooperatives is Coletti, *Le Associazioni Agrarie in Italia dalla Metà del Secolo Decimoottavo alla Fine del Decimonono e la Società degli Agricoltori Italiani* (Rome, 1900). Enea Cavalieri, *Le Origini del Consorzi Agrari e della Loro Federazione* (Rome, 1905), on the growth of the Federazione Italiana dei Consorzi Agrari, was written by the president of the organization.

A. Maffi, *Venticinque Anni di Vita della Cooperazione in Italia, 1866–1911* (Milan, 1912), and M. Ruini, *La Cooperazione in Italia* (Como, 1921), examine the role of cooperatives in the development of political awareness among farmers. Luciano Barbieri, *Il Mutualismo nell'Emigrazione Italiana* (Parma, 1909), focuses on how cooperatives provided both information on jobs available abroad and money for the journey.

The growth of militant organizations and the impact of peasant strikes are documented in Italy [32], [33], and [34]. For a compendium of the data from 1911 to 1923, see Ministero dell'Economia Nazionale, *I Conflitti di Lavoro in Italia nel Dodicennio 1914–1923* (Rome, 1924). Società degli Agricoltori Italiani, *I Recenti Scioperi Agrari*, is the most important publication on this topic. One of the best syntheses for the years 1901–26 is Zangheri, *Lotte Agrarie*; it deals mostly with the Emilia-Romagna and Apulia regions, where the emigration rate was the lowest in the country. S. Zaninelli, *Le Lotte nelle Campagne dalla Grande Crisi Agricola al Primo Dopoguerra, 1880–1921* (Milan, 1971), is equally impressive; it includes the decades not covered by Zangheri. An acute analysis of peasant unrest in the 1890's is A. Di Vito Di Marco, "Le Recenti Agitazioni Agrarie," *Giornale degli Economisti e Rivista di Statistica*, 15 (1897). Finally, for an impressive appeal to the Italian government to redistribute the land, see Giustino Fortunato, *La Terra ai Contadini* (Rome, 1919).

12. The Agricultural Depression

Gino Luzzatto's *L'Economia Italiana* and *Storia Economica dell'Italia Moderna e Contemporanea*, pt. 2, *L'Età Contemporanea* (Padua, 1960), contain lucid accounts of the depression of the 1880's and 1890's. On the 1870's see his "L'Economia Italiana nel Primo Decennio dell'Unità," *Rassegna Storica del Risorgimento*, 44 (1957). Luzzatto, "Gli Anni Più Critici," is a brief survey covering the years of mass emigration. Another important report, by a contemporary observer, is Giuseppe De Vincenzi, *Delle Vere Cagioni delle Attuali Sofferenze della Nazione* (Rome, 1890).

Several publications document the decline in farm prices. DGS, *Movimento dei Prezzi di Alcuni Generi Alimentari dal 1862 al 1885, e Confronto fra Essi ed il Movimento delle Mercedi* (Rome, 1886), compares farm prices and wages. An important source on this topic is the *Bollettino dei Prezzi*, published by the MAIC from 1873 to 1879, and by the Direzione Generale dell'Agricoltura since 1880. For an analysis of the data of the *Bollettino*, see Achille Necco, *La Curva dei Prezzi delle Merci in Italia negli Anni 1881–1909* (Turin, 1910). Another source is MAIC, Direzione Generale dell'Agricoltura, *Bilanci di Famiglie Coloniche* (Rome, n.d.). Although dealing only with the late 1870's—the years before the agricultural depression—the volume shows, by means of household budgets, how Italian families lived.

The decline in farm prices was not identical in all regions. For an introduction to regional differences, see A. Argentino, *Studi sulla Decadenza del Valore della Proprietà Rustica e delle Industrie Agricole in Italia* (Naples, 1891). Three economic historians have shown how prices fell throughout the nineteenth century in various parts of Italy: Felloni, *I Prezzi sul Mercato di Genova*, Bandettini, *I Prezzi sul Mercato di Firenze*, and Petino, *I Prezzi sui Mercati di Palermo e di Catania.*

On the impact of American competition, see Achille Montagna, *La Crisi Agraria in Italia* (Rome, 1889), and Corrado Massa, *Sull'Agricoltura, Crisi Agraria, e Concorrenza Americana* (Rome, 1885). Egidio Rossi, *Gli Stati Uniti*, is the best analysis. The best summary of foreign competition and its impact on the Italian economy is Necco, "La Curva dei Prezzi."

13. Italians in San Francisco

Both primary and secondary sources are rather limited. A useful demographic introduction is Warren S. Thompson, *Growth and Changes in California's Population* (Los Angeles, 1955). For the period 1850–1920 see also O. McEntire, "An Economic and Social Study of Population in California," Master's thesis (University of California, Berkeley, 1928). For specific treatments of San Francisco, see William Procter, *The Population of San Francisco: A Half-Century of Change* (San Francisco, 1954), and Margaret King, "The Growth of San Francisco, Illustrated by Shifts in the Density of Population," Master's thesis (University of California, Berkeley, 1928). Forest G. Hill, "The Shaping of California Industrial Patterns," in *Proceedings of the Thirtieth Annual Conference of the Western Economic Association* (1955), is a brief but illuminating periodization. For a more detailed account of the years 1900–1950 in California, see Gordon, *Employment.* On San Francisco, especially at the turn of the century, see Young, *San Francisco.*

There are no major statistical sources exclusively on Italians in San Francisco. The U.S. censuses show the size, geographical distribution, literacy or illiteracy, occupational profile, citizenship, and average family size of the Italian community. The Bureau of the Census issued some special reports useful in comparing San Francisco Italians, Italians in other cities, and immigrants of other nationalities. *Immigrants and their Children*, U.S. [18], is the most important. It explores the demographic characteristics of the immigrant population, and compares them with the native-born-of-foreign-parents and the native-born-of-native parents. *Population*, U.S. [19], offers important family data on each immigrant group in the city. U.S. [14] provides data on housing by block; and U.S. [15] breaks down the city's population by tract, with data on nativity, marital status, education, age distribution, and income.

Palmer, "Italian Immigration," is a very useful introduction to Italians in California and San Francisco. Radin, *Italians of San Francisco*, reports on a survey made in the early 1930's. Scherini, "Italian-American Community," is one of the most recent studies on San Francisco Italians, and stresses community organization. Raymond Dondero, "Italian Settlement," is also a good introduction. Paoli, "Italian Colony," is a popular account.

Besides naturalization records and vital statistics, there are three other important primary sources: reports by the Italian consuls, San Francisco Italian newspapers, and the files of the Italian Welfare Agency. The consular reports begin in 1861 and cover the next twenty years in detail. There are fewer reports for the years 1880–1915, and almost none after 1915. The reports are in the archives of the Ministry of Foreign Affairs in Rome. The Italian Consulate in San Francisco has no archival material for the years before 1946.

The Italian newspapers mainly report the activities of the mutual aid societies, but also other matters that affected San Francisco Italians and the city at large. The library of the University of Santa Clara has a complete set—several hundred volumes—of *L'Italia*, from 1877 until it was discontinued in 1964. There is no complete set of any other paper. The library of the University of California, Berkeley, keeps microfilms of several Italian newspapers; no set, however, is complete. Some issues of early Italian newspapers, sent by Italian consuls, can be found at the Ministry of Foreign Affairs in Rome. For a commentary on later newspapers, see De Medici, "The Italian Language Press."

The Italian Welfare Agency has about 500 files of families assisted since 1916. Although concerned only with poor families, the files are a rich source on family life, and on how Italians dealt with society at large. Each file contains reports of social workers and other documents.

A few other publications contain useful information. Società Geografica Italiana, *Memorie*, reports the results of a worldwide survey of the largest Italian communities abroad. Carlo Dondero, *Relazione sugli Italiani*, although brief, is excellent on the 1890's. Patrizi, *Gli Italiani*, is a promotional booklet written by a San Francisco Italian for Italians in Italy. A. Frangini, *Italiani*, G. V. Panattoni, *Professionisti Italiani e Funzionari Pubblici Italo-Americani in California* (Sacramento, Calif., 1935), and Tuoni and Brogelli, *Attività Italiane*, are three unreliable accounts, the last two clearly designed to promote Fascism.

The *Bollettino dell'Emigrazione*, issued by the Commissariato Generale dell'Emigrazione, has several reports on San Francisco Italians, written either by Italian consuls or by other government officials. See Adolfo Rossi, "Per la Tutela degli Italiani," on the oversupply of Italian labor in San Francisco, the tension it created, and the division within the San Francisco Italians on the issue of increased immigration. For the years before 1901 the *Bollettino Conso-*

lare, issued by the Ministry of Foreign Affairs, has a few items on San Francisco Italians.

Dessery, "Study of the Mental Inferiority of the Italian Immigrants," and Powell, "Mental Survey of the Three Lowest Grades," reflect how Americans looked at Italians in the 1920's. On housing and overcrowding, see Devine, "Housing Problem," Ihlder, "Fighting for Better Homes," and Griffith, "The Housing Awakening," the last of which comments on the exploitation of Italians by other Italians. Finally, Giovinco, "Democracy in Banking," is the best short account on how the expanding economy in San Francisco helped Italians to overcome their regionalism.

Bibliography

Bibliography

Abbate, P. A. "Stato di California al 20 Gennaio 1863," *Bollettino Consolare*, 2 (1863).

Adams, Frank. "The Historical Background of California Agriculture," in Claude B. Hutchinson, ed., *California Agriculture.* Berkeley, Calif., 1946.

Agresti, Olivia Rossetti. *David Lubin: A Study in Practical Idealism.* Berkeley, Calif., 1941.

Anfossi, Anna, Magda Talamo, and Francesco Indovina. *Ragusa: Comunità in Transizione.* Turin, 1959.

Angarano, Francesco. *Vita Tradizionale dei Contadini e Pastori Calabresi.* Florence, 1973.

Asbury, Herbert. *The Barbary Coast: An Informal History of the San Francisco Underworld.* New York, 1933.

Balletta, Francesco. *Il Banco di Napoli e le Rimesse degli Emigrati, 1914–1925.* Naples, 1972.

Bandettini, Pietro. *I Prezzi sul Mercato di Firenze dal 1800 al 1890.* Rome, 1957.

Banfield, Edward. *The Moral Basis of a Backward Society.* Glencoe, Ill., 1958.

Barton, Josef. *Peasants and Strangers: Italians, Rumanians and Slovaks in an American City, 1880–1950.* Cambridge, Mass., 1975.

Battaglia, Bruno. *Relazione sullo Stato Agricolo-Zootecnico delle Province di Calabria Citra.* Naples, 1870.

Bell, Alexander. *Arguments in Favor of Immigration, with an Explanation of the Measures Recommended by the Immigration Union.* San Francisco, 1870.

Bell, Rudolph. *Fate and Honor, Family and Village: Demographic and Cultural Change in Rural Italy Since 1800.* Chicago, 1979.

Beneduce, Alberto. "Saggio di Statistiche dei Rimpatri dalle Americhe," *Bollettino dell'Emigrazione*, 11 (1911).

Bernardy, Amy. "L'Emigrazione delle Donne e dei Fanciulli nel Nord America," *Bollettino dell'Emigrazione*, 1 (1909).

———. *Italia Randagia attraverso gli Stati Uniti.* Turin, 1913.

———. "Sulle Condizioni delle Donne e dei Fanciulli Italiani negli Stati del Centro e dell'Ovest della Confederazione del Nord degli Stati Uniti," *Bollettino dell'Emigrazione*, 1 (1911).

Bertani, Agostino. *Atti della Giunta per la Inchièsta Agraria e sulle Condizioni delle Classi Agricole*, vol. 10, *Provincie di Genova e Porto Maurizio.* Rome, 1883.

Bertozzi, Giuseppe. "Notizie Storiche e Statistiche sul Riordinamento dell'-Asse Ecclesiastico," *Annali di Statistica.* Rome, 1879.

Bianco, Carla. *The Two Rosetos.* Bloomington, Ind., 1974.

Blandini, Ettore. *Inchièsta sulla Piccola Proprietà Coltivatrice Formatasi nel Dopoguerra.* Rome, 1911.

Blasutti, Renato. "Per lo Studio dell'Architettura Rurale Italiana," *Rivista Geografica Italiana*, 33 (1957).

Boccardo, Gerolamo. "Spontaneità ed Artificio nell'Emigrazione Coloniale," *Giornale degli Economisti e Rivista di Statistica*, 34 (1886).

Bocci, Mario. *La Mutualità in Italia.* Ascoli Piceno, 1940.

Bodio, Luigi. "Dei Problemi del Dopoguerra Relativi all'Emigrazione," *Giornale degli Economisti e Rivista di Statistica*, 37 (1918).

Böhme, Frederick. "Vigna Dal Ferro's 'Un Viaggio Nel Far West Americano,' " *California Historical Society Quarterly*, 41 (1962).

Bohning, W. R. "Return Migrants' Contribution to the Development Process: The Issues Involved," in Ayse Kudats and Yilmaz Ozkan, eds., *International Conference on Migrant Workers.* Berlin, 1975.

Bonansea, Silvio. *L'Agricoltura in Sicilia e la Situazione Economica e Politica dell'Isola.* Milan, 1891.

Bonardelli, Eugenio. "L'Emigrazione Italiana in California," *Italica Gens*, 2 (1911).

Borghi, Armando. *Mezzo Secolo di Anarchia, 1898–1945.* Naples, 1954.

Borrie, Wilfrid. *The Cultural Integration of Immigrants.* Paris, 1959.

Branca, Antonio. *Atti della Giunta per la Inchièsta Agraria e sulle Condizioni delle Classi Agricole*, vol. 9, *Calabria.* Rome, 1883.

Briggs, John, *An Italian Passage: Immigrants in Three American Cities, 1890–1930.* New Haven, Conn., 1978.

Byington, Lewis. *The History of San Francisco.* Chicago, 1931.

Cagli, Cesare. *La Basilicata ed il Problema dell'Immigrazione e della Colonizzazione Interna.* Rome, 1910.

California Commission on Immigration and Housing. *Ninth Annual Report.* Sacramento, 1923.

California Immigration Union. *All About California and the Inducements to Settle Here.* San Francisco, 1871.

California State Legislature. *Report: Joint Fact-Finding Committee on Un-American Activities in California to the California Legislature.* Sacramento, 1943.

Callegaris, Giuseppe. *Relazione Riassuntiva dell'Opera della Camera di Commercio Italiana di San Francisco nei Primi Otto Anni della Sua Esistenza.* San Francisco, 1894.

Camera di Commercio di Genova. *Condizioni Economiche dell'Agricoltura Ligure.* Genoa, 1861.

Candeloro, Luigi. *Storia dell'Italia Moderna*, vol. 5, *Lo Sviluppo del Capitalismo e del Movimento Operaio.* Milan, 1970.

Cannistraro, Philip. "Fascism and Italian-Americans," in Silvano Tomasi, ed., *Perspectives in Italian Immigration and Ethnicity.* New York, 1977.

Capuana, Luigi. *Gli Americani di Rabbato.* Milan, 1912.

Caputo, Agostino. *L'Abitazione in una Città di Provincia.* Cosenza, 1912.

———. "Di Alcune Questioni Economiche della Calabria: L'Emigrazione dalla Provincia di Cosenza," *Giornale degli Economisti e Rivista di Statistica*, 35 (1907).

———. *Di Alcune Questioni Economiche della Calabria: L'Influenza dell'-Emigrazione sui Costumi.* Rome, 1909.

———. *Inchièsta sulle Condizioni del Lavoro Agricolo e sugli Effetti dell'-Emigrazione nella Provincia di Cosenza.* Rome, 1909.

Caracciolo, Antonio. *Il Movimento Contadino nel Lazio.* Rome, 1952.

Caroli, Betty Boyd. *Italian Repatriation from the United States, 1900–1914.* New York, 1973.

Carpi, Leone. *Delle Colonie e dell'Emigrazione Italiana all'Estero.* Milan, 1874.

———. *Dell'Emigrazione Italiana nei Suoi Rapporti coll'Agricoltura, l'Industria, ed il Commercio.* Florence, 1871.

Casper, Donald. "The San Francisco Story Italian Style: The Italians in the Early San Francisco," *Columbus Day Celebration Program.* San Francisco, 1969.

Cassels, Alan. "Fascism for Export: Italy and the United States in the 1920's," *American Historical Review*, 69 (1964).

Caughey, John W. *Gold Is the Cornerstone.* Berkeley, Calif., 1948.

Cenni sulla Provincia di Chiavari. Chiavari, 1863.

Cerase, Francesco. *Sotto il Dominio dei Borghesi: Sottosviluppo ed Emigrazione nell'Italia Meridionale, 1860–1910.* Rome, 1975.

Child, Irvin. *Italian or American? The Second Generation in Conflict.* New Haven, Conn., 1943.

Chudacoff, Howard. "A Network of Ethnic Neighborhoods: Residential Dispersion and the Concept of Visibility in a Medium-Size City," *Journal of American History*, 60 (1973).

Cinanni, Palo. *Emigrazione ed Imperialismo.* Rome, 1968.

Coletti, Francesco. "Le Associazioni Agrarie in Italia dall'Unità Politica ad Oggi," *Giornale degli Economisti e Rivista di Statistica*, 22 (1901).

———. "Dell'Emigrazione Italiana," in Regia Accademia dei Lincei, ed., *Cinquant'Anni di Storia Italiana.* Rome, 1911.

———. *Economia Rurale e Popolazione Rurale in Italia.* Piacenza, 1916.

———. "Esame Critico delle Fonti Statistiche dell'Emigrazione Italiana," *Giornale degli Economisti e Rivista di Statistica*, 45 (1912).

———. *La Popolazione Rurale in Italia.* Piacenza, 1925.

Corinaldi, Leopoldo. "L'Emigrazione Italiana negli Stati Uniti," *Bollettino dell'Emigrazione*, 2 (1902).

Corradini, Enrico. *Volere d'Italia.* Naples, 1911.

Corsini, Antonio. *Le Sofferenze della Nazione.* Milan, 1899.

Coulter, Charles. *The Italians of Cleveland.* Cleveland, 1919.

Covello, Leonard. *The Social Background of the Italo-American School Child: A Study of the Southern Italian Family Mores and Their Effect on the School Situation in Italy and America.* Leiden, 1967.

Crespi, Cesare. "Il Miraggio Californiese," *Il Messaggero*, Dec. 3, 1897.

———. *San Francisco e la Sua Catastrofe.* San Francisco, 1906.

Cressey, Paul. "Population Succession in Chicago, 1898–1930," *American Journal of Sociology*, 44 (1938).

Cronin, Constance. *The Sting of Change: Sicilians in Sicily and Australia.* Chicago, 1970.

Cyriax, Tony. *Among Italian Peasants.* London, 1919.

Daggert, Emerson. *History of Foreign Journalism in San Francisco.* San Francisco, 1935.

Dal Ferro, Vigna. *Un Viaggio nel Far West Americano.* Bologna, 1881.

Damiani, Abele. *Atti della Giunta per la Inchièsta Agraria e sulle Condizioni delle Classi Agricole*, vol. 13, *Sicilia.* Rome, 1885.

Dana, Julian. *Amadeo P. Giannini: Giant in the West.* New York, 1943.

Day, Helen. "Social Traits," in Harvey W. Zorbaugh, ed., *Gold Coast and Slums: A Sociological Study of Chicago's Near North Side.* Chicago, 1929.

De Conde, Alexander. *Half Bitter, Half Sweet: An Excursion into Italian-American History.* New York, 1971.

De Felice, Renzo. *Interpretations of Fascism*, tr. Brenda H. Everett. Cambridge, Mass., 1977.

———. *Mussolini il Duce: Gli Anni del Consenso, 1929–1936.* Turin, 1974.

———. *Mussolini il Fascista: La Conquista del Potere, 1921–1925.* Turin, 1966.

———. *Mussolini il Fascista: L'Organizzatore dello Stato Fascista, 1925–1929.* Turin, 1968.

———. *Mussolini il Rivoluzionario, 1883–1920.* Turin, 1965.

De Grand, Alexander. *The Italian Nationalist Association and the Rise of Fascism in Italy.* Lincoln, Neb., 1978.

De Luca, Paolo. *Dell'Emigrazione Europea ed in Particolare di Quella Italiana.* Turin, 1909.

Delzell, Charles. *Mussolini's Enemies: The Italian Anti-Fascist Resistance.* Princeton, N.J., 1961.

De Marco, Domenico. "Considerazioni sulle Vicende della Proprietà Fondiaria e delle Classi Rurali in Calabria dopo l'Unità," *Atti del Secondo Congresso Storico Calabrese.* Naples, 1961.

De Mauro, Tullio. *Storia Linguistica dell'Italia Unita.* Bari, 1963.

De Medici, Marino. "The Italian-Language Press in the San Francisco Bay Area from 1930 to 1940," Master's thesis, University of California, Berkeley, 1963.

De Nobili, Leonello. "Appunti sull'Emigrazione in Calabria," *La Riforma Sociale*, 17 (1907).

———. "L'Emigrazione in Calabria: Effetti dell'Emigrazione in Generale," *Rivista d'Emigrazione*, 1 (1908).

Dessery, Edna. "A Study of the Mental Inferiority of the Italian Immigrants," Master's thesis, University of California, Berkeley, 1922.

De Stefani, Antonio. "Sull'Emigrazione dalla Garfagnana," in Mazzini, cited below.

De Vincenzi, Giuseppe. *Delle Vere Cagioni delle Attuali Sofferenze della Nazione*. Rome, 1890.

Devine, Edward. "The Housing Problem in San Francisco," *Political Science Quarterly*, 21 (1906).

Diggins, John. *Mussolini and Fascism: The View from America*. Princeton, N.J., 1972.

Dondero, Carlo. *Relazione sugli Italiani della Costa del Pacifico*. San Francisco, 1897.

Dondero, Raymond. "The Italian Settlement of San Francisco," Master's thesis, University of California, Berkeley, 1953.

Dore, Maurice. *Catalogue of Valuable Business and Residence Property to Be Sold on April 20, 1876*. San Francisco, 1876.

Eisenstadt, Shmuel. *The Absorption of Immigrants*. London, 1954.

Falbo, Ernest. "Stato di California al 1856: Federico Biesta's Report to the Sardinian Minister of Foreign Affairs," *California Historical Society Quarterly*, 42 (1963).

———, ed. *California and Overland Diaries of Count Leonetto Cipriani from 1853 to 1871*. San Francisco, 1972.

Felloni, Giuseppe. *I Prezzi sul Mercato di Genova dal 1815 al 1890*. Rome, 1957.

———. *Popolazione e Sviluppo Economico della Liguria nel Secolo Decimonono*. Turin, 1961.

Felton, Katharine C. "The Charities Endorsement Committee," *Proceedings of the National Conference of Charities and Corrections*, 1906.

Fenton, Edwin. "Immigrants and Union, A Case Study: Italian and American Labor," Ph.D. dissertation, Harvard University, 1957.

Ferenczi, Junre. "A Historical Study of Migration Statistics," *International Labor Review*, 20 (1929).

Ferroni, Charles. "The Italians in Cleveland: A Study in Assimilation," Ph.D. dissertation, Kent State University, 1969.

Filippi, Michael. "I Distretti Italiani di San Francisco," in G. M. Tuoni, ed., *Attività Italiane in California*. San Francisco, 1930.

Fishman, Joshua, and Vladimir G. Nahirny. "American Immigrant Groups, Ethnic Identification, and the Problem of Generations," *American Sociological Review*, 13 (1965).

Fisk, Henry. "The Fishermen of the San Francisco Bay," *Proceedings of the National Conference of Charities and Corrections*, 1906.

Foerster, Robert. *The Italian Emigration of Our Times.* Cambridge, Mass., 1919.

Fortunato, Giustino. *Il Mezzogiorno e lo Stato Italiano.* Rome, 1911.

———. *Pagine e Ricordi Parlamentari.* Bari, 1920.

Franceschini, Vittorio. "Le Prime Lotte Operaie nell'Italia Unita," in Amintore Fanfani, ed., *Cento Anni di Vita Economica Italiana, 1861–1961.* Milan, 1963.

Franchetti, Leopoldo. *Condizioni Economiche ed Amministrative delle Province Napoletane.* Florence, 1875.

———. *Mezzogiorno e Colonie.* Florence, 1950. Reprint.

Frangini, A. *Italiani in San Francisco ed Oakland.* San Francisco, 1914.

Gans, Herbert. *The Urban Villagers: Group and Class in the Life of Italian-Americans.* Glencoe, Ill., 1962.

Gardella, John. *Reminiscences of Old Newtown.* Placerville, Calif., 1968.

Garosci, Aldo. *Storia dei Fuoriusciti.* Rome, 1953.

Gay, Peter. *Art and Act: On Causes in History—Manet, Gropius, Mondrian.* New York, 1976.

Giacosa, Giuseppe. *Impressioni d'America.* Milan, 1899.

Gilkey, George. "The Effect of Emigration on Italy, 1900–1923," Ph.D. dissertation, Northwestern University, 1950.

———. "The United States and Italy: Migration and Reemigration," *Journal of Developing Areas*, 2 (1967).

Giorgetti, Giorgio. "Contratti Agrari e Rapporti Sociali nelle Campagne," in Ruggiero Romano and Corrado Vivanti, eds., *Storia d'Italia*, vol. 5, *I Documenti.* Turin, 1973.

Giovinco, Joseph. "Democracy in Banking: The Bank of Italy and California's Italians," *California Historical Society Quarterly*, 47 (1968).

Glazer, Nathan, and Daniel P. Moynihan, eds. *Ethnicity: Theory and Experience.* Cambridge, Mass., 1975.

Gordon, Margaret. *Employment, Expansion, and Population Growth: The California Experience, 1900–1950.* Berkeley, Calif., 1954.

Gramsci, Antonio. "Alcuni Temi sulla Questione Meridionale," in Bruno Cajazzi, ed., *Antologia della Questione Meridionale.* Milan, 1950.

Gregory, Winifred. *Union List of the American Newspapers, 1821–1936.* New York, 1937.

Griffith, Alice. "The House Awakening: The Romeo Flat in San Francisco," *The Survey*, 26 (1911).

Hall, Charles. *California: The Ideal Italy of the World.* Philadelphia, 1875.

Hall, Michael. "The Origin of Mass Emigration to Brazil, 1871–1914," Ph.D. dissertation, Columbia University, 1969.

Hall, Prescott F. *Immigration.* New York, 1913.

Handlin, Oscar. *The Uprooted: The Epic Story of the Great Migrations That Made the American People.* 2d ed. Boston, 1973.

Harr, David. "Economic Development and Fertility Transition," in D. V. Glass and Roger Revelle, eds., *Population and Social Change.* New York, 1972.

Hilgard, Ernest R., and Daniel Lerner. "The Person: Subject and Object of Science and Policy," in Daniel Lerner and Harold D. Lasswell, eds., *The Policy Sciences.* Stanford, Calif., 1951.

Hill, Forest. "The Shaping of California's Industrial Patterns," *Proceedings of the Thirtieth Annual Conference of the Western Economic Association*, 1955.

Hittell, Theodore. *Brief History of California.* San Francisco, 1898.

Hogan, Elodie. "Hills and Corners of San Francisco," *The Californian*, 5 (1893).

Homans, George. "Bringing Man Back In," *American Sociological Review*, 29 (Dec. 1964).

Huganir, George, "The Hosiery Looper in the Twentieth Century. A Study of Family Process and Adjustment to Factory and Community Change," Ph.D. dissertation, University of Pennsylvania, 1958.

Ihlder, John. "Fighting for Better Homes in San Francisco," *The Survey*, 21 (1911–12).

Isaacs, Julius. *Economics of Migration.* London, 1947.

[The place of publication for all the following Italian publications is Rome.]

Italy [1]. *Atti della Commissione Reale per i Demani Comunali nelle Province del Mezzogiorno.* 1902.

———, Commissariato Generale dell'Emigrazione [2]. *L'Emigrazione Italiana dal 1910 al 1923.* 1926.

———, Direzione dell'Agricoltura [3]. *Bilanci di Famiglie Coloniche.* 1880.

———, Direzione Generale della Statistica [4]. *Annuario Statistico Italiano.* Annual.

———,——— [5]. *Statistica delle Società di Mutuo Soccorso e delle Istituzioni Cooperative, Anno 1885.* 1888.

———,——— [6]. *Elenco delle Società di Mutuo Soccorso Giuridicamente Riconosciute al 1897.* 1900.

———, Inchiésta Parlamentare sulle Condizioni dei Contadini nelle Province Meridionali e nella Sicilia [7]. vol. 5, *Basilicata e Calabria*, tomo 2, *Calabria, Relazione del Delegato Tecnico.* 1909.

———,——— [8]. *Ibid.*, vol. 5, *Basilicata e Calabria*, tomo 3, *Relazione della Sotto Giunta Parlamentare.* 1910.

———,——— [9]. *Ibid.*, vol. 6, *Sicilia,* tomo 1, pts. 1–2, *Relazione del Delegato Tecnico.* 1910.

———,——— [10]. *Ibid.*, vol. 6, *Sicilia*, tomo 1, pts. 3–5, *Relazione del Delegato Tecnico.* 1910.

———, Istituto Centrale di Statistica [11]. *Sommario di Statistiche Italiane, 1861–1955.* 1958.

———, Ministero di Agricoltura, Industria e Commercio, Direzione Generale della Statistica [12]. *Censimento della Popolazione del Regno d'Italia al 31 Dicembre 1871*, vol. 1, *Popolazione Presente ed Assente per Comuni, Centri, e Frazioni di Comune*. 1874.

———,——— [13]. *Ibid.*, vol. 2, *Popolazione Classificata per Età, Sesso, Stato Civile, ed Istruzione Elementare*. 1875.

———,——— [14]. *Ibid.*, vol. 3, *Popolazione Classificata per Professioni, Culti ed Infermità Principali*. 1876.

———,——— [15]. *Censimento della Popolazione del Regno d'Italia al 31 Dicembre 1881*, vol. 1, pt. 1, *Popolazione dei Comuni e dei Mandamenti*. 1883.

———,——— [16]. *Ibid.*, pt. 2, *Popolazione secondo la Qualità della Dimora degli Abitanti dei Comuni*. 1883.

———,——— [17]. *Ibid.*, vol. 2, *Popolazione Classificata per Età, Sesso, Stato Civile ed Istruzione Elementare*. 1883.

———,——— [18]. *Ibid.*, vol. 3, *Popolazione Classificata per Professioni e Condizioni*. 1884.

———,——— [19]. *Censimento della Popolazione del Regno d'Italia al 10 Febbraio 1901*, vol. 1, *Popolazione dei Comuni e delle Rispettive Frazioni Divisa in Agglomerata e Sparsa*. 1902.

———,——— [20]. *Ibid.*, vol. 2, *Numero delle Famiglie e Numero degli Abitanti Classificati secondo la Qualità della Dimora, il Luogo di Nascita, il Sesso, l'Età, lo Stato Civile e l'Istruzione*. 1903.

———,——— [21]. *Ibid.*, vol. 3, *Popolazione Classificata per Professioni e Condizioni*. 1904.

———,——— [22]. *Censimento della Popolazione del Regno d'Italia al 10 Giugno 1911*, vol. 1, *Popolazione Presente, Popolazione Temporaneamente Assente e Popolazione Residente*. 1914.

———,——— [23]. *Ibid.*, vol. 2, *Popolazione Presente Classificata per Sesso, Età, Stato Civile ed Istruzione*. 1914.

———,——— [24]. *Ibid.*, vol. 3, *L'Alfabetismo della Popolazione Presente*. 1914.

———,——— [25]. *Ibid.*, vol. 4, *Popolazione Presente di Età Superiore ai 10 Anni, Classificata per Sesso, e per Professione o Condizione*. 1915.

———,——— [26]. *Censimento degli Opifici e delle Imprese Industriali al 10 Giugno 1911*. 5 vols., 1913–15.

———,——— [27]. *Notizie sulle Condizioni Industriali delle Province di Catanzaro, Cosenza e Reggio Calabria*. 1894.

———,——— [28]. *Notizie sulle Condizioni Industriali della Provincia di Genova*. 1892.

———,——— [29]. *Notizie sulle Condizioni Industriali della Provincia di Lucca*. 1900.

———,——— [30]. *Notizie sulle Condizioni Industriali della Provincia di Palermo*. 1893.

———,——— [31]. *Popolazione: Movimento della Stato Civile*. Annual.

———, ——— [32]. *Statistica degli Scioperi Avvenuti nell'Industria e nell'-Agricoltura dal 1884 al 1891*. 1892.

———, ——— [33]. *Statistica degli Scioperi Avvenuti nell'Industria e nell'-Agricoltura nel 1894*. 1896.

———, ——— [34]. *Statistica degli Scioperi Avvenuti nell'Industria e nell'-Agricoltura dal 1892 al 1893*. 1894.

———, ——— [35]. *Statistica dell'Emigrazione Italiana all'Estero*. Annual.

———, Presidenza del Consiglio dei Ministri [36]. *Censimento della Popolazione del Regno d'Italia al 1 Dicembre 1921*, vol. 15, *Calabria*. 1927.

———, ——— [37]. *Ibid.*, vol. 5, *Liguria*. 1926.

———, ——— [38]. *Ibid.*, vol. 8, *Toscana*. 1927.

———, ——— [39]. *Ibid.*, vol. 13, *Sicilia*. 1927.

———, Statistica del Regno d'Italia [40]. *Società di Mutuo Soccorso, Anno 1862*. 1864.

———, SVIMEZ (Associazione per lo Sviluppo dell'Industria nel Mezzogiorno) [41]. *Un Secolo di Statistiche Storiche Italiane, Nord e Sud: 1861–1961*. 1961.

Izzo, Luigi. *Agricoltura e Classi Rurali in Calabria dall'Unità al Fascismo*. Geneva, 1974.

———. "Per la Storia Demografica della Calabria nel Secolo Decimonono," *Atti del Convegno Storico Calabrese*. Naples, 1961.

Jacini, Stefano. *Atti della Giunta per la Inchièsta Agraria e sulle Condizioni delle Classi Agricole*, vol. 1, *Proemio del Presidente*. Rome, 1881.

Jackson, William. *The San Francisco Wholesale Fruit and Produce Market*. San Francisco, 1926.

James, Marquis, and Bessie R. James. *Biography of a Bank: The Story of the Bank of America*. New York, 1954.

Jones, Maldwin Allen. *American Immigration*. Chicago, 1960.

Kessner, Thomas. *The Golden Door: Italian and Jewish Immigrant Mobility in New York City, 1880–1915*. New York, 1977.

King, Bolton, and Thomas Okey. *Italy Today*. London, 1904.

Koht, Halvdan. *The Agrarian Spirit in Europe: A Survey of Transatlantic Influence*. Philadelphia, 1949.

Lieberson, Stanley. *Ethnic Patterns in American Cities*. Glencoe, Ill., 1963.

Livi-Bacci, Massimo. *L'Immigrazione e l'Assimilazione degli Italiani negli Stati Uniti*. Milan, 1961.

Livingstone, Arthur. "Italian-American Fascism," *The Survey*, 57 (1927).

Lloyd, Benjamin. *Lights and Shades in San Francisco*. San Francisco, 1876.

Loncao, Enrico. *Contadini di Sicilia*. Palermo, 1897.

London, Jack. *Tales of the Fish Patrol*. New York, 1905.

Lorenzoni, Giovanni. *Inchièsta sulla Piccola Proprietà Coltivatrice Formatasi nel Primo Dopoguerra*. Rome, 1938.

Luzzato, Gino. *L'Economia Italiana dal 1861 al 1914*, vol. 1, *Dal 1861 al 1894*. Milan, 1963.

———. "Gli Anni Più Critici dell'Economia Italiana," in Amintore Fanfani, ed., *Cento Anni di Vita Economica Italiana, 1861–1961*. Milan, 1963.

MacDonald, John S. "Agricultural Organization, Migration, and Labor Militancy in Rural Italy," *Economic History Review*, 16 (1963).

———. "Institutional Economics and Rural Development: Two Italian Types," *Human Organization*, 23 (1964).

———. "Italian Migration to Australia," *Journal of Social History*, 3 (1970).

———. "Italy's Rural Social Structures and Emigration," *Occidente*, 12 (1956).

———. "Migration from Italy to Australia," Ph.D. dissertation, Australian National University, Canberra, 1958.

MacDonald, John S., and Leatrice MacDonald. "Chain Migration, Ethnic Neighborhoods, and Social Network," *Milbank Memorial Fund Quarterly*, 42 (1964).

———. "Urbanization, Ethnic Groups, and Social Organization," *Social Research*, 25 (1962).

McBride, Paul. "The Italian-Americans and the Catholic Church: Old and New Perspectives," *Italian-Americana*, 1 (1975).

Maggiore-Perni, Francesco. *Delle Condizioni Economiche, Politiche, e Morali della Sicilia dopo il 1860*. Palermo, 1896.

Mangano, Antonio. "The Effect of Emigration upon Italy: Ci Manca la Mano d'Opera," *Charities and the Commons*, 20 (1908).

———. "The Effect of Emigration upon Italy: Threatened Depopulation of the South," *Charities and the Commons*, 19 (1908).

———. "The Effect of Emigration upon Italy: Toritto and San Demetrio," *Charities and the Commons*, 20 (1908).

———. *Sons of Italy: A Social and Religious Study of the Italians in America*. New York, 1917.

Marazzi, Francesco. "San Francisco di California," in Ministero degli Affari Esteri, ed., *Emigrazione e Colonie: Rapporti dei Regi Agenti Diplomatici e Consolari*. Rome, 1893.

Marenco, Maria. *L'Emigrazione Ligure nell'Economia della Nazione*. San Pier d'Arena, 1923.

Massari, Giovanni, and Stefano Castagnola. *Il Brigantaggio nelle Provincie Napoletane*. Naples, 1863.

Matteuzzi, Alfono. *L'Emigrazione Italiana*. Bologna, 1973.

Mayor Des Planches, Edoardo. "Gli Italiani in California," *Bollettino del Ministero degli Affari Esteri*, 284 (1904).

Mazzini, Carlo. *Atti della Giunta per la Inchièsta Agraria e sulle Condizioni delle Classi Agricole*, vol. 3, *Toscana*. Rome, 1881.

Medici, Giuseppe. *I Tipi di Impresa nell'Agricoltura Italiana*. Rome, 1951.

Meritani, Giovanni. *Un Mese nel Brasile: Note ed Impressioni di Viaggio*. Verona, 1888.

Meyriat, Jean. *La Calabrie: Une Région Sous-Développée de l'Europe Méditeranéenne*. Paris, 1960.

Michels, Robert. *L'Imperialismo Italiano: Studi Politico-Demografici.* Milan, 1914.
Minuti, Luigi. *Il Comune Artigiano di Firenze della Fratellanza Artigiana d'Italia.* Florence, 1911.
Moore, Dorothea. "The Saving of Telegraph Hill," *Proceedings of the National Conference of Charities and Corrections*, 1905.
Moore, Wilbert. *Economic Demography of Eastern and Southern Europe.* Geneva, 1945.
Morasso, Mario. *L'Imperialismo nel Secolo Decimonono.* Milan, 1905.
Moss, Leonard. "The Passing of the Traditional Peasant Society in the South," in Edward R. Tannenbaum and Emiliana P. Noether, eds., *Modern Italy: A Topical History.* New York, 1974.
Naselli, Girolamo. "Il Distretto Consolare di San Francisco," in Ministero degli Affari Esteri, ed., *Emigrazione e Colonie: Rapporti dei Regi Agenti Diplomatici e Consolari*, vol. 3. Rome, 1909.
Necco, Achille. "La Curva dei Prezzi delle Merci in Italia dagli Anni 1881 agli Anni 1909," *La Riforma Sociale*, 21 (1910).
———. "Il Problema della Popolazione in Italia," *La Riforma Sociale*, 21 (1910).
Negri, Giovanni Battista. *Sulle Condizioni delle Classi Agricole in Italia.* Como, 1978.
Nelli, Humbert S. *The Italians in Chicago, 1880–1930: A Study in Social Mobility.* New York, 1970.
Nicosia, Francesco. *Italian Pioneers in California.* San Francisco, 1960.
Nitti, Francesco Saverio. "La Nuova Fase dell'Emigrazione Italiana," *La Riforma Sociale*, 3 (1896).
Norris, Frank. "Cosmopolitan San Francisco," in *Frank Norris of "The Wave": Stories and Sketches from the San Francisco Weekly, 1893–1897.* San Francisco, 1931.
Olin, Spencer. "European Immigrant and Oriental Alien: Acceptance and Rejection by the California Legislature of 1913," *Pacific Historical Review*, 35 (1966).
Pallavicini, Paolo. *Tutto il Dolore, Tutto l'Amore.* Milan, 1937.
Palmer, Hans C. "Italian Immigration and the Development of California Agriculture," Ph.D. dissertation, University of California, Berkeley, 1965.
Pancrazi, Giovanni. *L'Etrusca all'Ovest: Romanzo Semivero.* Lucca, 1914.
Paoli, Deanna. "The Italian Colony of San Francisco, 1850–1930," Master's thesis, University of San Francisco, 1970.
Paolucci, Paolo. *La Garfagnana Illustrata.* Modena, 1920.
Park, Robert, and Herbert Miller. *Old World Traits Transplanted.* New York, 1921.
Parker, Charleton. "The State Commission on Immigration and Housing," *Labor Clarion*, 13 (1914).
Pasquali, Aldo. *L'Emigrazione ed i Suoi Rapporti con l'Agricoltura in Provincia di Lucca.* Lucca, 1922.

Passi, Michael. "Myth as History and History as Myth: Family and Church Among Italo-Americans," *Journal of Ethnic Studies*, 3 (1975).

Patrizi, Ettore. *Gli Italiani in California*. San Francisco, 1911.

Paul, Rodman W. *California Gold: The Beginning of Mining in the Far West*. Cambridge, Mass., 1947.

Pecorini, Alberto. "The Italians as Agricultural Laborers," *Annals of the American Academy of Political and Social Sciences*, 33 (1909).

Peixotto, Ernest. "Italy in California," *Scribner's Magazine*, 48 (1910).

Perret, M. E. "The Italian-Swiss Colony in California," Master's thesis, University of California, Berkeley, 1971.

Pestalozza, Massimo. "Sulle Recenti Agitazioni Agrarie e sui Contratti Agricoli," *Giornale dell'Ingegnere Architetto Civile ed Industriale*, 38 (1890).

Petino, Antonio. *I Prezzi di Alcuni Prodotti Agricoli sul Mercato di Palermo e Catania dal 1801 al 1890*. Rome, 1959.

Piore, Michael. *Birds of Passage: Migrant Labor and Industrial Societies*. London, 1979.

Pitrè, Giuseppe. *Biblioteca delle Tradizioni Popolari Siciliane*. 25 vols. Turin, 1910.

Powell, Cora. "A Mental Survey of the Three Lowest Grades in One of San Francisco's Most Difficult Elementary Schools," Master's thesis, University of California, Berkeley, 1920.

Preti, Luigi. *Le Lotte Agrarie nella Valle Padana*. Turin, 1955.

Preziosi, Giovanni. *Gli Italiani negli Stati Uniti del Nord*. Milan, 1909.

Puzo, Mario. "Choosing a Dream," in Thomas Wheeler, ed., *The Immigrant Experience*. New York, 1971.

Radin, Paul. *The Italians of San Francisco: Their Adjustment and Acculturation*. San Francisco, 1935.

Ravaioli, Alessandro. "La Colonizzazione Agricola negli Stati Uniti in Rapporto all'Emigrazione Italiana," *Bollettino dell'Emigrazione*, 4 (1904).

Renda, Francesco. *L'Emigrazione in Sicilia*. Palermo, 1963.

———. *Il Movimento Contadino nella Società Siciliana*. Palermo, 1956.

Report of the Department of Public Health. San Francisco, 1901.

Resoconto della Società Italiana di Mutua Beneficenza. San Francisco, 1868.

Ricciardi, Giulio. "Le Condizioni del Lavoro e l'Emigrazione Italiana in California," *Bollettino dell'Emigrazione*, 8 (1908).

Riis, Jacob. *Out of Mulberry Street: Stories of Tenement Life in New York City*. New York, 1898.

Rinaudo, Paolo. "Il Lavoro delle Donne e dei Fanciulli Italiani in California," *Italica Gens*, 5 (1914).

Rolle, Andrew F. *The Immigrant Upraised: Italian Adventurers and Colonists in an Expanding America*. Norman, Okla., 1968.

Rossati, Guido. "Le Condizioni del Lavoro Italiano negli Stati Uniti," *Bollettino dell'Emigrazione*, 3 (1907).

Rossi, Adolfo. "Per la Tutela degli Italiani negli Stati Uniti: Dal Texas alla California," *Bollettino dell'Emigrazione*, 16 (1904).

———. "Vantaggi e Svantaggi dell'Emigrazione dal Mezzogiorno d'Italia," *Bollettino dell'Emigrazione*, 13 (1908).

Rossi, Egisto. *Gli Stati Uniti e la Concorrenza Americana*. Florence, 1884.

Rossi, Luigi. *Relazione sui Servizi dell'Emigrazione per gli Anni 1909–1910*. Rome, 1910.

Rossi-Doria, Manlio. "I Problemi della Trasformazione Fondiaria nel Mezzogiorno e nelle Isole," *Rivista di Economia Agraria*, 1 (1946).

Saloutos, Theodore. *They Remembered America*. Berkeley, Calif., 1965.

Salvadori, Massimo. *Resistenza ed Azione: Ricordi di un Liberale*. Rome, 1951.

Salvemini, Gaetano. "La Deviazione Oligarchica del Movimento Socialista," in Bruno Cajazzi, ed., *Antologia della Questione Meridionale*. Milan, 1950.

———. *Italian Fascist Activities in the United States*. Washington, D.C., 1944.

———. *Il Movimento Socialista e la Questione Meridionale*. Milan, 1963.

Samogyi, Stefano. "L'Alimentazione nell'Italia Unita," in Ruggiero Romano and Corrado Vivanti, eds., *Storia d'Italia*, vol. 5, *I Documenti*. Turin, 1973.

Sangree, Walter. "Mel Hyblaeum: A Study of the People of Middletown of Sicilian Origin," Master's thesis, Wesleyan University, 1952.

Sartorius Von Waltershausen, Wolfang. *Die Sizilienische Agrarverfassung und Ihre Wandlungen, 1870–1912*. Leipzig, 1913.

———. "Die Suditalienische Auswanderung und Ihre Volkswirtschaftlichen Folgen," *Jahrbuchen für Nationalekonomie und Statistik*, 41 (1911).

Scalise, Giuseppe. *L'Emigrazione dalla Calabria*. Naples, 1905.

Scanlan, J. M. "An Italian Quarter Mosaic," *Overland Quarterly*, 48 (1906).

Scherini, Rose. "The Italian-American Community of San Francisco: A Descriptive Study," Ph.D. dissertation, University of California, Berkeley, 1976.

Schuyler, Eugene. "Italian Immigration in the United States," *Political Science Quarterly*, 4 (1899).

Sereni, Bruno, "Caratteri dell'Emigrazione Barghigiana," Istituto di Studi Americani dell'Università di Firenze, ed., *Gli Italiani negli Stati Uniti*. Florence, 1972.

Serra, G. "Gli Italiani in California e gli Altri Stati della Costa del Pacifico," *Bollettino dell'Emigrazione*, 5 (1902).

Sforza, Carlo. *The Real Italians: A Study in European Psychology*. New York, 1942.

Shepperson, Wilbur. *Emigration and Disenchantment*. Norman, Okla., 1965.

Shinn, M. S. "Poverty and Charity in San Francisco," *Overland Monthly*, 14 (1889).

Smith, Dennis Mack. "Regionalism," in Edward R. Tannenbaum and Emiliana P. Noether, eds., *Modern Italy: A Topical History Since 1861*. New York, 1974.

Società degli Agricoltori Italiani. *I Recenti Scioperi Agrari in Italia ed i Loro Effetti Economici*. Rome, 1901.

Società di Mutuo Soccorso del Paese di Porcari. *Statuto.* Lucca, 1894.
Società Francese di Risparmio e di Mutua Beneficenza. *Contoreso del Secondo Semestre: 1866.* San Francisco, 1867.
Società Geografica Italiana. *Memorie della Società Geografica Italiana*, vol. 4, *Indagini sulla Emigrazione Italiana all'Estero Fatte per Conto della Stessa Società, 1888–1889.* Rome, 1890.
Solimani, Carlo. "Le Origini del Nazionalismo e l'Ideologia di Pascoli e D'Annunzio," *Società*, 14 (May 1958).
Sonnino, Sidney. "Le Condizioni dei Contadini in Italia," in *Scritti e Discorsi Parlamentari.* Bari, 1972.
———. *I Contadini in Sicilia.* Florence, 1877.
Sonnino, Sidney, and Leopoldo Franchetti. *La Sicilia nel 1876: Condizioni Economiche ed Amministrative.* Florence, 1878.
Spagnoli, Antonio. "Lo Sviluppo della Popolazione di Sicilia nei Cento Anni dell'Unità," *Rivista di Economia, Demografia, e Statistica*, 3–4 (1963).
Statuti della Società di Mutuo Soccorso di Lorsica. Chiavari, 1893.
Statuti della Società di Mutuo Soccorso di Porcari. Pescia, 1887.
Sturzo, Luigi. *La Mia Battaglia da New York.* Cernasco sul Naviglio, 1945.
Sulpizi, Francesco. *Il Problema dell'Emigrazione dopo la Rivoluzione Fascista.* Città di Castello, 1925.
Tapinos, Georges. *L'Economie des Migrations Internationales.* Paris, 1974.
Taruffi, Dino, Leonello De Nobili, and Cesare Lori. *La Questione Agraria e l'Emigrazione in Calabria.* Florence, 1908.
Thernstrom, Stephan. *The Other Bostonians: Poverty and Progress in an American Metropolis, 1880–1970.* Cambridge, Mass., 1973.
Thompson, Kathleen. "Aux Italiens," *Overland Monthly*, 44 (1904).
Tomasi, Silvano. *Piety and Power: The Rome of the Italian Parishes in the New York Metropolitan Area.* New York, 1975.
Tuoni, G. M., and G. Brogelli. *Attività Italiane in California.* San Francisco, 1929.

[The place of publication for all the following U.S. publications is Washington, D.C.]

United States, Bureau of the Census [1]. *Twelfth Census of the United States Taken in the Year 1900: Census Reports*, vol. 1, *Population*, pt. 1. 1901.
———,——— [2]. *Twelfth Census of the United States Taken in the Year 1900: Census Reports*, vol. 3, *Vital Statistics*, pt. 1, *Analysis and Ratio Tables.* 1902.
———,——— [3]. *Thirteenth Census of the United States Taken in the Year 1910*, vol. 1, *Population, General Report, and Analysis.* 1913.
———,——— [4]. *Ibid.*, vol. 2, *Population.* 1913.
———,——— [5]. *Fourteenth Census of the United States Taken in the Year 1920*, vol. 2, *Population, General Report, and Analytical Tables.* 1922.
———,——— [6]. *Ibid.*, vol. 4, *Population and Occupations.* 1923.
———,——— [7]. *Fourteenth Census of the United States: State Compendium—California.* 1924.

———,——— [8]. *Fifteenth Census of the United States, 1930, Population*, vol. 1. 1931.

———,——— [9]. *Ibid., Population*, vol. 2., *General Reports*, 1933.

———,——— [10]. *Ibid., Population*, vol. 4, *Occupations by States*, 1933.

———,——— [11]. *Ibid., Metropolitan Districts, Population and Area.* 1932.

———,——— [12]. *Sixteenth Census of the United States, 1940, Population*, vol. 1, *Number of Inhabitants.* 1942.

———,——— [13]. *Ibid., Population*, vol. 2, *Characteristics of the Population.* 1943.

———,——— [14]. *Ibid., Housing: San Francisco, Block Statistics.* 1942.

———,——— [15]. *1950, United States Census of Population; Census Tract Statistics, San Francisco–Oakland and Adjacent Area, Selected Population and Housing Characteristics.* 1952.

———,——— [16]. *Census of Manufactures*, vol. 1, *Report by States with Statistics for Principal Cities and Metropolitan Districts.* 1918.

———,——— [17]. *Historical Statistics of the United States from Colonial Times to 1957.* 1960.

———,——— [18]. *Immigrants and Their Children.* 1927.

———,——— [19]. *Population: Special Report on Foreign-Born White Families by Country of Birth of the Head.* 1933.

———,——— [20]. *Report of the Manufactures of the United States at the Tenth Census, 1880.* 1883.

———,——— [21]. *Statistics of Manufactures in Cities at the Eleventh Census, 1890.* 1892.

———, Immigration Commission [22]. *Immigrants in Industries*, pt. 25, *Japanese and Other Immigrant Races in the Pacific Coast and Rocky Mountains.* 1911.

Valenti, Ghino. *La Cooperazione Rurale in Italia.* Florence, 1902.

Vecoli, Rudolph. "Contadini in Chicago: A Critique of *The Uprooted*," *Journal of American History*, 51 (1964).

Venerosi, Raniero. "La Coscienza Nazionale tra gli Emigrati Italiani," *Italica Gens*, 1 (1910).

Villari, Luigi. *Italian Life in Town and Country.* New York, 1902.

———. *Gli Stati Uniti e l'Emigrazione Italiana.* Milan, 1912.

Villari, Pasquale. "L'Emigrazione Italiana e le Sue Conseguenze," *Nuova Antologia*, 45 (1907).

———. *Lettere Meridionali.* Florence, 1878.

Virgilio, Jacopo. *La Questione dell'Emigrazione.* Genoa, 1874.

Vöchting, Friedrich. *La Questione Meridionale.* Naples, 1955.

Von Borosini, Victor. "Home-Coming Italians," *The Survey*, 28 (1912).

Warner, Sam Bass, and Collin Burke. "Cultural Change and the Ghetto," *Journal of Contemporary History*, 4 (1969).

Weber, Eugen. *Peasants into Frenchmen: The Modernization of Rural France, 1870–1914.* Stanford, Calif., 1976.

Wells, Robert V. "Family History and Demographic Transition," in Michael Gordon, ed., *The American Family in Socio-Historical Perspective.* New York, 1978.

Wheast, Carl. "Pioneer Visitor to the Death Valley and the Forty-Niners," *California Historical Society Quarterly*, 18 (1939).

Willcox, Walter. *International Migrations*, vol. 2. New York, 1929.

Williams, Phyllis. *South Italian Folkways in Europe and America.* New York, 1938.

Wood, Samuel. "The California State Commission on Immigration and Housing: A Study of Administrative Organization and the Growth of Function," Ph.D. dissertation, University of California, Berkeley, 1942.

Wrigley, Edward. *Population and History.* New York, 1969.

Yans-McLaughlin, Virginia. *Family and Community: Italian Immigrants in Buffalo, 1880–1930.* Ithaca, N.Y., 1977.

Young, John. *San Francisco: Activity of the Pacific Coast Metropolis.* San Francisco, 1912.

Zangheri, Renato. "I Catasti," in Ruggiero Romano and Corrado Vivanti, eds., *Storia d'Italia.* vol. 5, *I Documenti.* Turin, 1973.

———. *Lotte Agrarie in Italia: La Federazione Nazionale dei Lavoratori della Terra, 1901–1926.* Milan, 1960.

Ziino, Nunzio. *Latifondo e Latifondismo: Studio di Economia Rurale.* Palermo, 1911.

Index